SOUTHERN BIOGRAPHY SERIES

The White Chief

Titles in the
SOUTHERN BIOGRAPHY SERIES

Edited by Fred C. Cole and Wendell H. Stephenson

FELIX GRUNDY, *by Joseph Howard Parks*
THOMAS SPALDING OF SAPELO, *by Merton Coulter*
EDWARD LIVINGSTON, *by William B. Hatcher*
FIGHTIN' JOE WHEELER, *by John P. Dyer*
JOHN SHARP WILLIAMS, *by George Coleman Osborn*
GEORGE FITZHUGH, *by Harvey Wish*
PITCHFORK BEN TILLMAN, *by Francis Butler Simkins*
SEARGENT S. PRENTISS, *by Dallas C. Dickey*
ZACHARY TAYLOR, *by Brainerd Dyer*

Edited by T. Harry Williams

JOHN BELL OF TENNESSEE, *by Joseph Howard Parks*
JAMES HARROD OF KENTUCKY, *by Kathryn Harrod Mason*
ARTHUR PUE GORMAN, *by John R. Lambert*
GENERAL EDMUND KIRBY SMITH, *by Joseph Howard Parks*
WILLIAM BLOUNT, *by William H. Masterson*
P. G. T. BEAUREGARD, *by T. Harry Williams*
HOKE SMITH AND THE POLITICS OF THE NEW SOUTH,
by Dewey W. Grantham, Jr.
GENERAL LEONIDAS POLK, C.S.A., *by Joseph Howard Parks*
MR. CRUMP OF MEMPHIS, *by William D. Miller*
GENERAL WILLIAM J. HARDEE, *by Nathaniel Cheairs Hughes, Jr.*
MONTAGUE OF VIRGINIA, *by William E. Larsen*
THOMAS MANN RANDOLPH, *by William H. Gaines, Jr.*
JAMES LUSK ALCORN, *by Lillian A. Pereyra*
ROBERT TOOMBS OF GEORGIA, *by William Y. Thompson*
THE WHITE CHIEF: JAMES KIMBLE VARDAMAN, *by William F. Holmes*

THE WHITE CHIEF
JAMES KIMBLE
VARDAMAN

by William F. Holmes

LOUISIANA STATE UNIVERSITY PRESS
BATON ROUGE

FOR MARGUERITE

Library of Congress Catalog Card Number 70–108201
ISBN 0-8071-0931-2
Manufactured in the United States of America by
The TJM Corporation, Baton Rouge, Louisiana

Designed by Jules B. McKee

PREFACE

On a warm summer evening in 1959 I read *Lanterns on the Levee,* wherein William Alexander Percy describes James K. Vardaman as "a kindly, vain demagogue unable to think, and given to emotions he considered noble." I had little knowledge of Mississippi history and it was my first reference to Vardaman, but it stuck. The next year at the University of Delaware, Dr. Walter Heacock suggested that I read W. J. Cash's *Mind of the South.* Not only did I find Cash's work exciting, but it sparked my interest in reading more widely in southern history. As a result, I wrote a seminar paper for Professor Morton Rothstein on southern politics in the early twentieth century. In preparing that paper two books particularly impressed me: C. Vann Woodward's *Tom Watson: Agrarian Rebel* and Francis Butler Simkins' *Pitchfork Ben Tillman: South Carolinian.* It was after reading those works that I began to think about writing a biography of James K. Vardaman. Later, at Rice University, Professor Frank E. Vandiver encouraged me to choose Vardaman as a dissertation subject. This I did, but the dissertation covered only Vardaman's early career, and five years passed before I managed to complete the biography.

The absence of a substantial body of Vardaman's private papers presented the chief obstacle in undertaking this work. Such a collection might have afforded far more insight into his personality and thought. It would certainly have made my work easier. The scarcity of Vardaman papers forced me to root out material in county courthouses, in the Mississippi Department of Archives and History, in the National Archives, and in the Library of Congress. I relied upon contemporary newspapers and periodicals, public documents, the correspondence of his contemporaries, and the newspapers that Vardaman edited. As a result, my study focuses chiefly upon Vardaman's public career.

A grant from the National Endowment for the Humanities enabled me to devote the 1967–68 academic year to the completion of my research and to begin a first draft of the manuscript. A fellowship from the American Philosophical Society permitted me to spend the summer of 1968 completing the first draft. A research grant from the University of Texas at Arlington facilitated my work during one summer.

The staffs of the Mississippi Department of Archives and History, Rice University Library, the University of Texas at Arlington Library, the National Archives, and the Library of Congress were always cooperative in fulfilling my numerous requests. Many people helped me at various stages of the work: Miss Charlotte Capers, Mrs. Laura D. S. Harrell, Mrs. Jane Melton, Mrs. T. Eugene Caldwell, James F. Wooldridge, Mrs. W. E. Noblin, Dr. John Hebron Moore, Mrs. J. H. Freeman, Douglas Robinson, Jr., Edwin R. Holmes, Jr., B. F. Ward, Miss Margaret Francine Morris, Dr. E. C. Barksdale, and Dr. Robert W. Griffith. While I taught at the University of Texas at Arlington, Mrs. Janice Maddox and Miss Patricia Berryman performed yeoman work as research assistants. James K. Vardaman, Jr., a man blessed with an amazingly accurate memory and an unusual sense of objectivity, helped me immensely through his candid discussions of his father's career.

Professor Frank E. Vandiver, my dissertation director, not only gave valuable encouragement and criticism but, by his own work, taught me how to approach historical research and writing. Professor Barnes F. Lathrop of the University of Texas at Austin and the late Professor Andrew Forest Muir of Rice University read parts of the manuscript and their criticisms proved valuable. Professor Willard B. Gatewood of the University of Georgia also helped me over several humps in the writing. Without the help and encouragement of my wife Marguerite I would never have completed the job. Not only did she maintain order in the household while I wrote, but she was my most demanding and constructive critic.

INTRODUCTION

LATE IN THE afternoon of July 4, 1911, thousands of people thronged the railway depot in Meridian, a town in eastern Mississippi near the Alabama line. Many had ridden for miles in horse-drawn wagons over dusty country roads to hear James K. Vardaman, candidate for the United States Senate, who was to speak that evening. The day had been so hot and humid that many of the early arrivals had bided their time in hotel lobbies, drugstores, and the homes of friends—any place to escape the blistering heat. Although some men wore coats and wide ties that hung to their belts, most were in shirt sleeves. Broad-brimmed Stetsons and black derbies spotted the crowd. Women wore long cotton dresses and carried fans and parasols against the heat. Shortly before the train's arrival a breeze suddenly began to stir giving some meager relief to those waiting.

When the train pulled in shortly before five o'clock, a wave of excitement rippled through the crowd. A few moments later Vardaman stepped onto the platform and was hailed with such deafening cheers and applause that the local band's rendition of *Dixie* could not be heard a block away. For more than five minutes the demonstration continued. Obviously pleased by the warm reception, Vardaman smiled and waved to the multitude. He made no effort to stop the applause. He enjoyed it too much. Members of the local Vardaman Club pushed through the crowd to welcome the senatorial candidate, and as the cheering subsided they led him to a waiting lumber wagon, hitched to a team of eighty oxen. Vardaman got on the wagon and sat in a seat mounted high in the middle. Then the parade began, led by bands from neighboring towns and accompanied by hundreds of men on horseback carrying red streamers and flaming torches. Many marched on foot and some bore signs with the captions "Rednecks,"

"Cattle," and "Hillbillies." Preceding the teamsters who led the oxen were two men carrying a banner proclaiming "The White Chief." Men struggled for the honor of leading the oxen, and the crowds lining the streets pressed forward to wave to Vardaman and, if possible, to touch him.

The parade culminated at the city park where Vardaman was to speak. If any strangers were present, they did not have to ask which person was Vardaman. Dressed in a white Prince Albert suit and wearing white boots, he stood out from all about him. With his fiftieth birthday only a little more than three weeks away, he still had a fine physique, for he stood six feet tall, had broad shoulders, and displayed no sign of a paunchy midriff. A dark-complexioned man, he wore his hair long and brushed it straight back from his forehead, allowing it to fall to his shoulders. Carrying himself erect and holding his head high, he exuded self-confidence. Some, undoubtedly, instantly disliked his cocky, high-falutin airs. Yet those who met him found a warm, friendly man who enjoyed meeting people and who quickly put those about him at their ease. As he made his way through the park to the speaker's platform, he shook hundreds of hands and surprised many whom he had met in earlier campaigns by remembering their names.

In the rural state of Mississippi there were few modes of public entertainment that equaled political rallies in popularity, especially those featuring colorful candidates who spoke enthusiastically and movingly. After almost twenty years of campaigning, Vardaman had developed a rapport with his audiences that few politicians ever equaled. In his opening remarks he flattered the crowd, giving a tribute to the women present, eulogizing the Confederate soldier, and recalling with great pleasure his earlier visits to Meridian. That he might have the opportunity to represent the good people of Mississippi in the Senate especially pleased him. There were no finer people, he boasted, than the Mississippi farmers who embodied the virtues of honest yeomen.

Turning to more serious issues, he declared that railroads, steel companies, and other powerful trusts dominated the nation. All too frequently the government ignored the interests of the common man. It was time for reform. If elected to the Senate, he promised to work for stringent railroad regulation, stricter antitrust laws, a low tariff, a graduated income tax, abolition of child labor, direct election of senators, and reform of the federal judiciary. Vested interests like railroads and lumber companies, he warned, were actively working for his defeat. Only honest, hardworking men could insure his victory.

Mississippi faced a graver problem, he went on, because more than half its population was black. As Negroes belonged to an innately inferior race, whites had to guard against blacks ever gaining social and political equality. That danger existed! During Reconstruction the vindictive Radical Republicans had tried to humiliate the South by passing the Fourteenth and Fifteenth amendments which, if enforced, would give blacks full equality. Although Mississippi, like other southern states, had effectively invalidated those amendments, someday the Republicans might again try to enforce them. The problem could be met in only one way: repeal the Fifteenth Amendment and dilute the Fourteenth, thereby removing the threat that Negroes posed to whites. As a senator he would work for white supremacy.

He assured his listeners that he did not hate Negroes. Throughout his life he had liked them. He even recalled the "old mammy" who had cared for him as a baby. Yet the towns and countrysides were infested with black fiends who lusted after white women! Then to the delight of many he described a rural home where the father and sons worked all day in the fields and the mother and daughters tended to household chores. It was a happy and content family until one peaceful summer day a "big, black buck" invaded the home and raped the women. By that act he forever destroyed the peace and serenity of the home. White men must forever be on their guard against such a menace.

When Vardaman stopped speaking, the people raised cheer after cheer. Two men standing near the platform hoisted him onto their shoulders and carried him through the exuberant crowd. Then all moved across the park and filed slowly by long tables where women passed out plates laden with hunks of barbecued goat and chicken and heaped with potatoes and slaw. Vardaman received a plate but he ate little. He greeted hundreds of people who wanted to meet him and talked about the coming election until late into the night.

During the summer of 1911 Vardaman reiterated the themes of that speech time and again. Even though no other demonstration matched the intensity of the Meridian parade, enthusiastic crowds greeted him wherever he spoke. That summer he reached the peak of his power. In the Democratic primary Vardaman swept to an easy victory over two opponents, carrying seventy-four of the state's seventy-nine counties. He then dominated Mississippi politics as has no other man before or since.

On July 4, 1918, seven years to the day after the spectacular Vardaman rally, Meridian witnessed another oxen parade. This time Congressman Pat Harrison, who was opposing Vardaman's bid for reelection, held center stage. Judge R. F. Cochran, organizer of the 1911 rally, recalled that earlier celebration in his speech introducing Harrison and in complete renunciation thanked God that the oxen were now pulling Vardaman out.

Vardaman's campaign in 1918 little resembled earlier canvasses. Before, he had always stumped the state for months in advance of the primary, giving speeches in every county. In 1918 he campaigned less than a month. In those towns where he actually spoke, he received rough treatment. In one small town on the night before his scheduled speech, someone painted the speaker's platform yellow and splashed yellow paint on his local campaign manager's front door. As he spoke, hecklers interrupted him with shouts of "Kaiser von Vardaman," and some demanded to know why he had not always supported President Wilson's conduct of the war. Vardaman did not cower at the abuse heaped upon him; he defended his Senate record and declared that even if he had the chance, he would not change a single vote. Not only had he supported every major social and economic reform of the past six years, but he had voted against war because of profound conviction.

Despite his attempts to explain, Vardaman was fighting a losing battle and he knew it. His stand against war made him so unpopular that he could no longer fire audiences with enthusiasm for his cause. Frequently he tried to bolster his popularity by appealing to racism. Declaring that the war filled Negro soldiers with ambitions to achieve full equality, he warned that whites must keep black veterans in their "place." In 1918 that appeal had no punch. The world conflict then presented a far more emotionally charged issue, one that Vardaman could not escape.

Ill health added to Vardaman's troubles, for he lacked the stamina that had carried him through past campaigns. Threads of white streaked his long hair and wrinkles creased his face. His once powerful frame had begun to shrink. Campaign speeches so strained his voice that many could barely hear him.

In the Democratic primary on August 19, 1918, Harrison beat Vardaman. That defeat ended Vardaman's political career, for he never again held public office. In 1911 no man could have predicted that within seven years he would be finished as a politician. Then, the very idea was preposterous, for he completely dominated Mississippi politics and continued to do so until 1915. After that, America's increasing involvement in the European war presented issues that proved politically disastrous to him. Even though Vardaman knew they would hurt him and knew he could have avoided them by following President Wilson's leadership, he refused to skirt those issues or to compromise his determined opposition to war. As a result, he lost his vast power and suffered political death.

Many hailed his defeat as a victory for political decency, for they considered him a contemptible demagogue. They had reason for that belief. For almost a quarter century Vardaman had incited racism in his every campaign. When he first ran for office, he advocated curbing Negro education, charging it wasted white taxpayers' money and spoiled good field hands. Later he attacked the Fourteenth and Fifteenth amendments. Frequently he baited audiences by describing attempts by black men to rape white women, and he even condoned white mobs lynching black rapists. More than any man, he instilled a blatant brand of racism into Mississippi politics that plagued the state into the late twentieth century. Critics charged he exploited Negrophobia merely to satisfy his personal ambitions; he so wanted the power and prestige of office that he stooped to Negro baiting to attain it. He posed as a friend of the common man, they said, shouted "nigger," and rode into office with the support of ignorant "rednecks."

Yet those who knew Vardaman best, both friends and foes, knew that the charge of being a racist demagogue was not entirely correct. As governor, despite his racist agitation, he intervened to save Negro prisoners from lynch mobs and even led a fight against white terrorists who intimidated Negroes. The animosity he held for blacks did not extend to other minorities. Throughout his life, for example, he vehemently opposed anti-Semitism.

He differed too from many southern politicians who also exploited racism. Senator "Cotton Ed" Smith of South Carolina stayed in office for years by riding the Negro question; but Smith left a negative record, one that showed little concern for those who voted for him. Vardaman, in contrast, left a record of positive accomplishment. If any southern politician of the early twentieth century could lay claim to being a progressive reformer, Vardaman could. In the end, moreover, he proved his integrity and dedication to principle, as he pursued the lonely course of opposing America's entry into war.

In Vardaman's career ran strains that affected southern politics throughout the twentieth century. On the one side there was the master demagogue who fanned the flames of racial hatred. On the other side there was the dedicated reformer who worked for programs he believed benefited small white farmers, laborers, and businessmen. In Vardaman the white masses of Mississippi found a spokesman and champion. His career, combining racism and reform, appeared to many baffling and paradoxical, and it was. It also affords insight into the history of the South.

CONTENTS

Preface   v

Introduction   vii

1   From the Hills to the Delta   3

2   The Country Editor   22

3   A Politician's Apprenticeship   43

4   The Emergence of a Popular Leader   81

5   The Administration   116

6   The Prisons and the Campus   150

7   Defeat   177

8   The "Secret Caucus"   196

9   Political Upheaval   230

10   Progressive Senator   267

11   Opponent of War   294

12   Political Demise   328

13   The Last Years   361

Epilogue   382

Critical Essay on Authorities   393

Index   403

The White Chief

CHAPTER I

FROM THE HILLS
TO THE DELTA

WINONA LAY IN the loess hill region of north-central Mississippi where fertile soil in combination with steep hills and narrow valleys made farms productive but small. A dusty little county seat town located on the Illinois Central Railroad, it lethargically served as the major trading center for the surrounding complacent countryside. Although many young men might have selected a more attractive place, James Kimble Vardaman, twenty-one, found Winona a most satisfactory town in which to begin his practice of law. He had, after all, spent much of his life in the adjacent and similar milieu of Yalobusha and Carroll counties. More important, a cousin, Hernando DeSoto Money, lived in Winona. The Moneys were an influential family, and Hernando himself represented the third district of Mississippi in Congress.[1]

During Vardaman's childhood his own family had neither the wealth nor influence enjoyed by the Moneys. His father William Sylvester came from a family of Swedish descent which had immigrated to America early in the eighteenth century, settling first in Virginia, then moving westward to Kentucky, and finally to Mississippi. William Sylvester's father Jeremiah served with a Mississippi militia company in the War of 1812 and afterward settled in the southwestern Mississippi county of Copiah, where a number of his relatives lived. The Vardamans of Copiah County were farmers, several of whom became small planters owning sizable tracts of land and a few slaves.[2]

[1] Dunbar Rowland, *The Official and Statistical Register of the State of Mississippi, 1908* (Nashville, 1908), 975.
[2] Vardaman family genealogy, in possession of Mrs. J. H. Freeman, Greenwood, Mississippi; National Archives and Records Service, Bounty Land Warrant, no. 47587–80–55; Manuscript Returns of the United States Seventh Census, 1850 (National Archives), Schedule No. 1, Free Inhabitants in County of Copiah, State of Mississippi, 92–94; *ibid.,* Schedule No. 2, Slave Inhabitants

By 1848 William Sylvester Vardaman, then twenty-two years old, moved north to Holmes County and there began buying land along the Big Black River. During the next four years he purchased more than a thousand acres and acquired nine slaves.[3] As the young planter cleared the land, he devoted it exclusively to cotton. In 1852 he married Mary Ann Fox of Carroll County, the daughter of a well-to-do family that had come from Virginia to Mississippi by way of northern Alabama.[4] The couple lived in Holmes County until 1858, when William Sylvester took his family and slaves on a long overland trip to Texas. There the following year he and Michael H. Laughter purchased sixteen hundred acres of land in Jackson County.[5] It was in that southeastern Texas county that Mary Ann Vardaman on July 26, 1861, gave birth to a son, James Kimble Vardaman. He was one of seven children, three daughters and four sons.[6]

The years in Texas proved difficult for the family. After serving with Confederate forces in the state during the Civil War, William fell into debt, and by 1868 he and Laughter sold their land to meet obligations.[7] The Vardamans then returned to Mississippi. During the long, tedious trip most of the family rode in mule-drawn wagons, but James, then seven, rode the entire way on horseback. They eventually settled near

in Copiah County, 413; *ibid.*, Schedule No. 4, Productions in Agriculture, Copiah County, 381.

[3] Deed Book of Holmes County (Office of the Chancery Clerk, Lexington, Mississippi), Vol. I, 478–79, Vol. L, 356–57, 362–64, 756, Vol. M, 464–65, 568, Vol. N, 221, Vol. S, 829; Manuscript Returns of the United States Seventh Census, 1850 (National Archives), Schedule No. 1, Free Inhabitants in County of Copiah, State of Mississippi, 270; Assessment of Persons and Taxable Property in the County of Holmes for Years 1848, 1853, 1855, Mississippi Department of Archives and History, Jackson.

[4] Fox family genealogy, in possession of Mrs. J. H. Freeman, Greenwood, Mississippi; *Tyler's Quarterly Historical and Genealogical Magazine*, XXI (1940), 217–90.

[5] Manuscript Returns of the United States Eighth Census, 1860 (National Archives), Schedule No. 1, Free Inhabitants in the County of Jackson, State of Texas, 28; *ibid.*, Schedule No. 2, Slave Inhabitants in Jackson County, 13; Deed Records of Jackson County, Texas (Office of County Clerk, Edna, Texas), Vol. E, 746–48, Vol. F, 46–48.

[6] Vardaman's three sisters, all older than he, were Sarah Talbot, Martha Elizabeth, and Margaret Newland; his older brother was John Fox Vardaman and his younger brother was William Sylvester. The youngest of the seven children, Gideon Smith Vardaman, died at birth.

[7] *L. M. Owen vs. W. S. Vardaman, et al., September 6, 1866,* in Civil Minutes, District Court, Jackson County, Texas, Vol. C, 225.

relatives in the village of Preston in Yalobusha County. James's father failed to recoup his financial losses, and during the remainder of his life he never acquired property on the scale he had during the 1850's.[8] It does not appear that he exerted much influence in molding the character of his son, but his wife did. Mary Ann Vardaman, a strong-willed woman, was a devout Methodist who believed there could be no compromise between right and wrong. Though she failed to make James a church-going man, she did instill in him her sense of moral righteousness.[9]

Because his family was poor, James knew austerity in his youth and later boasted that he spent many of his early years cutting and hauling timber. What physical labor he performed became more difficult soon after the move to Mississippi, when his right arm was mangled in a corn sheller. Although he was able to write with his right hand and could lift light objects, the arm remained small and withered. During his lifetime he occasionally experienced periods of acute pain which forced him to cancel appointments.[10] As he grew to maturity, only that single physical defect detracted from his strength and appearance. Compared to a man with two strong arms, he was at a disadvantage. Perhaps it was this flaw which led him, consciously or subconsciously, to strive for political power.

His disability may also have contributed to his becoming an avid reader while still a young boy. His formal education was meager, consisting only of rudimentary instruction in a one-room log schoolhouse in Yalobusha County. Acutely aware of his limited education and determined to widen it, he moved to Carrollton, Mississippi, at the age of eighteen to live in the home of an uncle, Pierson Money. Hour upon hour he spent engrossed reading the volumes of law, history, political theory, and literature found in the family's library. He also served as

[8] Deed Books, First District, Yalobusha County (Office of the Chancery Clerk, Coffeeville, Mississippi), Vol. 37, pp. 20–24, 249, Vol. 39, p. 238.

[9] Interview with James K. Vardaman, Jr., Wrightsville Beach, North Carolina, May 1, 1968.

[10] James K. Vardaman to John M. Allen, April 20, 1904, in Letter Book of Governor James K. Vardaman, Mississippi Department of Archives and History, Jackson. Hereinafter cited as Vardaman Letter Book; Jackson *Daily Clarion-Ledger*, April 11, 1904. Some believe that an attack of infantile paralysis in early childhood crippled Vardaman's arm. Interview with Mrs. J. H. Freeman, Greenwood, Mississippi, July 3, 1963.

clerk for a local law firm. Three years later, in 1882, he passed the state
bar examination, a feat that required only the barest acquaintance
with law, but one that gave him a sense of achievement.[11] By that time,
moreover, he knew what he wanted to do—practice law and later, like
his cousin Hernando DeSoto Money, enter politics.

Vardaman greatly admired his cousin. Twenty-one years older than
Vardaman and now a resident of Winona, Money grew up in Carrollton and later attended the University of Mississippi. After service as an
officer in the Civil War, he became a leader in the campaign to overthrow the Reconstruction government in Mississippi. With the return
of home rule in 1875 Money attained a seat in the state house of representatives, and thereafter for three decades he was a force to reckon
with in Mississippi politics.[12]

Money himself was a junior associate of the most powerful figure in
the public affairs of post-Reconstruction Mississippi—Senator James
Z. George. A resident of Carrollton, George had risen to prominence
during Reconstruction. As a leader in the election of 1875, and later as
the most influential man at the constitutional convention of 1890,
George became "the symbol of white supremacy triumphant." Although a rich man and a railroad attorney, he nonetheless supported,
on some issues, the interests of the small farmers.[13] Throughout their
careers George and Money remained close political allies. Like George,
Money frequently sided with the farmers and firmly supported the
doctrine of white supremacy.

The Carrollton leaders greatly influenced Vardaman's future. He
began his political career by supporting the Mississippi Democratic
Party led by George and Money. Like his political mentors, he demonstrated an awareness of the agrarian's aspirations and eventually be-

[11] A. S. Coody, *Biographical Sketches of James Kimble Vardaman* (Jackson,
1922), 14–16; Heber A. Ladner, "James K. Vardaman in Mississippi Politics"
(M.A. thesis, Duke University, 1938), 8.

[12] "Hernando DeSoto Money," *Dictionary of American Biography* (New
York, 1928–37), XIII, 85–86; Rowland, *The Official and Statistical Register of
... Mississippi, 1908,* 974–76.

[13] Charles Granville Hamilton, "Mississippi Politics in the Progressive Era,
1904–1920" (Ph.D. dissertation, Vanderbilt University, 1958), 62–64; May
Spencer Ringold, "Senator James Zachariah George of Mississippi: Bourbon or
Liberal?" *Journal of Mississippi History,* XVI (1954), 164–82; Ringold, "Some
Liberal Aspects in the Senatorial Policies of James Zachariah George during
the Period, 1881–1890" (M.A. thesis, University of Mississippi, 1950), *passim.*

came a champion of the small-farmer class. When he espoused the cause of white supremacy, he simply followed the earlier lead of George and Money. These post-Reconstruction Bourbons left, as part of their legacy to the state, Governor James K. Vardaman.

Once admitted to the bar, Vardaman wasted no time in moving to his cousin Hernando's town of Winona. It was with self-satisfied enthusiasm that he regarded the railroad depot, the bank, the hotel, the few general stores, the seven saloons, and the wooden frame homes of the twelve hundred residents that comprised this sleepy little town. Vardaman's arrival in Winona must have caused comment, for his trim, erect figure, six feet in height, was crowned by long black hair, combed straight back and allowed to grow to shoulder length. A large nose, full mouth, restless searching eyes, and dark complexion added to his striking appearance.

It was not long before Vardaman met Dr. B. F. Ward. Their lifelong relationship came to resemble that of a father and son, and Vardaman often sought the advice of this Confederate veteran who had served with distinction at Gettysburg. Ward was an unreconstructed Rebel who cherished the mythology of the antebellum South, who denounced Henry Grady and the New South spokesmen as traitors to their heritage, and who argued that Jefferson Davis had been a far greater leader than Abraham Lincoln. He was an outspoken foe of Negro equality, believing that black men belonged to an inferior race which must be confined to a caste at the bottom of society; he even justified mobs lynching Negro men who had raped white women. Ward helped to instill in Vardaman a belief in the righteousness of the Confederate cause, a hatred for Reconstruction, and an abiding devotion to white supremacy. Probably Ward did not impart all of his beliefs to Vardaman during the young lawyer's brief residence in Winona; during the next three decades, however, it became practically impossible to distinguish the views of one from the other.[14] Years later one observer of Mississippi politics speculated that "Vardaman had a brilliant political career opening out before him until he became the blind disciple of

[14] Greenwood *Yazoo Valley Flag,* April 30, 1887; Greenwood *Commonwealth,* May 13, 1897, May 16, 1902, January 2, 24, July 11, 1903; Jackson *Evening News,* September 8, 1905; Jackson *Issue,* September 12, 1908, October 9, 1909.

that aged, bitter old man of Winona, whose every thought of the past, present and future seems brewed on race and sectional gall." [15]

Five months after his arrival in Winona, James and his cousin William Vardaman Money became editors of the Winona *Advance,* the only newspaper that furnished news of the town and of Montgomery County. This event was brought about by Congressman Money, who purchased the *Advance* from B. H. Wear and gave his young relatives the job of running it. Evidently James's law practice amounted to little as yet, and editing a country newspaper could be a rewarding profession. Requiring no formal training and slight capital, it promised much prestige and might enable the editor to exert strong influence in his community. Vardaman's experience with the *Advance* taught him the importance of the press as an instrument for guiding public opinion and gave him his baptism in Mississippi politics.

The *Advance* was a small four-page weekly, its front and back pages filled with ready-print articles featuring current events, short stories, sermons, agricultural topics, women's fashions, and tales of murders, robberies, and mysterious visions. The editors prepared the two inside pages, one devoted to editorial comment on local, state, and national news, the other to social events in Winona and Montgomery County. In their first issue the young men cautiously described their editorial policy. Admittedly awed by their new job, they aimed to be just, to avoid fights, and to do their best. "We are not working for fun, nor glory, nor for our health; therefore we want the money." [16] In an early article they modestly urged the establishment of a chair of journalism at the University of Mississippi to impart training that would make newspapermen more efficient and give the press "a better tone intellectually and morally." [17]

At first Vardaman and Money abided by their declared editorial policy and published no controversial material. They frequently complimented friends, and they printed letters or speeches by state and local dignitaries on such timely topics as schools, religion, and social life. Special attention went to schemes for more efficient and productive farming. All Mississippians, they proclaimed, should support a

[15] Brookhaven *Leader,* July 8, 1903.
[16] Winona *Advance,* May 4, 1883.
[17] *Ibid.,* May 11, 1883.

bill sponsored by Congressman Money to establish experimental stations to provide agricultural information for farmers throughout the
nation. The *Advance* also took the agrarian side in condemning railroad rate discrimination against farmers and maintained that states
had the right to regulate railroads in the public interest.[18]

The race problem received little notice in the *Advance* except as
it related to Democratic solidarity. The editors faithfully supported
white supremacy and scorned anyone who did not. Thus they felt no
sympathy for whites in Nashville who were outraged when a Negro
constable shot a restaurant owner there; any town that tolerated a
Negro official had no right to complain.[19] To maintain white supremacy was to maintain the Democratic Party and to maintain the Democratic Party was of life-and-death importance.

Year after year, election after election, as long as we live and abide
in Miss[issippi] we must set ourselves firmly to the duty and toil of
holding up Democracy and defeating Republicanism. . . . With us it is
no strife for a political creed, but a battle for our very existence, so-
cially, materially, and politically. . . . It has no end. . . . Be sure that you
fight for Democracy; because you are then sure that you are opposing
your enemy. Let not any one surprising [*sic*] you with false face of
"Independence," or any other mask. . . . You are free to choose from
all men who are Democrats but note well that he is not an enemy.[20]

The editors had sound reasons for urging party solidarity in the early 1880's. The Mississippi Democracy had recently experienced its
first serious dissensions since the overthrow of the Reconstruction government. In the senatorial election of 1880 and the gubernatorial election of 1881, Ethelbert Barksdale and a group of dissatisfied Democrats had seriously challenged the dominant wing of the party led by
Senator George, Representative Money, and Senator Lucius Quintus
Cincinnatus Lamar. The Bourbon Democrats had put down this initial
challenge, but in 1882 a new threat arose in the form of a movement
led by James R. Chalmers, who attempted to forge an alliance between
Republicans, Greenbackers, and Independent Democrats. The threat
was particularly serious in Money's congressional district, but he

[18] *Ibid.*, May 4, 18, 1883.
[19] *Ibid.*, June 15, 1883.
[20] *Ibid.*, August 31, 1883.

managed to achieve reelection in 1882, and the Democrats presently quelled the danger in the state at large.[21]

It is against this background that the anxiety of the *Advance* for party regularity, even at the local level, is to be understood. When elections were to be held in October, 1883, the *Advance* asked everyone to abide by the county Democratic executive committee's ruling on whether nominations should be made by a convention, a mass meeting, or a primary. As it turned out, the executive committee called for a popular primary, a decision the *Advance* supported, even though the editors charged that the last primary held in Winona had been a farce in which many Negroes voted, even minors participated, and the vote cast exceeded the total number of registered voters. The editors urged that this time the candidates not employ the Negro vote and that the officials maintain a free and fair election.[22]

After only three months as an editor, Vardaman abandoned his original policy of avoiding controversial issues. At that time a Democratic nominating convention at Lexington, Mississippi, struggled for four days and cast more than seven hundred ballots before choosing Edmund F. Noel, an able young lawyer, to be the party's candidate for district attorney from the fifth judicial district. At first Vardaman and Money were pleased with the outcome, reporting that Noel had celebrated his victory by giving the members of the convention a champagne reception. But their pleasure changed to wrath when they discovered that the delegates of Holmes, Carroll, and Leflore counties had pooled their votes and selected the nominee by raffle. The *Advance* urged with angry indignation that such conniving delegates should never again be allowed to represent the people. Vardaman and Money immediately found themselves embroiled in a bitter controversy in which they were labeled as youngsters meddling in the affairs of older, more experienced men. Not one member of the convention had denied their version of what had taken place, they retorted; they would

---

[21] Willie D. Halsell, "Democratic Dissensions in Mississippi, 1878–1882," *Journal of Mississippi History*, II (1940), 123–35; Halsell, "Republican Factionalism in Mississippi, 1882–1884," *Journal of Southern History*, VII (1941), 84–101; Halsell, "James R. Chalmers and 'Mahoneism,' in Mississippi," *Journal of Southern History*, X (1944), 37–58.

[22] Winona *Advance*, July 27, August 31, September 14, 21, 1883.

retract their condemnation when and if proved wrong by the delegates' published statements.[23]

Vardaman further angered the defenders of the convention by making fun of Noel. In describing a political rally at Winona, he reported
that Noel had been "clearing away the mysteries that clung around
the fantastic tricks and games that were played at the convention."
When a pistol accidentally fell from the pocket of a deputy marshal
and discharged, "Noel stepped back, threw his hands to his side,
looked scared and fell to his knees." Those sitting on the platform with
Noel scurried under benches and tables and did not budge until the
commotion had settled. Vardaman's attempt at humor aroused the ire
of Noel's friends, one of whom asserted that the people wanted only
the facts and not "funny fictions." [24]

Increasing discontent with the "corrupt bargain" presently induced
opposition leaders to begin circulating petitions through the district
urging support for Colonel A. H. Brantley in place of Noel. The *Advance* continued for a time to maintain, as it had all along, that Noel
was the official party nominee no matter how illegal his nomination,
but it was not long before the youthful editors began defending the
privilege of petition as a basic American right. If a majority of voters
signed petitions for Brantley, they argued, this merely demonstrated
that they had not gotten their choice at the Lexington convention.[25] At
this the *Yazoo Valley Flag,* hot with indignation, charged the *Advance*
with causing disunity within the Democratic Party. Vardaman replied
that if the convention had conducted itself properly, no petition would
have been necessary. As it was, the petitions would serve as a "preven-
tative" against future trickery and corruption.[26] By late September the
Advance had gone completely over to the Brantley side by publishing

[23] Winona *Advance,* August 10, 24, 31, September 7, 1883; Greenwood *Yazoo
Valley Flag,* August 25, 1883. Twenty years later, when Vardaman and Noel
were opponents in the first state Democratic primary for governor, Noel maintained that he had not been aware of the actions of the Lexington convention
and had not approved its methods. Jackson *Daily Clarion-Ledger,* June 14,
1902.
[24] Winona *Advance,* September 28, October 5, 1883.
[25] *Ibid.,* August 31, September 14, 1883.
[26] Greenwood *Yazoo Valley Flag* quoted in Winona *Advance,* September 21,
1883; see also September 28, 1883.

a copy of a petition for his election instead of Noel's. Vardaman, in denouncing the convention, displayed an outspokenness that led some to consider him a smart aleck. Presenting himself as standing for honesty and openness, he appealed to his readers for their support by attacking the defenders of the convention with bursts of fiery indignation and touches of sardonic humor. In the ensuing election Brantley won.[27]

In the midst of the Noel controversy, William Money left the *Advance* because the paper was failing financially. He urged his former readers to "give Mr. Vardaman all your patronage, and if you can't give him any money or cloths [*sic*] or produce, then go every day and read his exchanges, and give him good advice." [28] Vardaman went on alone for another month and a half until the middle of October. Then he, too, gave up and Congressman Money sold the paper to Percy L. Moore. In his valedictory issue Vardaman explained that he had sought not a career in journalism but had wanted to make himself known to the local people upon whose patronage his practice as a lawyer would depend. Finding that he could no longer manage as both editor and lawyer, he had decided to devote full time to the law. No doubt this explanation was largely an attempt to save face. The financial plight of the *Advance*—accentuated perhaps by loss of patronage resulting from the Noel affair—drove Vardaman temporarily out of the newspaper business. Nonetheless, the *Advance* had played a leading role in disrupting the convention's work and in defeating Noel. Vardaman's reaction to Noel's nomination was typical of those he exhibited in his later journalistic and political career. Although as a young man he was conscientious about his manners and social niceties, he never attempted to water down his strong convictions and refused to compromise with what he believed to be wrong.

During Vardaman's editorship of the *Advance,* a struggle to establish prohibition had begun to divide the townspeople of Winona into opposing camps. The movement to stamp out "demon rum" had long existed in Mississippi, but by the 1880's it had intensified. In the South, post-Civil War developments had given new impetus to the temperance forces. Because after the war freedmen could buy liquor as readily as whites, many who had formerly opposed prohibition now sup-

27 Greenwood *Yazoo Valley Flag,* October 31, 1883.
28 Winona *Advance,* September 7, 1883.

ported legislation that would "keep whiskey away from the Negro." As a result the Mississippi legislature passed stringent laws regulating the manufacture and sale of alcohol. Men formed numerous prohibition clubs, Frances E. Willard came in 1882 to organize the state's first chapter of the Woman's Christian Temperance Union, and town after town prohibited the sale of liquor.[29] The movement had definitely taken a firm hold in Winona when Vardaman arrived. Letters advocating prohibition frequently appeared in the local newspaper, and in February, 1883, some temperance leaders formed the Prohibition Union of Montgomery County with the avowed purpose of stopping the sale, manufacture, and importation of liquor throughout the entire state.[30]

Vardaman and Money tried to keep the *Advance* out of the prohibition controversy. Even though they respected temperance and those who were trying to stamp out a known evil, they feared that bringing the prohibition question into politics might endanger white solidarity. They ridiculed the disposition of some reformers to believe that prohibition would solve all problems, "including that of running the government." The editors feared the rise of demagogues who would use the emotional issue of prohibition to undermine white solidarity in the Democratic Party. "The very life and soul of politico-prohibition is the ambition of its leaders to rise on the ruins of [the] party that has rendered your life in Mississippi even tolerable. The fires of ambition burns [*sic*] so fiercely in some men, that if they could, they would wreck the throne of Heaven and climb over its ruins to the seat of power." [31] Vardaman continued to oppose political prohibition until he left the *Advance*.

The prohibition campaign in Montgomery County began in earnest in January, 1884, after Vardaman resumed his law practice. Because the *Advance* under his successor supported the antiprohibitionists, temperance leaders established the Winona *Times* to champion their cause. They also organized their supporters thoroughly and cam-

[29] Daniel Jay Whitener, *Prohibition in North Carolina, 1715–1945* (Chapel Hill, 1945), 50, 57–58; James Benson Sellers, *The Prohibition Movement in Alabama, 1702 to 1943* (Chapel Hill, 1943), 50–51; Thomas Jefferson Bailey, *Prohibition in Mississippi; or, Anti-Liquor Legislation from Territorial Days with its Results in the Counties* (Jackson, 1917), 51–63.
[30] Winona *Advance,* February 9, 1883.
[31] *Ibid.,* June 15, 1883.

paigned intensively, outdoing the wets in both respects. Prominent state temperance leaders visited Winona and addressed large gatherings. Local prohibition clubs were organized and the drys circulated much literature supporting their cause.[32] The wets, on their side, argued through editorials and speeches that prohibition violated personal liberty, that it could never be enforced, and that it would hurt the economy of Montgomery County. The struggle soon gave rise to serious tensions as animosities developed and old friendships dissolved.

Despite his earlier uneasiness over prohibition as a threat to white solidarity, Vardaman entered the fight on the side of the drys. Certainly he must have been influenced by his friend Dr. Ward, who warned "that from the smallest dram to the most hilarious drunk, the use of alcoholic stimulant is only and continually evil." [33] Perhaps he reasoned, too, that an election would settle the controversy once and for all. More probably he was responding to popular sentiment, partly as one swept along by it, partly as an astute opportunist seeking to take advantage of it. Vardaman first indicated his new position in March by withdrawing his card as an attorney from the *Advance* and inserting it in the *Times*. By May he was speaking publicly in behalf of the cause, and he soon became a leader in organizing prohibition clubs in Winona.[34]

The struggle grew more serious in June after it was announced that a prohibition election would be held on July 8. The *Times* intensified its appeal, arguing that so many evils sprang from intemperance that the deadly cancer must be wiped out.[35] The antiprohibitionists retaliated with equal vigor, lambasting the whole movement as a "fanaticism born in New England, the hot-bed of isms, intolerance, and hatred toward the South." [36] Although the wets waged a hard fight, the prohibitionists on election day marched to the polls in groups to cast

[32] *Ibid.*, January 25, 1884; Mississippi Historical Records Survey, Service Division, *Mississippi Newspapers, 1805–1940: A Preliminary Union List of Mississippi Newspaper Files Available in County Archives, Offices of Publishers, Libraries, and Private Collections in Mississippi* (Jackson, 1942), 260–62.
[33] Winona *Times*, March 14, 1884.
[34] *Ibid.*, March 14, May 23, 30, 1885.
[35] *Ibid.*, June 6, 1884. To insure a fair election, the prohibitionists appointed election commissioners for each beat to supervise the voting and the ballot count. Winona *Times*, June 20, 1884.
[36] Winona *Advance*, February 8, 1884.

their votes. The emotional appeal of their cause and their superior organization carried the election. Admitting the election had been a fair one, the editors of the *Advance* accepted defeat and promised to abide by the results. They continued to believe in their cause, however, and predicted that liquor would still be sold even though the saloons had closed.

While the prohibition fight was still hot, Vardaman married Anna Burleson Robinson, a widow seven years his senior. After a lengthy courtship, they were married in June, 1884. Like Vardaman's, her roots were deep in the rural South. The daughter of a prosperous family from Decatur, Alabama, she remembered that when she was a small child, Union troops had plundered her home, forcing her mother to flee. In 1882 Anna's husband Douglas died, having bequeathed his property, totaling about three thousand acres, to his wife and unborn child. This plantation and her young son Douglas, she brought to her marriage with Vardaman.[37]

Immediately after their wedding, the couple began making trips to Sidon, the site of the plantation, and in September they left Winona, moving to Sidon. Vardaman had lived in Winona less than two years, but his stay was important as a formative period that to some extent foreshadowed his later career. He wanted to practice law, but he had discovered how difficult it was for an inexperienced lawyer to develop a practice. He had withdrawn from journalism, only temporarily as it turned out, because he spent much of his subsequent life as a newspaper editor. The Noel episode held particular significance for Vardaman's future: Noel sponsored the state's first Democratic primary law in 1902—Vardaman opposed him and won the governorship in what was the initial application of that law. The fight for prohibition, centering around an emotional issue and causing bitterness on both sides, resembled Vardaman's later vigorous statewide campaigns.

A new life was beginning for Vardaman. Along with many hill people, the couple moved to the Yazoo-Mississippi Delta just as thousands of Negroes and whites were migrating into the lowland region and vast acres of rich land were being cleared and planted with cotton.

[37] Vardaman family genealogy; Winona *Times,* June 6, 1884; Greenwood *Commonwealth,* July 27, 1900; Frank E. Smith, *The Yazoo River* (New York, 1954), 268–69.

The building of railroads, the beginning of federal flood control programs, and a relative stabilization of cotton prices accounted for the Delta boom of the 1880's.[38]

Sidon, located on the Yazoo River, was in one of the parts of the Delta first settled by white men.[39] The plantation lay in what was yet largely wild, untamed country, with towering forest covering much of the land. The spring brought floodwaters which inundated vast tracts of the Delta. Some hill people wrote off the entire Delta as swamp, but they were wrong. That sprawling lowland region was blessed with miles and miles of dark, rich soil—soil so rich that its cotton yield per acre exceeded that of all other regions in the United States. The silt deposited by floodwaters through hundreds of years drew men from near and far to the Delta.

Vardaman did not want to farm; therefore in January, 1886, he leased the land and moved his family to Greenwood, a town about ten miles north of Sidon in Leflore County, which was rapidly becoming a chief river port on the Yazoo.[40] Greenwood's economy centered around the buying and selling of cotton, and eventually it became the largest inland market for long-staple cotton in America.

After moving to Greenwood the Vardamans still maintained close relations with Sidon. Between 1887 and 1890 it appeared that Sidon might develop into a flourishing community. In 1886 the Yazoo and Mississippi Valley Railroad, a branch of the Illinois Central, was built through Sidon. With comparatively good roads to the hill country and a steamboat landing on the Yazoo River, the little village became more active as a trading center. A number of enterprising merchants came there hoping to profit by the area's expanding trade, and by 1890 there were eleven stores and two saloons. In 1887 the Vardamans had begun to sell some of their land, both in the town and in the adjoining countryside, and these sales contributed to Sidon's growth. Vardaman not only sold land but on one occasion, at least, built a store for a mer-

[38] Robert L. Brandfon, *Cotton Kingdom of the New South: A History of the Yazoo Mississippi Delta from Reconstruction to the Twentieth Century* (Cambridge, Mass., 1967), 73–74.

[39] Smith, *The Yazoo River*, 267; Mary K. Ward and Frank Smith, "A Short History of Sidon, Mississippi" (MS in Greenwood Public Library, Greenwood, Miss., 1937).

[40] Greenwood *Yazoo Valley Flag*, January 16, 1886; U.S. Bureau of the Census, *Compendium of the Eleventh Census: 1890* (Washington, 1897), I, 241.

chant who wanted to come to Sidon.[41] But the community did not develop as he hoped; Greenwood grew more rapidly and overshadowed its neighbor to the south. Then in 1894 a disastrous fire destroyed much of the smaller town, dooming most of its further economic growth. Although this outcome must have been distressing to the Vardamans, their rented property at Sidon helped sustain the family in its early years and would be used as collateral during the 1890's. The Robinson plantation enabled Vardaman to purchase one newspaper and to found another.[42]

For seventeen years James and Anna made their home in Greenwood. The first of their children, Bessie, born in Sidon in 1885, died the following year of influenza. Then came Aletha in 1887, James Money in 1891, James Kimble, Jr., in 1893, and Minnie in 1896. They and their half-brother Douglas brought the family number to seven. It was a closely knit unit. Anna was totally absorbed in the role of wife and mother, and James, despite the rising distractions of politics, devoted much time to his family, especially to the problems and interests of the children. He gave as much love to his stepson Douglas as to his own children. Although she had little interest in politics, Anna remained intensely loyal to her husband and always stood by him in his many political battles.[43]

To house their growing family the Vardamans bought a sprawling, two-story, seven-bedroom home. Wide porches encircled the house and towering oak trees shaded the front lawn; in the back and side yards were a vegetable garden, a well, and an outhouse. With friends and relatives dropping in from Carrollton, Winona, or Sidon, and with several school teachers usually boarding at the house, a number

[41] Deed Book of Leflore County (Office of the Chancery Clerk, Greenwood, Mississippi), vols. XI, XII, XIII, XIV, XV, XVI, XVII, XVIII, XX, XXXIV, XXXVII, *passim*; Greenwood *Yazoo Valley Flag,* March 10, 1888.

[42] The Vardamans had previously divided the land into two sections: James and Anna retained the ownership of one part; an equally large section, consisting of numerous lots in the town of Sidon, they registered in the name of Douglas Robinson, Jr. Until he came of age, his property remained in a trust under the supervision of the chancery court of Leflore County. Deed Books of Leflore County, XII, 123–24.

[43] Vardaman family genealogy; interview with Douglas Robinson, Jackson, Miss., August 23, 1963; interview with Mrs. W. T. Ratliff, Birmingham, Ala., September 3, 1963; Percy Bell to Mary Dinkins, January 26, 1938, in Kate M. Power Papers, Mississippi Department of Archives and History.

of guests frequently joined the family meals. The day began with a huge breakfast of fresh fruit, oatmeal, eggs, sausage, grits, hot biscuits, molasses, and coffee. A man who liked people, Vardaman habitually invited friends to the noon meal—without giving Anna forewarning. To accommodate these unexpected guests she always set extra places at the long dining room table. An unassuming woman without pretensions, she made her visitors feel welcome and served dinners of roast beef, hams, and chicken, along with heaping bowls of potatoes, green beans, corn, turnip greens, blackeyed peas, and okra. Despite his advocacy of temperance, Vardaman enjoyed a glass of claret with dinner and in the evenings sometimes had a bit of sherry. Meals were usually lively affairs, the eating interspersed with conversation and laughter. For supper—usually cold meats and leftovers—he sometimes stopped at Dantone's Restaurant on his way home from work and ordered several large, piping hot loaves of French bread stuffed with fried oysters.[44]

At six each morning he greeted the day leisurely, spending two hours at his meticulous toilet. While shaving carefully, so as not to nick his face, he frequently stopped to jot down notes of things to do that day. His long, black hair received hundreds of strokes with a brush until it glowed. Being a dandy, he wore only white shirts, freshly pressed suits, and polished shoes, and often sported a carnation in his lapel. A rare morning it was when he arrived at his office before nine.

Endowed with fine health and robust stamina, he was an expert horseman who loved to ride for sport and pleasure. In late afternoons he frequently took long rides into the countryside. Dressed elegantly and sitting erect in the saddle, he caused many to pause and watch as he rode through the streets of Greenwood. He was not a hunter, but during the spring and summer he often journeyed to lakes in the Delta and fished for bream and perch.

In Greenwood the Vardamans developed an active social life. James enjoyed playing the host, and his consideration for others, gracious manners, and personal magnetism attracted visitors to the household. Besides being a gifted mixer who had the ability to make and hold friends, he had a remarkable memory for names. Two months after

[44] Interview with James K. Vardaman, Jr.

taking his seat in the Senate in 1913 he knew the names of every fellow senator, as well as every representative. He could tell stories and jokes for hours, and when women were not present his language was apt to become salty. He enjoyed practical jokes and was particularly gifted at imitating people. As governor, years later, he took special delight in mimicking the state archivist Dunbar Rowland, a straight-laced gentleman who struck some as pompous.[45] James and Anna especially enjoyed the company of young people and gave frequent dances for them. Birthdays, weddings, and anniversaries were occasions for more general parties featuring dinners, games, and dancing into the early morning hours.[46]

While he lived in Greenwood, Vardaman often journeyed to Carrollton, Winona, Grenada, and Greenville, and sometimes as far afield as Memphis and New Orleans. In all his travels he easily won friends and made lasting impressions—an asset that would contribute to his later political success.

His most distinctive habit during his years in Greenwood, and a source of his abilities as a writer and speaker, was his avid reading. When not entertaining, he habitually spent long evenings in the solitude of his library.[47] Still acutely aware of his lack of formal education and determined to overcome that deficiency as best he could, he frequently read until early morning. As soon as he joined the state legislature his fellow members nicknamed him the "bookworm." When the Vardaman home burned in 1891, the loss of books, of which the usual price was then not above one to three dollars apiece, was estimated at $2,500. In 1895 he lost a second collection when his law office burned. At the time of his death in 1930 his library exceeded five thousand volumes.[48] Precisely what he read during these years is unknown, but from his editorials and speeches it is evident that he concentrated on classics, history, and poetry. He had a special passion for poetry and for language marked by rhythm and grace. During his years in Green-

[45] *Ibid.*

[46] Greenwood *Yazoo Valley Flag,* May 22, July 31, 1886, June 4, August 6, 1887, November 17, 1888, January 5, February 23, 1889; Greenwood *Enterprise,* June 2, 1893, July 5, 1895; Greenwood *Commonwealth,* June 17, 1897, August 17, 1900.

[47] Interview with James K. Vardaman, Jr.; interview with Mrs. J. H. Freeman.

[48] Greenwood *Enterprise,* August 20, 1891, December 20, 1895; interview with James K. Vardaman, Jr.

wood he often gave encouragement to young people who hoped to become writers.[49]

As a private citizen, Vardaman took an active role in the civic affairs
of Greenwood and the Delta. He cooperated with fellow citizens in appealing to the federal government for protection against caving banks
caused by the current of the Yazoo River. He set an example for the
residents of Greenwood by being one of the first to lay a sidewalk in
front of his home. In the summer of 1889 the Mississippi Hedge Company attempted to stimulate the development of Osage orange hedges
in the Delta, and Vardaman was among those invited to Union City,
Tennessee, to inspect the feasibility of the project. In 1896 he served
as one of the state commissioners for the Southern States Exposition to
be held in Chicago the next year, and under his leadership Leflore
County arranged a display there. He led the fight to reinforce the levees against the rising waters of the Mississippi and Yazoo rivers that
often endangered the Delta during the spring. When a yellow fever
epidemic threatened the county in 1897, he worked hard organizing
quarantine practices.[50]

Vardaman practiced law alone except for two brief periods. In 1887
he formed a partnership with J. E. Prewitt and Bonner Richardson that
lasted only six months; in 1892 he and R. G. Humphreys worked
together for about a year. Vardaman became an active member of the
Leflore County Bar Association and helped to draw up basic regulations
for the local profession concerning fees and expenditures. In 1893 he
served as city attorney of Greenwood, and in 1896 the board of supervisors appointed him county attorney.[51] Each of these positions he held
for only a short time, and it does not appear that his private practice
ever amounted to much. A survey of the criminal dockets and minute
books of Leflore County for the 1880's and early 1890's reveals that the

[49] J. K. Vardaman to Harris Dickson, November 7, 1899, October 31, 1903,
in Harris Dickson Papers, Mississippi Department of Archives and History.
[50] Greenwood *Yazoo Valley Flag,* September 17, December 3, 1887, January
5, 1889, July 27, August 17, 1889; Greenwood *Enterprise,* April 3, 1896; Greenwood *Delta Flag,* March 26, 1897; Greenwood *Commonwealth,* September 23,
1897.
[51] Greenwood *Yazoo Valley Flag,* January 8, 22, February 5, May 28, July 30,
1887; Greenwood *Enterprise,* May 20, 1892, March 31, September 15, 1893,
April 10, 1896.

firm of W. T. Rush and A. T. Gardiner handled the greater part of the legal business arising in Greenwood and that Vardaman participated in only a few cases. Perhaps his meager success at the law caused him to turn back to journalism, a calling in which he would become one of the leaders of the state.

CHAPTER II

THE COUNTRY EDITOR

IN 1890 GREENWOOD had two weekly newspapers, the *Yazoo Valley Flag* and the *Enterprise*. The *Enterprise,* edited by Will Cowan since 1889, was a four-page paper, similar in layout to Vardaman's Winona *Advance* of 1883. In the autumn of 1889 Cowan had announced that he wanted to sell the *Enterprise* and Vardaman expressed interest in it, but nothing came of this idea until that newspaper office was badly damaged in a fire that destroyed much of the Greenwood business district in May, 1890. Shortly thereafter Vardaman bought the paper from Cowan, probably for less than the previous price.

Following the custom of the times, Vardaman's fellow editors welcomed him to the profession. The Winona *Times* foresaw that he would make of the *Enterprise* "one of the ablest and best papers in the State." The Lexington *Bulletin* alluded to his having newspaper experience, called him "an able writer of broad liberal views," and joined in predicting success.[1]

That Vardaman intended to succeed, there can be no doubt. He began his editorship with a promise to revise and improve the *Enterprise* so as to warrant a greater circulation, and he soon proved as good as his word. In October, 1890, he purchased a new press, expanded the *Enterprise,* and gave it a new format. The paper became an eight-page publication and covered a wide range of topics. The front page was usually devoted to state and national politics, letters and speeches by Mississippi congressmen, and articles from other newspapers of the state. The inside pages were aimed at one and all, containing articles on agriculture to attract farmers, sentimental short stories to arouse female interest, Bill Arp's humor column, and reports of sensational crimes to capture everyone's attention. Vardaman expanded local

---

[1] Greenwood *Enterprise,* October 10, 1889, May 8, 1890; Winona *Times* and Lexington *Bulletin* quoted in Greenwood *Enterprise,* May 29, 1890.

news to cover the whole of Leflore County, with correspondents in each community reporting all arrivals, departures, births, deaths, marriages, and social events.

The improvements were rewarded by an increase in advertising and circulation. The new press, which produced larger and more attractive advertisements than had formerly appeared, brought patronage not only from Greenwood businessmen but also from merchants in adjoining towns. Vardaman soon boasted of a weekly circulation exceeding a thousand copies and covering Leflore, Carroll, Sunflower, and Holmes counties. The regular subscription rate was two dollars a year. In a further effort to expand circulation, he offered to send the paper free for two months to any new subscriber. At the same time, facing a problem universal to country editors, he constantly pleaded for his readers to pay the debts they owed him.

Except for the mechanical work and for temporary help from a cousin, George P. Money, Vardaman in the beginning edited and published the *Enterprise* singlehandedly. However, the job of a country editor was not easy. After Vardaman entered the state legislature, its sessions sometimes kept him away from Greenwood for months at a time. Lack of money also plagued him on occasion. By the beginning of 1892 his weekly paper had reverted to four pages. Because he needed editorial and financial help, he sold a half interest in the paper to J. L. Gillespie, formerly a member of the legislature and editor of papers in Tupelo and Oxford. Gillespie became business manager and served as editor when Vardaman was out of town; Vardaman retained control over editorial policy.[2]

Soon after Gillespie arrived, the *Enterprise* again assumed an eight-page format. Early the next year, however, fire destroyed the office and equipment. Publication was not interrupted, fortunately, because the printing was done in a neighboring town for almost six months, but the size fell back to four pages.[3] In September, 1893, Vardaman and Gillespie purchased the right to use the Taylor Chromatic Printing Process, which enabled them to produce a handsome paper with color printing and advertising.[4] By 1894 the editors had recovered suffi-

[2] Greenwood *Enterprise,* January 29, February 5, 1892.
[3] *Ibid.,* February 3, 1893.
[4] *Ibid.,* September 22, 1893.

ciently from their losses to return the paper to an eight-page format.

During the five years that Vardaman edited the *Enterprise* it became a leading paper in the Delta country. Its local rival, the *Delta Flag,* remained a four-page publication during much of this time, although it eventually assumed an eight-page layout similar to that of the *Enterprise.* Which paper was more widely read is not known, but by 1895 the *Enterprise* boasted a weekly subscription of 1,200.

As editor of the *Enterprise,* Vardaman carefully formed and maintained his policies. No longer did he try to avoid offending readers and remain friends with all, as he had when he first became editor of the *Advance.* Now he believed that an editor should, after mature deliberation, form opinions, announce them and stand by them. He also diligently strove to prevent his editorial page from becoming littered with petty compliments to friends and local personages. "There is nothing more contemptable [*sic*], and at the same time, more discouraging to the country editor," he complained, "than the disposition on the part of some little one by three-quarters money changer, penut [*sic*] merchant, jack-let lawyer, or patent medicine doctor, to speak disparagingly and lightly of the country newspaper. They seem to think that the newspaper is established and run solely for the purpose of paying cheap compliments and publishing senseless communications without charge." [5]

The hazards of editorial responsibility were at times serious indeed. In July, 1890, a group of pranksters cut from an illustrated newspaper a picture of the Chicago city council—recently accused of graft— wrote over the head of each councilman the name of a Greenwood city official and then posted the illustration on the Delta Bank. Evidently Vardaman thought the incident more than a harmless joke, for he condemned it in a stinging editorial: "The man who would assassinate your character, who would slyly and sneakingly attempt with vile tongue, pen or pencil to besmirch the fame of any man or body of men, would when occasion permitted stab you in the back or shoot you in the dark." His editorial enraged Walter Stoddard and T. H. Upshur, two of the pranksters. Early on the morning that the editorial appeared, before Vardaman had arrived at work, they barged into his office and demanded that his assistant tell them who had written the

[5] *Ibid.,* May 4, 1894. See also September 10, 1891.

editorial. The assistant refused to tell, but before leaving they warned that if the editorial was aimed at them, they would hold the "s. o. b." who wrote it responsible.[6]

Vardaman was at the Delta Bank when he learned that Stoddard and Upshur were looking for him. Fearing they were armed, a cashier gave Vardaman a thirty-two-caliber revolver. A few moments later Stoddard and Upshur confronted the editor in front of the bank. Had Vardaman written the editorial? Stoddard asked. He had. What did he mean by it? He meant exactly what he said. Stoddard slapped Vardaman. The editor struck back, knocking Stoddard to the ground. He quickly turned on Upshur and drove him back with three quick blows to the head. Then either Stoddard or Upshur pulled a pistol and shot at Vardaman. As Vardaman drew his gun and began to fire, his cousin James Money stepped out of the bank and joined the fray. Onlookers ran madly for cover; the four combatants fired time and again. When the shooting stopped, Stoddard lay dead, his body riddled by five bullets; a shot had broken Money's leg; Upshur had fled the scene; and although a bullet had ripped Vardaman's coat, he had not been hurt. No one pressed charges against Vardaman and Money because they had fought in self-defense. The shooting helped to establish Vardaman's reputation as an editor who would stand by his work. Many of his later editorials aroused anger, but no person ever repeated Stoddard's mistake.

As editor of the *Enterprise* he avoided sensationalism and vituperative journalism, deeming accurate reporting more important. When a fellow editor, for example, reported that officials at the Yalobusha County convict farm treated prisoners cruelly, Vardaman sent an agent to the farm to investigate the situation, concluded that the charges were groundless, and condemned his irresponsible colleague. He ordinarily wrote in a moderate tone, not resorting to invective or distortion. Those public officials whom he criticized could reply through the columns of the *Enterprise* free of charge. Indeed, he promised that the

[6] Winona *Advance,* August 1, 8, 1890; Yazoo *Sentinel,* August 7, 14, 1890; Jackson *Daily Clarion-Ledger,* August 1, 1890; Walthall *Warden,* August 6, 1890; Jackson *New Mississippian,* August 6, 1890; Greenville *Times,* August 2, 1890. The issue of the *Enterprise* for the week of the shooting is not on file in the Office of the Chancery Clerk in Greenwood nor in any other depository known to the author.

"most violent and uncompromising personal enemy will be accorded the same fairness of reply that would be given the warmest and most devoted personal friend." Sometimes men who opposed his views took advantage of this offer.[7]

Newspaper editors, Vardaman believed, had a special obligation to society. Usually they were the only medium for informing the public about current happenings. In a speech to the Mississippi Press Association in May, 1893, he called the attention of his colleagues to their responsibilities, asserting that there had never been "a more imperative demand for honest, intelligent and courageous journalistic work, than confronts us today." Too many accepted existing conditions without realizing that major changes might soon occur. The present was an age of transition: "We are in the very vortex of mutations—the old order of things is being displaced by the new—the multitudinous interests are demanding a change in our system." Change might represent progress and advancement, but many existing forces endangered the nation. "The concentration of wealth in the hands of a favored few,— the unholy greed for gold—the prostitution of the ballot—the subversion and subordination of every moral truth to sordid selfishness—the widespread want and discontent—the emasculating effect of inherited indigence—all brought about by unjust and immoral legislation— legislation enacted for the purpose of robbing the indigent many for the enrichment of the few, are the deadly germs of governmental destruction—the fatal symptoms of national death." Vardaman mined the wealth of his wide-ranging reading. Drawing an analogy from James Anthony Froude's *Caesar: A Sketch,* he warned that weaknesses similar to those that caused the downfall of Rome endangered America in the 1890's.[8] Editors must so inform their readers and arouse them to action.[9]

The young editor's enthusiastic sense of civic pride in his community and its citizens spurred him to work for Greenwood's advancement.

[7] Greenwood *Enterprise,* May 9, August 8, 1891, June 30, 1893, June 29, December 7, 1894.

[8] In his speech Vardaman did not refer to a specific work. James Anthony Froude's only major work on Roman History, however, was *Caesar: A Sketch* (London, 1879). British Museum, *General Catalogue of Printed Books* (New Edition, London, 1961), LXXX, 200.

[9] Vardaman's speech was published in the Greenwood *Enterprise,* May 12, 1893.

Since the Civil War the Delta's population had grown rapidly, and Greenwood had shared in this growth. Yet it remained a rural town, and in the early 1890's did not have the electric lights, waterworks, and telephones that other municipalities throughout the country were adopting.[10] Vardaman worked for these and other improvements not by attacking city officials or criticizing their lack of initiative but by directing his appeals to his readers. If he could arouse enthusiasm for improvements, their attainment would be only a matter of time, and to arouse animosities might make reform more difficult to achieve.[11]

To improve the city's business opportunities, Vardaman issued special trade editions which described the growth of Greenwood, the advantages of doing business with her merchants, and the possibilities of future expansion. Frequently having sixteen pages, these trade editions were distributed throughout Leflore and adjoining counties. He also encouraged the establishment of manufactories. Greenwood had a variety of small enterprises, such as stave companies, cooperages, foundries, and machines shops, but no large establishments. In an attempt to encourage industrial growth, the *Enterprise* advocated the formation of a businessmen's league, whose members should correspond with industrialists throughout the country interested in establishing factories in the South. When the citizens of Greenwood formed such a league in 1893, Vardaman became a leading member.[12]

That Greenwood needed better fire protection was well demonstrated by the fact that within a five-year period the *Enterprise* office burned twice. The town eventually provided for a volunteer fire company, and urgings by the *Enterprise* and various civic groups induced the county board of supervisors to order the erection of a fireproof vault in which to preserve public records.[13]

---

[10] *Compendium of the Eleventh Census: 1890*, I, 241. In its adoption of civic improvements at this time, Greenwood resembled hundreds of other cities and towns throughout the United States. Arthur M. Schlesinger, *The Rise of the City, 1878–1898* (New York, 1933), 92–106; Edward C. Kirkland, *Industry Comes of Age: Business, Labor, and Public Policy, 1860–1897* (New York, 1961), 241–44; Roger Burlingame, *Engines of Democracy: Inventions and Society in Mature America* (New York, 1940), 243–47; John W. Oliver, *History of American Technology* (New York, 1956), 349–51, 433–40.

[11] Greenwood *Enterprise,* June 19, 1890.

[12] *Ibid.,* August 14, 1890, September 10, 1891, January 1, 1892, September 22, November 3, 10, 1893.

[13] *Ibid.,* October 24, 31, 1890, February 3, July 28, 1893, October 5, 1894.

Even more serious was the lack of public utilities. Dependent upon wells for her water supply, Greenwood had neither running water nor a sewage disposal system. The *Enterprise* suggested that the experience of Yazoo City showed that river water could be filtered and pumped into an elevated tank to furnish an inexhaustible supply the year around. Despite Vardaman's pleadings, more than a decade passed before Greenwood got around to establishing a waterworks. In the early 1890's he did not oppose private ownership of utilities, but by the end of that decade he came to believe that municipal ownership of gas, electricity, water, and streetcar lines would best insure a community's welfare. "Municipal management and ownership of such things has passed the experimental stage," he wrote in 1901. If a private corporation could run a utility profitably, there was no reason a city could not, and probably at a saving to the taxpayers.[14]

What Greenwood needed above all else, Vardaman thought, was a public high school. If the city erected a suitable building, teachers and school would follow. He recommended a structure costing fifteen thousand dollars to be financed by twenty-year bonds. An adequate educational system would attract new people to the area; the money that wealthier parents now paid to boarding schools could be directed into Greenwood's economy; and children could remain at home throughout the year. Furthermore, society should assist those who could not afford a private education: "This class of children—the poor of society [—] are entitled to some consideration." In the long run, Vardaman warned, it would be wise for the wealthier people to provide this necessity for the poor.[15]

When the new state constitution of 1890 provided for a minimum of four months' public schooling to be paid from the state's general fund and authorized individual counties to extend the term by levying a special tax, the *Enterprise* became more vehement in demanding a school. After a time numerous citizens petitioned the city council to erect a frame schoolhouse costing not more than two thousand dollars. This Vardaman opposed, arguing that within a few years the cheap building would have to be abandoned. When the city council proceed-

14 *Ibid.*, October 31, 1890; Greenwood *Commonwealth,* September 29, 1899, July 14, 1901.
15 Greenwood *Enterprise,* May 29, June 19, 1890.

ed to order the construction of one costing three thousand dollars, he expressed his confirmed disapproval. Such a building would not insure a competent and efficient school system or attract men with capital "to come and cast their lot among us." Nevertheless, he accepted the proposal as better than none and as a final effort appealed for a ten-month school term.[16]

The five years during which Vardaman edited the *Enterprise,* 1890–1895, saw Greenwood gain not only a school of sorts, a fire company and a fireproof vault but also a streetcar system, an electric light plant, telephones, and an opera house. He had helped obtain these improvements by educating the public to the need, as well as by actively participating in the organizations formed to realize their establishment. Civic spirit motivated him, but so did enlightened self-interest. A town with an active spirit, an educated citizenry, and an expanding economy could better support its newspapers.

Having quickly become an influential figure among his fellow editors, Vardaman was instrumental in inducing the Mississippi Press Association to meet at Greenwood in May, 1893.[17] The *Enterprise* urged its readers to prepare for the occasion, and committees made plans to entertain the visitors with excursions, fishing parties, picnics and dances. In view of a strong prohibition movement in Leflore County at the time, the editor of the Oxford *Globe* asked if Greenwood was a dry town? "Yes," Vardaman replied, "but it is not exactly working at the business yet. . . . There will be enough on hand for the 'boys' on the 16th." [18] As Vardaman hoped, many of the editors returned to their homes after the meeting prepared to sing the praises of the progressive Delta town.[19]

While editing the *Enterprise* and later during his early years as editor of the Greenwood *Commonwealth,* Vardaman was well liked by most of his fellow Mississippi editors. In 1897 the state press association made an excursion up the Mississippi River to St. Louis. On the first night of the trip the editors and their wives retired early, and only a "few old stagers, sporty men and lively women" remained on the

16 *Ibid.,* October 24, 1890, February 20, March 21, April 4, 1891.
17 Tunica *Independent* quoted in Greenwood *Enterprise,* June 2, 1893.
18 *Ibid.,* May 11, 1894.
19 *Ibid.,* May 25, 1894.

passenger deck, where they gambled until the early morning. The night
was hot and the editors made frequent trips across the deck to the water cooler. Near midnight a tall man with flowing black hair and with
a sheet draped carelessly across his shoulders, approached the cooler
and "proceeded, a la Washington Irving's headless horseman, to drink
the vessel dry." As the women shrieked and the men swore, "the ap-
parition beat a hasty retreat." The next night R. H. Henry, soon to
become one of Vardaman's bitterest political critics, was arraigned
before a mock court and was "charged with walking in his sleep, and
dancing the can-can on the quarter-deck, thinly clad, to the shocking
amazement of lady passengers." Vardaman somberly presided over the
trial and, after hearing the evidence against the editor of the Jackson
Daily Clarion Ledger, declared Henry guilty and sentenced him to buy
drinks for the press party. "Then the company adjourned to the fore-
deck, where all 'took sugar in theirn', the judge and prisoner leading
the procession, arm in arm, the best of friends, for at the time factionalism had not been incorporated upon the body politic, to estrange men
and make political enemies of former companions." [20]

Even in his early public years Vardaman was a decided advocate of
certain humanitarian reforms and liberal positions. The most surprising of these, perhaps, was his conviction that capital punishment
should be abolished, and this in an era when southern life on its dark-
er side was characterized by much violence. Large crowds, for example, customarily assembled to witness public hangings. Despite the
strength of this frontier mentality, Vardaman considered the adage "an
eye for an eye and a tooth for a tooth" an indication of ignorance, barbarity, and revenge.[21] The Greenwood editor opposed capital punishment because he believed it did not deter crime: "You may hang,
burn or flay, but crime will be committed." [22] Capital punishment, he
argued, could be defended only on the grounds of revenge. Convinced
that the state should strive to deter crime and rehabilitate criminals, he
considered capital punishment to be no more justified than lynch law.

---

[20] R. H. Henry, *Editors I Have Known Since the Civil War* (New Orleans,
1922), 318–20.
[21] Greenwood *Enterprise,* June 29, 1894.
[22] *Ibid.,* July 21, 1893.

Nor had the state any greater right to hang a man than had a mob; if the state did not consider life sacred, neither would the mob.[23]

Far more important than capital punishment as a practical issue in the South was prison reform. The barbaric convict lease system still existing in Mississippi during the 1890's caused untold injustices.[24] Vardaman was the outraged witness of one tragic result of this system. On an April morning in 1894, at the request of the sheriff, he examined a Negro prisoner, Julius Adams, who had just escaped from the farm of J. H. Foltz. Convicted of petty larceny and unable to pay a fine of fourteen dollars, Adams had been leased to Foltz.[25] Adams told of being forced to work out of doors during the winter until his fingers froze; the skin burst and peeled off, exposing the bones. Foltz nevertheless forced him to continue working; no physician attended him. When his hands became gangrenous, an assistant of Foltz took Adams to a block and cut off each of his fingers at the first joint. Finally he could not work and Foltz locked him in a log cabin and chained him down each night. In March, Adams again began working, but fled at the first opportunity. Although pursued by dogs, he managed to reach the sheriff's office in Greenwood.

Vardaman's editorial on the inhumanity to Julius Adams opened with these lines:

> Nothing But a Convict!
> Man's inhumanity to man,
> Makes countless thousands mourn.

[23] *Ibid.*, June 19, October 31, 1890, March 21, July 4, 1891.

[24] In 1890 Mississippi became the first southern state officially to outlaw the convict lease system, but it lingered in the state on a small scale until 1906. J. H. Jones, "Penitentiary Reform in Mississippi," *Publications of the Mississippi Historical Society,* VI (1902), 111–20; C. Vann Woodward, *Origins of the New South, 1877–1913* (Baton Rouge, 1951), 424. Also see Fletcher Melvin Green, "Some Aspects of the Convict Lease System in the Southern States," in *Essays in Southern History Presented to Joseph Gregoire de Roulhac Hamilton, Ph. D., LL. D., By His Former Students at the University of North Carolina,* ed. Fletcher Melvin Green (Chapel Hill, 1949), 112–23; George W. Cable, "The Convict Lease System in the Southern States," in *The Silent South* (New York, 1885), 113–80; Blake McKelvey, *American Prisons: A Study in American Social History Prior to 1915* (Chicago, 1936), 180–85.

[25] "The so-called 'pig law' of Mississippi defined the theft of any property over ten dollars in value, or any cattle or swine of whatever value, as grand larceny,

In biting language he attacked the entire convict lease system and the society that tolerated it. For a minute crime the state had assigned this poor creature to a living hell: "In this day of bibles, boasted benevolence, charity and forgiveness . . . we find in our midst, committed by intelligent white people deeds of barbarity that would outrage the bloody instincts of the most conscienceless savage that ever roamed the wilds of the West! " True, many considered him nothing but a "damned negro convict," lacking even the rights of beasts of burden. Admittedly the Negro had no political rights in Mississippi, but Vardaman maintained that the white race must be humane to all. Even if half of Adams' story was true, "then there is enough [in it] to damn, to make crimson the souls of the whole community." It would be better to take a gun and blow out a prisoner's brains than subject him to the ordeal through which Adams had passed. Foltz published a statement in which he denied the charges leveled against him. He held that when Adams came to his farm he had syphilis, which rendered him liable to serious injury from even slight exposure. The outcome of the Adams case is unknown. Its barbarity was, however, inescapable. As Vardaman pointed out, one thing did not lie: "the mutilated disfigured hands." [26]

One reason the southern people lagged far behind the rest of the nation in the management of their penal institutions, Vardaman believed, was that many did not understand the cause of crime. He did not believe that man had complete free will and was responsible for all of his actions. Rather, he maintained that "it is quite probable that the actions of all men are determined by countless causes over which they have no control." Certainly in many cases, mental illness and environmental factors gave rise to crime. Convinced that many criminals were not responsible for their actions, he urged that prisons should be "moral hospitals," and "when the patient shows symptoms of returning or entirely recovers he should be released." [27]

---

with sentence up to five years." Woodward, *Origins of New South,* 213; Wharton, *The Negro in Mississippi,* 236–38.

[26] Greenwood *Enterprise,* April 13, 20, 27, 1894.

[27] Greenwood *Commonwealth,* April 15, May 6, 20, August 12, 1897, September 29, 1899, January 19, 1900, February 22, 1901. Vardaman's views on crime and prison reform may well have been influenced by John Peter Altgeld's *Our Penal Machinery and Its Victims,* published in 1884. Vardaman's views were

Throughout Vardaman's early writings ran a persistent note of optimism: he believed in progress. Some day, after time and education had done their work, man would end capital punishment and institute prison reforms. To insure his own advancement man must have complete freedom of thought. Intolerance, bigotry, and fanaticism had always "rested like a foul fog upon progress and prosperity." It did not matter what men might believe temporarily, if they came to their conclusions honestly and could express them freely. Mistakes would be made, but if men remained free all error would eventually be driven out. To those who feared unrestricted intellectual freedom, he pointed to scientific discoveries which the church had considered to be "an emanation from infinite wickedness." Copernicus, Bruno, and Servetus had suffered at the hands of the "ruling ignorance of their respective times." Modern men must follow the course of intellectual freedom.[28]

Because he believed in free inquiry, Vardaman sharply criticized religious groups desirous of imposing their views on others. Sunday blue laws particularly aroused his ire. In Tennessee a judge had fined a Seventh Day Adventist for working on Sunday. In reviewing the case Vardaman noted that the witnesses had not claimed that the accused had disturbed a religious meeting nor that he had violated their individual rights; he only had shocked their moral sense, and the court ruled that shock to be a nuisance. Vardaman doubted that the witnesses had a moral sense, for it "is a very common human frailty to mistake bigotry and intolerance for moral sense." [29] State laws should not attempt to control conscience but should allow the utmost freedom in individual matters. In his war against Sunday blue laws, he even leveled his guns at the Mississippi State Baptist Convention, which had opposed having the World's Fair open on Sundays. Arguing that many people could attend the fair only on Sunday, Vardaman hoped the authorities would pay no attention to such demands.[30]

---

similar to those expressed by the Illinois reformer. Ray Ginger, *Altgeld's America: The Lincoln Ideal Versus Changing Realities* (New York, 1958), 65–66.

[28] Greenwood *Commonwealth*, March 25, 1898; Greenwood *Enterprise*, June 30, July 21, 1893.

[29] Greenwood *Enterprise*, August 14, 1890, October 1, 1891.

[30] *Ibid.*, October 24, 1890, August 1, 1891. Vardaman's position can be more fully understood when one realizes that in the late nineteenth century, evangelical religious faiths formed a powerful force in rural southern life, and most

He had little respect for ministers who abused their positions by attacking individuals or groups. Resort to such vulgar and slanderous methods degraded their office. He considered that the attacks of evangelist Sam Small upon bootleggers, gamblers, and prostitutes—attacks widely reported in the southern newspapers—were "as much out of place in the pulpit as prostitution is out of place in the home of purity or around the fireside of virtue." When Small was beaten by a bartender, Vardaman believed he had gotten what he deserved. After hearing another well-known evangelist, Sam P. Jones, lecture in Greenwood, Vardaman described him as a cheap showman and reported that Jones's lecture offered nothing of value.[31]

In Vardaman's mind Thomas Paine was symbolic as a champion of intellectual freedom and a victim of ignorance and religious intolerance. More than any man, Vardaman believed, Paine had helped the cause of American independence, and at the end of the Revolution only Washington's popularity had exceeded his. Then Paine wrote the *Age of Reason,* "and the Christian world has waged cruel and relentless warfare against him from that time to this good day." For one indiscretion he lost all. Though Vardaman thought Paine erred in writing the *Age of Reason,* Paine believed what he wrote, and the treatment accorded him was a crime for which "the recipients of his benefaction must suffer in the judgment of coming generations." [32] Perhaps it was because Vardaman felt Christianity had so frequently stifled intellectual freedom that he rarely affiliated with an organized church, although he claimed to be a Methodist.

Despite the fact that his outlook on humanitarian reform and intellectual freedom, as well as his zeal for civic improvements, would be considered liberal by his own and later generations and would also help to explain why he became a progressive governor and senator, his views on other matters, especially the Negro, were far from enlightened. He was in truth a hard-shelled racist. In great measure his attitude reflected his time, place, and circumstances. Many people both

---

editors paid at least lip service to them. Thomas D. Clark, *The Southern Country Editor* (Indianapolis, 1948), 134–35.

[31] Greenwood *Enterprise,* November 17, 24, 1891; Greenville *Weekly Democrat,* March 3, 1898.

[32] Greenwood *Enterprise,* November 19, 1893; Greenwood *Commonwealth,* October 15, 1897.

North and South then regarded the Negro as an inferior being, and concern over his welfare had been muted since the end of Reconstruction. In the South the legacy of Reconstruction had given particular emphasis to the problem of "keeping the Negro in his place," and fear of Negro domination had been a chief concern of southern politics during the last quarter of the nineteenth century.[33] Finally, Vardaman had spent much of his life watching a white minority rule a society in which the blacks were a majority, often a vast majority.

As proof that racial conflict was a living reality and that whites must look to their supremacy, Vardaman recalled an incident in Leflore County, where Negroes then outnumbered whites 14,276 to 2,597.[34] In the late summer of 1889 racial violence erupted. At that time Oliver Cromwell, a Negro, was trying to persuade black farmers in the community of Shell Mound to form a Colored Farmers' Alliance store and to cease all business with white merchants. Because of his work, Cromwell was warned by whites to leave the county or be killed. He refused to cower and in response to his leadership about five hundred Colored Alliance members armed themselves and threatened to march on Greenwood, the county seat. The sheriff then wired Governor Robert Lowry for help, and the executive immediately ordered three companies of national guardsmen to proceed to Leflore County. With the arrival of troops and the organization of a large posse, the Negroes dispersed into small bands and fled into the canebrakes, but local whites hunted down and shot a number of them. Cromwell managed to escape and flee the state.[35]

At Winona, Vardaman had supported white supremacy as a politi-

[33] Rayford W. Logan, *The Negro in American Life and Thought: The Nadir, 1877–1901* (New York, 1954), *passim*; I. A. Newby, *Jim Crow's Defense: Anti-Negro Thought in America, 1900–1930* (Baton Rouge, 1965), *passim*; John Higham, *Strangers in the Land: Patterns of American Nativism, 1860–1925* (New Brunswick, 1955), 131–57; Wharton, *The Negro in Mississippi*, 216–33; Guion Griffis Johnson, "The Ideology of White Supremacy, 1876–1910," in Green (ed.), *Essays in Southern History*, 125–56.

[34] *Compendium of the Eleventh Census: 1890*, I, 241.

[35] *Journal of the House of Representatives of the State of Mississippi at a Regular Session Thereof, Convened in the City of Jackson, January 7, 1890* (Jackson, 1890), 594–98. Hereinafter cited as *House Journal, 1890*. The *Journals* for 1892, 1894, 1898, 1906, 1908, 1910 will be similarly denoted. *See also* Wharton, *The Negro in Mississippi*, 222–23; Winona *Times*, September 6, 1889; Jackson *Clarion-Ledger*, September 5, 1889; Raymond *Gazette*, September 7, 14, 1889; Natchez *Daily Democrat*, September 4, 1889, Jackson *New Mississippian*, September 4, 1889.

cal necessity, and at Greenwood he developed his views more fully and expressed them through his newspaper in concrete language. The Negro had to be barred from voting and holding office because he was incapable of self-government. For proof the editor pointed to the histories of Haiti and Santo Domingo, which he described as characterized by revolution, chaos, and despotism. Yet it was the race that ruled Santo Domingo which the "Republicans of the North have been trying for the last thirty years to place at the head of the governmental affairs of the South," most recently by the Force Bill of 1890.[36] The South would never submit to such domination. No matter how many laws Congress passed to insure the Negro's social and political equality, he would not be allowed to enjoy them. Southern whites would treat him properly "just so long as he keeps the place which nature designed for him." All white Americans should cooperate in meeting this problem, Vardaman urged, by supporting the passage of laws that prohibited Negroes from participating in governmental activities.[37]

His one exception to an abhorrence of capital punishment was his advocacy of lynch law to deal with Negro men who raped white women. Lynch law brought demoralizing and harmful effects to the whites, he realized, but when Negroes violated white women "there is nothing left to do with these human brutes but to kill them and at least get rid of them. That is all there is in it." [38] When a group of Negroes in Marianna, Arkansas, threatened an insurrection, he advised that the "judicious use of the noose and rifle might teach them a very salutary lesson." Allowing Henry Jones, "a 30 year-old-negro brute," to stand trial for having raped a seven-year-old white child enraged Vardaman. The blacks themselves should have dealt with him in short order.[39] He did make one compassionate concession, namely, that mobs should lynch their victims as quickly and simply as possible. He condemned the "brutal spirit" manifested by people in Paris, Texas, who had burned an alleged Negro rapist.[40]

[36] Greenwood *Enterprise,* July 25, 1891.
[37] *Ibid.,* May 26, 1893.
[38] *Ibid.,* May 27, 1892. On lynching in the South and the nation, see James Elbert Cutler, *Lynch-Law: An Investigation into the History of Lynching in the United States* (New York, 1905), *passim*; Southern Commission of the Study of Lynching, *Lynchings and What They Mean* (Atlanta, 1931), *passim*.
[39] Greenwood *Enterprise,* October 1, 8, 1891, September 7, 1894.
[40] *Ibid.,* February 10, July 28, 1893.

His concept of womanhood strongly influenced his justifying lynch law. As with many white men of that day, the fear of interracial marriage touched the emotional depth of his soul. Here his views on race stood out most clearly. The proudest boast of a southern man, he declared, was "the exalted virtue, the vestal purity and superlative qualities of Southern woman." He did not believe women to be inferior to men. If they wanted to enjoy equal political and economic opportunity, they had the right. In one area, moreover, women surpassed men: in religion and morals. Believing them to be of a finer moral fiber than men, Vardaman was certain that woman more frequently did the correct thing in matters of right and wrong. In turn, this female virtue exerted a decisive and much-needed influence upon men. "The truth is that quality in woman is the check and balance wheel to man's character." Men, for their part, should constantly strive to defend women's virtue, for their fall was "his saddest loss." Fathers and brothers had to protect their wives and sisters not only from Negro rapists, but from the evil intentions of dishonorable whites. Even the simple kiss could be a danger, "when given as an expression of lascivious emotions." Fathers and brothers who failed to regard it in that light might live to deplore their judgment. Since "promiscuous kissing" could become the "doorway of prostitution," the man who thus took advantage of a woman deserved death. "No, Brother, it is better that death be the penalty, than the debasement of the character of sublime womanhood." [41]

Vardaman's racist convictions accounted for his exalted view of southern women and his advocacy of lynch law. Convinced that Negroes belonged to an inferior race, he feared that sexual intercourse between a black man and white woman would cause the demise of the superior race. Whites had to maintain their racial integrity, for race played the major role in accounting for all human development. Wherever whites had maintained racial purity—as in America—there had been progress; where whites had intermarried with blacks—as in Haiti—all progress had ceased. In maintaining that line of thought, of course, he ignored the fact that for centuries southern white men had enjoyed sexual relations with Negro women, the result being an abund-

[41] *Ibid.,* August 11, 1893; Greenwood *Commonwealth,* March 9, 1900, November 7, 1902; Jackson *Issue,* December 5, 1908.

ance of mulattoes. Like most southern males, he skirted that paradox by accepting the popular theory that the offspring of a white man and a black woman always became a Negro. For the white South, maternity was the key to racial purity: should a black man father the child of a white woman, then the white race had been polluted.[42]

Vardaman was not alone in defending lynching and in exalting southern womanhood. In the late nineteenth century most southern white men shared his views. Newspapers frequently published editorials eulogizing women and defending lynching. In sharing those views he merely reflected the deeply embedded racist views of his contemporaries.

Many northerners often failed to realize, Vardaman thought, that the blacks received from the whites more advantages than they returned. The whites fed, clothed, and schooled them, receiving in return inefficient labor for six months of the year. The Negro was the greatest obstacle to material progress in the South, "a blight, a catapillar [sic] that destroys everything in sight and leaves nothing behind." All society suffered by his presence.[43]

Burdensome though he believed Negroes to be, Vardaman conceded that the South could not do without them. In his own Delta country, Negro field hands and sharecroppers supplied the only available labor for the large plantations. Any attempt to replace them would fail. "There is no man on earth," he warned, "who will take the negro's place in the South" under the existing system. However, he suggested that the system be changed. If western farmers could be enticed to the Delta and the large plantations broken up and sold to them as small farms, the Delta would become one of the wealthiest agricultural sections in the world. The Negro had failed as an agriculturist, and the South would never prosper until white farmers replaced him. But so long as the old system continued, "Sambo is the only man that will suit the Delta farmer." [44]

Even though Vardaman had by this time closely assumed his lifelong position on the race question, he was less extreme in the early

[42] Gunnar Myrdal, *An American Dilemma: The Negro Problem and Modern Democracy* (New York, 1944), 586–87, 591. For another view of the rape-lynch complex, see W. J. Cash, *The Mind of the South* (New York, 1960), 116–19.
[43] Greenwood *Enterprise*, May 26, 1893.
[44] *Ibid.*, May 18, 1894, January 4, 1895.

1890's than he later became. He did not, for example, use the word "nigger" in his writings, nor did he completely oppose Negro education. When Isaiah T. Montgomery, a Negro writer and lecturer, wanted to establish a grade school for black children at Cleveland, a Delta town not far from Greenwood, Vardaman published Montgomery's appeal for funds and quoted the Greenville *Times* in support of him: "The stand which this man has taken for the improvement and elevation of the negro . . . entitle[s] him to the hearty encouragement and material support of the white citizens and property owners of the Delta." [45]

The Italians apparently were the only other ethnic group that received his prejudiced disdain. When a New Orleans mob lynched eleven Italians in 1891, he supported the violence. He believed the victims had been members of the Mafia and justified the murders by the "law of self protection." Italians throughout the country, and especially those in New Orleans, should understand that if they attempted to retaliate, "the whole crowd will be wiped from the face of the earth." If necessary, the United States should go to war with Italy to settle the matter.[46] Fear of the Mafia, and general hostility toward Italians no doubt prompted this nationalistic bluster from Vardaman.

This violent attitude was not reflected in what he had to say about other racial or ethnic groups. Throughout his journalistic career he fought anti-Semitism. He could not understand prejudice against Jews. True, there were some "thieving rascals" among them, but no more than among gentile groups. He believed the Jews to be the most law-abiding people in the world: "Obedient to authority, patriotic, charitable, sympathetic—loyal to friend and fair to foe, they make the ideal citizen." Much of Greenwood's prosperity he attributed to its Jewish citizens, and on a number of occasions he defended Jews against unjust criticism. When a Memphis judge described a Jewish witness as having the "down-trodden look of his race," Vardaman protested that American Jews were not "down-trodden either in looks or in conduct."

[45] Greenville *Times* quoted in Greenwood *Enterprise*, November 10, 1891.
[46] Greenwood *Enterprise,* March 21, April 4, 1891. The New Orleans riot resulted from the murder of the superintendent of police under conditions which pointed to members of the local Italian population. The lynchings were widely supported by local newspapers and business leaders. Higham, *Strangers in the Land,* 90–91.

The idea that the Jews might establish a nation in the Turkish Empire seemed ridiculous to Vardaman. The American Jew loved his country as much as any citizen and would not give it up for any place on earth.[47] As editor of the *Commonwealth* in 1899, he advocated that the nations of the world express their disapproval of the Dreyfus case by withdrawing support from a world's fair to be held in France.[48]

A prohibition campaign in 1893 generated the most heated controversy of Vardaman's years as editor of the *Enterprise*. It resembled his earlier experiences in Winona, but this time he played a more definite role. Congruent with his views on blue laws, he did not believe it wise or possible to force moral views on others. For this reason he opposed prohibition at first but wanted rigid laws strictly enforced to regulate the sale of liquor. By such a course, many of the "little crossroad" saloons could be eliminated. He urged saloon owners to help enforce the laws, promising that if they did the "prejudice against the saloon in this country will die out entirely." He opposed all attempts to enact statewide prohibition; if temperance legislation must be adopted, let it be on a county-option basis.[49]

In Leflore County the movement began to gain momentum in June, 1893, when prohibition leaders began to circulate petitions requesting the board of supervisors to call a local option election. At first Vardaman did not endorse the prohibition cause, but he got into the fight in August, when the board of supervisors refused to call a local option election on the grounds that many signers of the petitions were not registered voters. Believing the board had violated the law, the editor now sided with the prohibitionists and, partly as a result of his writings, public opinion soon forced the supervisors to yield and order an election for October 14.[50]

[47] Greenwood *Commonwealth*, September 14, 1900; Greenwood *Enterprise*, February 24, 1893, June 15, 1894; Greenwood *Commonwealth*, September 9, 1897.

[48] Greenwood *Commonwealth*, September 15, 1899. The first anti-Semitic demonstrations in American history occurred in parts of the Lower South. In 1893 nightriders burned many homes belonging to Jewish landlords in South Mississippi, and many Jewish businessmen were terrorized in Louisiana. Higham, *Strangers in the Land*, 92.

[49] Greenwood *Enterprise*, September 10, November 24, 1891, February 4, 19, 1892.

[50] *Ibid.*, June 23, 30, August 4, 25, September 8, 1893; Greenwood *Delta Flag*, September 15, 1893.

The antiprohibitionists now directed much of their wrath at the editor of the *Enterprise*. Judge S. R. Coleman, the attorney for the board of supervisors, accused him of treating the board unfairly and of relying on secondhand reports and rumors. On the personal side, he accused Vardaman of hypocrisy and asserted that the action of the board had only given him an excuse to ally himself with the prohibitionists. "The Great Chief, and bottle-washer of the *Enterprise*," as Coleman described Vardaman, had debased the code of journalism by putting pressure on the board to call a local option election. He further accused Vardaman and other prohibitionists of having had Negroes sign the local option petitions. For a short while Coleman was editor of the *Delta Flag* and continued to attack Vardaman viciously.[51] As he replied to Coleman's attacks in kind, the feud between the two became so bitter that a group of mutual friends arranged a truce. The two editors agreed to retract everything of a personal nature written about each other and the bitterness between the two papers subsided.

The struggle for prohibition, however, continued at an even fiercer pace. Vardaman knew the saloon men were fighting for their lives, but he warned that they should not use Negroes in the coming election. Only white men must decide if Leflore County would be wet or dry.[52] He knew of what he wrote, because some antiprohibitionists did go through the county registering Negroes to vote. So serious did the situation become that the county Democratic executive committee issued a resolution urging all to work against the wholesale registration of Negroes. This enraged the antiprohibitionists, who interpreted it as an attempt by the Democratic leaders to side with the opposition.[53] The committee denied this charge and held it only wanted to maintain white control in Leflore County. The state supreme court settled the controversy by ruling that no one could vote who had not registered four months before the election. The antiprohibitionists accepted the court's decision as a death knell for their cause. Though they continued to struggle, on October 14 the prohibitionists won the election.[54]

Despite his strong convictions on many subjects and his vigorous

[51] Greenwood *Delta Flag,* August 25, September 1, 15, 1893.
[52] Greenwood *Enterprise,* September 22, 1893.
[53] *Ibid.,* October 13, 1893; Greenwood *Delta Flag,* September 15, October 13, 1893.
[54] Greenwood *Delta Flag,* October 2, 27, 1893.

participation in sometimes controversial matters, Vardaman was a popular editor, one who worked constructively for the betterment of his community. During the five years he edited the *Enterprise* he rarely criticized state or local officials, and his views on many subjects resembled those of other country editors throughout the South. At that time he was not the embittered critic of existing social and political conditions he would be by the early twentieth century. For this reason it must be noted that the prohibition fight during his editorship of the *Enterprise* was not representative of his public career up to that time. Although the gun battle with Stoddard and Upshur and his stands on prohibition and religious intolerance showed that he would stand by his beliefs in spite of their unpopularity, he rarely offended the sensibilities of his readers. In fact, he sympathized with the conservative forces that controlled Mississippi politics and entered their ranks when he began his own political apprenticeship.

CHAPTER III

A POLITICIAN'S APPRENTICESHIP

IN VIEW OF Vardaman's boyhood ambition to enter public life, it is not surprising that he should become active in local politics. He began his political initiation by becoming a delegate from Leflore County to the county and district Democratic nominating conventions. In October, 1890, he became chairman of the county Democratic executive committee, a position he held during most of the nineties. In 1885 he had tried and failed to win a seat in the state legislature, but he succeeded in the election of 1889, and the next year, at the age of twenty-nine, assumed his official duties in the house.[1] That conservative body was made up largely of old Confederates, with James S. Madison, a planter and merchant from Noxubee County, presiding as speaker. Vardaman found the atmosphere perfectly congenial. He was an ambitious young man who wanted to advance himself within the existing system, and he had achieved his political position thus far by supporting state leaders like his cousin Hernando Money and Senator George, whom their opponents labeled as "Bourbons." In Mississippi the Bourbons controlled the Democratic Party, but unlike their contemporaries in some southern states, they did not cater exclusively to the interests of railroads, planters, and businessmen.[2] Nevertheless, the attention that a sizable number of Mississippi Bourbons devoted to agrarian interests was not enough to placate the farming elements in their demands for sweeping social and economic reforms.

Agrarian pressure was largely responsible for the calling of a state

[1] Greenwood *Yazoo Valley Flag,* April 11, 18, May 9, 1885, July 10, 1886, June 25, 1887; Greenwood *Enterprise,* October 24, 1890; Greenwood *Yazoo Valley Flag,* March 9, 16, July 27, November 9, 1889.

[2] Willie D. Halsell, "The Bourbon Period in Mississippi Politics, 1875–1890," *Journal of Southern History,* XI (1945), 519–37; James Sharbrough Ferguson, "Agrarianism in Mississippi, 1871–1900: A Study in Nonconformity" (Ph. D. dissertation, University of North Carolina, 1953), 266–69.

constitutional convention in 1890—a landmark accomplishment of the legislature. The Reconstruction constitution of 1868 had based apportionment on total population, giving the Delta control of the state legislature. The Delta's dark, rich soil produced such an abundant per acre cotton yield that thousands of Negro laborers had been attracted to the area and by 1890 the blacks there greatly outnumbered the whites. Because Mississippi Negroes had little voice in politics, the small number of Delta whites—many of whom were planters—exercised far greater political power in proportion to their number than did the white small farmers in the northeastern and southern part of the state. Many whites, therefore, wanted a constitution that would disfranchise the Negro (eliminating him as an influence in Mississippi politics) and base apportionment on white population. The small farmers also opposed the existing per capita system of distributing the school fund. Because few Negroes attended school, the white children of the Delta enjoyed better schools and longer terms than did the children of other sections. Additional reforms demanded by the farmers included an elective judiciary, limitation on the repeated reelection of state officials, abolition of convict leasing, and the removal of tax exemptions for railroads.

During the 1880's agrarian pressure for a constitutional convention had steadily mounted, and in 1890 Senator George surprised many of his fellow Bourbons by announcing his support for a new constitution. George has sometimes been described as the father of the 1890 constitution, although he actually began to support the convention after the issue was decided. When the agrarians could no longer be stopped, George worked to control the convention and "even to tame it." He wanted disfranchisement of the blacks, but not the progressive reforms demanded by the agrarians. He explained that his decision had been prompted by Senator Henry Cabot Lodge's Force Bill of 1890, which provided for federal control of elections.[3] The explanation fell upon receptive ears, for the Republican victory of 1888, Lodge's Force Bill, and the fact that a convention of Mississippi Negroes in 1889 nominated candidates for all state offices had aroused many whites—both

[3] Ferguson, "Agrarianism in Mississippi," 448–52; Albert D. Kirwan, *Revolt of the Rednecks, Mississippi Politics: 1876–1925* (Lexington, 1951), 60–64, 70.

Bourbons and farmers—and prepared them for the total elimination of the Negro from public affairs.

In response to George's leadership, Vardaman became one of only three Delta legislators who voted for the constitutional convention.[4] He not only voted for the convention, but when it met in August, 1890, he also supported its work. Although he, too, wanted the Negro disfranchised, he opposed any type of suffrage qualification based on property ownership. Against the suggestion that a multiple vote be granted to property owners on a basis of one vote for each forty acres of land owned, he argued that the "fruits of cupidity, avarice, stinginess, and usury are not [to be] counted above brains and patriotism when we come to exercising the elective franchise." [5] Vardaman's own plan, offered the previous May, involved a residence requirement of three years in the state and one year in the county, a poll tax to be paid annually six months before general elections, and an examination to determine mental fitness. Plainly this plan could be expected to reduce greatly the number of voting whites as well as Negroes, but he professed himself willing to accept even a reduction in Mississippi's congressional delegation if it were the necessary price of restricting the black's franchise.[6]

In the course of the constitutional convention a split developed between the conservatives who wanted to restrict the suffrage by property or educational qualifications and the leaders of the small-farmer class who wanted no restrictions at all. Senator George then offered a compromise plan, almost identical to Vardaman's, which, by employing an increased poll tax and an educational requirement, would disfranchise many whites as well as most Negroes. To compensate the agrarians, George arranged to increase their strength in the state legislature by assigning thirteen new members of the house of representatives to the white counties.[7] After the convention accepted the essential parts of George's plan, Vardaman fully supported the new

[4] *House Journal, 1890,* 211–17, 238–39; Jackson *Daily Clarion-Ledger,* January 16, 1890; James P. Coleman, "The Origins of the Constitution of 1890," *Journal of Mississippi History,* XIX (1957), 88.
[5] Greenwood *Enterprise,* October 20, 1890.
[6] *Ibid.,* May 29, 1890.
[7] Ferguson, "Agrarianism in Mississippi," 467–73.

constitution. His primary objective of having the Negro disfranchised
was achieved. Furthermore, his section did not lose its political
strength as many Delta politicians had feared it would, for it continued
to control the legislature and the state Democratic conventions.[8] By
devoting its major attention to disfranchising the Negro, the constitutional convention had ignored many of the constructive reforms advocated by the agrarians.[9] Be that as it may, the outcome pleased
Vardaman.

Besides serving his party as a legislator, he campaigned for the
Bourbon Democracy when it was threatened by agrarian movements.
The Southern Farmers' Alliance, an organization of great strength in
Mississippi, advocated the subtreasury plan as a means of expanding
credit to farmers. Essentially the plan provided that in agricultural regions the federal government would establish warehouses where farmers could deposit their produce when market prices were low and obtain low-interest loans on the commodities they stored. Later, when
market prices rose, they could sell their produce—hopefully—at a
profit.[10] Most of the state's Democratic leaders, including Senator
George, denounced the plan as unwise and unconstitutional. When
Ethelbert Barksdale opposed George's bid for reelection in 1891, the
challenger endorsed the subtreasury in an attempt to win the Alliance's
support. The resulting campaign held national significance, for it tested
the subtreasury plan's strength as a political issue in an agricultural
state.[11]

Vardaman strove to avoid a party split and labored to unite the
Leflore County Democracy behind George. In accordance with his
urging, a primary election was not held, but a county convention chose
delegates for the state nominating convention. He was delighted; under his direction the county convention supported George. Through

[8] Albert D. Kirwan, "Apportionment in the Mississippi Constitution of 1890,"
Journal of Southern History, XIV (1948), 234–46.

[9] Ferguson, "Agrarianism in Mississippi," 477–78.

[10] For a description of the subtreasury plan, see John D. Hicks, "The Sub-
Treasury: A Forgotten Plan for the Relief of Agriculture," *Mississippi Valley
Historical Review,* XV (1928), 355–73; James C. Malin, "The Farmers' Alliance Sub-Treasury Plan and European Precedents," *ibid.,* XXXI (1944), 255–
60; John D. Hicks, *The Populist Revolt: A History of the Farmers Alliance and
the People's Party* (Minneapolis, 1931), 186–92.

[11] Theodore Saloutos, *Farmer Movements in the South: 1865–1933* (Los
Angeles, 1960), 122.

the columns of the *Enterprise* he championed the senator's cause and harshly rebutted attacks upon the Mississippi leader. He branded Barksdale's attempt to take the Alliance into politics as demagogic and as endangering the entire farmers' movement. The editor heaped his strongest abuse upon those who threatened to bolt the Democratic Party. All loyal Democrats must accept the dictates of the party; any man who could not, should get out. But woe to him who did! "Judas Iscariot was just about as good a friend to Jesus Christ as the man who will go over the country and denounce the action of the Democratic state convention." [12] Barksdale's followers did not attempt to bolt the party, even though George carried the state nominating convention which met in August. However, this did not mean they had abandoned the fight. Because the state legislature, not the convention, chose United States senators, the Alliance men continued to work during the fall to elect legislators who would support Barksdale. This second attempt to secure the election of Barksdale also failed.

Throughout his terms in the state legislature, Vardaman continued to side with the conservative interests. Agrarian leaders had long advocated popular election of judges, but in 1892 and 1894 he voted against elective judiciary bills. G. A. Wilson introduced a bill to repeal tax exemptions granted to railroads, but Vardaman defended the corporations' interests.[13] Many small farmers opposed the convention system for choosing party nominees, but in 1892 House Speaker Hugh N. Street and Vardaman put down a movement to establish popular primaries.[14] The Greenwood legislator also favored granting tax exemptions to state banks, and he voted against a state income tax. When the legislature elected United States senators, he voted for the incumbents, James Z. George and Edward C. Walthall, the state's two leading Bourbons.[15] In 1894 he voted for Anselm J. McLaurin, a rising power in state politics, to fill Walthall's unexpired term after

[12] Greenwood *Enterprise*, August 1, 1891. And see May 9, June 6, July 25, August 8, 14, September 17, 1891.
[13] *House Journal, 1892,* 523–24, 534, 560–62; *House Journal, 1894,* 328–29; Greenwood *Commonwealth*, February 16, 1900.
[14] *House Journal, 1892,* 686–88, 920–21; Jackson *Daily Clarion-Ledger,* March 31, April 1, 1892; Woodville *Republican,* April 16, 1892; Greenwood *Enterprise*, April 22, 1892.
[15] *House Journal, 1892,* 178–80, 862; *House Journal, 1894,* 447.

the senator resigned because of ill health.[16] The one area in which
Vardaman broke with the conservative interests was in supporting legislation to establish a penitentiary farm in the hope that it would end
convict leasing.[17] He also voted against leasing convicts to the Gulf
and Ship Island Railroad.[18]

Because the Greenwood representative favorably impressed his fellow legislators, they accepted him. During his first term he seldom
missed a vote, and his speeches were marked by moderation and "gen-
tleness." [19] His sense of humor and ability to take a joke added to his
popularity. By the opening of the 1892 session he had become known
as a leader of Mississippi's "young democracy," and a movement was
under way to elect him speaker. Older legislators could strengthen
party solidarity, some argued, by supporting a young man for the
speakership.[20] The race involved three candidates: James S. Madison
sought reelection and was opposed by Vardaman and Hugh Street, an
insurance adjuster from Meridian. Some strongly opposed Street's candidacy, accusing him of being a tool of the insurance companies operating in the state.[21] Since no one of the three candidates had majority
support, some feared an extended fight. Shortly before the balloting
began, however, Vardaman surprised the assembly by withdrawing
from the race "in the interest of party harmony." His move enabled
Street to win by the narrow margin of 61 votes to 60.[22]

---

[16] Jackson *Daily Clarion-Ledger*, February 8, 1894; *House Journal, 1894,*
273, 283, 294–97, 304–307, 317–20, 334–37, 358–61, 374–76. Because of poor
health, Walthall wanted someone to finish his term; then, after a year's rest he
would resume his place in the Senate to begin a new term to which he had already been elected. Kirwan, *Revolt of the Rednecks,* 96–97.

[17] *House Journal, 1894,* 164–65.

[18] *House Journal, 1892,* 349–50; Jackson *Daily Clarion-Ledger,* February 12,
1892.

[19] Jackson *Daily Clarion-Ledger,* February 13, 1890.

[20] The *Enterprise* reported articles from other papers favorably mentioning
Vardaman's candidacy for the speakership. Articles appeared in the Walthall
Warden, Carrollton *Conservative,* Greenville *Times,* Oxford *Globe,* Tupelo
Ledger, Brookhaven *Leader,* Raymond *Gazette,* Monticello *Lawrence County
Press,* Meridian *Standard,* Greenwood *Delta Flag,* Vicksburg *Herald,* Green-
wood *Enterprise,* September, October, 1891.

[21] Woodville *Republican,* October 24, 1891; Jackson *Daily Clarion-Ledger,*
January 13, 1892.

[22] Greenwood *Enterprise,* January 8, 1892. This election was settled in a
Democratic caucus. When the house convened, Street was officially elected
speaker, receiving 114 of 116 votes. *House Journal, 1892,* 5–6.

It was not unselfishness that caused him to leave the race. He had in effect formed an alliance with Street. The speaker rewarded his young colleague by appointing him chairman of the appropriations committee; the two men thereafter often cooperated on legislative business, and Vardaman frequently served as speaker *pro tempore* during Street's absences.[23] Vardaman's withdrawal also helped strengthen his position within the party. Because he was young, he might gain the speakership at a later election. J. M. McGuire, a fellow legislator, predicted "there are high honors in store for Mr. Vardaman, who is one of the recognized leaders of the legislature." [24]

As chairman of the appropriations committee, Vardaman continued to serve the legislature's conservative majority. Since the late 1880's a group of agrarian reformers, representing the interests of the impoverished farmers and led by Frank Burkitt, had sought to lower taxes and reduce all state expenditures that benefited the wealthier classes. Some advocates of retrenchment soon became Populists, as did Burkitt himself in the summer of 1892.[25] Vardaman, as chairman of the appropriations committee, worked to offset Burkitt's attempts to cut expenditures. The clash of interests did not become sharp, but it showed that Vardaman clearly sided with the conservative interests rather than the minority of reformers.[26] Because he later became an avowed opponent of Negro education, one observes with interest that as a legislator he favored appropriating funds to the state's Negro colleges.[27]

After the close of the 1892 legislative session Vardaman worked against another agrarian threat to Democratic supremacy. By 1892 the Populist Party, which had gained moderate strength in Mississippi, entered a full slate of candidates for state offices, and the local Populists

---

[23] Hamilton, "Mississippi Politics in the Progressive Era," 68–70; Jackson *Daily Clarion-Ledger,* January 13, April 1, 1892; *House Journal, 1892,* 143–45, 189.

[24] Yazoo City *Herald* quoted in Greenwood *Enterprise,* January 22, 1892.

[25] Ferguson, "Agrarianism in Mississippi," 192–208; Hurshel Henry Broadway, "Frank Burkitt: The Man in the Wool Hat" (M.A. thesis, Mississippi State University, 1938), 24–26. One of the basic grievances of the members of the Farmers' Alliance and the Populist Party was the heavy burden of taxation which they had to bear. Hicks, *The Populist Revolt,* 85–87.

[26] *House Journal, 1892,* 189, 219–20, 252, 284–85, 358, 386, 448–49, 612–13, 698, 757–58, 813, 854, 915.

[27] *House Journal, 1892,* 698, 757–58; *House Journal, 1894,* 214–15.

supported the party's presidential nominee James B. Weaver. The Democrats, who marshaled their full forces to crush their opponents, realized the necessity of choosing able and influential men to represent their party as delegates to the national convention and as presidential electors. Who could better fulfill these requirements than the young Vardaman? [28] There was only one objection: through his newspaper he had been supporting Senator David B. Hill of New York for the presidential nomination and had been opposing former President Grover Cleveland's candidacy. While Vardaman admired Cleveland's courage and integrity, he opposed the New Yorker's sound money policies. Because the Greenwood editor had frequently denounced Cleveland's candidacy, he was not selected as a delegate to the national convention.[29] When the former President won the nomination, Vardaman reversed his position and supported him. No longer did he mention free silver and no longer did he criticize Cleveland's anti-inflationist policies. "Cleveland and Stevenson—a good pair to 'draw' Democratic voters to!" became the battle cry of the *Enterprise*.[30]

Assured of Vardaman's party loyalty, a state Democratic convention chose him as a presidential elector for the state at large. He wholeheartedly responded to his party's call. He resigned from the legislature, worked with party leaders in formulating campaign strategy, and for the first time went before the Mississippi electorate as a campaign speaker.[31] An ambitious man who craved public attention, Vardaman enjoyed speaking to crowds throughout the state. He proved to be an able orator, speaking so movingly and with such enthusiasm that he readily won the support of many who heard him. In all of his speeches he agreed with Populist leaders who decried the plight of the farmer and the laborer, but he denied that the Democratic Party was to blame. The true culprits were the Republicans. They had controlled the federal government for the past thirty years; they had passed the high protective tariff; they wanted to restore Negro rule in

[28] Vicksburg *Post* quoted in Greenwood *Enterprise*, April 22, 1892.
[29] Greenwood *Enterprise*, February 20, April 4, September 17, November 24, 1891, February 5, March 25, 1892.
[30] *Ibid.*, July 1, 1892.
[31] *Ibid.*, September 9, 16, 30, October 14, 21, 1892; J. K. Vardaman to John M. Stone, September 19, 1892, in Letters Received by John M. Stone, Governor's Records, Mississippi Department of Archives and History. Hereinafter cited as Stone Papers.

the South through the Force Bill. The Populists, whose policies advocated government ownership of railroads and telegraph and telephone lines, he branded as socialistic. He became especially outspoken in attacking Frank Burkitt who ran for Congress as a Populist against Congressman Hernando DeSoto Money. Denouncing Burkitt and other Populist leaders as opponents of white supremacy, he urged their followers to return to the Democratic Party.[32]

Cleveland's victory and the Populists' failure to make serious inroads in Mississippi further strengthened Vardaman among his fellow Democrats. The editor of the *Delta Advocate* held that "no young man in Mississippi has contributed more to, nor has any man, to a greater extent, sacrificed his personal interests for the success of the Democratic Party than the Hon. J. K. Vardaman."[33] When Cleveland was inaugurated, Vardaman went to Washington for the festivities and Congressman Money saw to it that he met the newly elected President. At the time, some Mississippi newspapers reported that he had been offered the position of Assistant Secretary of Agriculture.[34] If the offer was actually made, Vardaman rejected it, for his ambition was for higher elective office. Believing that the best way to achieve his goal was through the state legislature, he ran for reelection to the Mississippi house of representatives without opposition in the fall of 1893.

Vardaman's increasing prestige within the Bourbon Democracy was evidenced at the legislative session of 1894, when Street resigned as speaker and the lawmakers elected Vardaman to the position.[35] The move appeared to have been an extension of the alliance formed between the two during the previous session: as soon as he became speaker, Vardaman appointed Street chairman of the powerful Ways and Means Committee. Additional explanation of the alliance may be found in family ties and political factions: Street was an ally of Congressman Money and Senator George and chances are strong that Money exerted influence in behalf of his young cousin. It is doubtful

[32] Yazoo City *Herald,* *Yazoo Sentinel,* Winona *Times,* quoted in Greenwood *Enterprise,* October 7, 1892.

[33] *Delta Advocate* quoted in Greenwood *Enterprise,* December 2, 1892.

[34] *Delta Advocate* quoted in Greenwood *Enterprise,* March 17, 31, November 10, 24, 1893; Natchez *Daily Democrat,* November 2, 1893.

[35] Street's only explanation for resigning was that he preferred "the freedom of the floor to the laborious and responsible duties of that office [the Speakership]." *House Journal, 1894,* 7–8.

that Vardaman was unaware of the fact that in the past the speakership had been a valuable stepping stone on the path toward the governor's mansion. However achieved, his election constituted a major triumph for a man of thirty-three.

Vardaman as speaker demonstrated his Democratic loyalty and his belief in party government. The Populist movement in Mississippi reached its peak in this legislature, claiming eighteen members of the house over which he presided.[36] Although this small number posed no serious threat to the Democrats, he did not want to give them a chance to hurt his party. He therefore reorganized the house committees to put the Populists "where they can do the least harm—the place our enemies should always occupy when we have the location of them." The speaker realized that reorganization along party lines would tend to unify the opposition to the Democrats, but he did not mind that, believing it would prove profitable in the long run. As he said: "Feeling for my own political creed, as they [the Populists] probably regard theirs, I want to preserve it in its purity and integrity, and for that reason I want no man who entertains views at variance with mine to act and think for me. I think there is a great deal of true patriotism in party discipline. No great question of political, economic or governmental measure was ever enacted into law, but that had behind it as an indispensable prerequisite a well-organized and disciplined political faction." [37]

The legislative session of 1894 Vardaman described as the most harmonious he had ever witnessed. The Populists had caused no serious trouble; even Frank Burkitt had maintained a gentlemanly bearing at all times.[38] Actually the placid surface was deceptive, for it was only their small number that prevented the Populists from making their presence felt. On many issues, such as appropriating money for state

---

[36] *House Journal, 1894,* 488–92; William David McCain, "The Populist Party in Mississippi" (M.A. thesis, University of Mississippi, 1931), 23.

[37] New Orleans *Picayune* quoted in Greenwood *Enterprise,* January 12, 1894. On most major committees the Populists numbered only two, and their membership never exceeded four. In the session of 1892 Frank Burkitt had served as chairman of the committee on registration and election; when he returned in 1894 as a Populist, the Democrats stripped him of his chairmanship. Only the Populist R. R. Buntin continued to hold the minor position of chairman of the joint committee on enrolled bills. *House Journal, 1894,* 382–98.

[38] Greenwood *Enterprise,* February 16, 1894.

institutions, they formed a solid block of opposition.[39] In removing them from all positions of power, Vardaman had acted wisely in his party's interests. Certainly his actions as speaker gave no indication that he would later lead the progressive movement in Mississippi.

By the close of the session Vardaman appeared to be a rising power in Mississippi politics. Indeed, he had achieved much during his first five years in public office: as a state legislator, as a presidential elector, and as speaker of the house, he had served his party well. He now wanted to become governor. Some state newspapers had mentioned him as a likely gubernatorial candidate in 1893, shortly after he had canvassed the state as a presidential elector.[40] By the time he achieved the speakership, one national publication reported that twenty-seven Mississippi newspapers had endorsed him for the governorship.[41] At the time he enjoyed wide popularity among his fellow editors and one observer believed it was the "zeal of Vardaman's newspaper friends [that] induced him to become a candidate." [42] During 1894 it was widely rumored that he would be the Delta's candidate, and in December he officially announced his candidacy. By the end of that month his two leading opponents had also announced. United States Senator Anselm J. McLaurin would run as a free silver Democrat, while Henry C. McCabe of Vicksburg would uphold the gold standard.

When Vardaman entered the gubernatorial race he, too, advocated free silver, but he had not always championed it. Having supported Cleveland for the presidency, he continued during 1893 to back the President's policies, even while a depression spread over the country and the demand for free silver as a measure to restore prosperity gained strength. But Vardaman realized there was no simple solution for the nation's economic ills, for he believed the depression had been brought on by the Republicans' high tariff policy, the demonetization of silver in 1873, crop failures in 1886 and 1887 in the West, labor troubles in the East, and the crash of securities in South American

[39] *House Journal, 1894,* 92–94, 110–11, 228–31, 405–407.

[40] Winona *Times* and Ripley *Sentinel,* quoted in Greenwood *Enterprise,* March 17, 31, 1893; Bay St. Louis *Gulf Coast Progress,* January 4, 1894.

[41] Washington *National View,* quoted in Greenwood *Enterprise,* February 16, 1894.

[42] J. M. Liddell to A. J. McLaurin, September 23, 1895, in Letters Received by Anselm J. McLaurin, Governor's Records, Mississippi Department of Archives and History. Hereinafter cited as McLaurin Papers.

countries and Australia.[43] Through the *Enterprise* he urged his readers
to remain faithful to the Democratic Party, while he condemned those
who criticized Cleveland for his lack of action. At the same time he
believed that both the Democratic platform and the desire of many
southerners and westerners for free silver made imperative legislation favorable to the silver interests.[44] After repealing the Sherman
Silver Purchase Act, the party should start anew with a more effective
silver policy. What that should be, he left extremely vague. Indeed, his
writings indicated no true faith in silver legislation in any form.[45] Yet
as economic conditions worsened and inflationary sentiment increased,
he went over to silver. By the fall of 1894, after Cleveland had vetoed
the seigniorage bill and refused to sign the Wilson tariff, Vardaman
believed that he no longer represented his party and repudiated him
completely.[46]

Free silver became, and remained, a leading issue in the gubernatorial contest of 1895; Vardaman centered his early speeches around it
and so did his leading opponent, Senator McLaurin. But Vardaman
soon realized that he must broaden the appeal of his campaign. As a
senator, McLaurin was stronger in the Democratic party than was Vardaman. Without new issues McLaurin would easily carry the nominating convention in August. Vardaman began therefore to emphasize
state problems, especially the distribution of the common school fund.
He surprised a Delta audience at Batesville in early April by asserting
that the present system of allocating the common school fund was unfair to the white people. Each year the whites paid the larger part of the
school tax, but the Delta counties, heavily populated with Negroes, received a greater share of the proceeds than did the hill counties of eastern Mississippi where whites predominated. As things were, many
Delta counties ran their schools five to seven months each year, where-

[43] Greenwood *Enterprise,* June 16, 1893.
[44] Actually the Democratic platform of 1892 had straddled the silver issue as
it had the tariff question. George Harmon Knoles, *The Presidential Campaign
and Election of 1892* (Stanford, 1942), 81–83.
[45] Greenwood *Enterprise,* June 30, July 28, August 25, October 13, 27, November 3, 1893.
[46] Greenwood *Enterprise,* April 6, September 7, November 30, 1894. Seigniorage is the gain to the government involved in minting coins that are worth
more than the bullion from which they are made. Allan Nevins, *Grover Cleveland: A Study in Courage* (New York, 1932), 600.

as some largely white counties could barely manage four. The system should be changed. Negroes should not be educated at the expense of white people. Whites should realize, he warned, that education only made the Negro dissatisfied with his lowly position in society—a position he would always occupy as long as white men dominated the country.[47]

Vardaman knew his Mississippi. Sentiment had long been growing among many whites for a change in the distribution of the school tax. It had, in fact, been one of the chief demands made by the Farmers' Alliance at the time of the constitutional convention of 1890. Throughout the South some whites had been advocating the abolition of Negro education.[48] He may not have realized how strong the issue was until he began to use it in campaign speeches, but from that time forward he knew that it ignited a strong response among Mississippi's whites, as did other issues touching anti-Negro sentiment. Consequently he never lost sight of racism as a stepping-stone in his rise to power. The Sardis *Reporter,* itself a Delta paper, speculated that nine-tenths of the white voters in the state would agree with Vardaman: "We have noticed a trend of public sentiment in that direction all over the State, Mr. Vardaman made a certre [*sic*] shot—a ten strike—right there." [49]

Vardaman's appeal to racism greatly disturbed white Democrats who were competing with the Populists for the Negro vote. Although the 1890 constitution had disfranchised most Negroes, as late as 1895 a sizable number of blacks still voted in some counties. In Marion County, located in the piney woods of South Mississippi, for example, Democratic leaders feared that Vardaman's Negro baiting had endangered the black vote. A year earlier a Whitecap organization, which consisted chiefly of dirt farmers, had terrorized Negroes in an effort to drive them from merchant-owned lands. Because local officials had successfully stopped the Whitecappers, Negro leaders announced they intended to vote Democratic. Vardaman's visit to Marion County greatly upset the Negroes, as one Democratic leader explained to Sen-

[47] Greenwood *Enterprise,* April 12, 1895.

[48] Jackson *New Mississippian,* August 28, 1889; Woodville *Republican,* March 26, 1892; Jackson *Daily Clarion-Ledger,* February 6, 1894; Woodward, *Origins of the New South,* 405; Anne Firor Scott, "Southern Progressives in National Politics, 1906–1916" (Ph.D. dissertation, Harvard University, 1957), 34–35.

[49] Sardis *Reporter,* quoted in Greenwood *Enterprise,* April 19, 1895.

ator McLaurin: "When Vardaman was here, he made a most impru-
dent speech using such expressions as these 'To educate a negro is to
spoil a good field hand,' 'I am opposed to educating negroes' etc. This
has imperiled the negro vote, when able to do so will you kindly write
me or Dr. Ford you[r] views briefly on this subject so that we may set
them right." [50]

As the campaign progressed Vardaman took up other state issues.
Proper immigration laws and a new landholding system would improve Mississippi's economic situation. If the large plantations were
divided into smaller units, industrious farmers from the North and
West could be induced to come South to try them. To encourage northern farmers, and manufacturers, too, the state must greatly improve
educational facilities for whites. Finally, to remove "a shame and disgrace upon the fair name of Mississippi," the penitentiary lease system
should be abolished once and for all. The Mississippi press applauded
his emphasis on state issues, while many papers sharply criticized Mc-
Laurin for devoting his speeches entirely to free silver. The senator
apparently believed that his strength among party leaders made unnecessary any mention of state problems. McCabe, however, followed
Vardaman's example in discussing a wider range of subjects, but his
defense of the gold standard eliminated him as a serious contender for
the nomination.[51]

The problem of how to choose the Democratic nominee aroused
much attention. Although the party still employed the convention system, many voters wanted a popular primary. The state Democratic
executive committee settled the controversy by ruling in favor of a convention. Both Vardaman and McLaurin constituents had mixed feelings regarding the committee's decision. J. L. Gillespie, Vardaman's
former partner, supported the committee, for he feared the party did
not have adequate machinery for holding a primary.[52] Because Gillespie supported Vardaman, he apparently believed his candidate would

[50] T. S. Ford to A. J. McLaurin, September 24, 1895, in McLaurin Papers.
[51] Greenwood *Enterprise*, June 28, July 5, 1895; Canton *Times,* Tupelo *Journal,* Oxford *Globe,* McComb City *Enterprise,* Wesson *Mirror,* quoted in Greenwood *Enterprise,* May and June 1895; Bay St. Louis *Gulf Coast Progress,* June
6, 12, 27, 1895; Woodville *Republican,* March 2, 1895; Indianola *Sunflower
Tocsin,* April 26, May 8, 1895.
[52] Greenwood *Enterprise,* March 1, 8, 29, April 26, 1895.

fare well in the convention. Papers supporting McLaurin did not clarify the problem: the *Yazoo Sentinel* and the Yazoo City *Herald,* for example, both endorsed McLaurin, but took opposing sides on the primary question.[53] Vardaman himself refused to say what he thought of the committee's action, but as a state legislator he had supported the convention system.[54]

During the campaign Vardaman canvassed the entire state, speaking three and four times a day. His forceful and colorful language held the listeners' attention for hours at a time. With his head erect, his jaw jutting forward, and his left arm flashing in gestures, he made a striking appearance. By combining his personal magnetism with his ability to meet people and put them at ease, this tall, handsome man favorably impressed many who came to hear him. As the campaign progressed many who saw and heard him rallied to his support.[55] Unfortunately for Vardaman, the rank and file of the white voters had little to say about the outcome of the contest.

Opposition to his candidacy was based less upon issues than upon his age. No one argued that he lacked experience or qualifications for the governorship. It was just that he was young enough to wait. As the Grenada *Sentinel* pointed out, "Vardaman is opposed because someone, consulting the life insurance statistics, had discovered that he has an 'expectancy' of about thirty years." [56] The impact of his emphasis on state issues is difficult to determine. He appealed to causes which agrarian leaders had advocated since the 1870's, and this despite the fact that he had opposed their interests during his brief public career. But this strategy held little political advantage. A state convention chose the Democratic nominee, eliminating true expression of popular sentiment. Although Vardaman's appeal to state issues added new life to the campaign, it did not change the attitude of the delegates to the Democratic state convention.

[53] Yazoo City *Yazoo Sentinel,* May 2, 1895; Yazoo City *Herald,* April 5, 26, May 3, 1895.
[54] Greenwood *Enterprise,* April 26, 1895.
[55] Greenwood *Enterprise,* February 8, 15, 22, March 1, 29, April 26, 1895; Jackson *Daily Clarion-Ledger,* December 3, 4, 1894, June 11, 1895; Indianola *Sunflower Tocsin,* June 14, 1895.
[56] Grenada *Sentinel,* quoted in Greenwood *Enterprise,* February 8, 1895; Yazoo City *Yazoo Sentinel,* June 6, 1895.

In the end he left his campaign unfinished, announcing on July 12 his withdrawal from the race. He explained to an audience in Greenwood that his candidacy had suffered because he had not fought in the Civil War and because he had not served in the United States Senate as had his leading opponent, who by distributing patronage had developed a solid core of supporters. For example, he had learned, although he did not announce it publicly, that despite widespread support for his candidacy in Sunflower County, the party leaders there had sewed up all the convention votes for McLaurin. Convinced that he could not carry the convention, he decided that it would be foolish to continue campaigning. He would wait and run again in 1899. His decision, of course, pleased McLaurin's supporters, one of whom predicted that he, "is young enough yet to be Mississippi's chief executive." [57]

For a year and more after the gubernatorial contest of 1895 Vardaman occupied himself practicing law and managing the family property at Sidon. Then in December, 1896, he began publishing the Greenwood *Commonwealth,* an eight-page paper much like the earlier *Enterprise* in both format and editorial policy. Although he usually took a definite position on controversial questions, he did not want the *Commonwealth* to become a "reform" sheet or a guardian of the community's morals: "Could not accomplish it if we would, and would not if we could." [58] More than in the past, however, he now sharply criticized state and national leaders who he believed fell short in the performance of their duties. His colorful and stinging criticisms of officials sometimes angered other Mississippi editors and resulted in heated verbal duals between the *Commonwealth* and rival publications. Once when Charles E. Wright, editor of the Vicksburg *Dispatch,* challenged him to prove a charge of wrongdoing that he made against Governor McLaurin, the Greenwood editor pen-lashed his foe:

While we dislike to dignify and lend respectability to that moral pervert and cowardly liar, C. E. Wright, editor of the *Dispatch,* of Vicks-

[57] W. D. Perry to A. J. McLaurin, February 11, 1896, in McLaurin Papers; Yazoo City *Yazoo Sentinel,* July 11, 1895.
[58] Mississippi Historical Records Survey, Service Division, *Mississippi Newspapers, 1805–1940: A Preliminary Union List of Mississippi Newspaper Files* . . . , 85; Indianola *Sunflower Tocsin,* February 4, 1897; Greenwood *Commonwealth,* July 29, 1897.

burg, by entering into a controversy with him—knowing him, as we do, to be a scurvy biped without courage, conscience or conviction— an irresponsible and unscrupulous cur fit only for things filthy—a scoundrel without the virtue of courage—an assassin of character without remorse who would strike you in the dark and then hide his cancerous carcass to avoid the just punishment which his damnable deeds deserve; yet, notwithstanding all that, considering the fact that other people are involved in the controversy, we are disposed to respond to the demands of the said C. E. Wright and give him some of the facts upon which the charges above were made.[59]

Such spice helped the *Commonwealth* to become one of the most widely read and frequently quoted weekly papers in the state.

Vardaman continued to express faith in progress and advocate civic improvements, municipal ownership of public utilities, and prison reform. While he applied progressive views to his fellow whites, he had nothing but increasing hostility for Negroes. After founding the *Commonwealth,* he assumed a more vindictive and radical stand on the race problem. The word "nigger" began to prevail in his public writings, as issue after issue of his paper warned that relations between blacks and whites constituted the South's most serious problem. "The man who says the race problem in the South is settled is just about as capable of judging and understanding such matters as the average nigger is capable of understanding the philosophy of the Decalogue." [60] In part Negroes had worsened race relations, he argued, by attending public schools; as they gained the rudiments of education, they wanted to vote, hold political office, and assume more active roles in all areas of society. In Mississippi the problem could be solved by dividing the school fund between the blacks and whites in proportion to the amount of taxes paid by each race. Such a solution would insure that the Negro remained a menial laborer. If the race problem was not solved, he warned, whites would continue to lynch and terrorize Negroes. Though aware that his statements would "grate upon the sensitive nerves of some folks" Vardaman believed that no southern white man could honestly deny the truth of them.[61]

[59] Greenwood *Commonwealth,* May 26, 1898.
[60] *Ibid.,* February 28, 1898.
[61] *Ibid.,* July 1, 15, August 12, 26, September 2, December 17, 1897; January 14, February 28, 1898.

Why Vardaman's anti-Negro writings became so much more vehement is difficult to determine. At a time when racist thinking was increasing in intensity he may have been convinced by current writings that the problem was more serious than he had earlier believed. He frequently extracted and published articles on the race problem from journals and newspapers throughout the country. Moreover, he remained a politically ambitious man who still wanted to become governor. During his first gubernatorial campaign he had evoked the strongest response from his audiences when he had urged that whites not pay for Negro education. Through the *Commonwealth* he became one of Mississippi's most outspoken advocates of white supremacy and clearly one of his objectives was to pave the way for future political success.

Although Vardaman did not hold elective office while editing the *Commonwealth,* he revealed his lingering political ambitions by remaining active in the politics of his county and of the Delta. After withdrawing from the gubernatorial campaign of 1895, he resumed his position as chairman of the Leflore County Democratic executive committee, an office he held for the next three years. He also played an active role at the state Democratic convention which nominated McLaurin for governor in August, 1895; not only did he serve on the credentials committee, but along with Senator James George he shared the honor of presiding as chairman of the convention. During the fall he actively supported McLaurin as the Democratic nominee, and on several occasions he campaigned in his behalf, even substituting for him in a debate with Frank Burkitt, the Populist candidate. Despite his work in behalf of McLaurin, relations between the two men were never close and Vardaman made it clear that he was only performing his duty as a member of the Democratic Party.[62] In fact, soon after McLaurin's election a bitter rift developed between them, so that upon founding the *Commonwealth* Vardaman became one of the governor's most scathing critics. To understand the causes and significance of the Vardaman-McLaurin feud, it is necessary to examine the effects of McLaurin's administration upon the Delta.

At the time McLaurin won the governorship in 1895, political pow-

[62] Greenwood *Enterprise,* September 27, October 18, 1895; J. K. Vardaman to A. J. McLaurin, October 13, 1898, in McLaurin Papers. In 1896 Vardaman again served as a presidential elector for the state at large.

er in the Delta had long been concentrated in the hands of a small group of leaders, some of the most notable of whom were LeRoy Percy and William G. Yerger of Greenville, Charles Scott of Rosedale, P. S. Stovall of Clarksdale, and J. S. McNeilly and Murray F. Smith of Vicksburg. The old leaders, most of whom were highly successful planters, attorneys, and businessmen, controlled the Democratic Party machinery in the Delta and also dominated the two levee boards which guarded the lowland area against the ever-present threat of floods.[63] Not only were the levee boards the most important institutions in the life of the Delta, but they were also sources of political power, for each year they let valuable contracts for levee construction and they offered such lucrative offices as engineers, attorneys, cotton tax collectors, secretaries, and treasurers. The governor controlled the board, for he appointed the levee commissioners who, in turn, named the various officers. For twenty years following the overthrow of the Reconstruction government in 1875, two men, John M. Stone and Robert Lowry, had dominated the governorship, and they had named levee commissioners from a select group of Delta leaders. Many of the commissioners and officers were related through kinship or had marriage and business connections.[64]

During Governor Stone's second administration, 1890–1895, demands arose in the Delta for reforming the levee boards by abolishing some of the offices, reducing salaries, and eliminating favoritism in awarding contracts. What most rankled critics of the existing system was that the boards had too long been dominated by one group of men; there was too much closeness and familiarity among the officers to insure sound business practices. Then in 1894 a scandal rocked the levee

---

[63] The Mississippi Levee District, formed in 1865, afforded protection to the counties of Bolivar, Washington, and Issaquena. In 1884 the Yazoo-Mississippi Delta Levee District was chartered and included the counties of Tunica, Coahoma, Quitman, and Sunflower, along with parts of DeSoto, Tallahatchie, Leflore, and Yazoo. Robert W. Harrison, *Levee Districts and Levee Building in Mississippi: A Study of State and Local Efforts to Control Mississippi River Floods* (Stoneville, Miss., 1952), 27–29, 75–83. Vicksburg, located in Warren County, is not in the Delta, but in the 1890's it was part of the congressional district consisting of Delta counties.

[64] Walter Sillers to A. J. McLaurin, August 21, September 8, 1896, W. D. Robinson to Walter McLaurin, August 15, 1896, in McLaurin Papers; Greenville *Times,* September 12, 1896; Greenville *Democrat,* September 24, 1896; Greenwood *Commonwealth,* August 11, 1898.

board headquarters at Greenville, when it was discovered that General S. W. Ferguson, the treasurer, had embezzled almost $40,000 of official funds. Adding to the embarrassment of the levee officials, Ferguson fled before he could be prosecuted and then it was discovered that his bond had been worthless for over six months.[65] So riled were many people by the levee board's handling of the Ferguson scandal that a public meeting was held in Greenville on August 15, at which the commissioners admitted that their carelessness had permitted Ferguson to embezzle funds.[66] Despite promises of reform by the commissioners, the Ferguson affair had so angered many people that discontent continued to smolder in the Delta during the remainder of Stone's administration.

The dissatisfaction surfaced during the gubernatorial election of 1895. In that contest the free silver question provided an issue that helped to polarize the factions that had begun to form as a result of the levee board controversy. Governor Stone and many of the Delta leaders who had enjoyed power under him defended the gold standard and lent no support to McLaurin's candidacy. Rallying to the support of McLaurin and free silver was a group of Delta men who had opposed Stone's appointment policies; the most important were Walter Sillers, Edward H. Moore, and H. L. Sutherland of Bolivar County, John W. Cutrer of Coahoma, J. M. Jayne of Washington, Lorraine C. Dulaney of Issaquena, and P. S. Somerville of Leflore. Like those Delta men who had enjoyed patronage under Governor Stone and who defended the gold standard, the leading advocates of free silver in the Delta were mainly successful lawyers and planters. It was a question of two similar cliques struggling for power. The "outs" wanted "in." During the contest vigorous infighting developed between the rival factions in most Delta counties, and in two—Coahoma and Bolivar—the election left the Democratic Party split between the gold and silver forces.[67]

When McLaurin took office in January, 1896, it was not clear what

[65] Greenville *Democrat,* July, 1894; Greenville *Times,* July 7, 14, 28, 1894.
[66] Greenville *Times,* August 18, 1894; Greenville *Democrat,* August 16, 1894.
[67] Sam C. Cook to A. J. McLaurin, February 10, 1896; W. H. Fitzgerald to McLaurin, September 28, 1895, J. Alcorn Glover to McLaurin, November 9, 1895, Richard T. Spann to McLaurin, February 2, 1896, H. L. Sutherland to McLaurin, February 12, 1896, all in McLaurin Papers. Greenville *Democrat,* January 16, 1896.

course he would follow in making appointments. Despite their advocacy of the gold standard, some of the old Delta leaders hoped to retain power under the new administration. Accordingly they circulated petitions asking that the incumbent levee commissioners be reappointed.[68] Some, such as Charles Scott and LeRoy Percy, warned McLaurin that it would be dangerous for him to become involved in the Delta's factional fights, and they advised him to avoid the trouble by permitting each county to select its levee commissioners. Under Percy's leadership the Washington County Democratic executive committee actually nominated Nathan Goldstein for levee commissioner and sent the nomination to McLaurin for approval.[69] The governor, however, had been well posted on conditions in the Delta,[70] and by the end of February he had removed every levee commissioner, circuit and chancery judge whose term had expired and replaced them with his own appointees. So openly and thoroughly were the old leaders swept out of office that McLaurin's appointments aroused much furor in the Delta. Not only did ousted officials damn the governor, but many who had not yet become involved in the emerging factionalism believed McLaurin had been ruthless in so blatantly wielding patronage.[71]

Vardaman played no part in the levee board controversy, but he was not happy with many of McLaurin's appointments. As a state legislator during Stone's second administration, he and the former governor had developed respect for one another. Although they had taken opposing positions on the silver question in 1895, it had not impaired their relations; after Vardaman had left the gubernatorial race, Stone had appointed him a delegate to a waterways convention in Vicksburg.[72] The removal of the Stone appointees in the Delta marked the beginning of Vardaman's dissatisfaction with McLaurin. The Delta's congressional election of 1896 soon added to that estrangement.

[68] Greenwood *Enterprise*, December 13, 1895, January 24, 1896; Indianola *Sunflower Tocsin*, January 3, 1896; Greenville *Times*, February 15, 1896.
[69] Charles Scott to A. J. McLaurin, January 29, 1896, LeRoy Percy to McLaurin, n.d., in McLaurin Papers; Greenville *Times*, February 8, 1896; Greenville *Democrat*, February 13, 1896.
[70] Walter Sillers to A. J. McLaurin, February 14, 1896, J. C. Burnes to McLaurin, February 12, 1896, in McLaurin Papers.
[71] Greenwood *Enterprise*, February 14, 28, March 6, 20, 1896; Greenville *Times*, February 22, 1896; Indianola *Sunflower Tocsin*, March 6, 1896.
[72] Greenwood *Enterprise*, September 27, 1895. See also J. K. Vardaman to John M. Stone, February 21, 1894, in Stone Papers.

The incumbent congressman was Thomas C. Catchings, a defender of the gold standard and a close ally of the old Delta leaders. As in the past, he ran for reelection, arguing that in the Delta no issue took precedence over flood control and that because of his seniority on the Rivers and Harbors Committee he could obtain more federal funds for levee construction than any newly elected congressman. Although Catchings remained in Washington and did not return to campaign, such supporters as LeRoy Percy and Charles Scott worked hard in his behalf.[73]

Catchings faced a serious challenge, for his persistent opposition to free silver provided his opponents with a lethal issue. By March, 1896, R. F. Abbay, a state legislator and wealthy landowner from Tunica County, entered the race as a free silver Democrat, but he failed to develop significant support. A more serious challenger was Andrew H. Longino of Greenville, whom McLaurin had recently appointed to a chancery judgeship. Longino also seized upon the free silver issue and immediately won the backing of those men who had supported McLaurin's levee board appointments: Walter Sillers, Lorraine Dulaney, John W. Cutrer, and P. R. Somerville all worked actively in his behalf. As Longino's campaign got under way, newspapers supporting him pictured Catchings as a "gold bug" and as a tool of the "old Delta bosses." [74]

Vardaman took a keen interest in the contest. Some had suggested that he enter the race, but he refused, explaining that his one political ambition was to serve as governor. Although he had little sympathy for the McLaurin administration, he had committed himself to free silver. Moreover, Judge Longino was his friend, for in 1893 he had lived in Greenwood and at that time had sided with Vardaman in the fight for prohibition in Leflore County. During the past gubernatorial campaign Vardaman had even asked his old friend for a loan of a hundred dollars. It was not surprising, therefore, that Vardaman announced his

[73] Greenville *Times,* March 4, 11, April 18, 1896; Greenwood *Delta Flag,* February 28, April 10, 17, May 1, 1898; Greenwood *Enterprise,* January 31, March 13, 1896; Greenville *Democrat,* March 12, 19, 1896; J. H. Stafford to A. J. McLaurin, March 2, 1896, in McLaurin Papers.
[74] Greenville *Democrat,* March 12, April 30, 1896; Indianola *Sunflower Toc-sin,* March 13, 20, April 3, May 8, 1896; Greenwood *Enterprise,* April 24, May 6, 1896.

support for Longino: "In my judgment this effort on the part of some of our people to subordinate the silver question to levee matters is just a nice little piece of stratagem used to entrap the unwary and secure the election of their man. I make this prediction right now: that if Gen. Catchings should be elected his supporters and himself will herald it all over the country as a victory for "sound money." For that reason I can not believe the people of the Third District will elect a goldbug to congress." [75]

Much to the disappointment of the Longino forces, the district Democratic executive committee—which was dominated by Catchings' supporters—met on April 11 and ordered that on May 18 a convention be held in Greenville to select the party's congressional nominee. Longino had hoped that the contest would be settled by a party primary in late summer, thereby enabling him to conduct a thorough canvass of the district. Although many of his supporters denounced the executive committee's ruling as unfair, they accepted it.

In the weeks prior to the district convention the Catchings and Longino forces conducted hard-fought campaigns in every Delta county. As chairman of the Leflore Democratic executive committee, Vardaman used his influence for Longino, as did his two friends and fellow townsmen J. L. Gillespie, editor of the *Enterprise,* and J. R. Bew, editor of the *Southern Farmer.* A Democratic mass meeting in Greenwood selected delegates for the district convention and instructed them to vote for Longino. Catchings' supporters strongly protested, charging that Vardaman and other party leaders had failed to give adequate notice of the mass meeting and thereby had been able to swing the county to Longino. Accordingly, the Catchings men in Leflore County selected a "protest" delegation to attend the district convention.[76]

What happened in Leflore occurred in almost every Delta county: the local parties split, as the minority factions formed contesting delegations and demanded prorated representation at the district convention. The county which held the key to determining the outcome of the contest was Bolivar. There Charles Scott led the Catchings forces and

[75] J. K. Vardaman to A. H. Longino, April 29, 1895, in A. S. Coody Collection, Mississippi Department of Archives and History; Greenwood *Enterprise,* April 10, 1896.
[76] Greenwood *Enterprise,* April 24, May 15, 1896; Greenwood *Delta Flag,* May 15, 1896.

Walter Sillers led the Longino forces; each headed a delegation at the Greenville convention and each group claimed to be the sole representative of Bolivar County. Should the contesting delegations from other counties not be recognized, Bolivar would become the pivot in determining victory, for its votes would enable either Catchings or Longino to become the Democratic nominee.[77]

Early in the morning of May 18 trains filled with Catchings and Longino partisans bustled into the little town of Greenville. Through broad, tree-shaded streets bands led parades in which exuberant men flourished banners proclaiming proud slogans about their candidates. In and out of the swelling crowds boys maneuvered their bicycles decorated with blue and white streamers for Catchings, crimson for Longino. Few conventions in the state had ever attracted so much boisterous attention.[78] But the festivities could not erase the underlying seriousness of the day. The stakes were high. With contesting delegations present from practically every county, there was imminent danger that the Democratic Party throughout the Delta might rupture.

Before the convention could assemble, the district executive committee met to determine which of the rival delegations would be seated. During the entire day the committee remained in session listening to arguments on how to dissolve the deadlock. LeRoy Percy, Charles Scott, and Pat Henry served as spokesmen for Catchings, while Walter Sillers and P. R. Somerville represented Longino. Finally in the late afternoon the committee acted. Over the vehement protests of Sillers and Somerville, the majority voted to dismiss all contesting delegations and to seat the Catchings group from Bolivar County. The committee's action was a pure power play designed to insure the congressman's renomination, for it gave him a majority of the delegates. As soon as word of the committee's decision spread to the delegates waiting in the courthouse, the Longino men marched off to the local opera

[77] Greenwood *Enterprise,* May 15, 1896; Greenville *Democrat,* May 14, 21, 28, 1896.

[78] This account of the district convention is based on detailed reports in the Greenwood *Enterprise* of May 22, 29, 1896, and the Greenwood *Southern Farmer* of June 1, 1896. Percy R. Somerville, Longino's campaign manager, published an account in the *Enterprise* on May 29. W. G. Yerger, who presided as chairman of the convention, presented another version in the *Southern Farmer* on June 1. For Vardaman's version of his role in the convention, see Greenwood *Commonwealth,* May 26, 1898.

house and organized a convention of their own. Convinced that the committee had acted in a ruthless and arbitrary fashion, they were determined that Longino should have the nomination. Now the feared party split was imminent.

At that point Vardaman broke with his fellow delegates from Leflore County and joined the convention of Catchings' supporters in the courthouse. Several delegates from Coahoma County, which was also pledged to Longino, followed Vardaman's example. He explained that he refused to participate in a rump convention because he did not want the party split. Since he was pledged to support Longino, he would not vote for Catchings, but he would uphold the rulings of the convention. The Catchings delegates loudly applauded this announcement, for his decision helped to maintain Democratic unity in the Delta. Longino did even more to preserve party solidarity, for he informed the opera house convention that he would not accept its nomination because that would split the Democratic ranks.

As soon as Longino announced his decision, the courthouse convention proceeded to nominate Catchings. Vardaman was well rewarded for his party loyalty. He served on the resolutions committee which drew up a platform endorsing free silver, for by that time Catchings had promised to abandon the gold standard if so instructed by the convention. Then a committee, consisting of such longtime Delta leaders as LeRoy Percy, Charles Scott, and Murray Smith, presented a list of nominees to serve on the district's new executive committee and the convention quickly elected the members, one of whom was Vardaman. Finally, after Catchings had received the nomination, Vardaman escorted the congressman into the courthouse "amid scenes of the wildest enthusiasm and patriotic demonstration."

J. L. Gillespie expressed the anger of many over Longino's defeat: "Mr. Catchings is no more the nominee of the people of the third district than Boss Tweed, but for the sake of party unity, and hoping that the questionable methods by which Gen. Catchings was nominated will never be resorted to again, the *Enterprise* will not oppose his election." [79] Although Catchings' nomination was accepted by the Longino supporters, it hardened those factional lines that the levee board dispute had formed. Catchings had been backed by the Delta leaders

[79] Greenwood *Enterprise,* June 5, 1896.

who had controlled the levee boards under Governor Stone, whereas Longino had won the support of the McLaurin lieutenants who had recently taken control of the boards.

Vardaman's refusal to join the Longino delegates in their attempt to bolt the district convention strongly affected his future career. Some of the Longino men denounced him for having sold out to the "old bosses." "Now, really people, what kind of Governor would the gentleman from Leflore have made?" asked the editor of the *Sunflower Toscin*. "The long haired gubernational [*sic*] possibility from Leflore, while strengthening himself with the gang, weakened himself with the people. He must remember that the Congressional Executive Committee of the 3rd district do not control gubernatorial canvasses, and while they are the MAJORITY in this district, they are mighty small potatoes in the state." [80] Vardaman's refusal to lend support to splitting the party definitely cooled his friendship with some of his former supporters. J. R. Bew, who had contributed financial support to Vardaman's gubernatorial race of the past year, now described him as one of "the gentlemen who went over to the enemy at the 11th hour." [81] Even though Longino had refused to condone a split in the Democratic Party, he was angered by Vardaman's cooperation with the Catchings forces; early the next year Walter Sillers reported to Governor Mc-Laurin that Longino was "after my son Absolom's (Vardaman) hair." [82] Most important, at the district convention Vardaman joined the anti-McLaurin camp, and in the future he sided with that Delta faction led by Percy and Scott in its battle against the state administration.

Having become a determined opponent of McLaurin by the time he founded the *Commonwealth* in December, 1896, Vardaman joined a number of other editors who consistently criticized the administration. Not only in the Delta but throughout Mississippi, McLaurin's distribution of patronage and his actions on certain key issues stimulated a bitter opposition to him that eventually gave rise to a new factionalism: the Mississippi Democracy divided into McLaurin and anti-McLaurin

[80] Indianola *Sunflower Tocsin*, May 22, 29, 1896.
[81] Greenwood *Southern Farmer*, June 1, 1896.
[82] Walter Sillers to A. J. McLaurin, February 9, 1897, in McLaurin Papers.

camps.[83] Vardaman's reasons for attacking McLaurin were varied. In part, he based his position on fundamental disagreements with the state's chief executive; in part, he sought to advance his own political fortunes by joining the anti-McLaurin forces.

As editor of the *Commonwealth* he continued to criticize many of McLaurin's political appointments, and he denounced the governor for not adopting the legislature's plan for constructing a new Capitol. At a special legislative session in 1897 the lawmakers passed a bill for erecting a new building, but McLaurin vetoed it, the question at issue being whether he or a legislative committee should supervise the construction. Vardaman condemned the veto, and when the legislature adjourned without providing for a new structure, he placed blame entirely upon McLaurin: "In the annals of Mississippi statesmanship he stands alone the most unique, absurd, and ridiculous character that ever varied the monotony, created a ripple in public affairs or disappointed and humiliated a constituency." [84]

In his attacks upon the governor, he sometimes resorted to personal accusations and innuendo. He did not in so many words accuse McLaurin of nepotism, but noted that the governor had given offices to six of his seven brothers.[85] He also devoted much attention to the charge that widespread drunkenness prevailed in the McLaurin administration. When the anti-McLaurin faction in the legislature attempted unsuccessfully to investigate the charges that Judge William K. McLaurin, the governor's brother, had been drunk while presiding at court, Vardaman held that the investigation should have been carried out so that the McLaurins might be in turn justified or censured.[86]

His persistent criticism of the administration became a key issue in dividing the *Commonwealth* from Greenwood's other two weekly papers. When McLaurin had first assumed office, both Gillespie's *Enter-*

<hr>

[83] Kirwan, *Revolt of the Rednecks,* 103–21. Robert E. Houston to A. J. McLaurin, November 25, 1896, W. G. Orr to McLaurin, March 30, 1897, Walter Sillers to McLaurin, July 1, 1897, H. C. Meadford to McLaurin, November 20, 1897, W. O. White to McLaurin, February 2, 1898, W. E. Chapman to McLaurin, July 3, 1898, all in McLaurin Papers.

[84] Greenwood *Commonwealth,* May 27, 1897.

[85] *Ibid.,* May 13, 1897.

[86] *Ibid.,* October 29, 1897, January 4, 21, 1898; *House Journal, 1898,* 64; J. McC. Martin to Harris Dickson, January 31, 1900, in Harris Dickson Papers.

prise and Bew's *Southern Farmer* criticized him for his wholesale removal of former levee commissioners and judges, but since the defeat of Longino at the district convention in 1896, the two editors had reassessed their earlier opposition to the administration. By the time Vardaman began assailing McLaurin in the *Commonwealth,* both Gil lespie and Bew had begun defending the governor.[87] As a result, he frequently clashed with his two former friends, and by 1898 the rivalry between them had become bitter; also by that time Gillespie and Bew had become trusted McLaurin aides, and they worked openly, as well as behind the scenes, to reduce Vardaman's political strength.[88]

As had happened two years earlier, the Delta's congressional campaign of 1898 revealed the factional strife which the McLaurin and anti-McLaurin forces were generating. Still determined to defeat Catchings, the McLaurin leaders from every Delta county met in Clarksdale in April and decided to back Pat Henry for Congress. Two years earlier Henry, a successful Vicksburg lawyer, had supported Catchings, but since that time he had joined the McLaurin forces. Henry ran as a free silver Democrat and promised that his election would end the rule of the Delta's "political bosses." Although Catchings had switched to free silver in 1896, Henry charged he had done it only to save his political hide.[89]

As did Henry, Vardaman changed politically between 1896 and 1898. Two years earlier he had dismissed Catchings' appeal to the flood control issue and had denounced the congressman as a "gold bug." McLaurinism convinced him to change. In 1898 he praised Catchings' work in behalf of the levee interests, and he branded Henry as a tool of the McLaurin faction.[90] As chairman of his county Dem-

[87] A. McC. Kimbrough to A. J. McLaurin, January 14, 1897, Walter Sillers to McLaurin, February 9, 1897, J. S. McDonald to McLaurin, May 15, 1897, all in McLaurin Papers. By 1897 Bew had abandoned the *Southern Farmer* and acquired the *Delta Flag.*
[88] Greenwood *Commonwealth,* October 15, 1897, January 21, 1898; Greenwood *Delta Flag,* March 5, 19, April 16, 23, 1897; J. L. Gillespie to A. J. McLaurin, February 27, March 1, 1899, Bew to McLaurin, March 21, 1899, in McLaurin Papers.
[89] Greenwood *Enterprise,* June 3, July 22, 1898; Greenwood *Delta Flag,* June 17, July 8, 1898; E. H. Moore to A. J. McLaurin, June 10, 1898, D. A. Griffing to McLaurin, June 14, 1898, J. L. Gillespie to McLaurin, July 8, 1898, in McLaurin Papers.
[90] Greenwood *Commonwealth,* May and June, 1898.

ocratic executive committee and as a member of the district executive committee, Vardaman played an active role in the contest. The bitter discontent, bordering on a party revolt, which Catchings' previous nomination had aroused, practically forced the district convention in 1898 to order a primary election. Vardaman supported the decision to hold a primary, and then he worked to see that Catchings would carry it.[91]

In May, 1898, the Greenwood editor infused new spirit into the campaign by announcing in the *Commonwealth* that a McLaurin lieutenant had attempted to make a deal with Catchings' friends. It was generally known that Senator Edward C. Walthall would resign from the Senate in 1899, and many anti-McLaurin men in the Delta wanted someone from their faction to replace him. Vardaman reported that a McLaurin aide had asked a Catchings supporter to persuade the congressman to withdraw from the race; if he did, and if the Catchings forces supported McLaurin's gubernatorial candidate in 1899, then the governor would appoint W. G. Yerger of the Delta to the senatorship vacated by Walthall. Vardaman did not believe Yerger was implicated in the sordid affair: "He is too clean to take the office under the terms proposed." If the governor had approved this offer, he maintained, then "he deserved the condemnation of every decent white man, woman, and child, and nigger, dago, 'yallar' dog and Chinaman in the state." [92]

When Vardaman first reported the proposed deal, he did not name those who were supposed to have attempted it. The Vicksburg *Dispatch,* a leading McLaurin paper, immediately accused him of lying and challenged him to name the individuals or "stand branded as a slanderer, himself." The editor quickly replied that Walter Sillers, "a close political friend, appointee and partisan" of McLaurin, had made the offer to LeRoy Percy, one of the Delta's most influential men. Vardaman implied that McLaurin had authorized Sillers to make the offer. Both Sillers and Percy wrote letters to the *Commonwealth* attempting to justify their own positions. Sillers claimed that the governor had no knowledge of the discussion and he had told Percy only that it might be possible to work out an arrangement. Percy reported he had laughed at

91 *Ibid.,* June 2, 9, 1898.
92 *Ibid.,* May 12, 1898; Greenville *Times,* May 21, 1898.

Sillers' proposition; he could not ask Catchings to withdraw from the race after having induced him to make it.[93]

The opposing factions continued to debate the issue, but Vardaman believed Percy. In fact, because he had become such an outspoken critic of the governor, he came to admire and support anti-McLaurin leaders Percy and Scott. He was particularly lavish in his praise of Percy, a man who, years later, would become his avowed opponent: "If I were called upon to name one of the most promising and gifted young men in the Third Congressional District, I should unhesitatingly name LeRoy Percy of Greenville. . . . He was born to rule—one of those peculiar characters whose influence is felt and obeyed." [94]

In the district primary of July 11, 1898, the electorate decided the contest, as Catchings won by a slim margin of 315 votes. Anti-McLaurin men claimed Henry's defeat reflected the governor's unpopularity. Friends of the administration, however, held that McLaurin had not affected the outcome: Catchings had won because as a congressman he had worked for flood control. In both Washington and Bolivar counties that issue had been stressed and those counties had given Catchings his largest majorities. In Warren and Leflore counties, however, the McLaurin issue had been emphasized and there the McLaurin forces had won. Murray F. Smith of Warren and Vardaman of Leflore had run as anti-McLaurin candidates for positions on the district executive committee and both had been defeated. Neither man had been able to carry his home county.

The reasons for Vardaman's defeat were uncertain. For one thing, he was out of the state at the time of the election and no one supervised his interests. Of greater importance, he led in a majority of the counties, but his name, either through "carelessness" or deliberate antagonism, was left off the ballot in Sunflower County, with the result that he got not a single vote there.[95] This "carelessness" in Sunflower appears to have been a deliberate strategem to undermine his political

[93] Greenwood *Commonwealth,* May 26, 1898; Walter Sillers to J. K. Vardaman, May 30, 1898, LeRoy Percy to J. K. Vardaman, n.d., both in Greenwood *Commonwealth,* June 9, 1898.

[94] *Ibid.,* February 9, 1900. For other references to Scott and Percy see *Commonwealth* of May 20, 1897, February 25, May 19, 1898, November 16, 1900.

[95] Greenwood *Commonwealth,* August 4, 1898; Greenville *Times,* July 30, August 11, 1898.

strength and bolster the McLaurin faction in the Delta. Some of the McLaurin men had never forgiven him for having abandoned Longino at the district convention in 1896; since that time, through his editorials in the *Commonwealth,* Vardaman had become a leading critic of the administration. In Sunflower, moreover, the McLaurin forces dominated the county Democratic executive committee.[96]

During the campaign of 1898 Vardaman's attention was diverted from politics by the worsening relations between Spain and the United States. He sympathized with the Cuban insurgents, believing their grievances against Spain to be justified and believing the United States should use its influence to secure Cuban independence peacefully. At first he did not want America to resort to war, for he believed that wars rarely accomplished anything worthwhile and that all too often they resulted only in loss and suffering for the belligerent nations. Eventually he became convinced that Spain was such a ruthless and barbaric power that only American military intervention could free Cuba. Yet there was little danger of America's going to war, he lamented, for wealthy bond owners with heavy investments in Cuba controlled the federal government and they would never condone war. During the early months of 1898, as his writings became more impassioned in favor of war, he appealed to a host of emotions to win support for intervention. The *Commonwealth* contained numerous articles describing Spanish atrocities and bemoaning the Cuban's plight. President McKinley was described as a tool of American corporations and too indifferent to defend the national honor. When the President finally gave in to the war hysteria that swept the country, Vardaman rejoiced.

In Mississippi, as in most states, officials made numerous mistakes in organizing troops and preparing for war. Vardaman blamed Governor McLaurin for all of this, and when McLaurin offered to lead the Mississippi forces in Cuba, he scoffed in rage: "He knows nothing about commanding an army—less probably than he does about properly performing the functions of his present office." [97] Because the governor lacked military training, the Greenwood editor considered his offer to be demagoguery.

[96] Greenwood *Commonwealth,* May 26, 1898.
[97] *Ibid.,* May 26, 1898.

Vardaman, who had less military training than McLaurin, also wanted to participate in the war.[98] No doubt he realized full well that an honorable war record would help his later political career. It might even compensate for his having missed the Civil War—a circumstance that he honestly believed had weakened his candidacy in 1895. The Water Valley Rifles gave Vardaman his first opportunity to serve by electing him their captain. He accepted the position, but his disabled right arm prevented his passing the usual physical examination. Such being the case, only the governor could authorize a commission, and McLaurin refused to do so unless Vardaman apologized for his many criticisms of the administration. He would not apologize; McLaurin refused to commission him.[99] Vardaman and his sympathizers took full advantage of the situation. They pictured the editor as a martyr who wanted to serve his country, McLaurin as allowing petty jealousy to degrade his office.[100] Even as he continued to excoriate the governor, Vardaman received a commission as captain in the Fifth Regiment of the United States Volunteer Infantry. On June 23, 1898, he bade farewell to the readers of the *Commonwealth* and left to join his regiment.

I have been an advocate of this war from its inception. . . . I believe that Cuba should be free, and I am willing to prove my convictions, to sustain my doctrine with my service, and if need be, my life. . . . The sacrifice so far as personal comfort goes, is a great one. To leave a comfortable home, a dear wife, and five sweet and loving children is a great sacrifice indeed. But as stated above, believing it to be my duty, I should be unworthy of them, disloyal to their better interest, were I to refuse to respond to the calls of my country at this time. To a loving God and a host of dear friends I leave them to their kind and generous keeping until I shall return.[101]

[98] McLaurin had served for one year as a private in the Third Mississippi Cavalry during the Civil War. Rowland, *The Official and Statistical Register of the State of Mississippi, 1908,* 976.

[99] Greenwood *Commonwealth,* June 2, 9, 1898; J. K. Vardaman to A. J. McLaurin, May 26, 1898, in McLaurin Papers.

[100] Greenwood *Commonwealth,* June 9, 1898. Newspapers throughout the state published articles denouncing McLaurin's refusal to commission Vardaman. See *Commonwealth,* June 16, 23, 1898. Earl Brewer to Walter McLaurin, June 6, 1898, Brewer to A. J. McLaurin, August 29, 1898, C. H. Doolittle to McLaurin, June 7, 1898, W. A. White to McLaurin, June 13, 1898, in McLaurin Papers.

[101] Greenwood *Commonwealth,* June 23, 1898.

His stay in Cuba was neither enjoyable nor exciting. He participated in no battles, but served the entire time with the Judge Advocate Corps in the forces occupying Santiago. There he presided over a board of claims and sat as a judge of a general court martial.[102] It was an assignment that brought heat, rain, mosquitoes, and the threat of yellow fever, but little glory. How much better it would be, he thought, to die in battle than "to remain here and become permeated with the poisons of this infernal pest hole, and die and rot like a dog."[103] The closest he ever came to actual fighting was a visit to the San Juan battlefield.

Long before Vardaman went to Cuba it had been generally known that he would run again for governor in 1899. Formal proclamation of his candidacy came in a letter from Santiago on November 6, 1898, describing the sacrifices he was making for his country and promising that on his return he would present his platform to the electorate.[104] In addition to Vardaman, five other candidates contested for the governorship. Andrew Longino, who had been appointed chancery judge by McLaurin and who had run for Congress against Catchings in 1896, became the leading contender and campaigned on the promise of a fiscally sound administration. Frank A. Critz, from the hill section of northeastern Mississippi, supported the national Democratic platform of 1896, advocated granting tax exemptions to encourage industrial growth in the state, and favored an elective judiciary. James F. McCool also spoke for tax privileges for industry and an elective judiciary; in addition, he wanted a distribution of the school fund more favorable to the white counties of eastern Mississippi and the establishment of a state uniform textbook law. Other candidates were Judge Robert Powell of Lincoln County and W. A. Montgomery of Hinds County.[105]

[102] Adjutant General Orders, Requisition Number 2920, May 23, 1900, Special and General Orders and Circulars, Department of Santiago and Puerto Principe, 1899, National Archives. See, specifically, Special Orders 22, 28A, 46, 93.
[103] J. K. Vardaman to editor, January 31, 1899, in Greenwood *Commonwealth*, February 17, 1898. See also George C. Osborn, "The Spanish American War as Revealed Through the Letters of Major James K. Vardaman," *Journal of Mississippi History*, IX (1947), 108–20. Vardaman was commissioned a Captain, but was promoted to Major on February 25, 1898 (Pension Number XC2633522, Spanish American War, National Archives).
[104] Greenwood *Commonwealth*, December 2, 1898; Jackson *Daily Clarion-Ledger*, November 26, 1898.
[105] Jackson *Daily Clarion-Ledger*, March 16, 1899; Kirwan, *Revolt of the Rednecks*, 118; Woodville *Republican*, March 25, 1899.

Accompanying the gubernatorial race in 1899 was a hot fight between Governor McLaurin and Congressman "Private" John Allen for the United States Senate. By that time McLaurin's political strength had reached its zenith, for he enjoyed wide popularity and his supporters controlled the political machinery in a majority of the state's counties. Because Democratic nominees were selected under the convention system, McLaurin had little difficulty in defeating Allen. As a candidate for office, however, McLaurin could not risk becoming openly involved in the gubernatorial contest. Moreover, Longino, McCool, and Powell had all supported his administration and were considered his friends. Although the governor avoided taking sides in the contest for his successor, Longino enjoyed the support of many McLaurin men in the Delta, and as the campaign progressed, his strength expanded throughout the state.[106] One thing was certain—having become an avowed critic of McLaurin, Vardaman stood little chance of carrying the state convention.

While Vardaman served in Cuba the *Commonwealth,* which he had left under the supervision of T. H. Crosby, became his chief spokesman. Vardaman's followers tried to bolster his cause by pointing to his war record. True, he had not been privileged to engage in any battles, but he had done his duty in the forces occupying Santiago. They also played up McLaurin's flight from Jackson during a recent yellow fever epidemic, whereas Vardaman had gone to an area infested with the disease.[107] In addition to making much of his participation in the war, his supporters based his early campaign on a denunciation of McLaurin. They equated McLaurinism in state affairs with Republicanism in national affairs; like the McKinley administration, McLaurin's had been marked by wasted money, the appointment of incompetent men to office, and disgraceful conduct by public officials. So strong was the McLaurin machine, they warned, that it covered the entire state; its power had to be broken in the coming election, or free institutions in Mississippi would be forever endangered. There was only one sure way to end the McLaurin influence: elect Vardaman.[108]

---

[106] A. McC. Kimbrough to A. J. McLaurin, January 9, 1899, J. L. Gillespie to McLaurin, February 11, 1898, January 1, 1899, in McLaurin Papers.
[107] Greenwood *Commonwealth,* August 11, 1898.
[108] *Ibid.,* September 15, 1898, January 27, March 3, 10, April 14, July 14, 1899.

Vardaman returned to Mississippi on June 2, 1899, and within a few days took the stump in a grueling canvass. Contrary to perhaps gleeful expectations in certain quarters, he did not engage in personal attacks on his opponents or brand any of them as tools of McLaurin. On national issues he supported the Democratic platform of 1896 and favored the nomination of William Jennings Bryan for the presidency. He opposed the expansionist policies of the McKinley administration and the existence of a standing army. Regarding state issues, he attempted, as he had in 1895, to broaden his appeal by advocating basic reforms that farmer movements had advocated since the 1870's. He favored the popular election of judges, primaries for choosing all state officials, and more liberal appropriations for the public schools; he opposed the granting of tax exemptions to railroads and industries.[109]

Above all, he stressed the need to change the system of distributing the state school fund under which the Delta counties, with their heavy Negro population, received larger appropriations than the white counties of eastern Mississippi. He had introduced this issue in the campaign of 1895. Since then, as he had devoted more attention to it, his thoughts upon it had become more rabid. A highly emotional issue, it touched two sensitive nerves of the Mississippi electorate: the all-prevailing race issue and the increasing class consciousness of rural whites. Under a system of popular elections, such an issue could carry a man far in the politics of the rural South. Vardaman presented it on the stump with brutal frankness:

There is no getting around the fact that the whole scheme of negro education in the South is a pitable [sic] failure. It is met by a barrier of race prejudice that is simply unsurmountable. I mean exactly what I say. We are charged with entertaining race prejudice. Well, I admit it. The charge is true. The prejudice exists, can't be eliminated, and may as well be considered as a factor of the problem. I am tired of this lying and shuffling in politics and platforms. It is time to face facts honestly and squarely and say what we mean and mean what we say. In educating the negro we implant in him all manner of aspirations and ambitions which we then refuse to allow him to gratify. It would be impossible for a negro in Mississippi to be elected as much as a justice of the peace, no matter how able, honest and otherwise unobjectionable

[109] *Ibid.,* June 23, 30, 1899; Bay St. Louis *Gulf Coast Progress,* June 29, August 10, 24, 1899; Walthall *Warden,* July 7, 1899.

he may be. Yet people talk about elevating the race by education! It is not only folly, but it comes pretty nearly being criminal folly. The negro isn't permitted to advance and their education only spoils a good field hand and makes a shyster lawyer or a fourth-rate teacher. It is money thrown away.[110]

In his campaign speeches he did not play upon his opposition to McLaurin. Perhaps by the time he returned from Cuba he realized the degree of McLaurin's strength and feared that by publicly denouncing the governor he would only hurt himself. He did, however, attempt quietly to align himself with the supporters of John Allen and in a few cases his strategy did succeed in winning some additional delegates.[111] Still, Vardaman's cause was hopeless, for the Allen delegates were themselves in a minority. The McLaurin forces would dominate the convention. A candidate for state railroad commissioner graphically described the situation on the eve of the convention: "All that remains now is to see what McLaurin is going to do with us." [112]

The state press neither supported Vardaman as it had four years earlier nor paid as much attention to him. Only a few newspapers endorsed his candidacy and even after his return from Cuba opposition to him remained vague and general. His adversaries ignored his extreme racial views and did not accuse him of demagoguery for using that highly emotional issue. The editor of the Tunica *Democrat,* a Delta paper, regretted Vardaman's entry into the race; he liked Vardaman personally but believed that his platform lacked substance and his political strength was too narrowly confined to win the governorship.[113]

The old state convention made its last stand in the election of 1899. Although the demand for a popular Democratic primary had grown stronger during the past four years, the state Democratic executive committee called for a nominating convention to meet in Jackson on August 23. Vardaman had wanted a popular primary to decide the contest, but he accepted the committee's decision.[114] There were to be 266 votes at the nominating convention, thereby making it necessary

[110] Greenwood *Commonwealth,* June 30, 1899.
[111] J. M. Parchman to A. J. McLaurin, August 20, 1899, in McLaurin Papers.
[112] Kosciusko *Attala Democrat,* August 15, 1899.
[113] Tunica *Democrat* quoted in Greenwood *Enterprise,* December 9, 1898.
[114] Greenwood *Commonwealth,* April 14, 1899.

for the nominee to receive 134. By late July fifty-one of the state's seventy-five counties had chosen delegates for the convention. Some counties had not instructed their delegates to vote for a gubernatorial candidate, because they wanted to leave them free to bargain in behalf of favorite candidates for other state offices. Those counties that did instruct gave Longino 61 votes, Critz 26, Vardaman 9, McCool and Montgomery 8 each, and Powell 4.[115] Obviously, Vardaman would be far behind Longino going into the convention, but his supporters hoped that if Longino failed to get the necessary majority, the convention might swing to Vardaman. It would be absolutely necessary, however, for all the candidates to remain in the race and hold their own against Longino.

On Sunday, August 20, friends of the various candidates began to converge on Jackson. By Monday night all the gubernatorial candidates were circulating among the delegates, shaking hands and asking for support. On Tuesday morning hotels and boarding houses were alive with activity, as the politicians worked to secure support for their cause. They especially besieged the uninstructed delegates. After two days of bargaining and trading, the outcome of the gubernatorial contest had been decided. It was reported that Powell and Montgomery had withdrawn from the race; on Wednesday morning these former candidates substantiated the report. Learning this news, Vardaman and Critz, who had more than eighty votes between them, realized they could not defeat Longino. They accordingly withdrew and left the nomination to him. When the convention assembled that day "a great many candidates were seen with lost expression[s] on their face[s]." [116] Surely Vardaman was one of them.

Vardaman had begun his political career as a Bourbon Democrat conforming to the political system as he found it and working within it for advancement. As a newspaper editor, as a state legislator, and as a presidential elector he had worked for the Democratic Party. Always he had opposed attempts by independents and third party movements to gain political power in Mississippi. During the Spanish-American

[115] Jackson *Daily Clarion-Ledger*, July 24, 1899.
[116] New Orleans *Times-Democrat* quoted in Greenwood *Commonwealth*, August 25, 1899.

War he had proved his devotion to his country by serving for almost a year in Cuba. Despite these efforts he had suffered political defeat twice at the hands of the state Democratic nominating convention. A majority of the established leaders of the state—the men who controlled the Democratic conventions—had instead supported McLaurin and Longino. But the days of the convention system were numbered. Throughout the 1890's a movement for adopting statewide Democratic primaries had been gaining momentum; soon Mississippi would use primaries to choose all state officials. Candidates would thereby be saved from exclusive dependence upon the will of party leaders and could—indeed would have to—appeal directly to the white voters of Mississippi, most of whom were farmers.

CHAPTER IV

THE EMERGENCE OF A POPULAR LEADER

IN SEPTEMBER, 1899, when Vardaman resumed his position as editor of the Greenwood *Commonwealth,* he began to devote much attention to foreign affairs and to the involvement of the United States in the Philippines and in Cuba. His views on American foreign policy are important because they reflect his thinking on certain domestic issues, and they also help explain why later he would oppose American entry into World War I.

Before the United States went to war with Spain, Vardaman had opposed all schemes for acquiring new territories. He had not, however, become an inflexible opponent of American expansion, for he had published articles by Senator Hernando Money favoring annexation of the Hawaiian Islands by the United States, while also publishing from the works of such expansion foes as Carl Schurz. Although he had believed America would eventually control these islands, he had not liked the idea, fearing that the abandonment of isolationist tradition would give rise to standing armies and thereby increase the danger of future wars. Above all, Vardaman had feared the acquisition of new territories would further intensify the race problem, saying that "with the negroes in the South, the mixed breeds in Cuba and the great variety of the genus homo in Hawaii this country will have a most homogenous [*sic*] citizenship." [1]

Vardaman's unfavorable attitude toward American expansion had been visible in 1897, and his experiences in Cuba hardened him into a determined opponent of all imperialistic schemes. His first impressions of Cuba pleased him. Mountains covered with green growth surrounded the harbor of Santiago, the most picturesque place he had ever seen. [2] The filth, disease, and poverty underlying this beauty soon in-

[1] Greenwood *Commonwealth,* June 24, October 7, 1897.
[2] J. K. Vardaman to Anna Vardaman, August 21, 1898, Osborn, "The

81

spired horrified revulsion, however. Never had he imagined there existed so many poorly fed children and half-clothed people! Because the town had no sewers or sanitary arrangements, "disgusting odors" filled the night air. People who would tolerate such conditions, Vardaman believed, were the lowest form of humanity he had ever encountered. He commented: "The Almighty when He made Cuba, did a pretty good job, but He turned it over to a class of people that would cause hell itself to deteriorate. I think of all the weak, weary and altogether worthless people that I have ever had the misfortune to come into contact with the Cuban is, and about Santiago is, the most triflying [sic]. The American nigger is a gentlemen and scholar compared with him. Indeed, I am disposed to apologize to the nigger for making the Comparison." [3]

Despite his cruel evaluation of the Cubans, Vardaman pitied them. He wrote: "It may be a weakness but I am so put together that where I see any sort of an animal, human or otherwise, suffering I cannot for the life of me help pitying them and making a little effort to 'help them out.' " [4] At first he could not understand how they had become degraded to their lowly state. The island had abundant natural resources, and the inhabitants enjoyed contact with the most civilized countries of the world. After serving as president of the court of claims in Santiago, Vardaman became convinced that all Cubans totally lacked honesty and that their chief ambition was to steal from the United States. The Catholic Church, he believed, was largely responsible for the wretched conditions in Cuba. Although he respected Catholicism in the United States, he believed the Church in Cuba cared little for the spiritual or material welfare of its members, once saying that "there is about as much sweet spirit in it [the Church] as there is in an old fangless snake." He was far more disturbed on learning that the Church had encouraged social equality between Negroes and whites and committed the hideous crime of permitting interracial marriage: "It is common (in fact, the usual) thing to see a big buck nigger sitting by the side of

---

Spanish American War as Revealed Through the Letters of Major James K. Vardaman," 109.

[3] J. K. Vardaman to Greenwood *Commonwealth*, August 21, 1898, *ibid.*, 112.

[4] J. K. Vardaman to Greenwood *Commonwealth*, September 17, 1898, *ibid.*, 114–15.

a well-dressed white woman listening to the glad tidings of salvation from a Spanish padre." Since Cuba contained largely a homogeneous race, Vardaman concluded, the islands would always be backward and dismal. Shortly before leaving Cuba, he warned that whites should never live there: "When the Great God created the universe he drew the line north of Cuba as the place for Anglo-Saxons to live. This country will do for land crabs, spikers, niggers, bilious half-breeds and 'critters' of that character, but it was not built for our sort of folks, and therefore does not suit them." [5]

After returning from Cuba, Vardaman became an embittered foe of imperialism throughout the world. United States involvement in the Philippines especially enraged him. He considered this venture, which cost millions of dollars and thousands of lives, to be the selfish scheme of a few wealthy men who wanted to exploit the resources and trade of the archipelago. The acquisition of the islands would not benefit the majority of American people, he argued, and would be possibly harmful to southern farmers, who would have to compete with Filipino cotton planters. He did not believe those who argued that the Filipinos could not govern themselves; any form of government would be superior to what they had known during Spanish domination. The fact that the Filipinos had rebelled against Spanish rule and now were fighting American control proved, he believed, that they were entitled to self-government. Perhaps they would not enjoy a government like that of the United States, but it would be one "good enough for them." [6]

Vardaman became convinced that America's Philippine policy completely violated the Constitution and that eventually it would weaken the nation's moral fiber. No country could murder, plunder, and oppress others, he warned, and hope to escape the consequences. Certainly the Filipinos hated Americans: "God hates a liar, hypocrit [sic] and tyrant, and why should not man. The treatment to which the Filipinos have been subjected by Americans is enough to embitter and make resentful the soul of infinite forgiveness and love. They have been robbed of their country, plundered, humiliated and otherwise harshly used." With equal disgust he attacked those who argued that American

[5] J. K. Vardaman to H. T. Crosby, April 2, 1899, *ibid.*, April 14, 1899.
[6] Greenwood *Commonwealth,* December 15, 1899, March 16, 30, 1900, September 1, 1901.

missionaries would take Christianity to the islands. Religion would not
mellow the natives; only American "rotgut" liquor and "16-inch guns"
would achieve that end. He commented in the *Commonwealth*: "It is
not surprising that the Filipinos should doubt our sincerity when we go
to them, read the sermon on the mount, sing psalms, proclaim the glad
tidings of salvation, and tell them of the doctrine of the fatherhood of
God and the Brotherhood of Man as taught by the loving Christ, and
then turn around and shoot the saw-dust out of them because they refuse to give up their country and renounce the right to rule themselves." [7]

Vardaman extended his anti-imperialistic views to other nations.
The English committed just as great a crime in their war against the
Boers in South Africa as the Americans committed in their war against
the Filipinos. The Boers, like the Filipinos, were fighting for their
homes and rights. Vardaman wondered how American newspapers
could condemn England's actions in South Africa, while they supported the American position in the Philippines. [8]

Although he opposed imperialism, his sense of nationalism remained strong. When in the summer of 1900, Chinese nationalists
murdered foreign missionaries in Peking, Vardaman called for retalia-
tory action. The United States should send armed forces to China and
teach that nation a lesson. This incident was a matter of national hon-
or, he believed, and did not involve an attempt at expansion. [9] Imperialism, on the other hand, was foolish and selfish: foolish, because it
would infuse more "inferior races" into American society; selfish, because it was a deliberate scheme of the McKinley administration to
benefit a few wealthy men. Indeed, Vardaman considered every American killed in the Philippines a victim of the Republican Party.

The *Commonwealth* is opposed to converting this Republic into an
Empire—It is opposed to changing the office of President of the United
States to President of the United States and Emperor of the Philippine
Islands, Cuba and Porto Rico—It is opposed to cruising the Pacific
Ocean and making slaves of 10,000,000 people in the interest of that
government-looting band of millionaire robbers of the [Mark] Hanna

[7] *Ibid.*, March 21, August 17, 1900, July 12, 1901.
[8] *Ibid.*, January 12, February 16, April 13, 1900, November 16, 1901.
[9] *Ibid.*, July 6, August 10, 1900.

type. The *Commonwealth* is opposed to the American flag being planted where the American Constitution is a meaningless collection of
words. It is opposed to injecting any more niggers, chinamen and other
mongrel races into the body politic of this country, with all the accompanying evils—bublonic [*sic*] plague, leprosy, ignorance and superstition.[10]

The development of Vardaman's attitude toward imperialism closely paralleled his thought and writing on other subjects. On resuming
his editorial duties, he began to be harsher, bolder, and more vindictive
on many issues than he had formerly been. He expressed old ideas in
new language, lashing out at trusts, financial magnates, Republicans,
and Negroes. In his intensified attacks upon state and national leaders,
he resorted with greater frequency to rumors and innuendo. His initial
editorial of September 15 announced that he would tell the truth regardless of whom it hurt. If the people of Mississippi liked "that platform," they could subscribe to the *Commonwealth* for one dollar a
year.[11]

That Vardaman's new style appealed to many seemed evident from
the fact that people throughout Mississippi began to subscribe to his
paper. The reader could easily identify his editorials, for he wrote in
the first person singular. Some of his fellow editors criticized his egotistical approach, but Vardaman argued that it was a matter of "taste."
Moreover, since he determined editorial policy for the *Commonwealth*, he would continue to use "I." [12] On occasion his writing offended readers because of its bluntness and harshness. To such persons
he could only suggest that they stop reading the *Commonwealth*, for he
would not change his style.

I have no apology to offer for the language used in The Commonwealth. I try to be just, candid and clear. I do not want anybody to remain in doubt as to my position on the question at issue. . . . An editor
is often called upon to discuss questions which are not altogether
agreeable. It becomes his duty to make exposures which are not pleasant for the refined to look upon. But it must be done. The sanitary
officer is as necessary as the florist. And it is the offensive fertilizer

10 *Ibid.*, March 16, 1900.
11 *Ibid.*, September 15, 1899.
12 *Ibid.*, October 20, 1899.

which makes the sweetest flower. No man admires purity of thought, grace and elegance of diction more than I do. I also despise a counter-fit [*sic*] and sham.[13]

Vardaman's new style may have been influenced by South Carolina's Senator Ben Tillman and by the Texas editor William C. Brann. Throughout the 1890's southern newspapers had frequently reported Tillman's rabid speeches and exploits. Vardaman's own comments showed a realization that Tillman was a man of strength, although he did not express admiration for the South Carolinian until after the Spanish-American war. Then he began to demonstrate a fondness for Tillman, as well he might, for their views on the issues of race, trusts, and imperialism were almost identical. He explicitly approved Tillman's forthright and fearless mode of expression: "Senator Ben Tillman of South Carolina is at times not very elegant in his language, but there is a virtility [*sic*] and wideopen honesty about the old fellow's speech which all honest men admire." [14] Brann edited *Brann's Iconoclast* from 1895 until he was shot to death in 1898 at Waco, Texas. Perhaps no editor in American history ever aroused as much furor and controversy as did Brann, whose bold and vigorous writings and scathing verbal attacks blasted many of the nation's most respected political and religious leaders. Like Vardaman he vehemently opposed Negro equality. Vardaman believed Brann was "the most brilliant newspaper writer on the American continent," and he may well have tried to follow the Texan's style and approach in his own editorials.[15]

Besides writing in a more dramatic style than formerly, Vardaman began to emphasize some new subjects. Beliefs and prejudices that were held by many southern farmers, but that had played a minor part in his earlier writings, now became major themes. He warned, for example, that one of America's greatest dangers was the growing influence of the "money power." This sinister force, centered chiefly in the large eastern cities, was led by John D. Rockefeller, J. P. Morgan, and

[13] *Ibid.,* January 4, 1901.
[14] Francis B. Simkins, *Pitchfork Ben Tillman: South Carolinian* (Baton Rouge, 1944), *passim*; Greenwood *Commonwealth,* August 9, 1901. See also May 6, 27, 1897, June 1, 1900, *ibid.*; Greenwood *Enterprise,* October 31, 1890, December 14, 1894.
[15] Greenwood *Commonwealth,* April 8, 1898.

Andrew Carnegie.[16] These men would go to any lengths to enrich themselves at the expense of the American people. So great was their power that they strongly influenced the national government and some state governments. As proof of this, Vardaman now condemned former President Grover Cleveland for having made a "dishonest deal" in 1894 and 1895 by selling government bonds to J. P. Morgan and Company. Ironically enough, Vardaman's criticism of Cleveland and Morgan was harsher in 1901 than it had been when the bond sale occurred.[17]

The growing power of concentrated wealth endangered many aspects of American life. It posed a special threat to academic freedom, for wealthy men frequently came to control American schools to throttle freedom of investigation and render the school subservient to their own wills. Endowments to universities by wealthy industrialists and financiers represented an attempt by the "money power" to instill its ideas of the value of "predatory wealth and commercialism" into the minds of the nation's youth. Far more serious was the danger that concentrated wealth posed to capitalism; it could destroy the entire American economic system! The unlimited accumulation of capital by a few could either drive many poor men to attempt social revolution or force the government to intervene and impose a system of socialism. Both of these alternatives, the Delta editor believed, should be avoided and could be simply by checking the "money power." Strong labor unions afforded the surest way to redress the influence of great wealth, to protect the interest of laborers, and to preserve American capitalism.[18]

As the United States rapidly developed into an industrial nation, Vardaman lamented, the older agrarian values were dying, the true spirit of Christianity was being forgotten, and far too many had the one goal of trying to amass money for themselves. While men spent thousands of dollars for churches and "high-priced ministers," a perfect "Niagara" of souls went to hell every day because they lacked the basic necessities of life and because they had no one to help them. The prob-

[16] *Ibid.,* April 29, July 1, 15, 29, 1897, April 12, May 31, 1901.
[17] *Ibid.,* April 29, 1897, January 18, 1901; Nevins, *Grover Cleveland,* 649–76.
[18] Greenwood *Commonwealth,* July 16, 29, September 16, 1897, January 26, 1900, June 14, August 2, September 27, 1901, October 17, 1902.

lem was worse in the cities, but even in the rural districts the spirit of commercialism was spreading.[19]

Since founding the *Commonwealth* in 1896, Vardaman had used its pages to voice his ardent support of white supremacy. Discovering with each editorial devoted to the danger of Negro equality the intense appeal that racism had among Mississippi's whites, especially those cursed with poverty and ignorance, Vardaman now constantly went to greater extremes. He continued to bemoan the folly of Negro education. Though he emphasized the value of education for whites, he did not believe it could settle the race problem. In fact, as he had long said, education only made the Negro dissatisfied with being a laborer or servant; no matter how much education a Negro gained, the whites would always force him to be a menial. It was "because he was a nigger." [20] Moreover, Negroes and whites could live together peacefully, Vardaman believed, only if the blacks willingly accepted a menial position at the bottom of society. Not only must Negroes be content with the barest rudiments of education, but they must abandon all pretense to social and political equality with the whites.[21] Above all, Negroes must never inflict crimes of violence upon whites, for such actions would result in the whites annihilating the blacks. As he had always believed, the most serious racial crime was for a Negro man to rape a white woman—the one offense that justified lynch law. One of Vardaman's most revealing editorials on this subject appeared in the fall of 1902 soon after an alleged Negro rapist had been burned to death by a mob at Corinth, Mississippi.

Much has been said and written about the people of Corinth burning the brute who killed Mrs. Cary Whitfield. I am sorry they burned him It would have been better to have buried him alive, or shot him, or hanged him in the jail. I think they did right to kill the brute, but it would have been better had the crowd been denied admission. It does not help a man morally to look upon a thing of that kind. It is rather hardening. But I sometimes think that one could look upon a scene of that kind and suffer no more moral deterioration than he would by looking upon the burning of an Orangoutang that had stolen a baby or

19 *Ibid.*, November 28, 1902, and January 18, 1901.
20 *Ibid.*, October 6, 1899.
21 *Ibid.*, September 29, October 20, 1899, January 19, 1900, March 29, November 8, 1901, June 20, 1902.

a viper that had stung an unsuspecting child to death. He ceases to be regarded as a human being, and is only looked upon as a two legged monster. But then, it is not elevating to even look upon the burning of a big monkey. However when one of these devils commit such deeds as this nigger did, somebody must kill him and I am in favor of doing it promptly. In this case I only regret the brute did not have ten thousand lives to pay for his atrocious deed. An eternity in hell will not be adequate punishment for it.[22]

This harsh editorial revealed how violent his racist beliefs had become during the past decade. His essential views had never changed, but they had hardened and become far more extreme.

Vardaman continued to voice his opinions on public education, arguing that during the past thirty years only a minority of Negroes had profited from education and that schools had not improved the majority either intellectually or morally. When some white Mississippi teachers held a summer school for Negro teachers, he bitterly denounced the entire plan: "Now it is almost an unpardonable offense for a white man or woman to teach [in] the ordinary nigger school. To do it means social ostracism. Will some one be kind enough to tell the difference? I had as soon teach a young as an old nigger. They both have the same fragrant accompaniment. . . . It should be prohibited by law. Let niggers teach niggers. I am opposed to mixing the races even in institutes." [23]

Some editors asked why Vardaman, a Delta man, should advocate the curtailment of Negro education, because the Delta counties, with their large Negro populations, received the greatest appropriations and their white children enjoyed better school facilities than did those in southern and eastern Mississippi. Vardaman replied that the issue should not cause sectionalism in the state, for all white children should receive the best possible education. "I deprecate most earnestly that spirit which would split the state into factions and array the hills against the delta," Vardaman asserted. "The interest[s] of the sections are one, and he [who] would favor one to the neglect or detriment of the other is a public enemy." [24]

Vardaman was especially hostile toward northerners who criticized race relations in the South. In his future political campaigns he would

[22] *Ibid.*, October 10, 1902.
[23] *Ibid.*, May 25, 1900.
[24] *Ibid.*, November 30, 1900.

often gain support by condemning outside critics. Believing that whites too frequently tried to appease northern opinion on the race problem, he declared that only southerners understood the Negro and could deal with him properly. When racial troubles flared in the North, Vardaman rejoiced. Such incidents, demonstrating that race prejudice existed throughout the country, might enable northerners to understand better the problem faced by the South. Vardaman's reply to an article in the New York *Independent* typified his reaction to northerners who condemned his views on race: "It matters very little with me what this blue belted, coon fascinated, south hatting [*sic*], vain glorious miscegenationist who presides over the editorial department of *The Independent* may think of me. I am not trying to please his kind of cattle. It is just such literary pole cats as he who have intimidated and bull-dozed the southern people and caused our public men to make egregious asses of themselves when dealing with the race problem." [25]

In still another area the Delta editor probably pleased his many readers—his coverage of state politics. Here Vardaman continued to attack Anselm J. McLaurin and many men whom he believed to be allied with the former governor. McLaurin's last senatorial appointment particularly irritated Vardaman. In the spring of 1898 Senator Edward Walthall had died and some observers believed McLaurin would appoint himself to fulfill the vacancy. The governor had, however, adopted a more cautious course and selected William V. Sullivan, a congressman from Lafayette County who wanted the distinction of having served for a short term in the Senate. Many believed that Sullivan and McLaurin made a deal whereby the governor appointed him to fulfill Walthall's term, which expired in 1901, on the condition that Sullivan would not run again. Whether the two men actually struck such a bargain is unknown, but Sullivan did serve for the short term and McLaurin won the full term. [26]

Vardaman took special delight in ridiculing Senator Sullivan: "Ten years ago such a man would no more have been considered in con-

---

[25] *Ibid.*, August 17, 1900, and November 10, 1899.
[26] Kirwan, *Revolt of the Rednecks,* 105–106. Later Sullivan claimed that McLaurin had promised to support him for both the long and the short terms, but had broken his promise.

nection with the United States Senatorship from Mississippi than for the presidency of the United States." Convinced that Sullivan was completely unqualified for his position, Vardaman accused the senator of sympathizing with McKinley's Philippine policies. He also supported as being true, rumors circulated by Sullivan's opponents, reporting that the senator had tried to violate the virtue of a young Mississippi woman whom he had promised to help find a job in Washington. Such an incident, Vardaman boasted, proved that Sullivan's political enemies were "those who stand for decency in politics, decency in the home: for the purity of our women and the honesty of our men." [27]

When Governor Longino assumed office Vardaman might have been expected to set upon his administration as he had McLaurin's. For almost two years, however, he refrained from such attacks. Although some argued that McLaurin supported Longino, Vardaman did not publicly accept this assertion. He described the new governor as an honest man who represented, so Vardaman hoped, a clean break with the government of the past four years. Such acts as Longino's refusal to reappoint Judge William K. McLaurin, Anse's brother, especially pleased Vardaman.[28] Initially he clashed with Longino on only one major issue: the governor wanted to encourage industry to come to Mississippi by offering a program of tax exemptions. Vardaman strongly objected. He, too, wanted more factories in the state, but he opposed any plan which discriminated in favor of corporate wealth.[29] Contrary to what Vardaman had feared, the legislature of 1900 did not grant tax exemptions; in fact, the state continued to press a suit initiated during the McLaurin administration against the Yazoo and Mississippi Valley Railroad, charging that the company owed a large amount of back taxes. After the Mississippi supreme court ruled against the railroad company, the case was appealed to the United States Supreme Court. Apprehensive lest the Longino administration compromise with

---

[27] Greenwood *Commonwealth,* October 13, 1899; Coffeeville *Courier,* quoted in Greenwood *Commonwealth,* November 3, 1899; Greenwood *Commonwealth,* February 15, 1901.

[28] Greenwood *Commonwealth,* March 2, 1900, July 12, August 30, 1901.

[29] *Journal of the Senate of the State of Mississippi at a Regular Session, January, February, and March, 1900* (Jackson, 1900), 88. Hereinafter cited as *Senate Journal, 1900.* The Journals for 1902, 1904, 1906, 1911, 1912 will be similarly denoted. And see Greenwood *Commonwealth,* January 26, 1900.

the railroad company, Vardaman devoted numerous editorials to this case. The administration attempted no compromise, however, and the Supreme Court ruled in favor of the state. The outcome pleased Vardaman. Longino was proving to be a much better governor than he had expected.[30]

Vardaman's attitude toward corporate wealth indicated how greatly he had changed his beliefs since the early 1890's. As a state legislator siding with the conservative faction of the Mississippi Democracy, he had defended a bill to grant tax exemptions to railroads. Beginning in 1897 and becoming more pronounced by 1900, he abandoned his conservative position and turned instead to supporting social and economic reforms that had long been advocated by agrarian movements in Mississippi. He also appealed to the small-farmer class by inciting Negrophobia. His attitudes toward corporate wealth, the trusts, poverty, and the Negro all reflected the general sentiment of the state's agricultural masses. By the turn of the century, moreover, these views had become stronger throughout the state and had become more widely accepted by men of all social ranks. If Mississippi abolished the old convention system and adopted popular primaries to choose state officials, the Greenwood editor, with his appeals for social reform and for suppressing the Negro, might become a new power in state politics.

Indeed, opposition to the convention system had been mounting throughout the 1880's and 1890's. The practice had been that counties frequently held primaries, but Democratic leaders always used conventions to nominate state officers. Since the end of Reconstruction the Bourbon wing of the Mississippi Democracy had maintained tight control over party machinery. Opposition to Bourbon domination through the convention system had at first stemmed largely from agrarian movements such as the Farmers' Alliance and the Populists. But unsuccessful politicians constituted another source of opposition, for the convention system offered them an increasingly strong issue upon which to attack their successful rivals. James Vardaman certainly had reason to want the convention system abolished and popular pri-

---

[30] Greenwood *Commonwealth*, February 2, 16, 23, March 9, 1900, January 11, 1901; *Yazoo and Mississippi Valley Railroad Company v. Adams*, 181 U.S., 530–33 (1901). Brandfon, *Cotton Kingdom of the New South*, 166–98.

maries adopted. After his second defeat in 1898 at the hands of a convention, he had begun to demand the passage of a primary law.[31]

A new wave of opposition to the convention system arose in April, 1900, when the state Democratic executive committee ordered primaries in all counties to choose presidential electors and delegates to the Democratic national convention but failed to provide for the meeting of a state convention. Some charged the proposed primary would have no importance, holding that it was a foregone conclusion that William Jennings Bryan would again be the Democratic nominee and he would have Mississippi's support. Traditionally, a state convention had assembled every four years to elect a new state executive committee, to ratify the results of the county primaries, and to draw up a state Democratic platform. The committee's failure to provide for a convention appeared to be an arbitrary attempt by its members to retain control of the state Democratic Party. Unless there was a state convention, the existing executive committee would retain power for the next four years and would canvass the vote of the county primaries. That it would conduct such a canvass fairly was highly doubted. The state press fiercely condemned the committee and its chairman C. C. Miller. Many county committees refused to hold primaries unless a state convention ratified the results.[32]

As fear grew that party machinery might break down, Vardaman assumed leadership of the opposition. In an editorial of May 11 addressed to the state executive committee, he accused the group of trying to mislead the people and asked the members whom they were trying to shield. Although he never named the persons responsible for the committee's action, he strongly implied that Senator Sullivan and Senator-elect McLaurin were behind it.[33] Other anti-McLaurin men pointed out that Miller had served as chairman of the state convention which had nominated McLaurin for governor and that the two men were close friends; from these facts they inferred that Mc-

---

[31] Kirwan, *Revolt of the Rednecks,* 122–23; Ferguson, "Agrarianism in Mississippi," 359–95; Greenwood *Commonwealth,* July 12, 1901.

[32] Jackson *Daily Clarion-Ledger,* April 30, May 1, 2, 3, 4, 7, 8, 10, 14, 22, 24, 28, 1900. Throughout May the *Clarion* reprinted editorials from Mississippi papers condemning the action of the executive committee. See also Woodville *Republican,* May 19, June 2, 1900; Bay St. Louis *Gulf Coast Progress,* May 5, 12, 1900; Kosciusko *Attala Democrat,* May 15, 1900.

[33] Greenwood *Commonwealth,* May 11, 1900.

Laurin, acting through Miller, had manipulated the executive committee. The charge may well have been valid. Only the strongest
pro-McLaurin newspapers, such as the Vicksburg *Dispatch,* defended
the committee's action.[34] Chairman Miller refused to comment on the
many demands that he reconvene the executive committee until he
made a hurried trip to Jackson for a meeting with McLaurin; then he
explained that he had no reason to call another meeting of the committee as it had carefully considered the vote for a primary.[35]

On May 25 Vardaman directed an appeal "To the Democracy of
Mississippi," urging county executive committees to send delegates to
a convention in Jackson on June 5. The convention would name its
own ticket of presidential electors and delegates to the national convention. It would also draw up a party platform to instruct the delegates to the national convention. Then in a state primary on June 21
the electorate would choose between the delegates nominated by the
excutive committee and those nominated by the convention.[36]

Twenty-nine counties responded to Vardaman's appeal and sent
more than three hundred delegates to the June convention. Many of
those in attendance, such as LeRoy Percy of Greenville, shared Vardaman's avowed opposition to McLaurin. Others, such as Governor
Longino, earlier had sympathized with McLaurin, but, in reaction to
the unwise ruling of the executive committee, now shifted to side with
the anti-McLaurin men.[37] The assemblage chose Vardaman as its
chairman and adopted the plan he had proposed. The party platform
closely resembled the national Democratic platform of 1896: it condemned the adoption of the gold standard, the trusts, imperialism,
and the tariff, and it supported the renomination of William Jennings
Bryan for the presidency. Disavowing any attempt to bolt the Demo-

[34] Vicksburg *Dispatch,* quoted in Jackson *Daily Clarion-Ledger,* May 21, 1900.
[35] Jackson *Daily Clarion-Ledger,* May 28, 1900. Miller and McLaurin were
indeed close personal and political friends. C. C. Miller to A. J. McLaurin,
February 10, March 2, 1896, December 30, 1898, May 4, June 11, July 12,
1899, in Letters Received by Anselm J. McLaurin, Governor's Records, Mississippi Department of Archives and History.
[36] Greenwood *Commonwealth,* May 25, 1900. The state press referred to the
call for a special convention as the Vardaman plan. Jackson *Daily Clarion-
Ledger,* May 26, 1900.
[37] Jackson *Daily Clarion-Ledger,* May 21, 1900. Longino had appealed to
Miller and the executive committee to reconsider its action. And see Kosciusko
Attala Democrat, May 29, 1900; Woodville *Republican,* June 2, 1900.

cratic Party, the convention nominated a ticket for the June primary that included all factions of the state party. Thus the delegates nominated to represent the state at large were Senator Money, Senator-elect McLaurin, Governor Longino, and R. H. Henry, editor of the Jackson *Daily Clarion-Ledger*.[38]

Despite its pretense of maintaining party unity, the convention's action widened the split between the McLaurin and anti-McLaurin factions. The state Democratic executive committee had nominated the same slate of delegates at large as had the convention, but with one exception: Senator Sullivan had been named in place of Henry. McLaurin, moreover, repudiated the convention's action by refusing to accept its nomination as a delegate to the national convention.[39]

The primary on June 21 resulted in a victory for the convention ticket, as Henry narrowly defeated Sullivan by a margin of about five hundred votes. This outcome pleased Vardaman, naturally, but he urged moderation in order to avoid a permanent party rupture. Many of those who had supported the June 5 convention urged that another convention be held in September to select a new state executive committee. Others, including Vardaman, believed that the party had already experienced enough infighting for that year. As the electorate had repudiated the existing Democratic executive committee, that body had had its authority undermined; there would be little danger in waiting until the next state convention met in 1903 to select a new executive committee.[40]

The interparty fight of 1900 held important implications for the future. In helping further to solidify opposition between the McLaurin and anti-McLaurin factions, it led to the formation of some new temporary alliances. John Sharp Williams, Mississippi's most distinguished young congressman, and LeRoy Percy had joined with Vardaman in fighting the McLaurin faction. In the state's next gubernatorial race Percy and Williams would support Vardaman against a candidate who enjoyed McLaurin's backing. Thus, by having seized upon the wave of protest to the executive committee's action, Varda-

[38] Greenwood *Commonwealth,* June 8, 1900; Bay St. Louis *Gulf Coast Progress,* June 9, 1900; Jackson *Daily Clarion-Ledger,* June 5, 1900.
[39] Jackson *Daily Clarion-Ledger,* June 9, 1900.
[40] Greenwood *Commonwealth,* June 15, 29, July 6, 13, 1900; Jackson *Daily Clarion-Ledger,* June 22, 25, 27, 1900; Woodville *Republican,* July 28, 1900.

man had assumed a commanding position among the leaders of the anti-McLaurin forces.

The factional struggle of 1900 also gave impetus to the movement for abolishing the convention system. Numerous scandals grew out of the June primary. In an effort to retain political power, some Delta politicians had resorted to ballot box stuffing and in that section there were many charges of fraud. Opponents of the existing system argued that Mississippi needed a uniform primary law that would be enforced fairly throughout the state. Political power, they believed, should be removed from the control of party "bosses" and placed directly in the hands of the white voters. During the next two years more and more state newspapers demanded that each voter should have the opportunity to express his individual choice. In 1902, in response to popular sentiment, Governor Longino urged the legislature to enact a state Democratic primary law. Opposition to popular primaries had always centered in the Delta—the section that had enjoyed the largest representation at state conventions. By the turn of the century, however, pockets of discontent with the convention system were numerous enough even in the Delta to undermine opposition to a primary law.[41] Edmund F. Noel, whose nomination for district attorney Vardaman had denounced so bitterly in 1883, had now become a state senator from Holmes County, and it was he who sponsored the state's first primary law, which the legislature passed on March 4, 1902.[42] Henceforth, party nominations in Mississippi would be made by primary elections. If no candidate received a majority in the first primary, a runoff election would be held three weeks later.[43]

---

[41] Kirwan, *Revolt of the Rednecks,* 125–26; Hamilton, "Mississippi Politics in the Progressive Era," 52–58.

[42] E. F. Noel, "Mississippi's Primary Election Law," *Publications of the Mississippi Historical Society,* VIII (1904), 239–45.

[43] "This was the first mandatory statewide primary in the country. . . . The legislature was required to ratify the selection of candidates for United States Senator who received a majority of the votes in the primary, thus bypassing constitutional election by the legislature and inaugurating a popular election of senator in fact. By providing for a run-off, in case no candidate had a majority in the first primary election, Mississippi established what has been considered by some as the first complete primary election system. . . . The primary system made the governor a more accurate reflector of statewide white opinion than the legislature." Hamilton, "Mississippi Politics in the Progressive Era," 58–59. For a more thorough discussion of the primary law, see Kirwan, *Revolt of the Rednecks,* 122–35.

Because the state committee ruled that only whites could vote in a Democratic primary and that party's nomination was equivalent to election, the primary law in effect placed another barrier between the Negro and the franchise. In that sense it was a move away from democracy. Otherwise, it was "the most democratic measure which the voters of the state had yet obtained." [44] Small groups of political leaders long had controlled the nominations of state officers, but after 1902 great numbers of white men would actually have a voice in the matter. A certain geographic shift in power and perhaps also a change in political emphasis might be expected, for the counties of eastern Mississippi had always cast the largest number of white votes and, in the future, political candidates would have to appeal strongly to the interests of that section.

Following the passage of the primary law, Vardaman abandoned his friendly attitude toward Governor Longino and became increasingly hostile toward his administration. When state newspapers began to report that corruption existed in the penitentiary system, Vardaman demanded an investigation. Something was "rotten and corrupt as hell," he warned, in the management of the penitentiary, and the responsibility for correcting the situation lay with the governor.[45] Vardaman reserved his harshest attacks for Longino's courageous opposition to lynchings. When on several occasions the governor personally stopped angry mobs from seizing Negro prisoners, Vardaman defended lynch law as a necessary evil.[46] He especially criticized Longino for trying to break up secret organizations, known as Whitecaps, which then were terrorizing Negroes in three counties of South Mississippi. Composed primarily of dirt farmers, the Whitecaps represented an extreme form of animosity against the Negro. When Longino attempted to suppress them, Vardaman accused him of making a "spectacular play" and of damaging the state's reputation by calling

[44] Kirwan, *Revolt of the Rednecks,* 131.
[45] Greenwood *Commonwealth,* October 17, November 7, 14, 1902. Vardaman held that Longino's administration had been "characterized by more 'filthy disclosures,' 'questionable transactions' and profound weakness than any democratic [sic] administration since the days of Winthrope [sic] Sargent." Greenwood *Commonwealth,* October 10, 1902.
[46] *Ibid.,* February 9, December 28, 1900, March 22, August 9, 1901; Jackson *Daily Clarion-Ledger,* June 11, 1902.

attention to a minute problem that local authorities could easily handle.[47]

One reason Vardaman attacked the governor so savagely was that in January, 1902, President Theodore Roosevelt appointed Longino's brother-in-law, Edgar S. Wilson, marshal of the Southern District of Mississippi. Wilson also became Roosevelt's patronage referee for Mississippi and worked closely with Booker T. Washington in attempting to revitalize the Republican Party in the state by selecting able and honest men for office. Roosevelt chose Wilson, a lifelong Democrat, because he had refused to support the free silver platform of 1896 and because, like Longino, he was a determined opponent of mob violence and apparently had a genuine concern for improving the lot of southern Negroes.[48] By working with Roosevelt and Washington, Wilson became a prime target for Vardaman, who described him as the "sublime embodiment of Gush, Gall and Guts, the honored brother-in-law of the governor, and Mark Hanna of the state administration." [49] Wilson's position soon enabled Vardaman to foster the belief that a cabal existed between Longino, Wilson, and Roosevelt. Indeed, by 1902 Roosevelt had become one of Vardaman's leading subjects, a convenient scapegoat upon which the Mississippian could vent his wrath.

Vardaman had disliked Roosevelt as governor of New York, but immediately after McKinley's assassination he predicted that the new President would purge the administration of its weak elements and would make an adequate leader.[50] His hopes for the new chief executive were short lived. Soon after becoming President, Roosevelt invited Booker T. Washington to dine with him at the White House. That act, which aroused condemnation throughout the South, moved Vardaman to the height of editorial fury. In denouncing the President

[47] Greenwood *Commonwealth,* January 2, 1903. For a discussion of the Whitecap problem, see Chapter 5 below.
[48] Mary Floyd Summers, "Edgar Stewart Wilson: The Mississippi Eagle, Journalist of the New South" (Ph.D. dissertation, Mississippi State University, 1962), *passim*; Edgar S. Wilson to Theodore Roosevelt, October 28, December 30, 1902, March 4, November 19, 1904, Roosevelt to Wilson, January 2, 1903, March 28, October 7, 1905, in Theodore Roosevelt Papers, Library of Congress.
[49] Greenwood *Commonwealth,* October 17, 1902.
[50] *Ibid.,* April 27, 1900, June 28, September 27, October 4, 11, 1901.

he gave vent to every prejudice and emotion at his command. Booker T. Washington, "the saddle-colored philosopher of Tuskegee," had been disgraced, he declared. Vardaman had hoped Washington had more self-respect than to accept the President's invitation and associate on terms of social equality "with a white man who had no more decency than to take a d——d nigger into his home." By this act the President had insulted every white man in America. "President Roosevelt takes this nigger bastard into his home, introduces him to his family and entertains him on terms of absolute social equality. He does more. He carries his daughter to another social function, where she and Washington are to be among the special guest[s] of honor." [51] Roosevelt's actions, Vardaman concluded, directly encouraged social equality and interracial marriage.

By picturing Roosevelt as an advocate of racial equality, Vardaman warned that no man was a greater enemy of the southern whites than the President. Governor Longino deserved the condemnation of those who had elected him because he officially welcomed the President to Mississippi in November, 1902, when Roosevelt went south to hunt bear in the Delta. Prior to his arrival Vardaman advertised in the *Commonwealth*: "WANTED, sixteen big, fat mellow, rancid 'coons' to sleep with Roosevelt when he comes down to go bear hunting with Mississippi's onliest governor Longy. Before Governor Longino invites any gentlemen to join Roosevelt in the bear hunt he should let them know who besides Teddy are expected. Teddy may bring Booker with him, and if he does Longy will have to entertain him, and of course gentlemen would not divide that honor with him." [52] Vardaman urged his readers to greet the President with "chilly courtesy" out of respect for his office, but he hoped they would not stoop to playing "the flunky, hypocrite or liar" in their dealings with Roosevelt.[53] At the conclusion of the bear hunt Vardaman resorted to verse in describing the President's visit. The lines illustrate well the extreme to which he went in exploiting the issue.

Teddy has come and Teddy has gone,
And the lick spittle spittled and the fawning did fawn.

[51] *Ibid.,* October 18, 25, 1901.
[52] *Ibid.,* October 31, 1902.
[53] *Ibid.,* November 14, 1902.

The coons smelt as loud as a musk rat's nest,
And Teddy licked his chops and said it smelt the best.[54]

Vardaman's rantings against Roosevelt might not have caused more than a passing sensation had the President not become involved in a Mississippi racial incident. During President Benjamin Harrison's administration, Mrs. Minnie M. Cox, a well-educated Negro woman, had been appointed postmaster at Indianola, a small Delta town about thirty miles from Greenwood. Local whites had accepted her and during McKinley's administration she had been reappointed with both Mississippi senators voting to confirm her. Trouble arose soon after Edgar S. Wilson took office, for the appointment of a white Democrat as patronage referee led some ambitious men to believe that Roosevelt would permit all Negro office holders to be replaced by whites. It was under such an erroneous assumption that some whites in Indianola initiated a movement in the spring of 1902 to oust Mrs. Cox by arousing concern over "Negro domination" and by warning that black officeholders were a "menace to white civilization." [55]

The movement against Mrs. Cox had gained momentum by the fall of 1902 when Vardaman seized upon the situation and exploited it for his own ends. By that time he again was running for governor and was basing his campaign upon anti-Negro agitation. Several times during the fall of 1902 he spoke in Indianola, taunting the people for "tolerating a negro wench as postmaster" and implying that Mrs. Cox had been appointed by Roosevelt and Wilson. Tension over the post office situation continued to increase and finally resulted in a meeting of local whites ordering Mrs. Cox to resign. Vardaman continued to inflame the situation by returning to Indianola and congratulating the whites for their stand. Through his newspaper he announced that "white people are going to rule this country and they *are not going to let niggers hold office.*" [56]

[54] *Ibid.,* November 28, 1902.
[55] For an account of the Indianola affair, see Willard B. Gatewood, "Theodore Roosevelt and the Indianola Affair," *Journal of Negro History,* LIII (1968), 48–69; United States House of Representatives, *Resignation of the Postmaster at Indianola, Miss.,* Document No. 422, 57 Congress, 2d Sess., *passim.*
[56] Greenwood *Commonwealth,* November 14, 28, December 5, 1902; Edgar S. Wilson, "Memoirs," Chapter 77, p. 1, in Edgar S. Wilson Papers, Mississippi Department of Archives and History.

In the face of the mounting opposition Mrs. Cox resigned as post-master on January 1, 1903. Roosevelt immediately retaliated by clos-ing the Indianola post office. The President's action ignited fierce opposition throughout Mississippi, and almost all of the state's white population denounced the action. Mississippi editors delivered scath-ing attacks upon the President, but no one exceeded Vardaman's editorial barrage:

In the annals of the political history of the world since the days of Nero there is not to be found a parallel to the pusillanimous lowdown, dirty and contemptible conduct of President Roosevelt regarding the Indianola post office. There have been deeds committed by heads of governments followed by more widespread and atrocious conse-quences but none that evidence a more craven and malignant spirit. It is the work of a human coyote who would destroy the civilization of the better and more respecting section of the country of which he by the accident of an assassin's shot is president; he would break down the barriers which keep back and hold in restraint the black waves of ignorance, superstition and immorality with which the South is per-petually threatened.

After reviewing the circumstances surrounding the Indianola incident, Vardaman concluded that Roosevelt had acted solely to advance his political career.

He had the power—not the right under law—but the power, and like the spectacular lion masquerading ass that he is, dared to prostitute that power. But probably I am a little harsh. It is remotely possible that I may not know any better. I would not be uncharitable. It is said that men follow the bent of their genius, and that prenatal in-fluences are often patent in shaping thoughts and ideas of after life. Probably old lady Roosevelt during the period of gestation was fright-ened by a dog and that fact may account for the qualities of the male pup which are so prominent in Teddy. I would not do her an injustice but I am disposed to apologize to the dog for mentioning it.[57]

When Vardaman ran for governor in 1903, he used anti-Rooseveltism as one of his chief appeals. Because the Indianola post office remained closed throughout 1903, anti-Roosevelt sentiment in-

[57] Greenwood *Commonwealth,* January 10, 1903.

tensified in Mississippi. Vardaman seized upon this sentiment, magnified it and used it for his political advancement. Unknowingly President Roosevelt contributed greatly to Vardaman's election as governor.

The gubernatorial contest of 1903 initiated a new era in Mississippi politics. After the passage of the primary law, candidates had to canvass the state more thoroughly than in the past, speaking to as many people as possible. It was no easy task. Railroads served the major towns, but much of the countryside was miles from any rail lines. Frequently office seekers had to travel in wagons or on horseback over dusty country roads. At a time when there was little political advertising, candidates had to meet voters personally by attending hundreds of barbecues, picnics, camp meetings, and political rallies. Vardaman was well fitted for such campaigning for he liked people, mingling easily with them, and being tall and a fastidious dresser, attracted attention, as always, wherever he went.

Three months after the passage of the primary law and more than a year before its first application, the gubernatorial canvass got under way with the candidates stumping from county to county. Among the first to enter the race was Vardaman. Having twice been defeated under the convention system, he now directed his campaign to the rural whites by appealing to issues that agricultural organizations had long advocated. In connection with schooling he observed that hundreds of parents simply could not afford to buy school books for their children. "In truth, there are thousands of families in this State wherein five or ten dollars will determine the question of whether or not the little children shall have shoes for the winter. That may sound incredible to some folks, but it is nevertheless true." Mississippi therefore needed a uniform textbook law to insure sound educational material for all the state's white children. Vardaman favored too an elective judiciary, construction of better roads, establishment of a state commissioner of agriculture, larger appropriations for white schools, abolition of convict leasing, and local option liquor laws. While he wanted industry to grow in Mississippi, he opposed granting tax exemptions to corporations. Since 1895 he had advocated distributing the school fund among the races in proportion to the taxes paid by whites and blacks, and he continued to hammer upon that issue. He played another familiar theme: Negro education was foolish

—because blacks belonged to an inferior race that was incapable of acquiring meaningful education—and dangerous because even a rudimentary education might rekindle the Negroes' ambitions to vote and hold office. To settle the race problem once and for all it would be necessary to abolish Negro education, repeal the Fifteenth Amendment, and greatly modify the Fourteenth. If elected governor, he promised to work for all three objectives. By then he knew that racist agitation gave him strong appeal among the voters and accordingly he rode that issue hardest. From the outset many hailed Vardaman as the leading candidate.[58]

Judge Frank Critz, from northeastern Mississippi, became Vardaman's closest rival. He, too, had run for governor four years earlier and lost. Like Vardaman, he favored a uniform textbook law, a state commissioner of agriculture, and larger appropriations for white schools. Unlike Vardaman, he believed industrial growth in Mississippi could best be assured by granting tax exemptions to corporations. Critz also clashed with Vardaman on the solution to the race question. Believing that his opponent appealed to racism solely to win votes, he argued that Vardaman's election would endanger race relations in the state. The constitution of 1890 had settled the problem in Mississippi, he claimed. Why foster unnecessary tensions and hatreds? Above all, he ridiculed the scheme to distribute the school fund in proportion to the taxes paid by each race. Even Vardaman admitted, he pointed out, that such a plan could not be enforced unless the Fourteenth Amendment was modified.[59]

Edmund Noel, author of the primary law, became Vardaman's leading Delta rival. Having studied Vardaman's legislative record, he held that his opponent had reversed himself on many issues: as a state legislator Vardaman had voted against an elective judiciary bill and

[58] Yazoo City *Herald*, August 3, 1900, May 8, 1903; Greenwood *Commonwealth*, April 25, 1903; Jackson *Daily Clarion-Ledger*, April 20, 1903.
[59] *Ibid.*, December 5, 1902, April 7, May 25, 1903; Yazoo City *Saturday Evening News*, March 7, 1903; Bay St. Louis *Gulf Coast Progress*, April 18, 1903; Meadville *Franklin Advocate*, April 30, May 21, 1903; Summit *Sentinel*, March 5, April 23, 1903. Frank A. Critz to J. C. Burrus, January 15, 1903, in John C. Burrus Papers, Mississippi Department of Archives and History. Hereinafter cited as Burrus Papers. Congressman Andrew F. Fox, who lived in Critz's home county of Clay, entered the race, but he dropped out, protesting that Critz had usurped much of his strength.

a primary election law; he had supported appropriations for the state's Negro colleges and had voted for a program to grant tax exemptions to corporations. Like Critz, Noel ridiculed as an impossibility Vardaman's scheme for distributing the school fund because it violated the United States Constitution. He argued, moreover, that the Delta counties actually contributed more money to the general school fund than they received in return.[60]

Noel was correct in asserting that since the early 1890's Vardaman had changed his position on many issues. As a member of the conservative faction of the Mississippi Democracy he had opposed such agrarian programs as retrenchment and an elective judiciary; he had fought against the sub-treasury plan and the Populist Party. But during the 1880's and 1890's, as the farmers struggled to improve their lot, the rural whites of Mississippi had begun to gain a sense of social and political unity. By the early twentieth century they were demanding reforms similar to those that had begun to develop strength throughout the nation and which became basic tenets for the progressive movement. Moreover, many Mississippi merchants, professional men, and planters had come to support some reforms that earlier had been voiced chiefly by the agrarians. The desire for greater popular participation in government through direct primaries and the demand for stricter regulation of corporate wealth, for example, were issues upon which most white Mississippians agreed.

The majority of white voters were also in basic agreement with the tenets of the white supremacy creed. Poverty and ignorance of many whites caused smoldering race prejudice to remain alive and Vardaman's blatant use of the issue simply poured fuel on the existing coals. Because President Roosevelt had dined with Booker T. Washington and because he closed the Indianola post office during the election year, Vardaman's appeal to racism came at an opportune time and allowed him to exploit anti-Roosevelt sentiment as well. During the campaign a report was circulated that Roosevelt had offered to contribute a year's salary if it would help to defeat Vardaman.[61] In capi-

---

[60] Jackson *Daily Clarion-Ledger*, September 10, 1902, April 4, May 9, July 24, 1903; Brookhaven *Leader*, September 17, 1902, April 22, 1903.
[61] Yazoo City *Herald*, March 20, 1903; Columbus *Commercial*, February 3, 1903; Aberdeen *Weekly*, September 4, 1903; Summit *Sentinel*, August 20, 1903; Brookhaven *Lincoln County Times*, January 7, 1903.

talizing on the opposition to Roosevelt, Vardaman and his followers resorted to many base and distorted appeals. They frequently pictured the contest as being between Roosevelt and Vardaman: *"A vote for Vardaman is a vote for White Supremacy,* a vote for the quelling of the arrogant spirit that has been aroused in the blacks by Roosevelt and his henchmen, a vote for the better education of *white* children, a vote for the *safety of the Home* and *the protection of our women and children."* [62] In speech after speech Vardaman attacked Roosevelt, sometimes describing him as a "coon-flavored miscegenationist," at other times as "that wild, untamed, self asserted, broncho busting negro dining man who sits in the chair of Washington, Jefferson, and Wm. McKinley." His attacks upon the President always evoked popular response, so Vardaman continued: "Let Teddy take 'coons' to the White House. I should not care if the walls of the ancient edifice should become so saturated with the effluvia from the rancid carcasses that a Chinch bug would have to crawl upon the dome to avoid asphyxiation." So extreme were Vardaman's attacks on Roosevelt that one observer reported that "for low-down vulgarity and indecency" they exceeded anything that ever fell from the lips of a public man.[63]

Vardaman was not alone in his extreme appeals to racism. In 1903 Governor Longino ran for the Senate against the incumbent Hernando DeSoto Money, Vardaman's cousin. Like Critz and Noel, Longino criticized the plan to divide the school fund between Negroes and whites on a tax basis as being unconstitutional and unfair. He also appealed for law and order and denounced the proponents of racial lawlessness. Money, however, ran on a platform identical to Vardaman's, arguing that education only spoiled Negro field hands. The senator also rivaled Vardaman in denouncing Roosevelt for having closed the Indianola post office. He accused Longino of sympathizing with the Republican administration because his brother-in-law Edgar Wilson was Roosevelt's patronage referee. Both Money and Vardaman presented themselves as working against the combined forces of the Longino administration in Mississippi and the Roosevelt admin-

[62] Greenwood *Commonwealth,* August 22, 1903.
[63] *Ibid.,* January 10, February 7, March 21, 1903; James W. Garner, "A Mississippian on Vardaman," *The Outlook,* LXXV (September 12, 1903), 139.

istration in Washington.[64] That Money, who had long served in Congress, based his campaign for the first time upon such an out and out racist approach well illustrated how the Indianola affair had ignited Negrophobia among the state's electorate.

Racism was only one emotional issue to which Vardaman appealed. The political machinery of the convention system supplied another issue. Agrarian leaders, Republicans, and unsuccessful Democratic candidates had long bemoaned the existence of a "Jackson ring" which supposedly controlled state politics. Although no one clearly defined the "Jackson ring," many believed in its existence. In general, the term denoted a group of professional politicians who supposedly had controlled the state government for the past quarter century. Vardaman charged that Governor Longino and Edgar Wilson were the current leaders of the "Jackson ring" and that they were working in cooperation with Roosevelt's "nigger loving gang in Washington" and the Union League in New York to insure his defeat. The Vardaman press never directly accused his rivals of being tools of the "ring," but some papers reported that Noel and Critz had resorted to sordid tricks in the hope of offsetting Vardaman's majority.[65]

Vardaman appealed to the white farmers to help him. Of the three gubernatorial candidates, he asserted, only he had risen from a humble background of poverty and hardship; only he represented the people in their fight against the politicians; only he stood against entrenched wealth. His election would prove that it was possible to elect a poor man governor.[66] He constantly stressed the importance of the sturdy farmer reasserting his control in Mississippi politics: "Take the history of our own republic from its birth, around whose cradle stood that coterie of undying patriots—Jefferson, Washington, Patrick Henry and others to this good day when the reigns [sic] of government

[64] Greenwood *Commonwealth*, April 18, 1903; Bay St. Louis *Gulf Coast Progress*, May 23, 1903; Brookhaven *Leader*, May 6, 1903; McComb City *Enterprise*, June 11, 25, July 30, 1903; Gatewood, "Theodore Roosevelt and the Indianola Affair," 66.

[65] Greenwood *Commonwealth*, December 19, 1902, April 11, June 27, August 1, 1903; Aberdeen *Weekly*, May 29, 1903; Yazoo *Sentinel*, July 23, 30, 1903; Ferguson, "Agrarianism in Mississippi," 338, 418. It was sometimes reported that in counties where Vardaman seemed to have the greatest support, Noel and Critz agreed to pool their votes in order to offset his lead.

[66] Greenwood *Commonwealth*, March 21, May 21, June 27, July 8, 18, August 6, 22, 1903.

have gone into the hands of that band of political bandits, vampires and vulgarians of the Roosevelt-Hanna brand, and you will find that *most all of our really great men*, in all of the walks of life, have been country raised boys. . . . I believe the 'ark of the covenant of American ideals' rests in the *agricultural sections of the South.*" [67]

During the campaign the *Commonwealth*, managed by Walter N. Hunt while the editor stumped the state, served as the leading Vardaman propaganda organ. It devoted special attention to answering attacks upon Vardaman. Thus when the editor of the *Mississippi Baptist* condemned Vardaman's appeal to Negrophobia, saying that any man who attacked an "inferior race" as Vardaman did should be "sent back to nature's mint and recoined as a counterfit [*sic*] on humanity," the *Commonwealth* published letters from ministers testifying that Vardaman was a practicing Christian.[68] On one occasion Vardaman himself answered the attacks of the *Baptist*: "Now I want to say that I yield to no one in my love, devotion and reverence for the church of the living God. For the faithful minister of the Gospel I have not words with which to express my admiration and respect. . . . But for one of these little nubbin-stud, self-sanctified, theological runts I have not the language to express my commiseration and contempt. He is a discredit to the Baptist church and ought to be pulling the bell-cord over a mule instead of misdirecting the official organ of that splendid sect of devoted Christian men and women." [69]

Opposition to Vardaman varied from enlightened criticism to personal attacks. Some denounced his plan to divide the school fund as unwise because southern whites should never forfeit control of Negro education, and unjust because the Negro contributed to Mississippi's economy and therefore deserved a fair share of educational benefits. The people should realize, the Columbus *Commercial* warned, that Vardaman was a demagogue who had taken advantage of the Indianola post office incident in the hope of exploiting the prejudice of the "ignorant and blood thirsty in the state." Some newspapers reported that if Vardaman won, many Negroes would leave Mississippi, thus creating a labor problem.[70] Others deplored his crude language, his

[67] *Ibid.*, June 20, 1902.
[68] *Ibid.*, October 10, 1902, February 7, April 25, May 9, 1903.
[69] *Ibid.*, April 25, 1903.
[70] Jackson *Daily Clarion-Ledger,* September 6, December 16, 1902, March 12,

attacks on the President, and his opposition to corporate wealth.[71] Typical of the campaign rumors spread against Vardaman were those describing him as being the candidate of the whiskey interests and of being an infidel.[72] In none of the criticisms leveled at him did anyone disagree with his belief in the inferiority of the Negro nor did any white doubt the necessity of rigid segregation.

As the candidates toured the state, speaking three and four times a day during the summer of 1903, excitement mounted. Of the three gubernatorial aspirants, Vardaman proved the master campaigner, always making a striking impression at public gatherings. He wore only white suits, shirts, ties, and boots, accentuated by a wide-brimmed, black Stetson. A man of great vigor and stamina, he conducted a far more gueling canvass than did his opponents. For fourteen months he campaigned through every county in Mississippi, shaking hands with "legions of men," bowing "gracefully to noble women," kissing "car-loads of babies," and all the while delivering over seven hundred formal campaign speeches.[73] As each address lasted two hours, Vardaman's throat frequently became raw and his voice hoarse.

Because he knew his audiences and shared many of their loves and hates, he managed to establish a rapport with them that his opponents failed to match. By speaking in graphic terms, by using stirring phrases, and by vigorously delivering his speeches, he captured the attention of his listeners and then proceeded skillfully to manipulate their emotions. He aroused admiration when describing the virtues of southern women and evoked tears when recalling the heroic efforts of the Confederate soldier. So moving was his eulogy upon women and his tribute to the Confederates, the Okolona *Sun* reported, "that he was able to reach down, take his entire audience by the hand and lift it

---

1903; Yazoo City *Herald*, March 6, July 31, 1903; Yazoo City *Saturday Evening News*, May 2, 1903; Aberdeen *Weekly*, August 1, September 19, 1902; Bay St. Louis *Gulf Coast Progress*, May 16, 1903; Biloxi *Daily Herald*, April 24, 1903; Columbus *Commercial*, July 28, 1903.

[71] Yazoo City *Saturday Evening News*, February 28, June 13, 27, 1903; Biloxi *Daily Herald*, April 7, 24, June 3, 1903; McComb City *Enterprise*, July 30, August 27, 1903.

[72] Greenwood *Commonwealth*, May 30, 1903; Yazoo City *Herald*, May 22, 1903; Brookhaven *Leader*, August 26, 1903; Summit *Sentinel*, May 21, 1903.

[73] Jackson *Daily Clarion-Ledger*, September 15, 1903.

as a whole to the heights few are ever able to ascend. The effects are simply impossible to portray." Always he appealed to local pride: "There is more sin in Boston in one night than in Mississippi in twenty-four months; Massachusetts beats the world in shoes, but Mississippi beats it in raising folks." Having aroused the sympathy and pride of his audience, he would suddenly incite fear and anger by describing the egalitarian policies of President Roosevelt and by warning that Negroes were determined to undermine white supremacy in the South. Sometimes, while taunting his audiences about the Indianola post office incident, "he would stamp furiously up and down the rostrum, his long black hair flying loose, his swelling voice resounding in the farthest reaches of the crowd." [74] Once, at Crystal Springs, while swept up in the excitement of the moment, Vardaman even publicly condoned lynch law: "I want to tell you just how far I am in favor of mob law. If I were the sheriff and a negro fiend fell into my hands I would run him out of the county. If I were governor and were asked for troops to protect him I [would] send them. but [sic] if I were a private citizen I would head the mob to string the brute up, and I haven't much respect for a white man who wouldn't. (Applause)" [75] So violently did Vardaman appeal to anti-Negro sentiment that without doubt he intensified Negrophobia in Mississippi and encouraged racial lawlessness.

Because he was such a dynamic speaker, "immense audiences met him everywhere and he swept them like a cyclone." Frequently on the days of his speeches, local businesses would close, courts would adjourn, and farm families would ride for miles in open wagons to hear him. As an accompaniment to his speeches, his followers often organized parades and demonstrations. In Chickasaw County, former Populist leader Frank Burkitt led hundreds of men on horseback, two abreast and with flying banners, to a Vardaman demonstration. At Water Valley, a blaring band and a booming cannon heralded his arrival. The excitement engendered by Mississippi's first Democratic

[74] Okolona *Sun,* April 7, 1903; Eugene E. White, "Anti-Racial Agitation in Politics: James Kimble Vardaman in the Mississippi Gubernatorial Campaign of 1903," *The Journal of Mississippi History,* VII (1945), 103.
[75] Jackson *Daily Clarion-Ledger,* July 24, 1903.

primary even gave rise to violence, for fistfights were not uncommon at political rallies. When a gun battle erupted in Yazoo City between Vardaman and anti-Vardaman factions, two men were killed.[76]

The first phase of the primary ended on August 6, 1903, when Vardaman received 39,679 votes, Critz 34,813, and Noel 24,233. The contest had been close, for of the nearly 99,000 votes cast, Vardaman had led by less than 5,000. Critz, moreover, had carried thirty-four counties to Vardaman's thirty-three; Noel had won only eight counties. Despite Vardaman's demand that the whites of the eastern counties be entitled to a larger share of the school fund, the vote did not fall into a rigid sectional pattern. The two areas in which Vardaman ran strongest were the hill counties in the extreme northeast and at the opposite end of the state in those counties that bordered the Mississippi River. In the hills the Negro population was relatively small, but the river counties of the southwest resembled the Delta in having a high proportion of blacks to whites. Vardaman also carried a large block of counties in central Mississippi, most of which had more Negro residents than white. Critz enjoyed his greatest strength in the white counties of the east and south and he also carried a number of counties in the northeast, his home section. Although Noel and Vardaman were both from the Delta, they carried between them only four counties in that section, while Critz led in the remaining seven. Since no one had a majority of the votes, a runoff between Vardaman and Critz was set for August 27.

Each side immediately began intensive campaigns in the hopes of winning the final contest. Critz denounced Vardaman's racist views as unattainable and dangerous to the state. Many of Vardaman's supporters in towns throughout the state organized clubs whose members actively campaigned in his behalf. Vardaman continued to hammer away at the issues of white supremacy, Theodore Roosevelt, and corporate wealth. Even more than in the first primary, he appealed to racism: "My election will mean and will be taken by the aspiring, trouble-breeding, ambitious negroes as a condemnation by the white people of Mississippi of Roosevelt's criminal policy of social and po-

[76] *Ibid.*, May 11, 29, 1903; Yazoo City *Herald,* February 27, July 31, 1903; Greenwood *Commonwealth,* July 18, 1903.

litical equality. It will have a most salutary restraining influence upon them. My defeat will, on the other hand, encourage these same negroes to aspire to the unattainable and trouble, discord and demoralization will follow. That is the real issue." [77] His Negro baiting became so venomous that some predicted his election would result in "four years of radicalism and riot; four years of whitecappism and lynching; four years of ignoring the law and of trampling the Constitution underfoot." In Tupelo, the Negro Pastor's Association became so alarmed that it issued a circular warning that a "grave evil confronts the colored people of Mississippi" and urging ministers to "call your people together in their churches and lodges and see if we can help defeat this man." [78]

Strongly affecting the outcome of the second primary was the influence of factional alignments. No longer a candidate, Noel gave his support to Critz, believing him to have a more enlightened view of race relations than Vardaman.[79] Of far more importance, Vardaman's old enemy, Senator Anselm McLaurin, entered the fight and announced he would support Critz. Actually the senator had opposed Vardaman from the beginning of the contest, but not until Noel had been eliminated from the race did McLaurinism become a live issue and thus help revive old factional lines.[80] In response to the senator's announcement, many of McLaurin's opponents rallied to Vardaman's cause. Senator Money, who had defeated Longino in the August 4 primary, and Congressman Wilson Shedric Hill and John Sharp Williams now joined the Vardaman forces. Williams even delivered speeches for Vardaman, and his brother Christopher Harris "Kit" Williams enrolled in the Vardaman statewide campaign committee. From the Delta, LeRoy Percy and Charles Scott, longtime foes of the McLaurin group, came out for Vardaman and fought to offset the influence of such McLaurin lieutenants as Walter Sillers, who was working to see that Critz continued to carry the Delta. From northeastern Mississippi,

[77] Greenwood *Commonwealth,* August 15, 1903; Yazoo City *Herald,* August 14, 1903; Summit *Sentinel,* August 27, 1903.
[78] White, "Anti-Racial Agitation in Politics," 98–99.
[79] Jackson *Daily Clarion-Ledger,* August 12, 1903.
[80] *Ibid.,* March 20, August 15, 1903; Walter Sillers to John C. Burrus, August 24, 1903, in John C. Burrus Papers.

former Congressman John Allen, defeated by McLaurin for the
United States Senate in 1899, campaigned for Vardaman in the second primary.[81]

In the runoff of August 27 Vardaman defeated Critz by 51,829 to
44,931. Critz won five counties that had earlier gone to Noel, while
Vardaman got the remaining three. Critz also led in two counties that
Vardaman had carried on August 6. More significant, Vardaman
took thirteen counties away from Critz. Especially did he gain strength
in the Delta, where he carried all but three counties; undoubtedly the
anti-McLaurin leaders there had boosted his cause.

The results of the second primary fell roughly along east-west lines.
Vardaman ran strong in the hills of the northeast. Except for that
northeast corner, Critz carried most of eastern Mississippi, while
Vardaman won all counties in the southwest, a sizable block in north-
central Mississippi, and most of the Delta. Since Vardaman captured
the counties that had more blacks than whites, his use of the school
fund issue apparently exerted little influence on the contest. Although
he had appealed strongly to the small farmers, he certainly had not
dominated that class as he would in later elections.

In the days following the primary, excitement ran high in Greenwood. Vardaman men in Jackson chartered a special train on which
they journeyed to Yazoo City, where they picked up more Vardaman
followers, and then pushed out into the Delta country. Over six hundred were jammed into the train when it arrived in Greenwood. In a
double column they marched from the depot to the hotel, many shouting and throwing fireworks along the way. Between deafening out-
bursts of applause Vardaman addressed the visitors and repeated
many of his campaign pledges. The crowd remained in Greenwood
until almost midnight, making it the most exciting night the little

[81] Jackson *Daily Clarion-Ledger*, August 10, 22, 24, 1903; Summit *Sentinel*,
August 20, 1903; Columbus *Weekly Dispatch*, June 11, 1903; Greenwood
Commonwealth, June 6, 1903. Percy endorsed Vardaman in glowing terms:
"He [Vardaman] will give us an administration unsmirched by scandal and un-
stained by political jobbery. Influenced by such motives, a lifetime resident of
the delta, thoroughly cognizant of the paramount importance of the levee question, conversant with the peculiar local condition existing here, the people
behind the levees could rest assured that their interest was in safe hands, entrusted to him; and this consideration is potential in influencing me to favor
his candidacy and to support him."

town had ever known. It was also the first time in the state's history that a chartered train had been run to the home of a gubernatorial nominee to celebrate his victory. Several days later another special train arrived from Columbus and again a celebration ensued. Each day Vardaman received hundreds of congratulatory telegrams and letters. In Vicksburg, Hattiesburg, and Gulfport his friends held banquets in his honor and he gladly attended them.

Immediately after the primary, newspapers beseiged Vardaman with requests to describe the policies his administration would pursue, but he ignored them, alleging that many papers had grievously misrepresented him during the campaign. Only once between his victory and inauguration did he let down his guard and talk freely, to a reporter from the New Orleans *Daily Picayune*. Because he had so frequently been misquoted, he felt that only a few people understood his views on the race problem: he intended to see that no Negroes received state offices, that their educational facilities were reduced to nil, and that they remained in their place as menial laborers. He would not tolerate racial lawlessness, however, and as governor he would do everything in his power to offset lynchings. He hoped that he could make strides toward dividing the school fund between the races and thereby give all the white children equal educational opportunities. The primary system, he believed, had placed political power in the hands of the white voters— exactly where it should be. Having been elected to office without obligations, he would assume his new duties with free hands. As governor he would be his own man and would not be manipulated by anyone.[82]

Despite the enthusiasm with which his followers greeted Vardaman's victory, others looked upon it with foreboding. Edgar Wilson believed the "primary system in Mississippi has elevated a lot of cheap men to high office." An editorial in *The Outlook* reported that the state had become "a promoter of ignorance and illiteracy." [83] A distinguished Mississippi historian, James W. Garner, described Vardaman as "a most violent negro-hater" and charged that he "has taken advantage of the passions and prejudices of the ignorant white population to arouse their hostility to the blacks, and by this means to ride

[82] New Orleans *Daily Picayune,* quoted in Summit *Sentinel,* September 3, 1903.
[83] Edgar S. Wilson to Thomas C. Rapier, August 22, 1903, in Edgar S. Wilson Papers; *The Outlook,* LXXV (September 5, 1903), 1–2.

into office." Having just visited his old home in Pike County near an area where whites had recently been terrorizing Negroes, Garner warned that Vardaman's election would encourage racial lawlessness and would probably lead to an increase in lynchings. Vardaman alone, Garner believed, was responsible for reviving the race issue and infusing it into Mississippi politics.[84]

Racism doubtless did contribute to Vardaman's victory. In an overwhelmingly agricultural state that had a population more than half black, Vardaman had directed his appeal to the rural whites, many of whom shared his views on the races. His use of racism had received an added boost as Mississippi's first primary had fallen in the same year that President Roosevelt had closed the Indianola post office. Certainly Vardaman had seized upon that issue and exploited it to the hilt during the campaign. Yet it would be a mistake to accept Garner's view that Vardaman was solely responsible for inciting Negrophobia in Mississippi. Racism had long been strong and widespread among the whites of that state; had it not, Vardaman's appeal would have fallen flat. In fact, throughout the South by the early twentieth century, anti-Negro seniment had become more heated. Writing a few years later, Ray Stannard Baker astutely observed that, despite frequent complaints that the masses of Negroes were ignorant, that was exactly what most whites wanted. The white South, Baker wrote, "loves the ignorant, submissive old Negroes, the 'mammies' and 'uncles'; it wants Negroes who, as one Southerner put it to me 'will do the dirty work and not fuss about it.' It wants Negroes who are really inferior and who feel inferior. The Negro that the South fears and dislikes is the educated, property-owning Negro who is beginning to demand rights, and take his place among men as a citizen." [85] It was the sentiment described by Baker that Vardaman had exploited in his rise to power.

Vardaman's view of the Negro actually differed little from that of most white southerners; his appeal to white supremacy aroused concern chiefly because of the blunt and dramatic way he presented it,

---

[84] *The Outlook,* LXXV (September 12, 1903), 139–40; Summit *Sentinel,* October 15, November 5, 1903.

[85] Ray Stannard Baker, "The Negro in Politics," *The American Magazine,* LXVI (June, 1908), 174.

not because of what he said. Governor Longino, for example, was known as a moderate on the Negro question because of his work to curb lynchings and maintain law and order; yet Longino also censured Roosevelt's handling of the Indianola post office affair, and he believed Negroes should hold a subservient position in society.[86] LeRoy Percy, who later acquired the reputation as an enlightened moderate on the race issue, displayed no hesitancy in endorsing Vardaman for the governorship.

Factors other than his racist rantings caused men to vote for Vardaman. His promise to curb the abuses of corporate wealth, to clean out the "Jackson ring," and to work for an elective judiciary touched issues that had long concerned the state's rural whites and that resembled issues which progressives throughout the nation, like Robert M. La Follette and Albert Cummins, were then advocating. Above all, old factional alignments contributed to his victory. With the infusion of McLaurinism into the contest, anti-McLaurin men with whom Vardaman had been aligned since 1896 began to work for him. This strong Delta faction probably accounted for Critz's losing five Delta counties in the second primary that he had carried in the first. Finally, Vardaman's personal magnetism and ability to sway crowds with his oratory contributed heavily to his success. His very appearance suggested strength and self-confidence. He looked and acted like a leader. In stump speeches he used such colorful language and spoke with such earnestness that he readily incited zeal among his listeners, who responded by rallying to his standard and carrying him to victory.

[86] Greenwood *Enterprise,* April 24, 1903.

CHAPTER V

THE ADMINISTRATION

On January 19, 1904, the sun rose bright and clear in Jackson, but dark clouds soon covered the sky, creating an aspect of gloom. Fortunately, rain did not begin falling until the late afternoon. Accompanied by his wife and his old friend Dr. Ward, the newly elected governor emerged from the state mansion at noon, wearing a dark broadcloth suit with a carnation pinned to the lapel. His long hair, as always, brushed to a brilliant luster, showed the first hint of gray. Vardaman had given his usual careful attention to what he wore and to how he looked.

In front of the mansion the official party entered an open carriage, which proceeded briskly to the recently constructed Capitol. Crowds lining the street applauded as the new executive passed, but for the first time in many years neither a band nor a military parade escorted mum of ceremony and pomp. It did not take the party long to reach the governor on inauguration day, for Vardaman had ordered a mini- the building, a sprawling structure set on a bald lot. Visitors and well-wishers, many of whom had come on specially chartered trains, filled the corridors to shake the governor's hand and congratulate him. Vardaman relished these ministrations and made little attempt to quicken the slow progress he was making through the crowd. He solemnly recited the oath of office before the supreme court judges and then proceeded to the house of representatives.

It was almost one o'clock before he arrived at the house chambers to address the legislators. When he entered the room and began to walk to the speaker's desk, the lawmakers stood and applauded. Former Governor Longino did not, as had been customary, introduce his successor. Vardaman's attacks upon him during the past two years had engendered too much bitterness to permit such courtesies.

116

Instead Emmet N. Thomas, the newly elected speaker of the house made the introduction. Vardaman's inauguration marked a momentous event in Mississippi's history, Thomas asserted, because he was the first governor chosen directly by the white voters without the aid of "convention, combinations or clique." [1]

Vardaman opened his address by asking that the bitterness born during the late primary be allowed to die. Admitting that freedom of speech had been abused in that contest, he nevertheless thought that the experience of directly choosing public officials had enhanced the Mississippi electorate's capacity for self-government. [2] In outlining the policies for which his administration would strive, Vardaman asserted that he would work neither for the benefits of a favored few nor for the interests of corporate wealth. He would try to ease the lot of the farmer, the "common laborer," and the "working man." In an age when materialism dominated American society, too many had forgotten "that the only real wealth is the labor of man." To keep the cost of the state's new Capitol from falling entirely upon the present generation, the legislature should, instead of increasing taxes, issue state bonds to be repaid over several decades. He wanted industry to come to the state, but he would not condone granting tax exemptions. Railroads, lumber companies, and other corporate interests should be made to bear their fair share of the tax burden. In addition, the legislature should impose stringent controls upon various financial interests that speculated too much at the common man's expense; for example, the state should force insurance companies to lower their rates. [3]

Mississippi could provide better educational opportunities, he urged, by appropriating more money to common schools. Increases for the state's colleges were unnecessary, for their costs could be borne by

[1] Jackson *Daily Clarion-Ledger*, January 19, 1904.

[2] The account of Vardaman's address is taken from *Inaugural Address: James K. Vardaman, Tuesday, January 19, 1904* (Jackson, n.d.); copy in Mississippi Department of Archives and History.

[3] Vardaman's demand for stricter regulation of corporate wealth was similar to that of progressive governors throughout the United States in the first decade of the twentieth century. George E. Mowry, *The Era of Theodore Roosevelt, 1900–1912* (New York, 1958), 8–9, 71–78; Russell B. Nye, *Midwestern Progressive Politics: A Historical Study of Its Origins and Development, 1870–1950* (East Lansing, 1951), 9, 206–32; Woodward, *Origins of the New South,* 374–77, 380–81, 384.

those who wanted to attain higher education. Many white children, especially those in the rural districts, were not receiving even the rudiments of education. "They [country students] need only the sunlight of an opportunity to awaken sleeping genius, one draught from the Pierian spring will create a thirst for knowledge that will remove mountains of obstacles to gratify it." It was a crime to deprive these children of even a bare education because they could not afford books. A uniform textbook law was sorely needed.

The judiciary and penitentiary too needed reform. Because governors frequently had appointed judges solely for political purposes, Vardaman suggested, an elective judiciary would end that problem. More competent men could then be attracted to the judiciary, provided the legislature increased the salaries of state judges. Turning to the penal system, he advocated a change in penitentiary management. Since 1895 the governor, the attorney general, and the railroad commissioners had managed penitentiary affairs. It would be far better to have a full-time board of trustees and a superintendent to direct the penal system. Under stricter supervision graft and inefficiency, so often characteristic of past management, might be eliminated.

Vardaman warned, as he had in his campaign speeches, that the greatest danger facing America was the presence of the Negro. He recommended several steps for meeting the problem. Most immediately the legislature could pass rigid laws to insure a separation of the races in all public places. Railroad companies and streetcar lines, for example, should furnish separate cars for blacks and for whites. To offset the "Republican crime" of having invested the Negro with all the rights of citizenship, Mississippi should lead the nation in a movement to alter the Fourteenth Amendment and to abolish the Fifteenth. Those amendments, Vardaman believed, posed the most serious threats to white supremacy. Pending change in the Fourteenth Amendment, Mississippi could curtail Negro education by investing the legislature with unrestricted control over public education. Vardaman never specifically said how the legislature was to reduce Negro education: apparently he contemplated that it would be accomplished by manipulating the school fund.

He concluded his inaugural address with an appeal to abolish the governor's mansion. Describing it as a relic of aristocracy, he argued that the mansion imposed undue social obligations upon the chief executive and forced him to devote less time to his official duties. As the first popularly elected governor, he asked that he be permitted to provide his own home as did other state officials.

The state press widely applauded the new governor's message. Some papers objected to his appeal to racism, but most considered the inaugural a sound and sensible document. Certainly it did not resemble his vicious, biting campaign speeches. His determination to maintain law and order especially pleased those who had feared he might condone racial lawlessness. After the inauguration, the Biloxi *Herald,* a strong anti-Vardaman paper, mused that the new administration might not be as "radical" as many had feared.[4]

By the time Vardaman took office, the legislature had been in session more than two weeks. Serving for the first time were many young men who had openly supported Vardaman during the primary.[5] Although he had visited Jackson several times in the weeks before his inauguration, Vardaman had taken pains, so he said, not to interfere with the work of the legislature, for he abhorred the idea of being a "political boss." Yet he was no political novice. Realizing that he would need the support of a majority of legislators if he hoped to get his programs enacted, the new governor consciously worked to win the friendship of many representatives and senators. On a cold, rainy night just prior to the inauguration the Vardamans had honored the legislators and their wives with a reception at the governor's mansion. Vardaman always enjoyed giving parties, and on that evening he moved among the guests, greeting the men with warm handshakes and flattering the women with compliments. Dr. J. M. Hoyle, a representative from Lee County, reported that the Vardamans "made it so pleasant for everyone, that it will not soon be forgotten." [6] During his administration Vardaman continued to cultivate legislative support. Whenever legislators were in Jackson they were welcomed at the

[4] Biloxi *Daily Herald,* January 20, 1904; Jackson *Daily Clarion-Ledger,* January 23, 1904; Aberdeen *Weekly,* January 22, 1904; Summit *Sentinel,* January 21, 1904; Meadville *Franklin Advocate,* January 21, 1904.
[5] Laurel *Chronicle,* January 6, 1904.
[6] J. K. Vardaman to W. P. Holland, July 25, 1904, in Vardaman Letter Book; Biloxi *Daily Herald,* January 5, 1904; Greenwood *Commonwealth,* January 2, 1904; Tupelo *Journal,* January 19, 1904.

governor's office and frequently received invitations to dine at the mansion.

It soon became evident that Vardaman's legislative strength centered in the house of representatives, where Emmet Thomas, who supported much of the governor's legislative program, had been elected speaker. Like Vardaman, he was from the Delta and had been aligned with the anti-McLaurin forces.[7] Other representatives who consistently worked for Vardaman's programs were William Calvin Wells, Jr., of Jackson, S. R. Coleman of Greenwood, Polk Talbert of Gloster, and Dr. Anthony Miller of Sharkey County. There were, of course, pockets of opposition within the house. Lorraine C. Dulaney of Issaquena County, for many years a leader of the McLaurin forces in the Delta, frequently worked against the governor. A more formidable remnant of the McLaurin faction remained in the senate, thereby limiting Vardaman's strength in that chamber. United States Senator McLaurin's brothers, William and Henry, represented Warren and Sharkey counties, respectively. Edward Harris Moore of Bolivar County, one of McLaurin's Delta lieutenants, also served in the upper house. Moore, in fact, was elected president pro tempore of the senate.[8] The senator who assumed leadership of the Vardaman forces was John L. Hebron, a wealthy Delta planter from Leland. Having long shared Vardaman's detestation of convict leasing, Hebron later became a leader in working to destroy that barbaric system on both the state and county levels.

During his administration Vardaman did not develop a highly tuned

---

[7] Jackson *Evening News,* January 6, 1904. The *News* commented: "The election of Mr. Thomas cannot but be regarded as a victory for the new administration which is to take charge on the 19th of this month. In the late campaign he was an ardent supporter of both Vardaman and Money, and that these forces contributed to his election yesterday there is little doubt." For Thomas' alignment with the anti-McLaurin forces, see Greenwood *Enterprise,* April 24, 1896, July 29, 1898; Greenville *Democrat,* April 30, 1896; Greenwood *Southern Farmer,* June 1, 1896; Emmet Thomas to J. K. Vardaman, August 10, 1905, in Letters Received by James K. Vardaman, Governors Records, Mississippi Department of Archives and History. Hereinafter cited as Vardaman Papers.

[8] Walter Sillers to A. J. McLaurin, January 6, 1898, E. H. Moore to McLaurin, May 23, 1899, L. C. Dulaney to McLaurin, August 20, December 27, 1897, February 2, March 21, 1898, May 21, 1898, in Letters Received by Anselm J. McLaurin, Governor's Records, Mississippi Department of Archives and History. See also Jackson *Daily Clarion-Ledger,* January 6, 1904.

political organization. His approach to politics was personal. By capitalizing on old divisions between McLaurin and anti-McLaurin forces and by employing his personal magnetism to persuade and cajole legislators, he succeeded in getting large parts of his program enacted into law. Though on occasion he was not above twisting arms and applying pressure to wavering legislators, he rarely had to resort to such tactics.

The brief legislative session of 1904 bore the stamp of Vardaman's influence. With almost unanimous support, the assemblage enacted a Jim Crow law by requiring streetcar companies to furnish separate facilities for Negroes and for whites. If a concern could not afford separate cars, its coaches had to be partitioned into sections. The legislature also passed a vagrancy law that provided stiff penalties for able-bodied persons who did not work and had no means of support. Though the law applied to gamblers, prostitutes, and bootleggers, it was directed chiefly against unemployed Negroes. In those counties where sheriffs strictly enforced the law, Negroes could be made to work cheaply for white farmers and planters.[9] The law probably relegated many blacks to peonage. Despite the statute's harshness, many newspapers enthusiastically supported it, hoping the law would end the " 'tin bucket brigade' of cooks who carry from the white people's tables food to support one or more . . . male vagrants, who when offered employment insolently decline and some of them boast that they do not have to labor." [10]

Vardaman delivered his most serious blow to Negro education by vetoing a bill to appropriate funds for the Holly Springs State Normal School, an institute in northeastern Mississippi that had been founded during Reconstruction to provide instruction for blacks who planned to teach in common schools. Although small and poor, the school had provided instruction for some Negro teachers. The house passed the appropriation by a vote of 70 to 19 and the senate by a vote of 25 to 13, but the governor rejected it, maintaining that literary educa-

---

[9] *Laws of the State of Mississippi Passed at a Regular Session of the Mississippi Legislature Held in the City of Jackson Commencing January 5, 1904, Ending March 22, 1904* (Nashville, 1904), 140–41, 199–203. Hereinafter cited as *Mississippi Laws, 1904*. Laws for 1906 will be similarly denoted.

[10] Aberdeen *Weekly,* January 29, 1904. Similar sentiment expressed in Laurel *Chronicle,* January 30, 1904 and Biloxi *Daily Herald,* March 28, 1904.

tion did not benefit the Negro.[11] He asserted that Negroes learned to read and write by imitation but never grasped the meaning of what they studied. "Literary education—the knowledge of books—does not seem to produce any good substantial results with the negro, but serves rather to sharpen his cunning, breeds hopes that cannot be fulfilled, inspires aspirations that cannot be gratified, creates an inclination to avoid honest labor, promotes indolence and in turn leads to crime." Negro schools, the governor maintained, should train only the pupil's heart and hands. After the house sustained the governor's veto, Speaker Thomas put down all further attempts to reconsider the measure.[12]

It is difficult to evaluate the effect of Vardaman's veto for, at the time, the Holly Springs school was barely managing to survive with an annual appropriation of two thousand dollars. Certainly the veto must have come as a blow to the advocates of Negro education. It also meant that during Vardaman's administration the only Negro college in Mississippi receiving state appropriations was Alcorn Agricultural and Mechanical College, which offered instruction primarily in farming and industrial training.[13]

The governor compensated the community of Holly Springs by having one of the state's two new agricultural experiment stations located there. In 1906 the legislature donated all the property and buildings of the defunct Holly Springs Normal College to the newly founded experimental station.[14]

While encouraging legislation detrimental to Negro education, Var-

[11] *House Journal, 1904*, 472–73; *Senate Journal, 1904*, 489.
[12] *House Journal, 1904*, 840–43, 867.
[13] The Holly Springs Normal School had been incorporated by the state in 1890 and by 1904 it had graduated about two thousand students. After its closing the only normal training provided for Negroes was in private institutions and in summer institutes sponsored by the state. Indeed, during the decade 1900–10 Negro education in Mississippi underwent a "decided retrogression," of which the closing of the Holly Springs Normal School was one cause. Stuart Grayson Noble, *Forty Years of Public Schools in Mississippi: with Special Reference to the Education of the Negro* (New York, 1918), 87–89. Vardaman's veto of the Holly Springs Normal bill evoked mixed reaction from the state press. Jackson *Daily Clarion-Ledger*, March 15, 1904; Jackson *Evening News*, March 15, 17, 1904; Biloxi *Daily Herald*, March 16, 1904; Natchez *Daily Democrat*, March 16, 1904.
[14] *Mississippi Laws, 1904*, 114–15; *Mississippi Laws, 1906*, 153. Jackson *Evening News*, July 28, 1904, January 6, 1906.

daman gave leadership to improving educational facilities for whites. Despite the active opposition of a publishers' lobby and after a lengthy struggle between the two houses, the lawmakers passed a sorely needed uniform textbook law. The senate passed a bill providing that a committee consisting of the governor, attorney general, state superintendent of education, and eight teachers choose the textbooks. The house objected to including the governor and attorney general on the committee. Although some feared the bill might be lost, the senate agreed to accept the house's version.[15] The legislature also followed Vardaman's recommendation and increased the appropriations for common schools. The sum provided, $1,125,000, represented an increase of $600,000 over the previous appropriation.[16]

Several other achievements are of note. Fire had destroyed the Deaf and Dumb Institute two years earlier and the legislature now empowered the governor to appoint a commission that would select a new site and plans for the school; it alloted $75,000 to cover the costs of construction. To provide care and housing for Confederate veterans, the legislature authorized the purchase of Jefferson Davis' former residence, Beauvoir, to serve as a home for veterans and their wives. The primary election law of 1902 was amended so as to eliminate minor problems relating to the time of runoffs, selection of election officials, and primary expenses.[17]

The legislature completed its business by late March and adjourned. Its work represented action upon some, but not all, of the new governor's programs. It had failed to reform the penitentiary system, to make the judiciary elective, or to curb the high rates charged by insurance companies. Vardaman's disappointment was not deep, however, because he realized that it was too early for him to exert his full in-

[15] Jackson *Daily Clarion-Ledger*, February 5, 11, 24, 27, March 15, 17, 1904; *Mississippi Laws, 1904*, 116–24.
[16] *Mississippi Laws, 1904*, 5. During the first decade of the twentieth century there were movements to improve educational facilities throughout the South. School terms were lengthened, teachers' salaries were improved, and new schools were erected. Still the "peculiar southern combination of poverty, excessive numbers of children over adults, and the duplication for two races proved in the end more of a problem than southern resources, philanthropy, and good intentions could solve." Woodward, *Origins of the New South*, 405–406.
[17] *Mississippi Laws, 1904*, 155–61, 178–82; Jackson *Evening News*, February 20, 1904.

fluence with the legislature. Two years later, having established his reputation as a strong governor, he would call a special session to take up unfinished business and then see more of his legislative program enacted into law.

An embarrassing inadequacy of funds in the state treasury caused much trouble during Vardaman's first year in office. Under the Longino administration the state had built a new Capitol costing over a million dollars. As the collection of unpaid railroad taxes was supposed to cover much of the construction costs, Longino had argued that the state would not have to impose new taxes or issue bonds. Vardaman necessarily disagreed, for it had become evident by 1904 that new sources of revenue must be secured to meet the state's basic needs. To avoid sharply increasing taxes, Vardaman urged the sale of state bonds. After much delay the legislature accordingly empowered the governor to sell 3 1/2 percent state bonds to the amount of $500,000 and to borrow $300,000 to cover the expenses of the state during 1905.[18]

By late spring of 1904 the state's financial resources reached low ebb and the need for additional revenue became imperative.[19] After several months of negotiation Vardaman arranged to sell bonds to N. W. Harris and Company of Chicago, but the company wanted time to investigate thoroughly because several of Vardaman's enemies complicated the transaction by warning the bond company that the state would repudiate the sale as soon as the money had been delivered.[20] As the company did not deliver the money until September, the resources in the treasury once sank to seventy cents, and many predicted the legislature would have to be called into special session.[21]

18 House Journal, 1904, 32–37; Jackson Daily Clarion-Ledger, January 21, 1904; Mississippi Laws, 1904, 42–43, 87–88.
19 Jackson Evening News, May 4, July 8, 1904.
20 J. K. Vardaman to Frank Burkitt, July 11, 1904, Vardaman to N. W. Harris and Company, July 13, August 25, 1904, Vardaman to Sidney L. McLaurin, July 14, 1904, in Vardaman Letter Book. Jackson Evening News, July 12, 1904. Mississippi had a reputation for repudiation dating from the 1840's. R. C. McGrane, Foreign Bondholders and American State Debts (New York, 1935), 193–222; B. U. Ratchford, American State Debts (Durham, 1941), 105–109.
21 Jackson Evening News, September 7, 8, 1904; Jackson Daily Clarion-Ledger, September 22, 1904.

The controversy resulting from the bond sale brought the first open break between Vardaman and the press, especially in Jackson. The governor believed some newspapers had unjustly blamed him for the financial troubles.[22] Throughout the remainder of his administration he accused the Jackson newspapers of open hostility toward him and frequently he was right.

From the beginning of his term Vardaman was under unusual pressure to prove himself an able administrator. Political opponents, who might admit that he was an effective speaker and writer, had argued that he totally lacked business sense.[23] The state's economic straits of 1904 certainly provided ammunition for these critics, but Vardaman's actions in meeting other problems won overwhelming praise. Immediately after the legislature passed the uniform textbook law, teachers throughout the state began bombarding Vardaman with applications to be appointed to the textbook commission. Publishers' representatives tried hard to discover who the commissioners would be. The new law did not go into effect until the fall of 1905, giving plenty of time for Vardaman to make sure that none of the commissioners had connection with any publishing company. The eight teachers eventually named were considered excellent choices.[24]

In July, 1905, a yellow fever epidemic broke out in New Orleans and soon spread to Mississippi. Vardaman assumed a leading role in maintaining order and in establishing quarantine regulations. He emphasized the importance of immediately reporting all new cases and promised to keep the public fully informed on the course of the disease. The last legislature had provided an emergency fund of five thousand dollars and Vardaman immediately wrote to each legislator asking for permission to borrow whatever additional money was necessary. With one exception, the lawmakers pledged their support. So thorough was the fight against the disease that the epidemic did not cause

[22] Jackson *Daily Clarion-Ledger*, October 1, 1904; Brookhaven *Lincoln County Times*, October 6, 1904. After the primary of 1903 Vardaman believed that many of the daily papers were deliberately working to undermine him. Vardaman to editor of Memphis *Morning News*, February 24, July 14, 1904, in Vardaman Letter Book.

[23] Jackson *Evening News*, February 2, 1904.

[24] Jackson *Daily Clarion-Ledger*, March 23, April 25, June 2, September 7, 1904, April 17, 1905.

widespread destruction as it frequently had in the past.[25] The governor received special citations for his leadership in the fight.[26]

Throughout his four years in office Vardaman was a conscientious and hardworking executive who gladly assumed the full burdens of his position. He rarely delegated responsibility to subordinates and to state officials, perhaps because he did not trust others, perhaps because he preferred to do the work himself. A strong and energetic man, he enjoyed the challenges presented by the governorship as well as the prestige and honor which his position brought to him. As governor he personally presided as chairman of the boards of trustees for the state's educational and benevolent institutions and rarely missed a meeting of those bodies. So active was he in supporting and supervising the construction of a new school for the deaf and dumb that, by the time he left office, Mississippi had one of the best of such special institutes in the South.[27] He also displayed a keen interest in encouraging the adoption of new methods and machinery that could be used in the treatment of the insane. After an inspection tour of several mental institutions in Illinois, he saw to it that Mississippi asylums installed hydrotherapeutic baths. A source of special pride to him was the establishment of the state's first open air sanatorium for the treatment of tuberculosis, a disease then widespread in the South.[28]

Although Vardaman personally tended to most duties of his governorship and failed to build a political organization, there was a small group of friends whose advice he frequently sought. His two brothers, John and Will, spent much time in Jackson during his administration, and they sometimes worked with legislators in behalf of their brother. Vardaman also received advice from his long-time friend, Dr. Ward of Winona; Ward was especially influential in helping Vardaman prepare his major legislative addresses. Two prominent Jackson men be-

[25] *Ibid.,* July 26, 27, August 3, 4, 12, 14, 1905; Jackson *Evening News,* July 26, 27, 1905; Meadville *Franklin Advocate,* August 31, 1905; "Yellow Fever at New Orleans," *American Monthly Review of Reviews,* XXXII (September, 1905), 273–74; Samuel H. Adams, "Yellow Fever: The Problem Solved," *McClure's Magazine,* XXVII (June, 1906), 179–92.

[26] Jackson *Daily Clarion-Ledger,* November 17, 1905.

[27] *Twenty-First Biennial Report of the Board of Trustees and Superintendent of the Mississippi Institution for the Education of the Deaf and Dumb for the Two Years Ending September 30, 1907* (Nashville, 1907), 9–10.

[28] Vicksburg *Herald,* October 29, 1907; Jackson *Daily Clarion-Ledger,* October 23, 1907.

came close confidants: Swep J. Taylor, a merchant, and H. Vaughn Watkins, a highly successful attorney. State Senator John L. Hebron was one of the few legislators who gained admission to the governor's inner circle of advisors. Throughout the rest of Vardaman's political career his two brothers, along with Ward, Taylor, Watkins, and Hebron, were his most trusted advisors. Except for Taylor, who later served as mayor of Jackson, and Hebron, who served in the legislature, none of Vardaman's close aides ever sought elective office. Content to work behind the scenes, not one of them ever attempted to push Vardaman out of the spotlight.

Throughout his political career Vardaman was a "loner." He never developed political protégées who might succeed him and continue his policies. Perhaps he realized that in the fluid structure of the one-party South there was little chance of forging a lasting political organization. Politics in the rural South was erratic, with political alignments frequently shifting and with old factions continually falling and new ones arising. Then, too, Vardaman's own political style was highly personal, for he had risen to power by relying upon his own dynamic personality and bold, aggressive stump speeches.

Inevitably, given the tone of the campaign that had put him in office, there had been fear that Vardaman would abuse his patronage power by appointing incompetent men to office. In general, however, Vardaman distributed patronage wisely. In spite of the fact that he rewarded many of his friends with offices, his appointees were recognized as men of ability. After he had been in office for less than a month the Jackson *Daily Clarion-Ledger,* an antiadministration paper, declared it no more than "the plain and simple truth to say that in this brief and trying time, when so many of his friends are clamoring for place and positions, that he has sustained himself ably and well, to the admiration of friends and to the satisfaction of opponents." [29] He demonstrated his moderation when confronted with a number of judicial appointments that Longino had made during his last months in office. In spite of much fear to the contrary, Vardaman decided after a thorough investigation not to disturb these "vacation appointments"; he would have the opportunity to appoint new judges during

29 Jackson *Daily Clarion-Ledger,* February 12, 1904.

the course of his administration.[30] On occasion Vardaman left political opponents in office, especially if they had proved to be competent and popular officials; thus he did not remove Circuit Judge W. F. Stevens, the son-in-law of Senator Anselm McLaurin.[31]

Having twice been the victim of conventions and having achieved power through the popular primary, Vardaman boasted that he did not want to be a "political boss." His sole objective, he avowed, in making appointments was to choose men of ability, regardless of their political views, and to a surprising degree he remained faithful to that promise.[32] During the course of his administration, however, he came to realize that the manipulation of patronage could greatly help to achieve some of his goals, as well as serve to reward those who had supported him. One of the most striking incidents occurred in 1906, when Vardaman refused to reappoint Judge Jeff Truly to the state supreme court and in his place named Chancery Judge Robert B. Mayes.[33] As will be discussed in the next chapter, Mayes upheld the governor in his fight to abolish convict leasing, while Truly sided with the opposition.

Of more serious political consequence was a key appointment to the Missisippi Board of Levee Commissioners. On first assuming office Vardaman swept the levee boards clean of practically all of the McLaurin and Longino appointees whose terms then expired. Although the levee commissioners he named failed to satisfy all of his Delta supporters, they were accepted without serious opposition.[34] Two years later Vardaman raised the ire of LeRoy Percy and other leaders in Washington County when he refused to reappoint Dr. J. T.

[30] J. K. Vardaman to William Williams, February 20, 24, 1904, Vardaman to J. A. P. Campbell, February 22, 1904, in Vardaman Letter Book; Jackson *Evening News,* January 6, 8, 22, March 22, 1904; Biloxi *Daily Herald,* January 9, March 2, 1904; Tupelo *Journal,* March 11, 1904. Attorney General William Williams ruled that Longino's appointments were legal and binding, but Judge J. A. P. Campbell held that they were unconstitutional and could be overturned. Jackson *Daily Clarion-Ledger,* March 3, 11, 1904.

[31] J. K. Vardaman to I. T. Blount, January 30, 1906, in Vardaman Letter Book; Brookhaven *Lincoln County Times,* March 10, 1904.

[32] J. K. Vardaman to W. P. Holland, July 25, 1904, in Vardaman Letter Book.

[33] J. K. Vardaman to Will C. Martin, February 23, 1906, in Vardaman Letter Book; Laurel *Chronicle,* March 3, 1906; Grenada *Sentinel,* March 3, 1906.

[34] J. K. Vardaman to H. Fitzgerald, February 1, 1904, Vardaman to G. R. Page, February 2, 1904, in Vardaman Letter Book; Jackson *Daily-Clarion-Ledger,* February 10, 24, 1904.

Atterbury to the levee board. Percy publicly censured Vardaman for ignoring the popular demand for Atterbury's reappointment, and he compared the governor's levee board policy to that of McLaurin. Percy even quoted from Vardaman's old editorials in the *Commonwealth* in which the governor had denounced McLaurin for ignoring the wishes of Delta residents in naming levee commissioners. Percy's criticism did not deter Vardaman from appointing state Senator John L. Hebron in place of Atterbury.[35] The decision fully justified itself, for Hebron became one of Vardaman's most loyal supporters, and he later played a major role in the most important achievement of Vardaman's administration—the reform of the state penitentiary system.

A realm in which Vardaman reversed past policies was that of appointing county electoral commissioners. The commissioners had usually consisted of two Democrats and one Republican, and in the Delta counties the Republican frequently had been a Negro. Vardaman announced that he would not appoint Negroes. In counties where the Populists had been strong he appointed Democrats and a Populist; in other counties he appointed a Republican, if a white one could be found. Republicans opposed this innovation, but acquiesced in it.[36]

In one instance Vardaman perhaps used his appointive powers for vindictive purposes. Governor Longino had appointed J. L. Gillespie as a trustee of Alcorn Agricultural and Mechanical College. It will be recalled that in the early 1890's Gillespie and Vardaman had been partners in the Greenwood *Enterprise*, but since 1896 they had been political enemies; Gillespie had joined the McLaurin forces, whereas Vardaman had become a determined opponent of that faction. On taking office, therefore, Vardaman did not reappoint Gillespie to the Alcorn board. Without informing Gillespie, the new board—of which Vardaman was president—accused him of having used his official position to obtain the contract for printing the college catalogue and stationery at excessively high prices. The sum of money involved was not large and Gillespie eventually cleared himself. One cannot but feel that if Vardaman and Gillespie had still been friends, the governor would have given him a chance to clear himself before the issue had

[35] Jackson *Daily Clarion-Ledger,* December 6, 1905; Jackson *Evening News,* December 4, 1905.
[36] Jackson *Evening News,* August 1, 31, October 10, 1904.

been made public. As it was, the state press reported the charge before Gillespie even knew about it.[37]

The preliminaries of the presidential election of 1904 brought on the first open political friction of Vardaman's governorship. He had originally favored not instructing the Mississippi delegates to the national convention, but because he suspected his old enemy Senator McLaurin of supporting William Randolph Hearst, he insisted that the delegation be pledged to Judge Alton B. Parker of New York. The state convention, led by Vardaman, Senator Money, and Representative John Sharp Williams, instructed the Mississippi delegation to support Parker.[38] When the Democratic national convention met at St. Louis in July, 1904, the struggle between the McLaurin and anti-McLaurin forces reached a new intensity. In view of their long-standing hostility, Vardaman and McLaurin refused to associate with one another. Taking advantage of the situation, Vardaman had the Mississippi delegation hold its meeting in his hotel room—a place he knew McLaurin would not go. This action enraged the McLaurin men in the Mississippi delegation, who appealed to Senator Money to intervene. Apparently Representative Williams tried to mediate, but his efforts were to no avail.[39] This new exchange between Vardaman and McLaurin would have a strong bearing upon future policies of the governor's administration.

Vardaman's opposition to the McLaurins probably contributed to friction that developed between him and state Attorney General William Williams. A young man of thirty-three, Williams was an ally of the McLaurins and was considered a rising power in Mississippi politics. In the summer of 1904 he and Vardaman became embroiled in a controversy over the construction of the new Deaf and Dumb Institute. After Williams disapproved an architectural plan favored by Vardaman, the governor issued an intemperate statement to the press advising the attorney general to "always 'give the state an honest job.' " Vardaman later apologized for this rash outburst, but relations between him and Williams remained strained and would lead to future collisions.[40]

[37] Jackson *Daily Clarion-Ledger,* July 28, August 1, 1904.
[38] *Ibid.,* May 18, 25, 27, June 15, 16, 1904; Biloxi *Daily Herald,* April 6, 1904.
[39] Jackson *Daily Clarion-Ledger,* July 16, 1904.
[40] *Ibid.,* July 1, 2, 1904.

Another who clashed vehemently with the governor on more than one occasion was the Methodist Bishop of Mississippi, Charles B. Galloway, who deplored Vardaman's "radical" racist beliefs. Fearing that the Negro would suffer even greater abuses under Vardaman than he had in the past, Galloway often publicly denounced the governor. Appalled by lynchings and other outrages long inflicted on black people, Galloway advocated "uplifting" southern Negroes by providing better educational opportunities and by impartial law enforcement. Although he did not recommend granting Negroes social and political equality, he objected strongly to Vardaman's crude racist views. Exactly how far the Bishop wanted Negroes to advance was not clear. Vardaman scorned Galloway's views, believing such schemes would only fire ambitions in Negroes that whites would never allow them to fulfill. The governor's advisor Dr. Ward answered the Bishop in a newspaper article, arguing as Vardaman did that Negroes had not improved during the past forty years, that education had failed to help the blacks, and that lynch law would remain a necessity as long as Negroes raped white women.[41] The contrast between Vardaman's and Galloway's views revealed a division among Mississippi whites on how to treat Negroes. Both believed blacks should be relegated to inferior social positions. Galloway wanted them treated as humanely as possible; Vardaman believed such a soft approach would only spoil able field hands. The Bishop's outlook offered some hope for Negroes, slight though it might be; for Vardaman the issue of Negro inferiority was closed.

To maintain popular support Vardaman continued to appeal to racism and to denounce those whom he considered enemies of white supremacy. During his first year in office the postmaster general of the United States, bearing in mind how virulently Vardaman had criticized President Roosevelt, refused to name a post office in honor of the new governor. This seeming triviality enhanced Vardaman's popularity in Mississippi. Even the Jackson *Evening News*, one of his leading critics, asserted that because of the postmaster's action, "it is time for all of us to be Vardaman men." [42] The following year

---

[41] *Ibid.,* April 26, 1904; Jackson *Evening News,* May 3, 1904.
[42] Jackson *Evening News,* July 28, 1904; T. C. Carter to Edgar S. Wilson, November 30, 1904, in Edgar S. Wilson Papers.

Vardaman refused to permit any official representatives of Mississippi to participate in Roosevelt's inauguration.

After he assumed office, Vardaman's racist views altered slightly; he ceased advocating his old plan of dividing the school fund in accord with the amounts paid by blacks and whites. Even though he had used the issue repeatedly in his rise to power, he had always known that it could not be achieved. Once in office, therefore, he dropped it. Aside from that change he remained an outspoken Negrophobe who rarely missed an opportunity to call attention to the race problem, especially the Negro crimes of violence. Vardaman noted that blacks committed more crimes during the summer months, and offered this demagogic explanation: "The heat of the summer sun seems to intensify the brutish negro's lust, as it causes the blood to flow in the body, and melts the virus in the fangs of the coiled serpent on the side of the rock in early spring. It seems to loosen within his soul the very fires of hell itself." [43] As an immediate solution to this problem he urged that law officers enforce the vagrancy law strictly, because most crimes were committed by "trifling, loafing, negroes"— not by those who worked honestly for their livings.[44] As a permanent solution he advocated his old plan of modifying the Fourteenth Amendment and abolishing the Fifteenth. It must be done quickly to meet an impending racial crisis. "The matter of white supremacy or black domination in the South is at fever heat and the sooner the North and West realize this, the better it will be for the nation." [45]

Vardaman's continual harping upon the Negro question contrasted sharply with his actual behavior as governor. Once in office he worked diligently to suppress racial lawlessness. Here he revealed the limits of his demagogery. Opponents had long accused him of inciting racism to win votes, and certainly that charge was true. As governor he continued to attack Negroes as a means of bolstering his popularity. Indeed some of his public utterances might have misled people into believing that he

---

[43] Jackson *Daily Clarion-Ledger,* January 28, 1905.

[44] *Ibid.,* March 9, 1905; Vicksburg *Herald,* September 26, 1906.

[45] Vicksburg *Herald,* September 25, October 19, 1906, November 2, 1907; Harris Dickson, "The Vardaman Idea: How The Governor of Mississippi Would Solve the Race Question," *Saturday Evening Post,* CLXXIX (April 27, 1907), 3–5.

would permit whites to beat and lynch Negroes. However radical the utterances by which Vardaman appealed to racism for political purposes, he realized the danger of permitting lawlessness to go unchecked and worked to maintain order. Shortly after his inauguration a mob at Doddsville captured a Negro man and woman accused of murdering a young white planter, James Eastland. The mob mutilated the man by cutting off his ears and fingers and then burned both Negroes to death.[46] Vardaman immediately contacted the local officials and urged them to restore order and to arrest those responsible for burning the alleged murderers. If needed, he offered to send the national guard.[47]

Except for rape, Vardaman believed, determined local officials could stop lynch mobs, and he continually urged sheriffs and policemen to give Negroes the full protection of the law. "I believe in making a negro keep his place, but when he does that, he is entitled to the protection of the law. The law is ample, if properly enforced, to protect every citizen." [48] To demonstrate his determination to maintain order, Vardaman personally intervened two weeks after the Doddsville murders to stop a lynching in Batesville. In protecting from mob action a Negro accused of killing a white man, Vardaman took a train to Greenwood, there enlisted the aid of the local national guard unit, and then proceeded to Batesville. Arriving after an all-night trip, he had the prisoner taken into custody and returned with him to Jackson.[49]

Perhaps the most inflammable situation with which Vardaman dealt occurred in Jackson in 1905 when a Negro raped a young white woman. Local men quickly organized search parties and as the crowd became embittered, some feared that innocent Negroes would suffer. Vardaman then made a public appeal, urging calmness and moderation. He, too, wanted the rapist punished, but he warned that "never in your history was it more necessary for your acts and utterances

[46] Greenwood *Commonwealth,* February 13, 1904.
[47] J. K. Vardaman to A. E. Anderson, Sam D. Neal, G. J. Weisinger, February 15, 1904, in Vardaman Letter Book.
[48] J. K. Vardaman to F. M. Lee, July 29, 1904, in Vardaman Letter Book.
[49] Jackson *Daily Clarion-Ledger,* February 29, 1904; Biloxi *Daily Herald,* February 29, 1904; Aberdeen *Weekly,* March 4, 1904; J. K. Vardaman to J. H. Harrahan, March 12, 1904, Vardaman to Sam C. Cook, March 31, 1904, in Vardaman Letter Book.

to be characterized by prudence and conservatism than in this emergency." [50] The Jackson citizenry responded to the governor's appeal and did not try to lynch Stewart Johnson, a Negro arrested for the crime. In fact, when Johnson was tried, the jury declared him innocent. The Jackson *Daily Clarion-Ledger* reported it may have been the first time in Mississippi that a Negro had been acquitted for such a crime.[51]

Altogether Vardaman intervened on at least nine occasions to prevent lynchings.[52] Such vigorous action against lawless mobs by one of America's most outspoken Negro baiters proved baffling to many. In earlier editorials and campaign speeches Vardaman had condoned lynching. As governor, however, he found himself in a position of public responsibility. It was his duty to suppress lawlessness, and to fulfill that obligation he worked to suppress lynchings in spite of his private feelings on the subject. Given the racist overtones of his campaigns, moreover, had he failed to check violence, lawlessness might have engulfed Mississippi during his administration. Vardaman was evidently well aware of this fact, as is demonstrated by his handling of the unrest that plagued certain parts of south Mississippi at the time he took office.

On assuming office Vardaman discovered that a serious race problem existed in parts of South Mississippi, where secret societies, known as Whitecaps, had been terrorizing Negroes for some time in an attempt to drive them off land they owned or rented. Ten years earlier Whitecaps had first appeared in the southwestern counties of Amite, Franklin, and Lincoln. There poverty and frustration resulting from agricultural depression had partly explained why some farmers resorted to violence. After local merchants foreclosed farm mortgages, they sometimes employed Negroes to work their newly acquired lands.

[50] Jackson *Daily Clarion-Ledger,* February 24, 25, 1905; Summit *Sentinel,* March 2, 1905. Vardaman considered hiring a Pinkerton Detective to catch the rapist. J. K. Vardaman to Pinkerton's National Detective Agency, February 24, 1905, in Vardaman Letter Book.
[51] Jackson *Daily Clarion-Ledger,* April 22, 1905.
[52] *Ibid.,* February 24, April 13, 19, 1905, February 1, 17, 1906; Vicksburg *Herald,* December 25, 27, 28, 1906; Jackson *Evening News,* April 5, June 29, 1904, January 23, August 17, 1905; Meadville *Franklin Advocate,* February 2, 1905; Summit *Sentinel,* May 26, 1904, January 26, 1905; J. K. Vardaman to Arthus Fridge, April 5, 1906, in Vardaman Letter Book.

In an effort to strike back at the merchant supply system some white farmers had formed secret clubs that became popularly known as Whitecap societies and had begun to terrorize Negroes living on merchant-owned land; soon the nightriders broadened their attacks to include other Negroes.[53] So serious had the problem become by the spring of 1893 that local officials began vigorously working to curb the lawlessness and soon Whitecapping subsided.[54]

In the same counties Whitecapping again broke forth during the fall of 1902 when labor problems caused unrest among local farmers. Some feared that merchants, through their control of credit and supplies, would soon monopolize all Negro tenants and thereby create a labor shortage among white farmers. Others believed themselves victims of a conspiracy in which white merchants and Negroes worked jointly to gain control of all valuable farm lands.[55] Moreover, newspapers reported that labor agents were at work persuading Negroes to go to plantations in Louisiana and the Yazoo-Mississippi Delta.[56] In October, 1902, a rumor spread through Amite, Franklin, and Lincoln counties that local Negroes were forming a secret organization to resist white control. Reports of uprisings had been common in Mis-

[53] Anti-Semitism also characterized this initial Whitecap movement; at first the night riders announced they would attack only Negroes living on land owned by Jewish merchants. W. T. Raulins to John M. Stone, October 29, 1893; A. E. Perkins to Stone, October 18, 31, 1892; Charles H. Otken to Stone, November 22, 1893, in Stone Papers. See also Jackson *Daily Clarion-Ledger,* January 12, 13, February 14, March 3, 22, June 1, 1893; Natchez *Daily Democrat,* January 14, 17, 20, February 3, 1893; Woodville *Republican,* January 14, 1893; Bay St. Louis *Gulf Coast Progress,* January 19, 1893. The origin of the term "Whitecap" is unknown. Perhaps it stemmed from the Reconstruction era when Klansmen sometimes wore robes and hoods to disguise themselves; the Whitecaps, in fact, modeled themselves partly on earlier terrorist groups such as the Klan, Knights of the White Camellia, and rifle clubs. There is no evidence, however, that Whitecaps wore costumes. For a more detailed account of whitecapping, see William F. Holmes, "Whitecapping: Agrarian Violence in Mississippi, 1902–1906," *Journal of Southern History,* XXXV (May, 1969), 165–85.

[54] Jackson *Daily Clarion-Ledger,* April 14, 21, May 4, 5, 8, 13, 1893; Woodville *Republican,* April 22, May 6, 13, 20, 1893; Natchez *Daily Democrat,* May 6, 7, 10, 16, 1893; Aberdeen *Examiner,* May 12, 19, 1893; Bay St. Louis *Gulf Coast Progress,* May 11, 18, 1893; R. E. A. Stuart to J. M. Stone, August 15, 1893, George S. Dodds to Stone, June 2, 1893, in Stone Papers.

[55] Liberty *Southern Herald,* September 23, 1904.

[56] Brookhaven *Lincoln County Times,* November 13, 27, 1902; January 7, 15, 1903; Brookhaven *Leader,* January 7, 1903; Summit *Sentinel,* November 6, 13, 1902, January 29, 1903; Liberty *Southern Herald,* December 26, 1902; Meadville *Franklin Advocate,* January 15, 1903.

sissippi during the past three decades, but they had rarely amounted to more than rumors. Although there was no proof of a Negro conspiracy in 1902, such a rumor moved many white farmers to action.[57]

First in Amite County and shortly thereafter in Lincoln and Franklin counties, farmers joined organizations designed to control Negro labor. In Amite they took the name Farmers' Protective Association; in Franklin County, the Farmers' Industrial League; and in Lincoln County, the Farmers' Progressive League. Despite differences in name, the groups had essentially the same organization and objectives. They wanted to reduce the influence of merchants in the farming community; they did not want merchants to furnish credit and supplies to Negro tenants without the approval of their white landlords and were convinced that merchants should never place Negro tenants on lands without white supervision. Furthermore, they opposed ownership of land by Negroes, wanting them to work only the lands of white farmers.[58] Although most Negroes were tenants, some had purchased land and some had acquired homesteads. By the secret oath of membership, those who joined the clubs promised to "assist in every way directed by the organization to compel negroes to vacate any and all property owned by merchants, and to assist to put out of the way any and all obnoxious negroes within the jurisdiction of this club." Moreover, they swore that if called to sit on a jury they would never vote to convict a fellow member. The penalty for violating the oath was death.[59]

In all three counties hundreds of men joined, but, as later investigations revealed, most members did not intend to terrorize Negroes. Some joined without realizing fully the objectives of the clubs; others joined out of fear, believing that membership would insure their personal safety. Not long after the organization of these groups, the more

[57] Meadville *Franklin Advocate,* January 1, 1903, March 20, 1905; Summit *Sentinel,* December 4, 1902; Jackson *Evening News,* March 22, 1905. For information on earlier reports of Negro uprisings, see Wharton, *The Negro in Mississippi,* 221–24.

[58] Summit *Sentinel,* November 6, December 4, 1902; Brookhaven *Leader,* December 17, 1902, September 21, 1904, April 18, 1906; Liberty *Southern Herald,* December 5, 1902, February 6, 1903; Hamburg *Gusher,* December 12, 1902, quoted in Meadville *Franklin Advocate,* March 2, 1905.

[59] Brookhaven *Leader,* February 25, 1905; Jackson *Evening News,* July 21, 1904; A. J. H[oyt] to H. W. Minster, July 2, 13, 18, 1904, in Vardaman Papers.

reckless members began to attack Negroes. At night, bands of men posted notices warning blacks to leave the lands they occupied and to go to work for white farmers. In Franklin County on the night of December 11, 1902, Whitecappers posted warnings on more than fifty Negro homes.[60] In all three counties nightriders burned homes, beat Negroes, and fired shots into residences.[61] While the trouble was serious in Lincoln and Franklin, the situation in Amite County had become especially alarming by December. There Whitecappers not only terrorized blacks but also attacked some whites who, for unknown reasons, had incurred their wrath.[62]

In response to the outbreak of lawlessness, concerned citizens appealed for state and federal help. Governor Longino offered a fifty-dollar reward in connection with each Whitecap conviction and urged all law-abiding citizens to oppose the nightriders. At public meetings in all three counties local leaders denounced the terrorism. Perhaps as a result of Longino's action and perhaps because of the concern expressed by many residents, the violence subsided early in 1903.

The determined action of officials in Amite County actually ended the trouble there permanently, but not before almost a thousand Negro field hands had been driven from the county.[63] To offset the danger of a serious labor shortage, local officials had obtained indictments against the men suspected of leading the terrorist bands. Then after several months of negotiations the entire membership of the Farmers' Protective Association, which numbered more than seven hundred men, agreed to disband their organization and to work for law and order in the county. The indicted leaders then submitted themselves to the judgment of the court and in return received suspended sentences.[64]

[60] Summit *Sentinel,* December 25, 1902; Brookhaven *Leader,* December 17, 1902; Meadville *Franklin Advocate,* December 18, 1902; Liberty *Southern Herald,* January 30, 1903.
[61] Brookhaven *Lincoln County Times,* December 25, 1902, January 1, 15, 1903; Summit *Sentinel,* December 25, 1902, January 8, 15, 29, 1903; Liberty *Southern Herald,* December 28, 1902; Meadville *Franklin Advocate,* January 15, 1903.
[62] Summit *Sentinel,* January 23, 1903.
[63] Brookhaven *Lincoln County Times,* April 2, 1903; Brookhaven *Leader,* April 22, 1903; Summit *Sentinel,* February 26, March 19, October 1, 1903.
[64] Liberty *Southern Herald,* September 25, 1903; Meadville *Franklin Advo-*

But the Whitecap problem continued in Franklin and Lincoln counties. During 1903 the farmers' leagues met secretly in these counties, and in the primaries of that summer they pledged their support to various candidates. It is difficult to say how much influence the leagues exerted on the elections. In Lincoln County, some members of the Farmers' Progressive League won minor office.[65] In Franklin County, however, the Farmers' Industrial League proved to be more politically effective. There, A. M. Newman, former president of the league, ran for sheriff and won. Because Newman was known to sympathize with the Whitecaps, the local business community strongly opposed his election. At least six other members of the League in Franklin County won elections, and other county officials who were not League members sympathized with its objectives.[66]

Certainly the gubernatorial primary, in which Vardaman's Negro baiting became a key issue, may have encouraged Whitecapping. The impression that his use of racism created in the minds of some Mississippians can be surmised from a Lincoln County newspaper article in which a farmer reported that some of his neighbors were going to vote for Vardaman because they believed he would pardon any white man convicted of killing a Negro if three whites signed a petition for pardon.[67] Although Vardaman made no such promise, some of his campaign speeches could have created that impression. Moreover, he had criticized Longino for his action against the terrorists: "This outside play, this gubernatorial stage thunder, is worth nothing. It only serves to magnify and give wider publicity to the unfortunate condition which prevails in a small subdivision of the state. If the sheriff of the "whitecap" infested counties would summons [sic] twenty-five brave and determined men and make them deputies, they could bag every "whitecapper" in that county within sixty days. No trouble about it. Yes it would be better if the counties would manage

---

cate, October 1, 1903; Brookhaven Leader, October 7, 1903; Summit Sentinel, October 1, 1903.

[65] Brookhaven Leader, September 21, December 14, 1904; A. J. H[oyt] to H. W. Minster, April 29, July 3, 7, 8, 9, 14, 1904, in Vardaman Papers.

[66] Brookhaven Leader, December 14, 1904, April 18, 1906; Meadville Franklin Advocate, December 15, 1904.

[67] Brookhaven Lincoln County Times, August 20, 1903.

their own affairs and let the governor and Federal judge alone." [68] In both Lincoln and Franklin counties the farmers' leagues supported Vardaman.[69]

Soon after the election, Whitecapping broke forth with renewed violence. While nightriders made raids in Franklin County, the most serious lawlessness developed in Lincoln County. There on the night of November 28, 1903, a band of riders shot and killed Henry List; soon afterward someone murdered Eli Hilson. List and Hilson, both Negro farmers who owned their own land, earlier had received notices warning them to abandon their farms.[70] The murders of List and Hilson were by far the most serious Whitecap crimes, but nightriders also threatened, beat, and shot other blacks.[71] Labor agents further complicated the problem as they attempted to exploit the racial violence in the hopes of persuading Negroes to move to Delta plantations.[72] The problem had become so critical in Lincoln County by early 1904 that many Negroes left, fifty of them passing through Vicksburg on a single day in January on their way to the Delta.[73]

Because local officials were apathetic in coping with the lawlessness and because some feared the situation would worsen, Vardaman decided, soon after taking office, that the trouble was serious enough to demand action. A number of developments must have prompted him. Despite his race-baiting oratory and his criticism of Longino for trying

[68] Greenwood *Commonwealth,* January 2, 1903.

[69] Brookhaven *Leader,* May 2, 1906.

[70] A. J. H[oyt] to H. W. Minster, March 22, April 2, 28, 1904, in Vardaman Papers; Brookhaven *Leader,* November 28, December 23, 1903; Gloster *Record,* December 4, 1903; Brookhaven *Lincoln County Times,* December 24, 1903; Summit *Sentinel,* January 14, 1904; Cutler, *Lynch-Law,* 168.

[71] A. J. H[oyt] to H. W. Minster, March 28, April 4, 7, 11, 26, 1903, in Vardaman Papers; Brookhaven *Leader,* November 25, December 2, 30, 1903; Meadville *Franklin Advocate,* November 26, 1903, March 17, 1904; Brookhaven *Lincoln County Times,* November 26, 1903; Gloster *Record,* November 27, 1903; Summit *Sentinel,* November 26, 1903, March 17, 1904; Liberty *Southern Herald,* March 11, 1904.

[72] Statement of L. W. Jones as Taken by A. J. Hoyt, July 1, 1904; Statement of Sam Jones, Given Voluntarily, April 20, 1904; A. J. H[oyt] to H. W. Minster, April 1, 5, 6, 7, 14, 15, 19, 20, 26, 27, May 2, July 9, 1904, in Vardaman Papers. Since the Civil War, large planters had used agents to procure laborers for them. Wharton, *The Negro in Mississippi,* 106–10.

[73] Vicksburg *Herald,* quoted in Summit *Sentinel,* January 28, 1904; Meadville *Franklin Advocate,* January 21, 1904; Brookhaven *Leader,* February 3, 1904; A. J. H[oyt] to H. W. Minster, April 19, 1904, in Vardaman Papers.

to stamp out lawlessness, he knew that Whitecapping was unfair and unjustified, and he realized it hurt Mississippi economically. It had forced some businessmen to leave the state and it had discouraged others from coming. Bankers had threatened to halt loans, for during the past year they had lost money on cash advances made to Negro farmers who had been forced to leave their lands. Finally, the terrorist activities threatened to create a badly feared labor shortage.[74]

In response to these conditions the state legislature in February, 1904, appropriated $2,500 "to suppress whitecapping," and Vardaman employed Albert J. Hoyt, a Pinkerton detective, to investigate conditions in Lincoln County. Vardaman probably chose Lincoln County because List and Hilson had been murdered there. By March 21, Hoyt had begun gathering evidence. For a month he worked quietly, interviewing victims. Hoyt was assisted by another employee of the Pinkerton Detective Agency, "#20," who posed as a laborer on the farm of a man suspected of having engaged in Whitecapping. It may well be that #20 was a Negro. Although Hoyt did not tell local residents of his work, he kept the governor closely informed of his activities through daily reports.[75]

After Hoyt had collected evidence for a month, Vardaman instructed him to contact the business leaders of Lincoln County and inform them of his investigation. Vardaman wisely went over the heads of county officials in his attempt to gain local support, for Hoyt discovered that some of these officials sympathized with the Whitecaps.[76] The business and professional men were surprised and pleased that the gov-

[74] Brookhaven *Lincoln County Times*, January 1, 7, 1903, December 15, 1904; Jackson *Daily Clarion-Ledger*, quoted in Summit *Sentinel*, December 31, 1903, January 7, 1904; Meadville *Franklin Advocate*, January 1, 1903; Brookhaven *Leader*, February 3, 1904; A. J. H[oyt] to H. W. Minster, April 12, 1904, in Vardaman Papers.

[75] Each day Hoyt sent a report of his activities to H. W. Minster, the resident superintendent of Pinkerton's National Detective Agency in St. Louis, Missouri. Minster then sent copies of Hoyt's reports to Governor Vardaman. The reports that have been preserved in the Vardaman Papers begin on March 20, 1904, and continue through April 30, 1904. The reports resume on July 1, 1904, and continue until the middle of that month. For those reports which best describe Hoyt's investigation see: H[oyt] to Minster, March 24, 27, April 18, July 5, 13, 1904, in Vardaman Papers.

[76] A. J. H[oyt] to H. W. Minster, April 21, 29, July 3, 7, 8, 9, 11, 14, 1904, in Vardaman Papers; Meadville *Franklin Advocate*, June 2, December 15, 1904; Brookhaven *Leader*, December 14, 1904.

ernor was working to end lawlessness, for many had blamed Vardaman's racist campaign of 1903 for the renewed vigor of Whitecapping. After these men met with the governor in Jackson, they pledged their moral and financial support to the investigation and created a "Law and Order Executive Committee," consisting of five business and professional men.[77] Of the five, Thomas Brady, Jr., a young attorney, assumed the leading role in vigorously prosecuting the terrorists.

Once the connection had been made between the businessmen and Vardaman, the investigation gained momentum and there is no evidence that county officials opposed it. Moreover, the Law and Order Executive Committee worked to gain popular support for the campaign. At a public meeting in Brookhaven on May 21, Brady and other leaders described some of the activities of Vardaman, Hoyt, and the committee in gathering evidence. Local newspapers supported the investigation and kept readers informed of new discoveries and arrests. This publicity, plus the knowledge that the investigation had the governor's backing, helped strengthen public support for an end to lawlessness. Some Whitecappers became so alarmed that they threatened to kill Hoyt and Brady.[78]

During the summer of 1904 Hoyt and the executive committee persuaded Jeff Wills and W. P. Adams, both of whom had belonged to farmers' leagues in Lincoln and Franklin counties, to supply evidence. Not only did the informants describe the oaths, rituals, passwords, and organizations of the leagues, they also described their objectives.[79] Wills even went through the tax rolls of Lincoln County and named every man he knew to be a member of the Farmers' Progressive League.[80] Both informants revealed that most members had not actually participated in the lawlessness, and they were able to name the men responsible for much of the nightriding. More important, they named the murderer of Henry List. Hoyt and the committee thus discovered

---

[77] A. J. H[oyt] to H. W. Minster, April 12, 13, 22, 25, 1904, in Vardaman Papers. The committee consisted of Thomas Brady, Jr., W. J. McGrath, D. J. Batchelder, Jr., W. H. Seavy, and B. T. Hobbs.

[78] A. J. H[oyt] to H. W. Minster, April 28, July 2, 1904, in Vardaman Papers.

[79] A. J. H[oyt] to H. W. Minster, July 1, 13, 14, 1904, in Vardaman Papers; Jackson *Evening News,* July 21, 1904.

[80] A. J. H[oyt] to H. W. Minster, July 2, 1904, in Vardaman Papers. The state eventually paid Wills $150 for the evidence he supplied. George R. Edwards, Jr., to T[om] Brady, Jr., February 7, 1905, in Vardaman Letter Book.

that most of the trouble had stemmed from an organized Whitecap band that had come from within the Farmers' Progressive League. They also learned from the informants that the League still held meetings in Lincoln County.[81]

From the evidence supplied by Hoyt's investigation and by the informants, in December, 1904, Whitecapping was crushed in Lincoln County. Five men received long prison sentences for having participated in List's murder. Oscar Franklin, the actual murderer of List and Hilson, was sentenced to life imprisonment.[82] The court did not stop with sentencing those guilty of actual crimes; it also destroyed the Lincoln County Farmers' Progressive League. Prior to imposing sentences on the List and Hilson murderer, Judge M. H. Wilkinson called for all members of the League to surrender on the charge that they had been part of a conspiracy to obstruct justice. In response to this appeal more than three hundred men, including three county officials and a member of the state legislature, admitted they had belonged to the league. Because of the large number of men involved and because most of them had not engaged in actual lawlessness, the court ordered that proceedings against them cease, but warned that the proceedings could be revived if necessary. In return, the Farmers' Progressive League was disbanded once and for all. With this action Whitecapping ended in Lincoln County.

In January, 1905, the campaign shifted to Franklin County. In the previous year the investigation in Lincoln County had disclosed that Whitecap bands in Franklin had intimidated Negroes living on federal homesteads. In November, 1904, on the basis of that evidence, a federal grand jury at Jackson had indicted seventeen men and set their trials for the following spring.[83] Despite this action by the federal court, local

[81] A. J. H[oyt] to H. W. Minster, July 11, 14, 1904, in Vardaman Papers.

[82] Brookhaven *Leader,* December 21, 1904; Brookhaven *Lincoln County Times,* December 22, 1904; Summit *Sentinel,* December 22, 1904. During the summer of 1905 friends of the convicted men appealed to Vardaman for a pardon, but he refused. In September, 1907, he did pardon the five men convicted of murdering Henry List. He did not pardon Oscar Franklin. Jackson *Evening News,* June 23, August 12, 29, 1905; Meadville *Franklin Advocate,* June 29, 1905; Brookhaven *Leader,* July 12, 1905; Summit *Sentinel,* June 29, 1905; Jackson *Daily Clarion-Ledger,* September 13, 1907.

[83] Brookhaven *Leader,* November 19, 1904; Brookhaven *Lincoln County Times,* November 24, 1904; Summit *Sentinel,* November 24, 1904; Jackson *Daily Clarion-Ledger,* November 12, 17, 1904.

officials did not move against Whitecappers, some of whom had terrorized Negroes as early as 1902. Moreover, some feared that the terrorists still held meetings in the county. The failure of Franklin County
officials to act prompted Vardaman in January to employ Hoyt to resume his investigation. Immediately a group of local business leaders
promised to support the investigation, and, as in Lincoln County, they
formed a Law and Order Executive Committee to assist Hoyt.[84] Other
residents, however, opposed Hoyt's work. Sheriff A. M. Newman, for
example, strongly denounced the investigation, charging that the committee—which he had not been asked to join—consisted of his political enemies, whom he branded as "crap shooters, gamblers, and
crooks." [85] One group of citizens urged that the investigation be
stopped as Whitecap lawlessness had already ceased.[86]

Despite persistent opposition, Vardaman pushed the investigation
and Hoyt successfully amassed evidence. He obtained 198 signed con-
fessions from former members of the Farmers' Industrial League.[87]
Hoyt discovered that the terrorism in Franklin County had stemmed
from the league, as it had in Lincoln and Amite.[88] In May, largely on
the basis of evidence supplied by Detective Hoyt, a federal grand jury
in Jackson indicted over three hundred Franklin County residents on
the charge of intimidating federal homesteaders. The first indictment
was against Sheriff Newman. Six other county officials were also indicted.[89] One observer noted that most of the indicted men did not

[84] Jackson *Daily Clarion-Ledger*, December 29, 1904, January 18, March 16,
1905; Brookhaven *Leader*, December 28, 1904, March 15, 1905; Meadville
Franklin Advocate, January 5, 1905; Summit *Sentinel*, January 19, 1905; Jackson *Evening News*, March 14, 17, 22, May 10, 12, 1905.
[85] Summit *Sentinel*, January 19, 1905; Meadville *Franklin Advocate*, January
19, March 22, 1905; Jackson *Daily Clarion-Ledger*, January 23, 1905. J. K.
Vardaman to A. M. Newman, March 25, October 16, 1905, in Vardaman
Letter Book.
[86] Brookhaven *Leader*, March 15, 1905; Meadville *Franklin Advocate*, March
9, 23, April 27, 1905.
[87] Brookhaven *Lincoln County Times*, April 12, 1906.
[88] Jackson *Evening News*, February 27, March 25, 1905; Meadville *Franklin
Advocate*, March 2, April 20, 1905; Summit *Sentinel*, March 2, 1905.
[89] Jackson *Evening News*, May 1, 4, 8, 10, 11, 12, 13, 1905; Jackson *Daily
Clarion-Ledger*, May 12, 1905; Brookhaven *Lincoln County Times*, April 20,
1905; Brookhaven *Leader*, May 10, 1905; Summit *Sentinel*, May 11, 18, 1905;
Meadville *Franklin Advocate*, May 18, 1905. H. G. Butler and M. F. Byrd to
William Moody, April 14, 1906, R. C. Lee to Moody, April 26, 1906, A. J.

wear "collars, and neckties seemed to be strictly tabooed. But there were broad-brimmed wool hats and unshaven faces in abundance, while a few wore long, sunburned locks that clustered about their shoulders in reckless profusion." [90] The court set the trials for the following November but later found it necessary to delay them until May, 1906.

Despite several attempts to quash the indictments, the trial was held as scheduled. Sheriff Newman and the six county officials pleaded not guilty. Their attorneys tried to have the cases dismissed, charging that Hoyt, although employed by the prosecution, had been allowed to talk to members of the grand jury while they were deliberating on the indictments and that John P. Butler, a member of the grand jury, had assisted Hoyt in securing evidence against the indicted. United States Attorney R. C. Lee denied the charges and Judge Henry Niles ruled that the indictments were valid.[91] Newman and the other leaders then changed their pleas to guilty, as did all 309 indicted men. They were sentenced to pay fines of twenty-five dollars and to serve three months in jail. The sentences were promptly suspended.[92]

The Franklin County Whitecappers had received the lightest penalties permitted by law. As in Amite and Lincoln counties, they deserved more severe treatment; however, under the circumstances, there was little chance of their receiving it. To sentence more than three hundred men to long terms in prison would have imposed serious hardships on their families and on the county. Too, many members of the Farmers' Industrial League had not actually been parties to the violence. Finally, many who condemned lawlessness did not consider crimes against Ne-

---

Hoyt to Moody, March 19, 1906, all in Justice Department Records, File Number 10132–03, National Archives.

[90] Jackson *Evening News,* May 12, 1905.

[91] *U.S. v. A. M. Newman, et al.,* No. 6811 (MS in Federal Records Center, East Point, Ga.); Jackson *Evening News,* May 8, 9, 1906.

[92] *U.S. v. Willie Evans, et al.,* No. 6787; *U.S. v. Jeff T. Cotten, et al.,* No. 6808; *U.S. v. W. E. Evans, et al.,* No. 6810; *U.S. v. A. M. Newman, et al.,* No. 6811; *U.S. v. E. C. Adams, et al.,* No. 6812; *U.S. v. Jim Coffee, et al.,* No. 6813; *U.S. v. J. T. Cain, et al.,* No. 6814; *U.S. v. Will Harvard, et al.,* No. 6815; *U.S. v. Emmit McMannus, et al.,* No. 6816; *U.S. v. A. M. Newman, et al.,* No. 6916; *U.S. v. E. C. Adams, et al.,* No. 6917 (MS in Federal Records Center); Jackson *Daily Clarion-Ledger,* May 9, 1906; Brookhaven *Lincoln County Times,* May 10, 1906; Summit *Sentinel,* May 10, 1906.

groes to be as serious as crimes against whites. The principal accomplishment of the investigations was the destruction of the Whitecap societies. By his leadership Vardaman had helped to end widespread racial terrorism. It may be that his office-seeking speeches in 1903 had encouraged atrocities, but by leading the fight against the terrorists he had proved that he could and would maintain law and order.

In January, 1906, Vardaman called the legislature into special session. The ostensible reason was to consider a new state code drawn up by a three-man commission authorized by the legislature and appointed by Vardaman in March, 1904. Actually the code was not all the governor had in mind. He announced that the lawmakers could take up any business they desired, and that he would, if necessary, extend the session into the spring.[93] Evidently Vardaman now felt himself strong enough to try again to secure enactment of his legislative programs.

His address to the special session renewed many recommendations he had made two years earlier: larger appropriations for the common schools as well as for the state insane asylum and the institutes for the deaf and blind, penitentiary reform, and an elective judiciary. Vardaman expanded his original program by calling for additional reforms. He recommended the creation of an office of commissioner of agriculture, an expanded program of highway construction, a law limiting the interest rate on loans to eight percent, the appointment of state bank inspectors, and a child labor law. From his experiences in coping with the outbreak of yellow fever the previous year, he suggested that the governor and the state board of health be given greater authority to declare and enforce quarantines during future epidemics. To overcome the revenue deficit from which the state had long suffered, he advocated a system of equally and uniformly assessing taxable property for, at the time, each county made its own assessments with the result that property was rarely taxed at full value. Repeating many of his old racist views, Vardaman now urged the legislature to provide the death penalty for the crime of rape; so long as ten years' imprisonment remained the maximum penalty, lynch mobs would continue to burn and hang suspected Negro rapists. Finally he wanted more Jim Crow laws by re-

[93] Jackson *Daily Clarion-Ledger,* March 24, 1904, January 2, 1906; Jackson *Evening News,* September 4, November 26, 1905.

quiring railroads operating in the state to provide separate sleeping and dining cars.[94]

From the time the legislature convened in January, Vardaman urged stricter regulation of railroads and other corporate enterprises. His actions were in accord with a strong antimonopoly and antirailroad movement that reached a high point in the South, as it did in other parts of the nation, in 1906 and 1907. Especially in the South did the progressive movement in its early stages take the form of antimonopoly drives against such enterprises as insurance, oil, tobacco, and railroads. In 1904 the legislature had passed an act to permit the Mobile and Ohio Railroad and the Southern Railroad to merge their operations in Mississippi. Vardaman had not signed this bill, and at the opening of the 1906 legislative session he vetoed it, notwithstanding intensive pressure applied by such railroad lobbyists as former Congressman John Allen. Maintaining that the act would encourage railroad consolidation, he asserted that only competition would protect the people's interest by insuring lower rates and better service. "Give the railroads in America the power," he warned, "and they will rule the Legislatures, dominate the courts, and ultimately enslave the people." His veto stood.[95]

Soon after Vardaman's veto of the railroad merger bill, the legislature began to investigate the possible existence of a lumber trust in the state. Many lumber companies were then operating in southern Mississippi, and some people had become alarmed over their increasing size and apparent influence and power. Until 1876 federal lands in Mississippi had been limited to homestead grants of eighty acres. In that year, in response to the growing needs for new lumber, federal lands were opened to unrestricted cash entry, and during the next twelve years thirty-two northern companies acquired 889,359 acres and eleven southern groups bought 134,270 acres. In 1888, "under the spur of

[94] *Biennial Message of Gov[ernor] James K. Vardaman to the Legislature of Mississippi, January 3, 1906* (Jackson, n.d.), *passim.* Copy in Mississippi Department of Archives and History.

[95] J. K. Vardaman to John Allen, April 20, 1904, in Vardaman Letter Book. Although they took opposing positions on the merger question, Vardaman urged Allen not to let it impair their friendship. "I wish you would come to Jackson to see me, and if this matter can't be settled any other way, we will call for unloaded pistols and a bottle of Extra Dry, and I will make you take it all back." And see *House Journal, 1906,* 45–50.

agrarian alarm," southern representatives tried to restore some of the 1866 restrictions, but by that time the rising lumber companies controlled the best stands of longleaf pine.[96] Mississippi had tried to curb corporate landholdings in 1892 when the legislature passed an act limiting real estate holdings of manufacturing and banking corporations to $1,000,000 in value, and of other corporations to $250,000. Despite this legislation, consolidation of large tracts of land continued in the years between 1890 and 1906. Indeed, some lumber interests advocated removing all restrictions on property holdings.

After investigating the timber industry, a legislative committee reported that no lumber trust existed, although the business had expanded greatly during the past twenty years. However, the committee recommended more stringent laws to regulate lumbering. Senator Horace Bloomfield, a member of the committee, issued a minority report supporting the industry and urging that lumber companies be allowed to own as much as $20,000,000 worth of property.[97]

The legislature did not follow Bloomfield's recommendation, but it did provide that corporations could own a maximum of $10,000,000 worth of property. Vardaman immediately vetoed the bill and strongly admonished the legislators for passing it. Believing the law would place even more of the forests of southern Mississippi "within the hands of a few people to be exploited," he urged the legislature to reconsider its action by setting the limit of corporate property holdings at $2,000,-000.

The policy of our laws, for many years, be it said to the credit of her law-makers, has been against the concentration of wealth in the hands of the few, for the elimination of trusts and against the fostering of monopoly. This section, if it becomes a law, places the pine forests of South Mississippi within the hands of a few people to be exploited, used and employed for the benefit of the few against the interests of the many. If the Legislature had undertaken in definite terms to create a lumber trust and place the long leaf pine industry in the hands of a limited number of men to be used as their cupidity and self-interest might dictate, I cannot conceive of a method or a means by which it

[96] Paul W. Gates, "Federal Land Policy in the South, 1866–1888," *Journal of Southern History,* VI (1940), 303–30; Woodward, *Origins of the New South,* 115–20.
[97] *House Journal, 1906,* 520–24; Jackson *Evening News,* February 24, 1906.

could have been more effectually done than is proposed to be done by the enactment of this law. . . . The effect of such legislation will be to close the door of opportunity and hope in the face of the struggling youth of the State and make of them the toilers of the favored rich.[98]

To the disgust of some lumber companies and land speculators, the legislature followed the governor's advice and reduced the limit of corporate holdings from $10,000,000 to $2,000,000.[99]

In pursuance of Vardaman's radical scheme to abolish Negro education, Senator James Alcorn Glover introduced a resolution to amend the state constitution by providing that no child be admitted to public school whose father had not paid the poll tax for the current year. Almost no Negroes paid this tax, and the amendment would have barred most black, as well as many white, children from school. Fortunately, Glover's resolution failed to pass the senate.[100]

Vardaman's other recommendations fared variously in the legislature. Nothing was done about child labor or an elective judiciary. In the matter of annual appropriations for the common schools, an attempted reduction of $125,000 was beaten off and the figure continued at $1,250,000. Another issue of state bonds, recommended by Vardaman as necessary because the state was still burdened with the debt from the new Capitol, was authorized. Finally, in accordance with Vardaman's repeated request in behalf of the agrarian interests, the legislature created the office of commissioner of agriculture. This officer came to assist farmers by collecting and making readily available information on agricultural conditions throughout the state. As an indirect means of aiding agriculture, the commissioner also sought to encourage industries to come to Mississippi.[101]

By the time Vardaman called the special legislative session of 1906, he had proven himself to be a competent and strong governor. In spite of his racism, he had not condoned terrorist lawlessness, and he had worked to maintain orderly, if not just, relations between the two races. Few people could criticize the able administration of his office or his

[98] *House Journal, 1906,* 1306–1308.
[99] *Ibid.,* 1315–16; Biloxi *Daily Herald,* April 24, 1906.
[100] *Senate Journal, 1906,* 137, 1041.
[101] Vicksburg *Herald,* February 9, 1906; *Mississippi Laws, 1906,* 54–55, 83–87. Vardaman appointed H. E. Blakeslee as the first commissioner of agriculture and commerce. Jackson *Daily Clarion-Ledger,* April 29, 1906.

laudable efforts in fighting yellow fever, in standing against legislation to permit railroad mergers and greater corporate landowning, and in working for white schools and agricultural interests. Contrary to widespread anticipatory fears, he did not use his patronage power to repay incompetent supporters but rather was generally praised for his discretion in making appointments. The response of the special legislative session to yet other programs of his administration proved the popularity and strength he enjoyed among the lawmakers. When the legislators enacted the penitentiary reforms he advocated, despite opposition by vested interests, they gave Vardaman the biggest personal victory of his career.

CHAPTER VI

THE PRISONS
AND THE CAMPUS

WHEN VARDAMAN BECAME governor in 1904, he had long been an advocate of prison reform. His editorials of the 1890's had indicated wide reading on penology and close observation of penitentiary conditions in Mississippi. Indeed, as governor, he showed more concern for the penal system than for any other state institution. It was well he did, for conditions were barbaric. At the Rankin prison farm, prisoners ate meals in an open shed with no protection against rains and freezing winter weather; they were not permitted to use knives or forks, only spoons. No prisoner there slept on pillows or sheets. After taking office Vardaman had a dining room built at Rankin, saw that knives and forks were issued, and made sure that all prisoners slept on pillows and sheets.[1]

Having long been an accomplished horseman, he frequently went for long rides before breakfast during his governorship. As the Rankin farm was only a short distance from Jackson, he sometimes rode there on horseback. Several times each year he and state supreme court Justice Albert H. Whitfield rode to the farm to help train the state's kennel of bloodhounds. Early in the morning on those days a trusty would leave the prison farm and light out through heavy woods. Several hours later the hounds were loosed, and then the governor, judge, and several prison guards followed on horseback as the dogs tracked the trusty. After several hours of hard riding, and after the hounds had treed the prisoner, then all—including the trusty—enjoyed a picnic lunch.[2]

Vardaman's interest in the penitentiary system went beyond training dogs and improving the physical surroundings of the inmates. All too

[1] Jackson *Daily Clarion-Ledger,* November 2, 1904, August 7, 1905; Brookhaven *Leader,* December 16, 1905.
[2] Interview with James K. Vardaman, Jr., May 1, 1968.

150

often the prisoners found even harsher conditions at places where they were leased as cheap labor. Until 1890 the state's convicts had been leased to railroad companies and private cotton planters who worked them as they pleased. So unjust and inhumane was the lease system that, during the 1880's, opposition had mounted increasingly against it. Small farmers were especially vocal in their opposition to the convict lease system because they felt the system enriched a few large Delta planters at the state's expense.[3] When Mississippi adopted the new constitution in 1890, the agrarians won a partial victory by including a provision that, after 1894, leasing would be abolished and convicts worked only upon state-owned farms. This provision also placed supervision of the penitentiary system under a board of control consisting of the governor, the attorney general, and the three state railroad commissioners.

Compliance with the constitution eliminated the worst aspects of convict leasing after 1894. The state purchased three farms—the Hunter and Stevens in Rankin County, Oakley in Hinds County, and Belmont in Holmes County—and the board of control assigned most prisoners to them. However, despite the creation of the state penal farms, the new constitution permitted the temporary leasing of some prisoners because at first the state would not have enough land under cultivation to absorb all the convicts.[4] Consequently, the board still leased prisoners to a select group of planters, thereby keeping the old system in vogue.

From the outset the state-owned plantations were successful, at least financially, netting $60,000 in the first year. Governor McLaurin was so pleased that in 1897 he urged the state to buy enough additional lands to absorb the entire prison population and thereby abolish the last remnants of leasing. Three years later the state purchased a Delta plantation of 13,789 acres in Sunflower County. But because the new tract required clearing before it could be cultivated, the board of control continued to lease some prisoners to plantation owners.[5]

[3] Lyda Gordon Shivers, "A History of the Mississippi Penitentiary" (M.A. thesis, University of Mississippi, 1930), 26–45; Ferguson, "Agrarianism in Mississippi," 304–22.

[4] Shivers, "Mississippi Penitentiary," 70–71.

[5] Ibid., 75–79; Paul B. Foreman and Julien R. Tatum, "A Short History of Mississippi's State Penal System," Mississippi Law Journal, X (1938), 262–67.

Not only did vestiges of convict leasing remain, but instances of mismanagement and corruption also plagued the penitentiary system. A legislative investigating committee reported in 1902 that the control board had kept its records carelessly and inefficiently. The committee discovered that the warden had used one hundred and fifty convicts to clear land belonging to himself or to a neighbor, and that the Yazoo Delta Railroad had employed almost two hundred convicts. There was no record that the railroad had paid the state for the convicts' labor. While most prisoners received adequate care, the committee noted, many sick convicts were forced to work. Finally, the committee reported that despite the good intentions of the board, its members had so many other official duties they could not devote adequate time to the penitentiary. Although the warden resigned after the legislative investigation of 1902, penitentiary management remained unchanged.[6]

In his inaugural address of 1904 Vardaman advocated abolishing the board, arguing that the governor, the attorney general, and the railroad commissioners could not properly manage the penitentiary. Under the present system, authority was so dispersed among the five officials that it was impossible to determine who was responsible for mistakes. In place of the board he wanted a new agency, headed by a superintendent, that would be solely responsible for penitentiary affairs; authority would be concentrated in the superintendent. It would then be easier to discover who was to blame if the penitentiary was mismanaged.[7] Despite the governor's appeal, the legislature took no action on prison affairs during the 1904 session.

As governor, Vardaman was automatically a member of the board of control and during the next two years he devoted much time to the penitentiary. To insure that convict leasing would be ended once and for all, he strove to increase the efficiency of each prison farm and make the entire system self-sustaining. He first sought to improve the Oakley farm which served as a prison hospital. Rented in the past to local farmers to work, Oakley had rarely brought profit to the state, and Governors Stone, McLaurin, and Longino had recommended its sale. Vardaman ordered the director of the state's agricultural experiment

[6] Shivers, "Mississippi Penitentiary," 80–82; Foreman and Tatum, "Mississippi's State Penal System," 267–68; *Senate Journal, 1902,* 47–55.
[7] *House Journal, 1904,* 149.

stations to inspect the place. Upon the director's recommendation the board converted Oakley to a stock farm so that it could supply draft animals and meats for the entire penitentiary system.[8] Changes were also made at other prison farms, not only to improve them but also in the hope that they would become models. Thus the board reduced cotton acreage on state farms and encouraged the cultivation of cereal crops. If other farmers would do the same, the governor argued, cotton prices might rise and thereby improve agricultural conditions throughout the South. Mississippi farmers failed to follow the good example set them, however, even though the penitentiary system benefited from the changes.[9]

Vardaman's fellow board members were the attorney general, William Williams, and the three railroad commissioners. Williams and Commissioner James Clayton Kincannon had served on the board during Governor Longino's administration; Stephen D. McNair and Richard L. Bradley were new appointees.[10] As if to signify a break with past management, Vardaman allowed members of the press to attend all board meetings.[11] Another innovation was his call for the immediate concentration of prisoners on state lands and the cancellation of leases with plantation owners. Despite the increased profits derived from state-owned farms, the governor pointed out, the board of control continued to lease land from five planters. Why, he asked, should these men be allowed to profit at the state's expense?

Also, he asked, why shouldn't the board concentrate the management of the entire penitentiary system at the Sunflower plantation so that all officials could have firsthand knowledge of prison conditions and thereby be able to render better service? The monthly meetings of the board and the office of its secretary should be moved to Sunflower, and the warden should make his home there.[12] Defenders of the exist-

[8] *Biennial Report of the Board of Control, the Warden and Other Officers of the Mississippi Penitentiary from October 1, 1903 to October 1, 1905* (Nashville, 1905), v–viii. Hereinafter cited as *Board of Control Report, 1905.* Jackson *Daily Clarion-Ledger,* January 12, February 17, March 22, June 12, 1905; Jackson *Evening News,* October 6, 1904.

[9] *Board of Control Report, 1905,* 3–4; Jackson *Daily Clarion-Ledger,* March 28, 1905, February 9, 22, 1906.

[10] *Board of Control Report, 1905,* iii; Dunbar Rowland (ed.), *The Official and Statistical Register of the State of Mississippi, 1904* (Nashville, 1904), 456–57.

[11] Jackson *Evening News,* May 3, 1904.

[12] *Ibid.,* July 26, 1904; Jackson *Daily Clarion-Ledger,* July 25, August 5, 1904.

ing system replied that the governor's recommendations were imprac-
tical: the railroad commissioners had to spend much time in Jackson
and it would be hard for them to attend meetings at the Sunflower
farm; the secretary of the board had to consult frequently with the state
treasurer; and the board's records could be kept more safely at the capitol.[13] Ironically, the arguments of the board demonstrated the cardinal
weakness of the existing system—namely, that the board could not devote to the penitentiary the full attention that strict and careful supervision demanded.

Vardaman's attempts to reform the prison system produced bitter
dissension within the board. Commissioner Bradley usually voted with
him, while the other members usually opposed him. Behind Vardaman's opponents stood most of the persons who had been connected
with penitentiary affairs, especially the five Delta planters who still enjoyed the fruits of convict leasing. Most formidable among the planters
was Henry McLaurin, a powerful political figure, not only as a state
senator himself but also as the brother of the governor's old enemy
United States Senator Anselm McLaurin. McLaurin had leased his
plantation, Sandy Bayou, to the state for the past seven years. Another
planter who had long benefited from the convict lease system and who
later would exert a decisive influence on Vardaman's political fortunes
was Lorraine C. Dulaney, a leader of the McLaurin forces in the
Delta.[14]

Vardaman's initial attempt to abolish the last vestige of convict leasing came at a meeting of the control board in August, 1904, when he
proposed to have all convicts concentrated on state farms the following
year. The board delayed a decision in order to give the planters an opportunity to protest the governor's recommendation. At the next meeting Commissioner Bradley moved that there be no leases in 1905.
Vardaman supported Bradley, arguing that the change would unques-
tionably benefit the state. To strengthen his argument he cited a recent
report by Warden John J. Henry advocating such a change. Attorney
General Williams immediately challenged Vardaman by pointing out

---

[13] Jackson *Daily Clarion-Ledger*, July 27, 1904; Jackson *Evening News*, August 6, 1904.
[14] *Board of Control Report, 1905*, 90; Jackson *Daily Clarion-Ledger*, August
2, September 6, 1904.

that he had misinterpreted the warden's report, which recommended the leases be reduced in number but not totally abolished. Consequently, a majority of board members voted to drop four of the five leases for 1905 but to retain Senator McLaurin's plantation, Sandy Bayou. The decision incensed the governor. If one lease had to be renewed, he demanded, why should it be with a state senator? Commissioner Bradley suggested that another plantation be leased instead of McLaurin's, but the group again voted to retain Sandy Bayou. As a last resort Vardaman proposed that the board advertise for a plantation in at least three state newspapers and then choose the best bid offered. Again the board voted against him.[15]

Even though the board of control had worked to improve the state farms, and more and more land had been cleared on the Sunflower plantation, Vardaman remained acutely dissatisfied with the existing arrangements. Not only had he long opposed any form of convict leasing, but he numbered the McLaurins among his most outspoken opponents. He continued to demand the termination of McLaurin's lease as well as the abolition of the board of control. Fortunately, during his first two years in office several incidents occurred that strengthened his position by stimulating public interest in prison reform.

Shortly before the board of control met in November, 1904, Vardaman learned that Sergeant E. E. Jackson of Oakley had been working convicts for his own use, and he immediately asked the board to investigate the charge. After a brief inquiry the officials learned that Jackson had used convicts in working two farms near Oakley. One farmer had repaid Jackson with half the profits of his crop. In another instance the sergeant had allowed a farmer to use his name in selling cotton, because the farmer's crop had been heavily mortgaged. When confronted with the evidence against him, Jackson claimed that Warden Henry had permitted him to use prisoners in performing small tasks for farmers in the Oakley neighborhood. Henry admitted he had allowed Jackson to make such use of the prisoners but denied having any knowledge of his recent activities.

After various witnesses had testified, Vardaman and Commissioner Bradley urged that the board dismiss Jackson. Attorney General Wil-

[15] Jackson *Daily Clarion-Ledger*, September 6, 1904; Jackson *Evening News*, September 6, 1904.

liams advised moderation, arguing that Jackson had not received a full hearing and cautioning the board not to damage Jackson's reputation unduly. Prominently present at the hearing was state Senator Henry J. McLaurin who pleaded in behalf of Jackson. Undoubtedly angered by McLaurin's intervention, Vardaman argued that since Jackson had abused his position, he should be fired. The majority of the board, however, decided to postpone action until the following day and at that time all prison officials, including Vardaman, agreed to allow Jackson to resign. The *Daily Clarion-Ledger* reported that although most members believed Jackson guilty of indiscretion, they did not think he had done anything criminal. Vardaman maintained that Jackson was the victim of the existing system of penitentiary administration: the loose methods that had characterized prison management and the past incidents of corruption in penitentiary affairs probably had encouraged him to exploit convict labor. If the state adopted a stricter system of supervision, the governor advised, such incidents might not arise in the future.[16]

Two months after Jackson resigned, a sergeant cruelly beat a convict at the Rankin farm. A white prisoner had escaped and ridden away on Sergeant David Puckett's horse. When authorities captured the convict, Puckett and an aide, Joe Strong, whipped him unmercifully, lacerating his back and seriously damaging one of his kidneys. By the time prison officials discovered this atrocity, Puckett's term of employment had expired and he resigned. Vardaman did not let the matter end. As early as 1894, when he had seen the mutilated hands of Julius Adams, the cruel treatment of convicts had repulsed him. He was determined, therefore, to make an example of Puckett in the hopes of ending cruelty in the penitentiary. He quickly employed William Calvin Wells, Jr., a lawyer and member of the state legislature, to prosecute the case.[17] When the authorities began to investigate conditions

16 Jackson *Evening News,* November 2, 3, 1904; Jackson *Daily Clarion-Ledger,* November 2, 3, 1904.
17 Jackson *Evening News,* January 3, 4, 5, 1905; Jackson *Daily Clarion-Ledger,* January 5, May 19, 1905; Summit *Sentinel,* January 12, 1905; J. K. Vardaman to Sylvester McLaurin, January 3, 1905, Vardaman to J. R. Enochs, May 19, 1905, Vardaman to W. Calvin Wells, May 10, 17, 1906, in Vardaman Letter Book.

at the Rankin farm, they discovered that for many years Puckett had beaten prisoners. Although Wells failed to secure Puckett's conviction, this case provided another example of the need for more efficient and enlightened prison supervision. It was the duty of the board of control, some argued, to know that Puckett had been terrorizing prisoners.[18]

In 1905 Vardaman directed Wirt Adams, state revenue agent, to examine the financial affairs of all educational, eleemosynary, and penal institutions. After months of investigation Adams reported that the records of the Oakley farm had been so badly kept—the board had never employed an auditor to examine them—that the financial condition of the farm could not be determined.[19] Adams discovered that between 1895 and 1899 the state had lost money in the sale of cotton seed, and he attributed much of the loss to state Senator Henry J. McLaurin's Sandy Bayou plantation.[20] Adams' report gave further impetus to the movement for prison reform.

After these revelations of mismanagement and cruelty, the board met in December, 1905, to consider leasing Sandy Bayou plantation for another year. Henry McLaurin aroused Vardaman's ire by announcing that he would fight for the renewal of his lease; for several days the two men exchanged insults through the columns of the Jackson newspapers. McLaurin claimed that the governor had shown poor business sense by selling state cotton for a ridiculously low price. Vardaman defended his cotton sales and asserted that he would "see to it that the special favors enjoyed by State Senator H. J. McLaurin will not be perpetuated if in my power to prevent." A majority of the board nevertheless voted to renew the Sandy Bayou lease, the alleged reason being that the Sunflower plantation still could not employ all state convicts.[21] As in the past, McLaurin agreed to supply land, animals, wagons, implements, and seed, while the state board agreed to furnish

[18] Jackson *Evening News,* June 5, November 10, 29, December 1, 1905, May 12, 31, 1906. The fact that Puckett was sick and near death probably accounted for his case not being tried.

[19] *Report of the Penitentiary Investigating Committee on Oakley Farm and Hospital: As Submitted to the Legislature, Special Session, 1906* (Nashville, 1906), 108–109. Hereinafter cited as *Penitentiary Investigation Report.*

[20] Jackson *Evening News,* July 29, 1905; Vicksburg *Herald,* July 1, 1906.

[21] Jackson *Evening News,* December 2, 1905; Jackson *Daily Clarion-Ledger,* November 26, December 3, 6, 1905; Aberdeen *Weekly,* December 1, 1905.

seventy convicts to work the crop. The state would be paid $25,000, and McLaurin would enjoy all profits over that amount.[22] Both Vardaman and Commissioner McNair voted against the lease, but only the governor refused to sign it.

Vardaman refused to accept a second defeat on the leasing of Mc-Laurin's plantation. Immediately after the renewal of the lease he filed suit for a writ of injunction against the board and McLaurin. The attorneys he employed to argue the case before Chancellor Robert B. Mayes in the Jackson chancery court contended that the contract was unconstitutional because it was not a lease of land, but a lease of convicts. McLaurin's attorneys defended the contract on the grounds that it was a lease of land and that the governor had no authority to institute proceedings in the case.[23] On December 18, 1905, the chancery court upheld Vardaman's position and issued an injunction against the lease with McLaurin.[24]

In rendering his decision Chancellor Mayes ruled that the board had violated the state constitution because the contract was, despite its wording, in reality a lease of convicts. McLaurin was not paying the state $25,000 for the use of land, seed, or equipment, but for convict labor. Even if the contract were a lease of land, Mayes ruled, it still violated the "spirit and letter" of the constitution by giving McLaurin, a private individual, an interest in the convicts' labor. Mississippi had abolished the lease system to protect convicts, the chancellor maintained, but by providing that McLaurin pay the state a fixed sum regardless of how much cotton he produced, the Sandy Bayou contract practically invited him to overwork the prisoners. Mayes also defended the governor's right to institute the suit. Manifestly, the attorney general, who as a member of the board of control had voted for the lease, could not be expected to sue for an injunction. It was therefore

[22] *Sandy Bayou Injunction Case: John J. Henry, Warden of the Penitentiary, et al., v. State of Mississippi,* 87 Miss., I (1906), 83–84.

[23] Jackson *Evening News,* December 7, 1905; Jackson *Daily Clarion-Ledger,* December 7, 9, 1905; Biloxi *Daily Herald,* December 11, 1905; J. K. Vardaman to Frank Johnston, J. A. P. Campbell, January 24, 1906, in Vardaman Letter Book.

[24] Jackson *Daily Clarion-Ledger,* December 7, 9, 20, 1905; Jackson *Evening News,* December 7, 1905; Aberdeen *Weekly,* December 22, 1905.

the duty of the chief executive to prevent the board from violating the law.[25]

Only a month after Chancellor Mayes undertook to enjoin the board of control, the state supreme court in a two-to-one decision reversed the lower court's ruling.[26] In delivering the majority opinion Chief Justice Solomon S. Calhoun held that only the attorney general had authority to institute a suit in behalf of the state. If the attorney general refused to bring suit, it simply meant there was a "hiatus" in the law; but better a "hiatus" than violate the constitution. Justice Jeff Truly's concurring opinion declared that the chancery court had no authority to regulate the action of an executive board. Truly also held that the contract was a lease of land and that the board had the right to make it. Justice Albert H. Whitfield's dissenting opinion upheld the chancery court's power to issue the injunction, supported the entire decision of Chancellor Mayes, and disagreed emphatically with Justice Calhoun's opinion that the governor had no right to bring a suit.[27]

Following the supreme court's decision, Warden Henry had seventy prisoners transferred to Sandy Bayou. But Vardaman did not give up. He now instituted proceedings to secure a writ of mandamus compelling the return of the convicts to the prison farm. Again by a vote of two to one the state supreme court ruled against the governor and refused to allow him to remove the prisoners from the McLaurin plantation.[28]

After Mayes issued the injunction against the board and before the supreme court annulled it, the 1906 legislative session convened. A commission, appointed by Vardaman two years earlier to draw up a new state code, now recommended that the board of control be abolished and replaced by a superintendent of prisons to be elected every four years. As the committee's plan accorded with the governor's recommendations, he urged it upon the legislature, devoting the major part of his legislative address to prison reform. Repeating ideas he had

[25] Sandy Bayou Injunction Case, 2–10.
[26] Jackson Daily Clarion-Ledger, January 2, 3, 9, 23, 1906.
[27] Sandy Bayou Injunction Case, 25–33, 42–78, 79–125.
[28] Sandy Bayou Mandamus Case: State of Mississippi, et rel. J. B. Greaves, District Attorney, v. John J. Henry, Warden of the Penitentiary, 87 Miss., I (1906), 125–69; Biloxi Daily Herald, March 8, 1906.

advanced as a newspaper editor, he emphasized that the penitentiary should be operated for the benefit of the prisoners. The chief object should be reform: "Man is the creature of heredity and environment, and the influence of the latter is more potential [sic] in the formation of character than the former. Therefore, the environment of the convict in the penitentiary should be so ordered and colored that the unfortunate individual would be better for having suffered imprisonment there. Punishment under our system is not inflicted in the spirit of revenge, but rather for correction—in love, rather than hate." All too frequently, he recalled, the penitentiary had served instead to benefit a few wealthy men who had exploited the convicts' labor and had been a source of graft and corruption. Even though the constitution of 1890 supposedly had abolished convict leasing, for over a decade the board of control had skirted the law and rewarded powerful Delta planters with prison labor.[29]

Vardaman's message deeply angered the McLaurins, because in it he charged that Henry McLaurin's " 'fertile land,' hypnotic power, political pull, and long enjoyment of a robust share of the revenues arising from convict labor, seems to have clothed him with the modern brand of Divine right to the perpetuation of that special privilege." He also asserted that not a single warden during the past ten years had worked for the well-being of the convicts and the public interest. Because his dead brother Walter had been a warden within the decade, even United States Senator Anselm McLaurin rushed into the battle by publicly denouncing Vardaman for having attacked his brother.[30]

In his reply Vardaman noted it was during McLaurin's governorship that his brother Walter had been appointed warden and the board of control had first leased the Sandy Bayou plantation.[31] This exchange between the senator and the governor aroused excitement and helped to solidify factional lines in the state legislature. Vardaman men prepared to work for prison reform; McLaurin supporters readied to fight the change. Vardaman's strength centered in the house, the McLaurins' in the senate.[32]

[29] House Journal, 1906, 17–23.
[30] Jackson Daily Clarion-Ledger, January 5, 1906; Laurel Chronicle, January 13, 1906.
[31] Jackson Daily Clarion-Ledger, January 7, 1906.
[32] Jackson Evening News, January 12, 1906; Brookhaven Leader, January 10, 1906; Biloxi Daily Herald, January 10, 15, 17, 1906.

The house of representatives began by authorizing its penitentiary committee to investigate thoroughly all the state's prison farms. The committee could subpoena witnesses, examine any pertinent records, and even make arrests. Under the chairmanship of Anthony Miller, the committee consisted largely of pro-Vardaman legislators who favored abolishing the board of control.[33] To insure secrecy of the proceedings a policeman constantly guarded the committee room and the participants refused to make public statements.[34] Actual examination was confined to the Oakley farm, partly because the affairs of Sergeant Jackson demonstrated the need for prison reform, partly because Oakley took up so much time that the committee could not devote attention to other prison farms. Representative Wells, the young lawyer whom Vardaman had appointed to prosecute David Puckett, became the driving force behind the inquiry. His intensive questioning produced spirited exchanges as well as objections from some witnesses, but the committee always supported him.[35]

The legislators dug more deeply into conditions at Oakley and into Jackson's use of convicts than had the board of control. They found that, partly because of the sergeant, the farm had lost money every year since 1900, the cumulative loss coming to $24,000.[36] The committee interviewed not only persons on the farm but also merchants, farmers, and cotton gin operators who lived near Oakley. They found that although he had not worked prisoners when they were sick nor treated them cruelly himself, Jackson had "beyond any doubt whatever" exploited convict labor for his own benefit in 1903 and 1904. He had even been heard to boast that he might be called "Jack" then, but if he could remain at Oakley for another year he would be "Mr. Jackson." [37]

The committeemen did not confine themselves to Jackson's activities, for they found others were implicated. If he had been working convicts, they asked, why had this not been reported by the prison

[33] *House Journal, 1906,* 50, 62, 65–66, 74, 85.
[34] Jackson *Evening News,* February 21, 1906.
[35] *Report of the Penitentiary Investigating Committee on Oakley Farm,* 5, 298–99, 313, 319–51.
[36] *Ibid.,* 5–6.
[37] *House Journal, 1906,* 617–19; *Report of the Penitentiary Investigating Committee on Oakley Farm,* 63.

physician J. P. Berry? The doctor denied knowledge of the sergeant's activities, but the committee found strong circumstantial evidence that Berry had permitted healthy prisoners to remain in the hospital and work for Jackson. As Jackson had occasionally lent money to Berry, the committee intimated that the doctor had repaid his debt by keeping his mouth shut about the sergeant's activities. A more serious indictment against Berry was the discovery that he had bought drugs for the Oakley hospital at prices higher than those to which the state was entitled. The committee also emphasized that he had ordered excessive quantities of whiskey and suggested without any semblance of proof that Oakley was the center of a large-scale bootlegging operation. That Berry was the son-in-law of United States Senator Anse McLaurin added not a little to the political overtones of the investigation.[38]

Throughout the proceedings Representative Wells's questioning had emphasized the inability of the board of control to manage penitentiary affairs adequately. The committee reported itself appalled at the immense ignorance of the board and the warden "with reference to theft, incompetency, extravagances and other irregularities" at Oakley farm and hospital. The incumbent warden was either "utterly incompetent, or grossly and practically criminally negligent in the discharge of his duties." The state should sell Oakley farm, concentrate all prisoners on the Sunflower plantation, and build a new prison hospital on the Rankin farm. Above all, the board must be abolished and a superintendent placed in charge of the penitentiary system.[39]

One member of the house penitentiary committee, Emmett Cavett, issued a minority report defending Dr. Berry, the warden, and the board of control. He denied that the entire penitentiary system should be condemned because of conditions existing at one farm. Cavett even blamed Vardaman for not prosecuting Jackson, for he noted that after the board of control had probed the case, it had authorized the governor to investigate further the sergeant's activities.[40]

The penitentiary committee issued its report the day after the state

[38] Report of the Penitentiary Investigating Committee on Oakley Farm, 10–12, 14–17, 383.
[39] House Journal, 1906, 620, 626–27.
[40] Ibid., 638–44.

supreme court had turned down Vardaman's appeal for a writ of mandamus.[41] Inevitably, the controversy produced a barrage of charges and countercharges in the state press between supporters of the governor and defenders of the board. Pro-Vardaman newspapers especially censured Cavett's minority report.[42] So also did the governor himself, asserting that Cavett was "trying to defend or excuse somebody connected with the Board of Control." He admitted that the board had empowered him to investigate Jackson further and to prosecute him. But the district attorney of Hinds County had ruled that Jackson was not amenable to prosecution, and the governor had neither money nor authority to investigate the situation as thoroughly as could a legislative committee. Vardaman had therefore postponed action until the legislature convened.[43]

Dr. Berry denied the charges against him and condemned the methods used by the penitentiary committee. He claimed that a key witness and a committeeman were leading enemies of the McLaurins and had special reasons for attacking their friends. The doctor strongly implied that Vardaman had instituted the investigation to advance his political career.[44] After Berry's statement appeared, the Jackson *Evening News* remarked:

Politics is sizzling and popping around the state house like a pan of frying frog legs, and the issue of Vardaman vs. McLaurin is now more squarely before the legislative body than at any time since the beginning of the session.

The air is so heavily charged with political electricity around the big building that its presence can be instinctively felt, even by a stranger, the moment his foot hits the marble floors of the main entrance.[45]

An incident that proved embarrassing to Vardaman, and that certainly supplied ammunition to the opponents of prison reform, had occurred at the governor's mansion just about the time the penitentiary investigation was beginning. Hezekiah Planer, a Negro convict working at the mansion, was drunk one night and raising a row when

[41] Jackson *Evening News,* March 6, 1906.
[42] Vicksburg *Herald,* March 8, 9, 10, 1906.
[43] *Ibid.,* March 9, 1906.
[44] Jackson *Evening News,* March 11, 1906.
[45] *Ibid.,* March 12, 1906.

a policeman arrested him. After Planer had been returned to the mansion, Vardaman castigated him for his behavior. At the time Planer
was squatting to polish the governor's shoes and when he made a
"sassy" reply, Vardaman booted him, toppling him over. Vardaman
then grabbed a hearth broom and hit him several times. When word
of the incident leaked out, anti-Vardaman newspapers denounced the
governor for losing his temper and reported that he had splintered a
broomstick in beating Planer. He was a hypocrite to condemn men
such as Puckett, they charged, when he committed similar atrocities
himself.[46] Representative Wells defended the governor by asserting
that Planer had insulted him and had gotten off with only a light whipping.[47] The incident continued to be discussed and added spice to the
excitement surrounding the penitentiary controversy.

Vardaman's fight with the board of control and Henry McLaurin
over renewal of the Sandy Bayou contract kindled popular support
for the final abolition of convict leasing in Mississippi. As a result, the
legislature, soon after assembling, passed a bill providing that prisoners could work only on public roads, levees, and state-owned lands;
they could not be employed upon privately owned plantations or in
other enterprises.[48] Although this constituted a victory for Vardaman
over the McLaurins, he still wanted to have the board of control
abolished.

About a week after the house penitentiary committee issued its report, the fight for prison reform entered its final phase with the introduction of a bill to reorganize the prison system. Newspapers dubbed
it the "administration bill," but it differed from Vardaman's original
proposal in that it divided authority between a prison superintendent
and a board of trustees, whereas the governor had wanted all power

[46] *Ibid.,* January 18, 19, 1906; Biloxi *Daily Herald,* January 20, 22, 1906.
[47] Vicksburg *Herald,* January 20, 1906; Meadville *Franklin Advocate,* January
25, 1906; Laurel *Chronicle,* January 27, 1906. Soon after the incident Vardaman had Planer returned to the Oakley prison farm because he suffered from
rheumatism. About a year later a convict at Oakley cut the throat of a prison
guard and then proceeded to incite a riot among some of the prisoners. Vardaman rushed to the farm and confronted the leader of the rebellion, who
threatened to kill anyone who tried to disarm him. At that point Planer stepped
forward and after a short fight disarmed the riot leader. Vardaman was so
moved that he took Planer back to Jackson and granted him a pardon. Vicksburg *Herald,* December 16, 1906.
[48] *Mississippi Laws, 1906,* 142–43.

vested in the superintendent.[49] Beginning in 1907 the trustees would be popularly elected, but the governor would appoint the superintendent. The newly elected trustees would not take office until 1908, thus Vardaman would appoint the first set of officials in January, 1907. He supported this bill, although he denied being its author. The "administration bill" easily passed the house, but it met sturdy opposition in the senate, whose committee on penitentiary affairs opposed the governor's plan to abolish the board of control. Some observers predicted that the bill would not pass during the 1906 session.[50]

While the bill was pending before the senate committee, the house penitentiary committee issued a second report—this one on conditions at the Rankin farm. As in the case of Oakley, the committee had concentrated upon an area of known mismanagement and corruption. The short report, based on quick investigation, disclosed that the abuses at Rankin had been more shocking than those at Oakley. Although various officials at Rankin limited their activities to petty graft, the most serious evil had been the punishments inflicted on prisoners by Puckett and his assistant Strong. Not only had they whipped prisoners unmercifully, but Strong had ordered one convict to murder another. The committee emphasized, as it had in the Oakley report, the inability of the board of control to supervise the prison system properly and recommended its abolition.[51]

The report on the Rankin farm did not, however, alter the determination of the senate penitentiary committee, which voted soon afterward against abolishing the board. The *Daily Clarion-Ledger* hailed the vote a victory for the "conservative and safer body of the legislature." [52] The Vardaman forces now put logrolling to the service of reform. William Wailes Magruder, an anti-Vardaman senator from Starkville, was trying to obtain for the Mississippi Agricultural and Mechanical College a large appropriation which he wanted deposited in his home-town bank. Other anti-Vardaman senators wanted the college appropriation fund kept in the state treasury. Leading the fight in the senate for the "administration bill" was John L. Hebron, the

[49] Jackson *Daily Clarion-Ledger,* March 16, 1906.
[50] *Ibid.,* March 30, April 1, 1906; Jackson *Evening News,* March 30, 1906.
[51] *House Journal, 1906,* 916–18; Laurel *Chronicle,* April 7, 1906.
[52] Jackson *Daily Clarion-Ledger,* April 6, 1906.

same man whom Vardaman had appointed to the Mississippi levee board over the protests of LeRoy Percy. Hebron now took advantage of the rift in the anti-Vardaman forces to arrange a deal whereby the pro-Vardaman senators voted against the attempt to move the college appropriation to Starkville, and the opponents of Magruder's financial plan voted for the penitentiary reform. The senate then passed the penitentiary bill by a vote of 23 to 13.[53] After the governor signed the bill, the Vicksburg *Herald* reported, he gave the pen to "Chairman Miller of the [house] penitentiary committee which was a fitting recognition of the chief victor; next to Vardaman himself." [54]

As a result of the penitentiary controversy Vardaman had become bitterly estranged from the other members of the board of control, as well as Warden Henry. Consequently, he refused to appoint any of them to the new penitentiary agency that assumed authority in 1907. Instead, he named William Alexander Montgomery, Charles C. Smith, and LeRoy Taylor as trustees and appointed C. H. Neyland, a farmer from Wilkinson County, superintendent of the penitentiary. The new trustees supposedly shared Vardaman's views on what a penitentiary should be.[55]

The enactment of prison reform constituted the major progressive achievement of Vardaman's administration. By two acts the legislature had abolished convict leasing once and for all and had created a more efficient system of penitentiary management. He had led the fight for reform, and by sheer political power plus a touch of shrewd compromise had attained victory. In part, personal animosities and politics had motivated him. The McLaurins were his old enemies, and he might well consider the leasing of Sandy Bayou a personal affront. But there were more important reasons why he worked for prison reform. Throughout the late nineteenth century, the state's small farmers had regarded the convict lease system as serving the interests of a few wealthy planters; by abolishing the last vestiges of it, Vardaman was championing the interests of those who had helped bring him into office. More important, during the 1890's he had advocated humane

---

[53] Shivers, "Mississippi Penitentiary," 86; Jackson *Evening News,* April 7, 11, 1906.

[54] Vicksburg *Herald,* April 17, 1906.

[55] Jackson *Daily Clarion-Ledger,* December 5, 28, 1906; Vicksburg *Herald,* March 12, 1907.

and enlightened treatment of convicts. As governor he had managed to translate part of his proposals into concrete action.

In fighting for prison reform Vardaman won praise throughout the state. Some of his avowed opponents admitted that he made an able governor, and even his outspoken racism and his work further to suppress Negroes did not evoke much criticism during his governorship nor for many years thereafter. Critics did not begin serious attacks on Vardaman until he had the chancellor of the University of Mississippi removed from office. At the time some believed that the governor had abused his powers to serve petty political whims. Years later others charged that he had initiated an era in which state politicians intervened in the University's internal affairs, thereby seriously weakening the school.

A board consisting of sixteen trustees, the governor, and the state superintendent of education directed the University. The governor, besides serving as president of the board, appointed the trustees, one from each of the eight congressional districts, the others from the state at large. Because trustees served six-year terms, two years were required for a new governor's appointees to become a majority on the board. The trustees relegated much work to an executive committee that met more frequently than the board and that handled much of the University's business. Because of his appointive power and his membership on the executive committee, the governor could control, if he were so minded, all aspects of the University, "from the janitor to the Chancellor and faculty, and from the selection of textbooks to the kind of buildings constructed." [56]

When Vardaman became governor in 1904, Robert B. Fulton had served the University for thirty-three years, the first twenty-one as teacher and the last twelve as chancellor. Under Fulton's administration the University had enjoyed rapid progress, for the student body, teaching staff, and annual revenues had doubled; schools of education, engineering, and medicine had been added; and numerous educational improvements had been introduced. In addition, the University not

[56] Grover Cleveland Hooker, "The Origin and Development of the University of Mississippi with Special Reference to Its Legislature Control" (Ph.D. dissertation, Stanford University, 1932–1933), 2–4, 151–53. In 1904 the state legislature increased the number of trustees from fifteen to sixteen. *Mississippi Laws, 1904*, 172.

only became a charter member of both the National Association of State Universities and the Southern Association of Colleges and Secondary Schools but also enjoyed the distinction of seeing its chancellor serve as president of each of those organizations.[57]

Unfortunately, the University's progress under Fulton was paralleled after 1900 by the rise of disciplinary problems that stimulated opposition to the chancellor and reached a peak during Vardaman's administration.[58] Much of the trouble stemmed from fraternities which were of long standing at the University. The school then had an enrollment of about three hundred, many of whom belonged to fraternities. Division between fraternity and nonfraternity men ran along social class lines, for the clubs usually accepted as members only the sons of wealthy parents or the descendants of respected families. Those students who did not belong to the clubs believed that fraternity members received undeserved privileges from some faculty members and the administration. The nonfraternity men frequently felt the sting of social ostracism. Many young women of Oxford, for example, would associate only with fraternity members, who were accused of deliberately fostering the impression "that non-fraternity men are rather second-class men, and unfit to associate with the girls of that good old town." Opponents of the exclusive societies argued that their members usually started campus disorders: "Fraternity men spend too much of their time in frequent carousals, making the night hideous with unearthly yells, with midnight wassail, and bacchanalian revelry." So serious had the problem become by 1902 that the board of trustees enacted stringent regulations to govern the fraternities.[59]

Difficulties over the fraternities continued after Vardaman became governor. In 1904 a majority of the joint legislative committee on

[57] Fulton graduated from the University of Mississippi in 1869 and from 1871 to 1892 he served on the faculty, teaching astronomy and physics. James Allen Cabaniss, *A History of the University of Mississippi* (University, Mississippi, 1949), 119–30; "Robert Burwell Fulton," *Dictionary of American Biography* (New York, 1928–37), VII, 27; Alfred Hume, "Robert Burwell Fulton: Chancellor of the University of Mississippi," *Southern Association Quarterly,* III (1939), 537; Annie Berry, "University Land Grants," *University of Mississippi Magazine,* XXVII (1904), 27–31.

[58] Cabaniss, *University of Mississippi,* 130–31.

[59] *House Journal, 1904,* 406–407; Cabaniss, *University of Mississippi,* 131–32; Hooker, "Origin and Development of the University of Mississippi," 155–56.

colleges and universities reported that friction between fraternity and nonfraternity men had become so serious that it was impeding the work of the University and recommended that no student be allowed to join a fraternity until successfully completing a year of course work.[60] A minority report from the same committee contended that the problem was more serious than the majority had indicated:

But we are constrained to believe our beloved University is sick of a fever. The "old home is not what it used to be." She is like the young man who went to Christ—"one thing she lackest," and that is the total abolition of the secret societies once and for all, now and forever. We may say not because we dislike the fraternities without a cause, but because we love the University more. We want to see her unshackled in every limb, erect, full and free, growing grander, better and brighter as the years shall circle away. The rich and the poor, when they enter her door, must have an equal chance in the great battle of life. No high-flown artificial distinctions, social or otherwise, should ever be permitted to sully her honor. The rank is but the guinea stamp. A man's a man for a' that.

W. A. Ellis, one author of the minority report, soon introduced a bill to abolish "fraternities and sororities and all secret orders" at state supported schools.[61] Ellis' bill failed to pass, however, and the legislators did nothing to offset the mounting discontent over fraternities. Chancellor Fulton may have been partly responsible for the failure to reform the societies, for he assured his friends in the legislature that although "some parties may be trying to stir up the fraternity matter in Jackson," all was peaceful at the University and "there was never a better spirit in the student body." [62]

From the beginning of his administration Vardaman was concerned about the management of the University. Although he never commented publicly on the fraternity problem, it should be remembered that he had risen to power by appealing to the small farmers, many of whom had no sympathy for "aristocratic" social clubs. He definitely wanted to end the friction that had begun to develop within the school,

[60] *House Journal, 1904,* 346–47.
[61] *Ibid.,* 348–49, 374, 406–408; Brookhaven *Lincoln County Times,* February 18, 1904; Laurel *Chronicle,* March 5, 1904.
[62] R. B. Fulton to W. B. Walker, January 12, 1904, in William Burwell Walker Papers, Mississippi Department of Archives and History.

but it would be a mistake to assume, as some have, that he immediately began appointing trustees hostile to Chancellor Fulton. In fact, on taking office he reappointed two trustees who had originally been appointed by Governor McLaurin and whose original terms expired in 1904.[63] Yet it was evident that he and his appointees intended to play a larger role in managing the University than had earlier boards. At a meeting on June 3, 1904, the first after Vardaman's inauguration, the trustees ordered that faculty members prepare reports of their departments. Then, before most had managed to submit their reports, the board ruled all faculty positions open and subject to being filled. Immediately thereafter the trustees unanimously agreed to reappoint Chancellor Fulton and all the faculty members except J. W. Johnson, Alexander L. Bondurant, and D. H. Bishop, all three of whom were considered incompetent teachers by some board members. Not until the board convened in a special meeting the following month, and only after active lobbying with the trustees by friends of the three professors, were they too reappointed to the faculty. None of the three was elected unanimously. Even R. H. Thompson, a trustee appointed by Longino and an intense foe of Vardaman, admitted that "the new blood on the board" had struck the faculty at its "weak points" in balking over the reappointments of the three.[64]

In more and more matters during the next two years the board exerted its authority in directing the University, sometimes against the advice of Chancellor Fulton. Some duties formerly exercised by him and by the proctor were assigned to a business manager; then the executive committee, by control of the University's finances, increas-

[63] *Announcements and Catalogue of the University of Mississippi . . . Fifty-Second Session . . . , 1903–1904* (n.p., n.d.), 8–9; *Announcements and Catalogue of the University of Mississippi . . . Fifty-Third Session . . . , 1904–1905* (n.p., n.d.), 8–9; *"Ole Miss" 1904,* edited annually by the fraternities and sororities of the University of Mississippi (n.p., n.d.), 7. For the charge that Vardaman deliberately worked for Fulton's dismissal from the beginning of his administration, see Hooker, "Origin and Development of the University of Mississippi," 155–56.

[64] R. H. Thompson to J. A. Orr, June 10, 1904, in Jehu A. Orr Papers, Southern Historical Collection, University of North Carolina. Dunbar Rowland to R. B. Fulton, June 13, 1904, Rowland to C. M. Williamson, June 13, 1904, Rowland to A. L. Bondurant, June 25, July 22, 1904, in Dunbar Rowland Papers, Mississippi Department of Archives and History; Hooker, "Origin and Development of the University of Mississippi," 159–61.

ingly assumed direction of school affairs. One of the most startling decisions came in 1905 when the board rejected an offer Fulton had obtained from the Carnegie Foundation to grant twenty-five thousand dollars for a library. At the time the University had no library. The board also turned down the chancellor's request that the University participate in a faculty retirement plan sponsored by the Carnegie Foundation.[65] Vardaman's belief that corporate wealth threatened academic freedom may explain the rejection. Whatever the trustees' motives, Chancellor Fulton must have found the board's opposition frustrating and it probably contributed to his eventual resignation.

Before the board met in June, 1906, new troubles had arisen at the University. They had begun the previous year when seven seniors had been suspended for violating fraternity regulations. Professor Garvin D. Shands, the dean of the law school, had assumed a leading role in demanding the suspensions. The seven students, all sons of well-to-do families, appealed to the governor for help, and he promised an immediate investigation. Apparently Vardaman demanded that the suspensions be dropped, for the faculty reversed its ruling and permitted the students to graduate. Unaware of why the suspensions had been lifted, nonfraternity students accused the faculty of bowing to the demands of the fraternities.[66]

Especially angered by the pardoning of the seven was a law student at the University, Duncan H. Chamberlain, Jr., whose experiences had converted him into a bitter foe of fraternities. Convinced that state newspapers would not report how "corrupted the management" of the University had become, he believed the "common people" should know that the University's administration had been catering chiefly to "the so-called upper classes." Just as the legislature convened in January, 1906, Chamberlain published, at his own expense,

[65] Hooker, "Origin and Development of the University of Mississippi," 161–63; Cabaniss, *University of Mississippi,* 133.
[66] Jackson *Evening News,* May 18, 1905; J. K. Vardaman to J. M. May, July 23, 1905, in Vardaman Letter Book. Those expelled were Lucius Mayes, son of Judge Edward Mayes who had formerly been Chancellor of the University and grandson of L. Q. C. Lamar; Murry Powell, son of Judge Robert Powell; James and Will Elmer, two well-known figures in college sports; Jim Stone, "son of one of the most prominent families in North Mississippi"; and W. F. Cook and Stokes Robertson, honor students. And see D. H. Chamberlain, Jr., *The Facts About the Troubles of the University of Mississippi: The Jim Crow Laws Against Whites at the University* (n.p., n.d.), 2–7.

a pamphlet describing the dominance of the fraternities.[67] Not only did many students belong to them, he charged, but influential men throughout the state were alumni members, and their combined influence gave the fraternities power to control the University with an iron grip. To support his argument that nonfraternity men suffered gross discrimination, he recalled an incident of 1903 in which he alleged that Rupert C. Morris, a student then struggling to pay his way through the University, had been unfairly suspended after having fought in self-defense against a fraternity man. Chamberlain accused Chancellor Fulton of having deliberately discriminated against Morris because the fraternity member's family recently had made generous financial contributions to the University.[68]

At Fulton's request the legislative committee on colleges and universities investigated Chamberlain's charges. During the ensuing investigation a clear division developed within the committee, as a majority of the members stoutly defended Fulton, but a minority held that some of Chamberlain's accusations were true. Chamberlain himself became the target of many critics. So infuriated was he by Senator James Alcorn Glover's denunciation of his pamphlet that he confronted the legislator in the lobby of the Edwards House and knocked him over a chair. Chamberlain was even more peeved by the results of the investigation, for a majority of the committee held that the chancellor had not abused his powers and exonerated him. A minority of three, however, issued a report denouncing Fulton for suspending Morris and urging the University board of trustees to take up the matter.[69]

---

[67] Chamberlain, *Facts About . . . the University,* 14–15. Duncan Holt Chamberlain entered the University law school in 1902 and graduated with distinction in 1905. In addition to winning several prizes for oratory, he was awarded the Edward Thompson Law Prize in 1905. *Historical Catalogue of the University of Mississippi, 1849–1909* (Nashville, 1910), 283–87, 293–96.

[68] Chamberlain, *Facts About . . . the University,* 1–10; *Record of the Testimony Taken by the Joint Committee on Universities and Colleges in the Investigation of the Charges Made Against Chancellor Robert B. Fulton by D. H. Chamberlain* (n.p., n.d.), 36–37, 46. Chamberlain described Morris' opponent only as a "Ricks boy" from Yazoo City. According to the *Historical Catalogue of the University of Mississippi,* the only student with that name who was enrolled for the 1903–04 academic year was John Ricks of Canton, Mississippi. Between 1900 and 1903 Mrs. Fanny J. Ricks of Yazoo City made large contributions to the University. Cabaniss, *University of Mississippi,* 123, 125.

[69] Jackson *Evening News,* February 8, 10, 13, March 3, 1906; Vicksburg *Herald,* March 15, April 5, 1906; *House Journal, 1906,* 372, 630–31; R. B.

Despite the majority report defending Fulton, the long-standing fraternity troubles—especially Chamberlain's recent disclosures—disturbed many people. One of Vardaman's correspondents alleged that Chamberlain's accusations had been correct and that Fulton's friends had controlled the legislative investigation. The writer also warned that if the "University is ever to become worthy of the money the taxpayers of Miss[issippi] are spending upon it, it will be when the fraternities and Chancellor Fulton, their logical head, are thrown out." [70] Chamberlain published a second pamphlet accusing the faculty members who had testified in Fulton's behalf of resorting "to sophistry, confusion, misdirection, and trimming of quotations" in trying to save the chancellor. He explained that his only motive in publishing the first pamphlet had been to inform the "taxpayers of the state" of the abuses that the fraternity system produced—"discord, favoritism, snobbery, clannishness and sycophancy." [71]

After the legislature adjourned in April, 1906, the issue shifted to the Board of Trustees. By that time Vardaman had become convinced that the University's troubles could be ended only "if a stronger man than Mr. Fulton were at its head." [72] To insure the chancellor's dismissal, Vardaman appointed three new trustees, S. A. Morrison, W. F. Tucker, and Judge Robert Powell, all of whom shared his belief that Fulton had to go.[73] Powell's appointment was particularly significant, for his son had been one of the seven students expelled for fraternity violations the previous year. Convinced that Professor Shands had been chiefly responsible for the suspensions, the vindictive judge wanted him driven from the University. If necessary, he would vote for removing Fulton from the chancellorship if it would insure Shands's dismissal.[74]

Fulton to Dunbar Rowland, January 25, February 9, 1906, in Dunbar Rowland Papers.

[70] N. A. Moore to N. C. Knox, February 12, 1906, in Vardaman Papers.

[71] D. H. Chamberlain, Jr., *The Mud Beneath the Whitewash* (n.p., n.d.), *passim.*

[72] J. K. Vardaman to _____, April 14, 1906, in Vardaman Letter Book. The name of the addressee has been blurred beyond recognition.

[73] Jackson *Evening News,* May 25, 1906; Rowland, *The Official and Statistical Register of the State of Mississippi 1908,* p. 285.

[74] Dunbar Rowland to R. B. Fulton, October 10, 1906, in Dunbar Rowland Papers.

For a month before the new trustees officially assumed their duties in June, reports circulated in the state press that the board intended to dismiss Fulton. In early May a report reached Fulton that a "plot" was under way to oust him from office. The chancellor's friends tried to intercede with trustees in his behalf. State Archivist Dunbar Rowland, for example, tried in vain "to set Judge Powell right." [75] When the board assembled at Oxford for its June meeting, a group of students tried to present a petition supporting Fulton, but Vardaman ordered them to "take the damned thing out of here." Even though Fulton had announced earlier that he would not quit, he discovered at the June meeting that he had lost the support of a majority of the trustees. He accordingly offered to resign, and after a determined fight by his friends on the board that lasted late into the night, the trustees accepted his resignation by a vote of 10 to 8.[76] Fulton did not know if Vardaman alone was responsible for his defeat or if other opponents on the board had plotted against him. "But under a board that would act as a majority of these men did," he wrote, "whether bound by any plot on me springing of their own making, or swayed by the will of their master, Vardaman, I could not serve with self respect even my own *alma mater* whom I love more than all others." Not only was Fulton pushed out, but Judge Powell had the satisfaction of seeing the board force Professor Shands to resign by cutting his salary four hundred dollars.[77]

Although the board elected Fulton professor of astronomy, he left

[75] Jackson *Evening News,* May 23, 25, 26, June 4, 1906; Tupelo *Journal,* June 1, 1906; R. B. Fulton to J. A. Orr, June 6, 1906, in Orr Papers; Fulton to Dunbar Rowland, October 3, 1906, in Dunbar Rowland Papers.

[76] Jackson *Evening News,* June 9, 1906; Jackson *Daily Clarion-Ledger,* June 10, July 1, 1906. Eight of the trustees who voted with Vardaman to accept Fulton's resignation were State Superintendent of Education H. L. Whitfield, C. Kindrick, S. A. Morrison, W. F. Tucker, Robert Powell, J. W. T. Falkner, J. D. McKie, and J. M. Acker. Summit *Sentinel,* June 21, 1906; Vicksburg *Herald,* June 17, 1906. With the exception of Falkner, all those voting against Fulton had been appointed by Vardaman. The ninth trustee who voted with Vardaman was probably John L. Hebron, one of the governor's most trusted lieutenants.

[77] R. B. Fulton to Dunbar Rowland, October 3, 1906, in Dunbar Rowland Papers. Later Fulton became convinced that Vardaman alone was responsible for his dismissal. Fulton to Rowland, March 4, 1908, April 27, 1910, in Dunbar Rowland Papers; Jackson *Daily Clarion-Ledger,* August 10, 1906. Shands had served as lieutenant governor of Mississippi from 1882 to 1890. It is not known if his former political activities had any bearing upon his forced resignation.

the University and moved to Virginia, where he became superintendent of the Miller School in Albemarle County. That his forced resignation created trouble for the University was demonstrated by the difficulty the trustees had in finding a successor to him. After two men refused the position, the board raised the salary, provided an official residence on campus, increased the chancellor's powers to nominate and to remove faculty members, and gave him more authority to arrange courses of study. Andrew Armstrong Kincannon, former state superintendent of education and president of the state woman's college, finally accepted the position.[78] Fulton's dismissal also demoralized some of the abler faculty members and eventually contributed to the departure of at least one of them from the University.[79]

Fulton's dismissal gave rise to charges and countercharges. The governor's opponents accused him of having forced the chancellor to resign for political reasons, among them that Fulton was known to have opposed Vardaman's election and that he was related to the wife of Representative John Sharp Williams, who had already announced that the next year he would run against Vardaman for the senate. Others concluded that since the fraternity issue cut across class lines, Vardaman had Fulton dismissed to bolster his own popularity with the small farmers.[80] Political considerations may have had some bearing on Vardaman's decision to stack the board against Fulton, but that had not been his chief concern. For one thing, he had not always sympathized with the antifraternity forces; he had, after all, used his influence in 1905 to have reinstated the seven students suspended for fraternity violations. He had even appointed as a trustee

[78] Cabaniss, *University of Mississippi,* 133–38. Vardaman wanted the chancellor's salary increased from $3,500 to $7,500 in the hope of getting Chancellor E. Benjamin Andrews of the University of Nebraska to accept the position. Andrews had formerly been forced to resign from the Presidency of Brown University because he had supported free silver and free trade. Andrews was interested in the position, Vardaman later recalled, but he feared he was too old to "make the adjustment to the south at this late stage." *Vardaman's Weekly,* January 29, 1920.

[79] Franklin L. Riley to R. B. Fulton, June 23, 1911, in Franklin L. Riley Papers, Southern Historical Collection.

[80] Summit *Sentinel,* June 14, 1906; Biloxi *Daily Herald,* June 23, 1906; Brookhaven *Lincoln County Times,* June 28, 1906; John Sharp Williams to Woodrow Wilson, August 1, 1914, in John Sharp Williams Papers, Library of Congress. Hereinafter cited as Williams Papers, Library of Congress. And see Hooker, "Origin and Development of the University of Mississippi," 163–66.

Judge Powell, a man so angered by his son's suspension that he was determined to force Shands out of the University. Fulton's dismissal, moreover, never became a meaningful political issue, for neither Vardaman nor John Sharp Williams devoted any attention to it during the senatorial campaign of 1907. Vardaman never publicly sympathized with the fraternity nor antifraternity advocates. He had come to believe, however, that the animosity between the two groups was seriously hurting the University, and accordingly he became convinced that only a new chancellor could end the "friction and bickering" that had plagued the school for the past six years.[81] That was the reason he had worked for Fulton's dismissal. C. F. Holmes, a trustee who had voted against accepting Fulton's resignation, publicly defended the governor by explaining that too many people had lost confidence in the chancellor's ability to direct the University.[82]

The University controversy was a complicated affair. There was no justification for the treatment meted out to Shands: he was the victim of a vengeful parent. Then the dismissal of Robert Fulton, a man who had served his school over thirty years, marked a tragic ending to a distinguished career. Vardaman has been criticized for his part in the Fulton affair on the basis that he hurt the University by inaugurating an era in which state politicians intervened in the school's affairs. The charge is not justified. For one thing, he was not the first Mississippi politician to concern himself directly in University affairs. On past occasions, state politicians had decisively interfered in the school's realm.[83] Nor was he responsible for later political intervention in the University. Although intervention in a university's internal affairs by a governor might frequently hurt the institution, it is incorrect to assume that it is always harmful. On occasion intervention might be necessary. Vardaman felt, and justifiably so, that the Fulton affair was such an occasion. Although the chancellor had rendered valuable service to the school, he had long been unable to cope with the disciplinary and social problems stemming from the fraternity controversy— problems that were hurting the University. It was with an eye toward ending the internal dissent that Vardaman decided the time had come for a change in leadership.

81 Vicksburg *Herald,* June 17, 1906.
82 *Ibid.,* June 26, 1906.
83 Hooker, "Origin and Development of the University of Mississippi," 335–36; Cabaniss, *University of Mississippi,* 79–92, 133.

CHAPTER VII

DEFEAT

IN FEBRUARY, 1905, Senator Hernando DeSoto Money announced he would not seek reelection to the United States Senate in 1907. Even though state legislatures still elected senators, Mississippi had used primaries since 1903 to select Democratic nominees. The Democratic nomination was tantamount to election, therefore the primary gave the white voters the only opportunity to express their preference. Money's natural successor, so to speak, was John Sharp Williams, Democratic minority leader of the United States House of Representatives, but Vardaman was not slow to let it be known that he intended to vie for the seat.[1] The two men had long been aligned politically. Ever since Williams had entered the House in 1893 Vardaman had praised him as one of the South's outstanding young congressmen and had predicted that someday he would become a distinguished senator.[2] Because both men had opposed McLaurinism, Williams had actively supported Vardaman in the gubernatorial campaign of 1903. Soon after Money had announced that he would retire, Williams' brother Christopher wrote to Vardaman's private secretary George R. Edwards asking if the Governor intended to run for the Senate vacancy. Edwards replied that he would run, but added that Vardaman "wants you and John S. to understand that his friendship for you both will in no way be affected." [3] In the face of rival political ambitions the old friendship did not long survive. By the spring of 1905 Williams began complaining to Vardaman that he was being unfairly attacked by the governor's newspaper

[1] Jackson *Evening News,* February 20, 1905; Jackson *Daily Clarion-Ledger,* April 18, 26, 1905.
[2] Greenwood *Enterprise,* November 10, 1893; Greenwood *Commonwealth,* May 27, November 26, 1897, April 28, 1898, July 6, 1900.
[3] G. R. Edwards to John Sharp Williams, March 5, 1905, in Vardaman Letter Book.

friends, and Vardaman replied that he had no control over the press; the governor did point out, however, that he was being slandered by the pro-Williams editors.[4]

Mississippi's two most popular politicians were pitted against one another, and the contest promised to be hard fought—one that would attract wide interest. The candidates presented a striking contrast in appearance, background, and style. Having grown up during the impoverished times of Reconstruction, Vardaman had acquired education through his own avid reading. The practice of law had not proved to his liking, and he had turned instead to newspaper editing and to politics and in both endeavors had enjoyed success. His stirring oratory and bold campaigning had enabled him to rise to power in the first state-wide primary. He conducted his campaigns like a showman and entertained his audiences with graphic descriptions of Negro crimes.

Williams came from a background of wealth and culture. He had been educated at the University of the South, the University of Virginia, and at Heidelberg, and he had been a successful lawyer. Also, he had inherited a large plantation which provided him a profitable income. At the time he ran against Vardaman for the Senate he had been in Congress for fourteen years, the last four of which he had served as House minority leader. The base of his political strength had been a block of counties that stretched directly across the center of the state from the Alabama line to the Mississippi River—a conglomerate area consisting of hills, prairie, and piney woods. Even though he did not represent the Delta, he was popular in that section. A small man, not physically imposing, who rarely gave careful attention to his dress, he spoke forcefully and entertainingly on the stump. Confident of his ability, he preferred to take on opponents in public debate.[5] His national reputation and popular appeal combined to make him a man of power in Mississippi and the most able opponent Vardaman ever faced.

The Williams-Vardaman campaign held more significance, how-

[4] J. K. Vardaman to John Sharp Williams, May 19, 1905, October 23, 1906, Vardaman to G. A. Wilson, July 17, 1905, in Vardaman Letter Book.

[5] George C. Osborn, *John Sharp Williams: Planter-Statesman of the Deep South* (Baton Rouge, 1943), passim. John Sharp Williams to Joseph P. Tumulty, January 31, 1917, in Woodrow Wilson Papers.

ever, than a contrast in personalities and campaign styles. Williams supposedly represented a more moderate approach to the race problem than did Vardaman, but in reality both wanted Negroes always to be only menial laborers. Yet there were important differences between the two, because they had begun to appeal to different social and economic groups. Williams favored such moderate progressive reforms as a lower tariff, a mild, graduated income tax, and stricter railroad regulation. He was, nevertheless, a laissez-faire reformer who strongly opposed programs calling for dynamic intervention by the federal government in attempting to alleviate social and economic problems. Throughout his career, for example, he opposed most reforms that the Populists had advocated, and as an old man he would describe Populism as "a revolt against superiority of intellect, of education, of birth." [6] In contrast to Williams, Vardaman had begun appealing more to the dirt farmer and laboring class. As governor he had best demonstrated his radical agrarianism by vetoing a railroad merger bill and the timber landowning bill. He was on his way, in fact, to adopting the entire body of Populist reform programs. [7] The split between the laissez-faire reformer Williams and the agrarian radical Vardaman was most clearly illustrated in 1907 by their reaction to William Jennings Bryan's proposal for government ownership of railroads: Vardaman favored Bryan's plan, Williams denounced it. [8]

Although the two were fast moving toward opposing poles within their party, issues in this campaign did not become as clearly drawn as they would in the next decade when the two sat together in the Senate. In 1907 Vardaman frequently avoided discussing government ownership of railroads, believing that appeals to racism would win more support. Williams was too shrewd a politician to risk openly alienating the laborers and small farmers. Like Vardaman, he professed to sympathize with their problems and as the campaign progressed he worked to offset the governor's appeal to them. Once, before attending a gather-

[6] John Sharp Williams to Cecil Johnson, December 14, 1923, in Cecil Johnson, "A Letter from John Sharp Williams," *Journal of Mississippi History*, XXIII (1961), 229–30.

[7] *Congressional Record*, 63 Cong., 2d Sess., 2159.

[8] John Sharp Williams to C. L. Tubb, June 10, 1907, in Williams Papers, Library of Congress.

ing of railroad workers in McComb, he urged his secretary to find his old membership card in the "Isthmian Canal Locomotive Engineers Union." [9]

With issues not sharply drawn, the campaign largely developed into a popularity contest between the congressman and the governor, and thousands of voters found it a difficult choice. The Vicksburg *Herald,* which previously had supported both men, remained neutral during the contest. Some anti-McLaurin leaders even suggested that the two men should not oppose one another. LeRoy Percy, for example, recommended that Money not resign and thereby avoid the risk of splitting the anti-McLaurin faction by a fight between Williams and Vardaman. Others suggested that one replace Money while the other agreed to wait for Senator McLaurin's seat, but McLaurin's term did not expire until 1913 and neither was willing to wait that long.[10] Thus by the spring of 1907 both were determined to fight it out in the August primary.

Williams launched his campaign by stumping through North Mississippi. Time and again he challenged Vardaman to meet him in joint debates and on receiving no reply, he accused the governor of being afraid to discuss the issues. He based his campaign largely upon his fourteen years' experience in Congress and upon his position as minority leader: the chief question that Mississippians had to decide was who was "better fitted by training, experience, study and natural ability" to represent the state in the Senate.[11] He agreed with Vardaman that the government should do more to help farmers by expanding rural free delivery of mail and by increasing appropriations for agricultural colleges and experimental stations, but he denounced government ownership of railroads as dangerous and foolish. Socialism could not solve the problem of high freight rates that railroads charged farmers, but strict government regulation of common carriers would. More ridiculous still, Williams asserted, was Vardaman's plan to solve the race problem by changing the Fourteenth Amendment and abolishing the Fifteenth.

[9] John Sharp Williams to N. T. Currie, February 12, 1907, Williams to Robert Bowman, Jr., May 27, 1907, in Williams Papers, Library of Congress.
[10] J. K. Vardaman to LeRoy Percy, May 19, 1905, in Vardaman Letter Book. Yazoo City *Herald,* quoted in Jackson *Evening News,* February 20, 1905.
[11] John Sharp Williams to W. J. Fortinberry, January 11, 1907, Williams to J. F. Gray, January 10, 1907, Williams to J. E. Warnock, February 9, 1907, in Williams Papers, Library of Congress.

Even if the nation were ready for this change, Vardaman could not achieve it through his radical rantings. On the contrary, the governor's extreme denunciation of the amendments reduced the chances of getting rid of them. Williams claimed that he, too, favored repeal and would begin to work for it at the proper time. It was more important, he urged, that the people should realize Vardaman was using racism solely to win votes. Did anyone actually believe Negroes posed a threat to white supremacy? Had not the state constitution of 1890 already voided both of the amendments in Mississippi? [12]

As a solution to the race problem, Williams suggested that white immigrants be attracted to the South. By buying land and becoming prosperous farmers, the immigrants could end the South's economic dependence upon the Negro. To offset the danger of Negro violence, about which Vardaman talked in such an inflammatory fashion, Williams suggested the organization of companies of mounted rural policemen similar to those maintained in some African colonies. The creation of such a constabulary, together with strict enforcement of the vagrancy law, would greatly reduce Negro crime.[13]

While Williams toured North Mississippi, Vardaman began his campaign along the Gulf Coast. Because much of Vardaman's persuasiveness rested upon his ability to excite emotions and admiration among his listeners, he was less likely to do well in direct give-and-take than in one-man oratory. He therefore ignored Williams' challenge to debate.[14] He devoted little attention to his constructive record as governor and largely avoided discussing government ownership of railroads. Without denying that he favored nationalizing railroads, he asserted that the issue had no place in the present campaign, for even Bryan had declared that it would not be included in the Democratic platform of 1908. Williams, he charged, was trying to create a false issue.[15] After skirting the railroad question, he appealed to his rural audiences by

[12] Jackson *Evening News*, April 3, 9, June 7, 1907; Batesville *Weekly Panolian*, April 4, 1907; Biloxi *Daily Herald*, May 29, 1907.

[13] Jackson *Daily Clarion-Ledger*, November 14, 1906.

[14] John Sharp Williams to J. K. Vardaman, November 24, 1906, February 16, 25, March 1, April 2, 1907; Vardaman to Williams, November 26, 1906, February 21, March 1, 1907, in John Sharp Williams Papers, Mississippi Department of Archives and History. Hereinafter cited as Williams Papers, Mississippi Department of Archives.

[15] Jackson *Evening News*, May 14, 1907.

lavishly praising farm life and reminding them that he had spent his boyhood working on a farm. He accused Williams of never having known the rigors of rural poverty. Had he ever gone barefoot as a boy? Had he ever suffered a genuine stone bruise? Did he eat black-eyed peas with a knife? [16]

As in the past, he rode racism, reiterating the necessity of abolishing the Fifteenth Amendment and warning that the foolish policy of educating Negroes only caused the blacks to commit more crimes. He was able to bring off one maneuver implementing his racial views just as the campaign got actively under way. As president of the Board of Trustees of Alcorn Agricultural and Mechanical College, a state Negro school, Vardaman had the board slash the salaries of all the "literary" teachers and make corresponding increases in the salaries of all vocational teachers. This change, the governor argued, would have the salutary effect of discouraging higher education among Negroes and of insuring that the blacks remained agricultural laborers.[17]

As the campaign mounted, it produced changes in old factional lines. The McLaurins chose whom they considered the lesser of two evils and supported Williams.[18] Vardaman's fight with Henry McLaurin over prison reform had removed any possibility of that family's supporting him. Williams accepted the endorsement of his former opponents and thereby helped to crack the solidarity of the anti-McLaurin faction. Some men who had supported Vardaman in 1904 chiefly because of his opposition to McLaurinism now endorsed Williams. LeRoy Percy, for example, warned in 1907 that the governor's radical opposition to Negro education was dangerous and unfair; four years earlier, despite Vardaman's denunciation of Negro education, Percy had had no scruples about endorsing him for governor.[19]

Yet McLaurinism still exerted some influence on Mississippi politics, as the gubernatorial contest revealed. Six candidates entered the

[16] Frederick Palmer, "Williams-Vardaman Campaign," *Collier's: The National Weekly,* XXXIX (July 27, 1907), 11–12.
[17] Jackson *Evening News,* April 9, 1907.
[18] Lexington *Advertiser,* January 11, 1906; Water Valley *North Mississippi Herald,* June 8, 1907.
[19] LeRoy Percy, "A Southern View of Negro Education," *The Outlook,* LXXXVI (August 3, 1907), 730–32.

race for governor: Charles Scott of Bolivar County, Earl Brewer of Coahoma, Jeff Truly of Jefferson, Edmund F. Noel of Holmes, Emmett N. Thomas of Washington and T. W. Sisson of Montgomery. At the time not one of the candidates was closely allied with Vardaman, but he endorsed Scott—a man who was not only one of the largest cotton planters in the entire South but was also a corporation lawyer, railroad promoter, and banker. The two men had little in common politically, for Scott was still a conservative corporation lawyer, while Vardaman had become a proven foe of corporate wealth and a spokesman for the agrarian masses. The reason for this seemingly paradoxical choice by the radical agrarian governor was simple: the two men had long worked together against the McLaurins, and in 1903 Scott had helped Vardaman carry the Delta.[20]

As Vardaman's senatorial campaign progressed, his appeal to the dirt farmer class became stronger than in earlier campaigns. Though Williams did not allow himself to be estranged from the small farmers, knowing it could lead to his defeat, it was Vardaman, not Williams, who was asked time and again to address county chapters of the Farmers' Union.[21] More important, he received the support of other noted agrarian spokesmen. When South Carolina's Senator Ben Tillman, one of the South's most outspoken racists and an advocate of agrarian reform, visited Mississippi in April, 1907, he endorsed Vardaman's stand on repealing the Fifteenth Amendment.[22] Arkansas' Jeff Davis, the "Karl Marx for Hill-Billies," did not enter the contest only because he feared his presence might be considered outside interference and thereby hurt Vardaman's cause. The man who became especially active in the governor's behalf was the Georgia Populist, Tom Watson. Despite their party differences the two men realized by

[20] J. K. Vardaman to Charles Scott, May 4, 1905, in Vardaman Letter Book. In discussing Scott's candidacy Vardaman wrote: ". . . . I do not hesitate to say to you (out of a heart full of gratitude for what you have done for me in the past) that there is no man in Mississippi, who would make a better Governor, and whose election would give me quite as much pleasure." And see Jackson *Evening News,* June 4, 1907.

[21] Brookhaven *Lincoln County Times,* June 4, 1906, August 9, 1906; Batesville *Weekly Panolian,* July 18, 1907; John Sharp Williams to N. T. Curris, June 10, 1907, in Williams Papers, Library of Congress. Some charged that in every speech during the campaign Vardaman tried to "prejudice the country against the town." Brookhaven *Lincoln County Times,* August 8, 1907.

[22] Jackson *Evening News,* April 8, 1907.

1907 that their views on the Negro, the dangers of corporate wealth, and the need for Populist-type economic reforms all combined to put them in "the same school of politics." [23] Through his *Weekly Jeffersonian* Watson actively worked for Vardaman's election and during the closing weeks of the campaign he distributed his writings widely through Mississippi. Typical of his work was an article that appeared on the front page of the *Jeffersonian* a week before the primary.

If the Hon. John Sharp Williams should win out in the fight with Governor Vardaman, the corporations would have just one more doodle-bug in the United States Senate.

Every time that a Railroad lobbyist stopped over the hole and called "Doodle, Doodle, Doodle"—soft and slow—the sand at the little end of the funnel would be seen to stir, and then the little head of J. Sharp would pop up.

Would I dare to say this if the record didn't justify me? Certainly not. If a sense of honor had no restraining power . . . , common purdence would sound its warning against a reckless accusation.

But the official record of John Sharp Williams proves that he belongs to the Wall Street element of the Democratic Party.[24]

Watson's support, which Vardaman welcomed, revealed the governor's intensified appeal to the small-farmer class, and the Georgian probably convinced many former Populists to vote for Vardaman.[25]

As the senatorial campaign approached full intensity in June, an evangelist, George C. Cates, was conducting a revival in Jackson. Each night large crowds flocked to his services and many "sinners" came to the mourner's bench. One evening a crowd of two thousand was startled to see among thirty converts who marched to the front the tall, athletic figure of Governor Vardaman. Excitement swept through the tent as Vardaman acknowledged his sins and announced that he "surrendered everything to the service of Christ." Certainly

[23] Jeff Davis to D. G. Haley, July 10, 1907, in Vardaman Papers; J. K. Vardaman to Thomas E. Watson, January 14, 1907, in Thomas E. Watson Papers, Southern Historical Collection.

[24] Watson's *Weekly Jeffersonian,* July 25, 1907, in Williams Papers, Mississippi Department of Archives.

[25] R. E. Thompson to T. E. Watson, June 28, July 27, August 2, September 14, 1907, A. L. Monroe to Watson, July 9, 1907, Gerrard Harris to Gordon Nye, July 19, 1907, in Thomas E. Watson Papers.

the governor's conversion must have marked a high point in the Reverend Cates's career! And Vardaman's "getting religion" won him much favorable comment in the state press.[26]

Williams continued to challenge Vardaman to meet him in debate, and Vardaman continued to refuse, saying that he felt bound to address as many people as possible and had not the time to listen to his opponent.[27] Finally, by resort to an unauthorized announcement that kindled popular interest too strong for Vardaman to ignore, the Meridian, Mississippi, Board of Trade managed to schedule for the Fourth of July a joint debate between the senatorial candidates.[28] On the day before the debate, trains from throughout the state brought many excited spectators to Meridian. Because every room was quickly taken, some spent the night in hotel lobbies. Even though it was blisteringly hot on the Fourth, many families rode for miles in open carriages and wagons to see the confrontation, and by nine o'clock crowds were streaming into the park grounds where the debate would be held. A small speaker's stand and a few rows of rough board benches had been erected in a grove for the event. Early arrivals quickly filled the benches and left most of the audience to sit on the ground. While Williams' followers mingled throughout the crowd, a large body of Vardaman supporters, accompanied by a band, marched into the park, wearing badges and shouting to prepare the way for their candidate.[29]

Williams rose to speak at ten o'clock. He tried first to embarrass his opponent by offering to cancel all his speaking engagements if Vardaman would but consent to debate him every day during the remainder of the campaign. Williams then asked the audience to consider whether he or Vardaman was better qualified to be United States Senator. Would it not be sensible, he asked, to elect the man who had served for fourteen years in the Congress and had proven his

[26] Jackson *Evening News,* June 25, 1907; Vicksburg *Herald,* June 26, 1907. Later it was reported that Vardaman had not actually joined the penitents at the revival: he had only knelt and prayed with a number of local ministers. Jackson *Evening News,* July 2, 1907.

[27] Jackson *Evening News,* June 13, 1907; Jackson *Daily Clarion-Ledger,* May 29, 1907; Vicksburg *Herald,* June 27, 1907.

[28] Jackson *Evening News,* July 2, 1907. On the day of the debate Vardaman asked to have the privilege of speaking first, explaining that he did not want a rejoinder. Some speculated that he wanted to leave immediately after delivering his speech.

[29] Jackson *Evening News,* July 4, 1907; Vicksburg *Herald,* July 14, 1907.

ability by becoming Democratic leader of the House of Representatives?

Williams devoted most attention to attacking Vardaman's racist agitation, especially his demand concerning the Fourteenth and Fifteenth amendments. Holding out a pencil and a copy of the Constitution, he challenged Vardaman to come forward and strike out those sections of the Fourteenth Amendment which he believed should be removed. The country was not ready for such a change, Williams argued, and it could never be accomplished by the likes of Vardaman. The constitution of 1890 had eliminated the Negro's participation in Mississippi politics, and there was no danger that the situation would change. The most ominous aspect of the race problem, Williams warned, was the way demagogues like Vardaman used it to enhance their political careers. Vardaman ought instead to consider the major problems confronting the nation, such as government ownership of railroads, which Williams deplored and which he challenged his opponent to discuss. If Vardaman became a senator he would accomplish nothing, Williams concluded, for he would spend all his time futilely urging the repeal of the Fifteenth Amendment. For the past three years as governor why had he failed to get the Mississippi legislature to initiate the work of repealing the Reconstruction amendment? [30]

When Vardaman's turn came his followers cheered as he rose to speak. As the applause lasted several minutes, Vardaman appealed for quiet, but the slight smile on his lips indicated that he enjoyed the cheering and wanted it to continue. Dressed in an immaculate white Prince Albert suit and with his long black hair and dark complexion, he probably looked to his opponents like an overdressed medicine show man. Having overworked his voice during the grueling canvass, he spoke in deep, gravelly tones and as he began, everyone strained to hear him. In his opening remarks he felt out his audience, talking about the importance of popular elections, expressing his faith in the voters, and describing how rural simplicity and honesty prevailed in Mississippi. "I thank God that we have not great cities. I thank God that we have very few multi-millionaires; I thank God we

[30] Vicksburg *Herald,* July 6, 1907; Jackson *Daily Clarion-Ledger,* July 14, 1907; Natchez *Daily Democrat,* July 5, 1907.

have not paupers. . . . In my state next to the virtue of our women the most sacred thing is the ballot."

To show that he did not, as Williams claimed, avoid national issues, he launched into a discussion of the need for lowering the tariff and followed up by attacking the imperialist policies of the Roosevelt administration. Most serious of the dangers posed by imperialism was that of infusing more inferior races into American society. President Roosevelt directly had encouraged this foolish policy, the most recent instance being his attempt to force white Californians to accept Japanese children in their schools. For Mississippians the lesson was obvious: "The Little wild man in the White House sent a man to California to say that the action the state had taken in the matter was in violation of the constitution of the United States. Now, the little Jap boys and girls have a right to sit next to our children in San Francisco and the president thinks they have. That same executive can say that your children shall sit next to the little black, unwashed Mississippi 'nigger' boys and girls."

As to government ownership of railroads, it was misleading for Williams to accuse him of supporting that. The country was not ready for such a step, because it would take time to educate and prepare the people for public ownership of transportation facilities. Even William Jennings Bryan had said it was not a live issue. Williams men immediately began to boo and hiss, demanding to know when and where Bryan had made any such statement. Vardaman's reply was virtually unimpeachable: Bryan had told him privately during a recent visit to Jackson.[31]

Turning away from national issues, Vardaman delighted his listeners by attacking advocates of Negro equality. After first arousing the audience's sympathy by describing the "ante-bellum mammy," he then went on into grave warnings of the ever-present danger of the Negro "fiend."

My friends, the mounted constable gets on his horse and starts out for his ride. He meets a young buck negro. He accosts him. Where are you going, Buck? Going to town. Where have you been? Been out here working at a saw mill. Buck passes down the street. He spies a

[31] Vicksburg *Herald,* July 6, 1907.

little cottage; he enters that cottage; he finds a mother and daughter there, the husband and brother out in the field at work. The beast goes in and commits that crime which forever blasts the peace, the purity, and the happiness of that home. The constable comes along. He may possibly arrest him and visit upon him punishment. But he has not brought back the love and light and purity of that home.

Vardaman closed by describing the ordeal of a white girl who had been ravished by a Negro.

This little girl languished for some time upon a sick bed; she got able to go into court; we had arrested a man to whom the hand of guilt pointed. I never shall forget that morning when the little girl came into the courtroom; the leading negroes about Jackson had hired counsel, or had gotten counsel somewhere. . . . This little girl came into court that morning, and here is the picture burned upon my heart: A little woman, with her eyes red with weeping. She speaks, her voice is broken. From eyes like hers and tones like hers, a man may learn much. She tells the story of the assault, tells it amid the insults from a shyster lawyer privileged through his employment to ask what he shall please; tells it from start to finish, and is not spared a word, until at last a pitiful, living corpse, she falls back into fearful senselessness. And facing her is a monster, composed, whispering at times into the attorney's ears, suggesting as to questions to be asked, and though the fear of death may be there, unable quite to hide a grin of delight.[32]

By the time Vardaman stopped speaking, sweat ringed his coat. He had become so hoarse that those on the fringe of the crowd could barely hear him. Williams then made a short rejoinder, again attacking his opponent for advocating abolition of the Fifteenth Amendment and for supporting government ownership of railroads. Vowing that the next day he would go to the hospital and have his left arm amputated if it would insure the repeal of the Fifteenth Amendment, he warned that Vardaman's agitation would only arouse the conscience of the North and result in the race question being settled by the "Yankees." If demagogues like Vardaman would leave the problem alone, it would ultimately be solved by whites' forcing black tenants off farms and into cities where the Negro death rate was steadily increasing. "I would not deceive you on this race question," Williams concluded,

[32] Jackson *Daily Clarion-Ledger,* July 21, 1907.

"for a United States senatorship or the presidency of the United States."[33]

Vardaman defended himself by arguing that his position on the Fifteenth Amendment would awaken the entire nation to the dangers confronting the South. After several interruptions by Williams' followers, he ended by citing the achievements of his administration as governor. When the debate ended, after four and a half hours, the crowd of more than five thousand broke into loud applause. Vardaman's partisans lifted him bodily from the platform and carried him on their shoulders through the park to a waiting carriage. Although both sides claimed victory in the debate, Vardaman's supporters were more numerous and more vocal.[34]

The Meridian encounter awakened Williams to Vardaman's strength and spurred him to more strenuous campaigning during the remainder of the contest. Vardaman and Williams followers organized clubs throughout the state, both groups staged frequent demonstrations in behalf of their candidates and distributed so much campaign literature that postal clerks in Jackson frequently had to work overtime.[35] Rumors were circulated against Williams alleging that he represented the commercial and financial interests of the state, that he was a drunkard, and that Negroes were supporting his candidacy.[36] The Williams forces retaliated with counter rumors charging that Vardaman had the backing not only of Tom Watson but also of Negroes, who knew that his radical ravings would never lead to the abolition of the Fifteenth Amendment.[37] Despite these rumors and the intensity of the contest, the campaign did not degenerate into one of personal vengeance and viciousness. A week before the end both sides agreed not to distribute new campaign literature; leaders in the Vardaman camp denounced the rumor that Williams had been drunk during the can-

[33] Jackson *Evening News,* July 4, 1907.
[34] Vicksburg *Herald,* July 6, 1907; Jackson *Daily Clarion-Ledger,* July 6, 11, 1907; Water Valley *North Mississippi Herald,* July 13, 1907; Brookhaven *Lincoln County Times,* July 11, 1907.
[35] Jackson *Daily Clarion-Ledger,* July 13, 17, 18, 24, 1907.
[36] *Ibid.,* July 21, 30, 1907; John Sharp Williams to Hunter Sharp Walker, June 10, 1907, W. L. Pryor to Williams, September 4, 1907, in Williams Papers, Mississippi Department of Archives.
[37] Jackson *Daily Clarion-Ledger,* July 26, 1907; Jackson *Evening News,* July 6, 15, 26, 1907.

vass, and Williams men quashed certain accusations against the governor.[38]

On the day before the primary both candidates arrived in Jackson aboard a train from southern Mississippi. The local Vardaman club, accompanied by a band from Brookhaven, paraded down one side of Capital Street, while at the same time a Williams parade started down the other side of the street. That night both men addressed large gatherings.[39]

In the early returns of the next day's voting, Williams took a commanding lead over Vardaman. Pro-Williams newspapers, though receding from earlier boasts of victory by 30,000 votes, were still able to predict that Williams would win by a margin of 10,000 to 20,000. The Jackson *Evening News* was full of glee:

> South Carolina has her Tillman, Arkansas her Jeff Davis, Tennessee her Bob Taylor, but Mississippi has thrown her Vardaman in the political discard.
>
> Fellow Mississippians, the News greets you and congratulates you on rising to an opportunity and electing to the highest office within the gift of the people of Mississippi a man who has made the name of Mississippi famous; a man who stands for the best traditions of the south, the democratic party and the white man.[40]

As returns from the state's rural districts mounted, however, Williams' supporters became alarmed. Hour after hour Vardaman cut his opponent's lead until many believed the governor would win. Once, while the contest was still in doubt, Vardaman even delivered a victory address to several thousand supporters who had gathered in front of the governor's mansion. So close was the election that Vardaman refused to admit defeat until the state Democratic executive committee, having officially canvassed the returns, announced that out of a total of 118,344 votes cast Williams had a majority of 648. Despite charges of corruption in some counties, Vardaman did not contest the primary.[41]

---

38 Vicksburg *Herald,* July 27, 1907.
39 Jackson *Daily Clarion-Ledger,* August 1, 1907.
40 Jackson *Evening News,* August 3, 1907.
41 Jackson *Daily Clarion-Ledger,* August 6, 9, 1907; Vicksburg *Herald,* August 9, 1907.

The vote in this spectacularly close election fell along sectional lines. Four years earlier Vardaman had carried all of the southeast and most of the Delta, those sections in which Negroes greatly outnumbered whites and in which most of the state's large plantations were centered. In 1907 he lost every county in those sections. In addition, Williams swept that area stretching across central Mississippi that had formerly made up his congressional districts, and he carried the entire Gulf Coast and a number of counties in the pine woods section of South Mississippi. Vardaman's strength centered entirely in the hill section of the northeast and in a block of counties in south-central Mississippi. Typical Vardaman counties were those where white small farmers predominated, the Negro population was relatively low, and the Populists had been strong in the 1890's. That Williams' margin of victory was so narrow, despite his carrying ten counties more than did his opponent, graphically illustrated that by 1907 Vardaman's strength had shifted to the white counties.

A number of developments explained the sectional shifts in Vardaman's strength. Four years earlier he had enjoyed the backing of the anti-McLaurin forces, which explained why Williams had then campaigned for him and why he had done well in the Delta where the opponents of McLaurin were strong. By 1907 the old alliances had shifted, for then the McLaurins transferred their support to a former opponent, Williams. Vardaman had won the first statewide primary by appealing to the rural whites and his three years in office had not weakened that appeal. In fact, by vetoing bills favoring railroad and lumbering interests and by ending convict leasing he had strengthened his hold on the small-farmer class. In his race for the Senate he had directed his campaign even more to rural whites, as was so clearly revealed by the help which he received from Tom Watson.

The results of the hard-fought contest left both candidates dissatisfied. Williams actually hurt his popularity by refusing to attend a victory rally; charging that the old Populists had almost defeated him, he announced that the election had been too close to warrant celebrations. In contrast, Vardaman issued a statement accepting defeat gracefully and thanking his many followers. Actually he was more angered than Williams by the election, and he privately attributed his defeat to the work of corporations and to the large campaign fund that he alleged had been used against him. He was especially incensed by Williams' complaint that the election had been too close: "He is the vainest and most egotistical little ass in public life," he wrote Tom Watson, "and why he expected more than he got I cannot understand unless he is blinded by an exaggerated idea of his own importance." [42]

Despite his defeat, Vardaman believed his political strength had not been impaired, and he intended to enter the next senatorial primary in 1911. He began preparing for that comeback during the runoff primary for governor in 1907 between Edmund Noel and Earl Brewer. Vardaman's first choice for his successor, Charles Scott, had attempted a spectacular campaign by wearing a Confederate uniform and riding horseback from the Tennessee line to the Gulf of Mexico, giving speeches along the way. Scott had fizzled as a campaigner, however, and ran third in the field of six.[43] Vardaman then supposedly sent aides to Brewer and Noel asking if either intended to run for the Senate in 1911; because Noel denied having any senatorial ambitions, Vardaman supported him and in the second primary Noel won.[44] Both Noel and Brewer had run on platforms containing many of the reforms that Vardaman had advocated as governor. Even more revealing of the influence Vardaman exerted on Mississippi politics was that all gubernatorial candidates favored curtailing Negro education.

In the five months following his senatorial defeat Vardaman remained active in performing his official duties, and early in 1908 he delivered his final address to the state legislature. More than any single document, it best expressed the objectives he had pursued as governor and the goals for which he believed future administrations should strive.

Mississippi still needed many reforms which he had advocated earlier: an elective judiciary, higher salaries to insure the services of able judges, a child labor law, greater road construction, state bank exam-

---

[42] J. K. Vardaman to T. E. Watson, August 15, 1907, in Thomas E. Watson Papers.

[43] R. B. McKinney to John C. Burrus, August 13, 1907, in John C. Burrus Papers; "Charles Scott," *The National Cyclopaedia of American Biography* (New York, 1891—), XVII, 231.

[44] Kirwan, *Revolt of the Rednecks,* 187; Hamilton, "Mississippi Politics in the Progressive Era," 134–35.

iners, and limitation of the maximum interest rate on borrowed money to 8 percent. His four years in office had convinced him that other programs were also needed, the most important being stricter regulation of railroads, greater protection for railroad employees, a reformatory for delinquent children, rural high schools, an institute for feeble-minded children, a home for the aged, and statewide prohibition. He hoped the legislature would continue to pump money into the state's schools, hospitals, and institutions for the deaf and blind; only the assurance of increased appropriations could insure continued progress. With pride he pointed to the achievements of his administration, especially in the area of penitentiary reform. Still more was needed. The prison system should be further remodeled by adopting more programs to rehabilitate prisoners, so that, hopefully, they might become useful citizens after serving their terms. Although the last remnants of convict leasing had been abolished in the state penitentiary, county convict farms still leased prisoners and that too should be ended. Finally, he called attention to the growing population of South Mississippi and recommended that that section be given greater representation in the state legislature.

Had Vardaman confined himself to outlining constructive reforms he could easily have taken his place among the most progressive governors of his time. But as in the past, he mixed progressivism with racism. The Negro, he warned, belonged to "a race inherently unmoral, ignorant and superstitious, with a congenital tendency to crime, incapable unalterably of understanding the meaning of free government, devoid of those qualities of mind and soul necessary to self-control." The only way to deal with blacks, he explained, was to keep them rigidly segregated and confined to the lowest social class. Mississippi could immediately meet the race problem by curtailing Negro education, imposing the death penalty on black rapists, strictly enforcing the vagrancy law, maintaining a strong state militia, and passing more Jim Crow laws. The state could also begin a movement to abolish the Fourteenth and Fifteenth amendments. Vardaman even urged the legislature to push for a national constitutional convention. In addition to repealing the Reconstruction amendments, he believed, there were other issues that could rally northern support for overhauling the

Constitution, the most important being the popular election of United States senators, woman suffrage, an income tax, popular elections of the President, and reform of the federal judiciary.[45]

Soon after delivering his final message Vardaman left office. Many state editors, relieved that his term had ended, admitted that he had been a better governor than they had expected.[46] His administration had not encouraged racial lawlessness as some had feared during the campaign of 1903. In fact, he had personally intervened to stop lynchings and had led the fight to stamp out Whitecap terrorism.

Despite his work to suppress racial violence, Vardaman had remained a determined racist who had consistently strived further to suppress black people. His advocacy of the Jim Crow law and the vagrancy law, along with his destruction of the Holly Springs State Normal School, all represented more setbacks for blacks. Then by constantly appealing to racism through speeches and other public statements he strengthened Negrophobia. Certainly his administration represented a low point for Mississippi Negroes. However shamefully he appealed to racism, no Mississippi whites challenged his basic views on the Negro. All agreed that blacks should remain menials. At the Meridian debates John Sharp Williams, who many well-to-do southern whites held as an ideal congressman, had even advocated the gradual extermination of blacks! It is not surprising, therefore, that Vardaman's racist agitation caused little disturbance among white Mississippians. Because he maintained law and order, few complained about his constant harping on race problems.

Aside from encouraging racism, he had proved to be a strong and able governor. Corruption did not mar his administration and he had not abused his patronage powers. Although the dismissal of Chancellor Fulton disturbed many, Vardaman believed Fulton was unable to cope with the festering fraternity problem and therefore worked for a change in the school's administration. Throughout his term he advocated a constructive legislative program and was able to obtain reforms that agrarian movements had long advocated. A uniform text-

[45] *Biennial Message of Governor James K. Vardaman to the Legislature of Mississippi, January 8, 1908* (n.p., n.d.), *passim.* Copy in Mississippi Department of Archives and History.

[46] Jackson *Daily Clarion-Ledger,* January 22, 1908; Vicksburg *Herald,* February 19, 1908; Baker, "The Negro in Politics," 172–73.

book law, increased appropriations for common schools, a new state code, improvements in the state's institutions for the deaf and the insane, the beginning of a tuberculosis sanatorium, stringent regulation of railroads and lumber companies, the creation of a commissioner of agriculture, the establishment of two new agricultural experimental stations, the abolition of convict leasing, and the reorganization of the penitentiary system all constituted the major achievements of his administration. He had been a progressive governor who had given impetus to reform in his state. By the time he left office the movement for reform had gained momentum, and in 1908 the legislature enacted a number of reforms recommended by the outgoing governor.

Despite his achievements and popularity, Vardaman lost to John Sharp Williams in a tight race for the Senate. At the time only a man of Williams' strength could have beaten him. Even in defeat Vardaman made an impressive showing, for Williams—whose national reputation gave him a distinct preeminence among Mississippi politicians— beat him by fewer than a thousand votes. The election marked a significant change in the state's politics, for it demonstrated that Vardaman's strength now rested almost exclusively with the rural whites of northeastern and southern Mississippi. In him they had found a champion who appealed to their needs and their prejudices. Despite defeat in 1907, victory could come to them again under Vardaman.

CHAPTER VIII

THE "SECRET CAUCUS"

DURING THE LAST months of his administration, Vardaman decided not to return to Greenwood, but to make his home in Jackson. It is not surprising that a defeated, yet still ambitious, politician should seek to stay in public view. Thus it was that on February 1, 1908, the state's capital saw the opening of Vardaman's weekly newspaper, *The Issue*.[1] Designed to expound views and causes in which he believed and consisting of his own editorials and of articles by state and national figures, *The Issue* did not resemble his Greenwood newspapers, for it presented no systematic coverage of state and local news. *The Issue* chiefly served his political ambitions by enabling him to remain before the people, and in future campaigns it attempted to rally support for him. As the forty-seven-year-old Vardaman was frequently away from Jackson lecturing and politicking, assistants performed much of the editorial work, and for that reason *The Issue* failed to develop the color and personality that had characterized the *Enterprise* and the *Commonwealth*.

As did Robert La Follette in his *Weekly Magazine* and William Jennings Bryan in his *Commoner,* Vardaman devoted much of his paper to advocating progressive causes. He praised the work of the Republican insurgents in Congress, especially the revolt led by George W. Norris against the entrenched powers of House Speaker Joseph G. Cannon.[2] Fearing that big business threatened the foundations of American life, he advocated plans for regulating corporations and wealthy men who might abuse the public welfare. Like some other

---

[1] Vicksburg *Herald,* August 31, 1907, January 18, 19, February 7, 1908; *The Issue,* February 1, August 22, 1908, July 24, 1909, August 26, 1910, March 10, 1911.

[2] *The Issue,* March 7, May 23, June 12, July 11, 1908, June 19, July 17, 1909, March 19, 26, 1910.

politician-editors he frequently oversimplified what caused economic and social problems in his age: he usually pictured corporations and Wall Street bankers as deliberately working to exploit the public, and industrial and financial leaders such as John D. Rockefeller, Andrew Carnegie, and J. P. Morgan provided ready targets for his wrath.[3] In spite of his sometime oversimplification of complex problems, he did have a genuine desire to alleviate social ills, as he illustrated in supporting such reforms as a graduated income tax, a national child labor law, and a federal program of old-age pensions.[4] Clearly illustrating the progressive, reform objectives of his new publication was an offer Vardaman made his readers beginning in December, 1909: two dollars could buy a year's subscription to both *The Issue* and La Follette's *Weekly Magazine*.[5]

He wanted his paper, like La Follette's, to become widely read by progressives throughout the nation, but it never was. In part, the reason for that failure may have been because Vardaman combined his appeals for economic and social reform with rabble-rousing racist agitation. *The Issue* "was born of the desire of its editor to promote a movement which will ultimately result in making this republic a white man's government." [6] In an age when numerous racist publications appeared, *The Issue* may well have been the most persistent and outspoken foe of Negro equality in the United States. Every week it contained such articles as "Sexual Crimes Among Southern Negroes Scientifically Considered," "Cannibalism in Hayti," and "The Negro a Different Kind of Flesh." Although southerners like Thomas Dixon wrote many of the racist articles, a substantial number came from physicians and academicians in leading northern universities.[7]

Vardaman himself frequently wrote about the race problem, reiterating themes he had developed over the past twenty years. He continued to harp upon the danger of Negroes attacking whites, especially the threat of black men raping white women. More and more he

[3] *Ibid.*, February 1, 22, 29, March 14, 1908, March 6, October 16, 30, November 6, 13, 1909, May 14, 1910, March 3, April 21, 1911.
[4] *Ibid.*, January 23, April 24, 1909, March 19, 26, September 30, 1910, March 3, 1911.
[5] *Ibid.*, December 4, 1909, March 26, 1910.
[6] *Ibid.*, September 25, 1909.
[7] *Ibid., passim.*

strove to foster a growing fear that southern white women faced ever present danger at the hands of Negro rapists.

The white women of the South are in a state of siege—The cloud of this black peril hovers about them as a deadly vapor.

Their very hearts are perturbed and they live in constant fear and painful apprehension.

And what is said of the women of the South may be truthfully said of the women in certain sections of the North. It is becoming more so in the latter section as the years roll by.

The pestilence is spreading.[8]

As he had since the early 1890's, Vardaman urged that white men break the necks of Negro rapists to defend southern womanhood. For their own self-protection, he believed, white women should learn to shoot.[9]

In addition to expounding his racial views in *The Issue,* Vardaman spread them to many parts of the nation by giving public lectures. Shortly after leaving office he signed a contract for ten thousand dollars to give Chautauqua lectures during part of the next year. Accordingly, in the spring of 1908 he began traveling through parts of the South and Southwest delivering again and again a single lecture, *The Impending Crisis.*[10] The greatest danger threatening America, the ex-governor warned his audiences, was the desire of Negroes to achieve social and political rights equal to those of the whites. For Negroes to strive for such an objective was foolish, because by nature they were inferior to the whites. To substantiate his assertion Vardaman described in detail a belief widely held at the time: white and black children were equal in mental ability until the age of puberty, at which time the white child continued to grow intellectually, but all progress for the Negro child ceased. Nature had also short-changed the Negro by failing to endow him with a sense of right and wrong. Having described the Negro as being cursed with the mind of a twelve-year-old and as being

    [8] *Ibid.,* November 27, 1909.
    [9] *Ibid.,* August 22, September 5, November 14, 28, 1908, February 13, 20, 1909, September 16, 1910.
    [10] Vicksburg *Herald,* January 31, 1908; *The Issue,* December 12, 1908, April 17, May 29, July 24, 1909, October 27, 1911; Yazoo City *Yazoo Sentinel,* July 29, October 7, 1909; J. K. Vardaman to Adam Reeler, September 4, 1907, in Vardaman Letter Book.

amoral, Vardaman warned that should Negroes obtain social and political equality in the United States, it would result in marriage between
whites and blacks. Intermingling of the races, in turn, would cause the
white race to deteriorate and then all intellectual, social, and economic
progress in America would end. That was "The Impending Crisis!"
There was only one way to avoid it and that was to repeal the Fourteenth and Fifteenth amendments. Vardaman concluded: "Repeal the
fourteenth and fifteenth amendments to our constitution and you shut
in the face of the negro the door to political equality. Shut the door of
political equality, and you close the door of social equality in the face of
the black man; shut the door of social equality and you smother in his
native savage breast the fury of his passion, which is but the blind crav-
ing of his soul to be equal of the white man, and the partner of the
white man. Ambition in the negro is concreted in lust." [11]

From 1908 to 1916, between political campaigns and sessions of
Congress, Vardaman took to the lecture circuit and described "The
Impending Crisis" to audiences in the South, Southwest, Midwest, and
the Plains. Lecturing became his chief means of making a living, for
The Issue never proved to be a moneymaking enterprise. Through
constant practice he developed expressions, gestures, and a sense of
timing, all designed to capture the attention of his listeners. That he
continued to be booked for engagements year after year indicates that
he became a popular lecturer. Americans living in that age widely believed the racist views of writers like Charles Carroll and Thomas Dixon and Vardaman's message of impending danger, combined with his
striking appearance and his spellbinding ability, proved to be entertaining and sobering.

Vardaman continued to follow closely the political developments in
Mississippi after leaving the governorship. He was especially interested
in the policies pursued by his successor, Edmund Noel. While having
served in both the Mississippi house and senate, Noel had become an
advocate of progressive legislation and held the distinction of having
introduced the primary election law of 1902. It will be recalled that
Vardaman had defeated him for governor in the first application of that
primary law, but Noel had run again in 1907 and won. The programs

[11] Yazoo City *Yazoo Sentinel,* May 5, 1910; Magnolia *Gazette,* August 28,
1915; Webster City (Iowa) *Daily Tribune,* July 21, 1915.

supported by the new governor closely resembled those of Vardaman. In his inaugural address Noel, like his predecessor, advocated a child labor law, an elective judiciary, rural high schools, stronger railroad regulation, and a constitutional convention to reapportion the state legislature in accord with the expanding population of southern Mississippi.[12] Although Noel and Vardaman advocated many of the same reforms, the two men differed in personality and public appeal. A small, bald man, Noel lacked the colorful and dynamic personality that enabled Vardaman to develop a devoted following. His opponents dubbed him "Granny Noel." [13]

In response to the appeals of Vardaman and Noel, the legislature of 1908 established an elective judiciary, increased the powers of the state railroad commission, outlawed the blacklisting of labor, abolished convict leasing by counties, and passed a child labor act, state antitrust laws, and a workman's compensation act.[14] Through *The Issue,* Vardaman commended the legislature for its work. He especially praised his old friend Senator John Hebron, to whom he attributed credit for a law abolishing convict leasing in the counties.[15] The failure to call a constitutional convention to give South Mississippi fairer apportionment disappointed Vardaman, but he did praise the unsuccessful attempt to provide for such a convention by a young, first-term senator, Theodore Gilmore Bilbo. "The people of south Mississippi," Vardaman noted, "have an able champion in the person of Senator Bilbo of Pearl River County." [16]

At the time Noel became governor, he and Vardaman appeared to be on friendly terms, but that facade of cordiality quickly disappeared. By the fall of 1908 they became locked in a spiteful controversy over the collection of a fund with which to purchase a silver service for the newly constructed battleship, the U.S.S. *Mississippi.* While still governor, Vardaman had collected $1,704.80 for the silver service. Then in 1908 the legislature appointed him, Noel, and State Archivist Dunbar Rowland to a committee to collect additional funds. When the commit-

[12] *House Journal, 1908,* 214–48.
[13] Yazoo City *Yazoo Sentinel,* July 15, 1909.
[14] Charles Granville Hamilton, "The Turning Point: The Legislative Session of 1908," *Journal of Mississippi History,* XVI (1964), 93–111.
[15] *The Issue,* February 1, 22, 29, March 21, 1908.
[16] *Ibid.,* February 29, 1908.

tee met to consider its task, Vardaman refused to turn over the money he had previously collected. He arrogantly charged that Noel and Rowland were his political enemies and that he could no longer trust them. His high-handed behavior probably stemmed from a personality clash with Noel and Rowland; furthermore, he was trying to win attention by presenting himself as a defender of the public interest. For several months Vardaman refused to cooperate with his fellow committeemen, and many state newspapers denounced his petty behavior. Perhaps the unfavorable publicity caused him to relent early in 1909 and relinquish the money to the committee.[17] He had failed, however, to keep a list of those who had made contributions; in future political campaigns some would strongly criticize his carelessness in record keeping and charge that he had stolen from the fund. Of more immediate importance, the silver service controversy openly alienated Vardaman and Noel and in so doing deeply affected their future careers. Soon Noel would have at his disposal the power to select a United States senator for Mississippi, and he would use that power against Vardaman.

The question of selecting a senator confronted Noel on December 22, 1909, when Senator Anselm McLaurin suddenly died with more than three years of his current term remaining. At that time it was widely known in Mississippi that in the next senatorial primary, scheduled for 1911, Vardaman planned to run against McLaurin. Even during the summer of 1909, with the election two years away, the opponents had begun sparring.[18] McLaurin's death ended the promise of what some had believed would be a close fight between two of the state's most popular politicians. The immediate question now confronting Vardaman, as well as other political hopefuls, was how would a successor be chosen? The authority to chose rested with Governor Noel. While Vardaman and his friends demanded an early primary election

[17] Eunice Miller Lockwood to James K. Vardaman, November 9, 1908, Vardaman to Lockwood, November 10, 1908, January 23, 1909, T. P. Scott to Vardaman, February 10, 1909; E. F. Noel to Lockwood, February 17, 1909, Vardaman to Noel, March 8, 1909, J. B. Stirling to Mississippi Battleship Commission, February 6, 1909, in Battleship *Mississippi* Silver Service Records, Mississippi Department of Archives and History.

[18] Yazoo City *Yazoo Sentinel,* July 22, August 26, September 30, October 21, 28, November 11, December 16, 1909; Newton *Record,* December 23, 1909; Macon *Beacon,* November 26, 1909; *The Issue,* December 18, 1909.

as the fairest means of filling the vacancy, Noel met the problem in a fashion pleasing to anti-Vardaman men. The governor appointed Colonel James Gordon, a seventy-six-year-old Confederate veteran, to replace McLaurin until the state legislature could meet and choose a successor.[19] As the legislature would assemble soon at its regular session in January, 1910, many hoped a new senator would be elected quickly and quietly.

To the surprise of no one, Vardaman immediately announced that he would be a candidate for McLaurin's unexpired term. The prospect of getting to the Senate three years earlier than he had expected was indeed a pleasing one. Not only would he be able to avoid a long, costly primary fight against an incumbent, but he would have the added pleasure of actually taking his seat in the Senate sooner than his former opponent John Sharp Williams, whose term did not begin until March, 1911. Confident of victory, Vardaman asserted that any man familiar with Mississippi politics knew he was the choice of a majority of the white voters. He strongly denounced those who asserted that he was an irresponsible radical, pointing out that as governor he had disproved that charge. As a senator, he promised, he would again disprove it.[20] Despite his public display of confidence, he was concerned over a "disposition on the part of certain gentlemen to form any sort of combination, make any character of deal to defeat Vardaman." He expected strong, well-organized opposition in his fight for the Senate, but he hoped to overcome it.[21]

He had sound reasons to fear opposition to his candidacy, for the news of McLaurin's death set many ambitious politicians to work organizing a coalition against him. Exactly who forged a coherent opposition and exactly how they accomplished it is unknown, but between the time of McLaurin's death and the meeting of the state legislature the feat was achieved. The plan to defeat Vardaman rested on a number of requirements. First, as many candidates as possible—each of whom could command some legislative votes—must enter the contest and thereby prevent his nomination on the first ballot. Then the oppo-

[19] Vicksburg *Herald,* December 28, 1909; Newton *Record,* December 30, 1909.
[20] Newton *Record,* December 30, 1909.
[21] James K. Vardaman to J. C. Burrus, December 27, 1909, in John C. Burrus Papers.

sition candidates had to agree not to drop out of the race except with the stipulation that their votes would not go to Vardaman. Finally, the opposition had to secure a secret ballot in the legislature's nominating caucus and thereby protect lawmakers whose constituents might not have approved of their voting against Vardaman. How many legislators were party to the combination is unknown, but it was evident that an organized opposition existed. A "steering committee," consisting of the anti-Vardaman candidates and the legislators who served as their floor leaders in the caucus, met frequently to plot strategy and assess their coalition's strength.[22] Thus it was that by the time the legislature assembled in 1910, the requirements for Vardaman's defeat had been met, for "a careful poll made by men who are intimately acquainted with the legislative personnel and the political affiliations of each and every member" revealed that a majority of lawmakers "cannot be induced to vote for ex Gov[ernor] Vardaman under any circumstances." [23]

Of the six candidates who entered the race against Vardaman, LeRoy Percy, wealthy lawyer and planter from the Delta town of Greenville, proved to be the strongest. Percy served as an attorney for some of the major railroads and utilities operating in Mississippi—an unpopular position in an age when many believed such corporations guilty of

[22] House of Representatives, *Inquiry Into the Charge of Bribery in the Recent Senatorial Contest* (Jackson, 1910), 158–59, 193–94, 299–313, 346–53, 394–96. The most obvious evidence that there was an organized opposition to Vardaman was the actual manuevering of the legislative caucus in attempting to elect a senator. From the beginning of the caucus the legislative majority made every effort to defeat Vardaman, as is discussed in the text below. Some members openly admitted that they were part of an organized opposition that was determined to defeat Vardaman. Senator W. D. Anderson, for example, proudly announced that he had been part of a "common cause" against Vardaman. John Sharp Williams, who tried to persuade every legislator he knew not to vote for Vardaman, believed that the men who had stood against Vardaman should be proud of their actions and admit to them. Those candidates and their floor leaders who comprised the anti-Vardaman "steering committee" were Charlton H. Alexander and Senator James McDowell, LeRoy Percy, and Representative Van Buren Boddie, Adam Byrd and Senator George H. Banks, Frank A. Critz and Senator Stacy Hibbler, and John Curtis Kyle and Senator Hugh Kirby Mahon. For Anderson's statement see Newton *Record*, January 27, 1910. For Williams' views, see John Sharp Williams to G. H. Alford, December 29, 1909, Williams to William Tucker, March 26, 1910, Williams to LeRoy Percy, September 1, 1910, Williams to B. F. Cameron, September 12, 1910, in Williams Papers, Mississippi Department of Archives.

[23] Macon *Beacon*, January 7, 1910.

paying low wages, charging unfair prices, and giving careless service. He had formerly been allied with Vardaman against the McLaurins and in 1903 had praised Vardaman as a champion of the Delta and as the man whom he endorsed for governor.[24] Once in office, however, Vardaman had angered Percy by refusing to reappoint Dr. J. T. Atterbury to the Mississippi board of levee commissioners, and during the senatorial race of 1907 Percy had sharply criticized Vardaman's plan for curtailing Negro education.[25] Percy had long been a power in Delta politics, but he had never held elective office. He was, in fact, devoid of those qualities essential to a successful politician, for by nature he was cold and shy. "Father couldn't get chummy with people," his son recalled, "and, though his friends worshipped him and would have died for him, they did not call him LeRoy." [26] Until he entered the senatorial contest few voters outside the Delta had ever heard of him. Even his brother Walker admitted that LeRoy "had a very slight acquaintanceship in Mississippi." A group of able and persuasive aides, plus sizable campaign funds, however, helped to overcome Percy's anonymity with the Mississippi legislature. Two of his ablest supporters were his brothers Will, a lawyer and a man of influence in Tennessee politics, and Walker, who had long been active in Alabama politics. Former United States Congressmen Wilson Shedric Hill and "Private" John Allen, both determined Vardaman foes, actively lobbied with legislators in Percy's behalf. Friends, and even some former opponents from the Delta, came to Jackson and worked for Percy's victory.[27]

[24] Jackson *Daily Clarion-Ledger*, August 12, 1903.
[25] *Ibid.*, December 6, 1905; Jackson *Evening News*, December 4, 1905. It should be noted, however, that Noel had also displeased Percy by refusing to appoint Atterbury. *The Issue*, March 28, 1908.
[26] William Alexander Percy, *Lanterns on the Levee: Recollections of a Planter's Son* (New York, 1941), 145.
[27] Vicksburg *Herald*, December 26, 28, 1909, January 2, 1910. As members of the anti-McLaurin faction in 1903, both Wilson Shedric Hill and John Allen had supported Vardaman for governor, but by 1910 they strongly opposed him. Allen, a railroad lobbyist, had been angered by Vardaman's veto in 1906 of a bill permitting a merger between the Mobile and Ohio Railroad and the Southern Railroad. Vardaman to Allen, April 20, 1904, in Vardaman Letter Book. Hill had formerly represented a strong pro-Vardaman district in Congress. Partly because he had openly supported John Sharp Williams instead of Vardaman in the senatorial race of 1907, he was defeated in his bid for reelection the following year. John Sharp Williams to William H. Taft, September 13, 1912, in Williams Papers, Mississippi Department of Archives.

Appeals to patriotism, ambition, and vanity persuaded five other candidates to enter the race. Charlton H. Alexander, a Jackson lawyer known for his outstanding educational and family background, formerly had served in the state legislature and in 1908 had introduced the act that established statewide prohibition. Adam M. Byrd also had been in the state legislature representing Neshoba County, but since 1902 he had served as a representative in Congress. John Curtis Kyle of Panola County had not held public office since he had resigned from Congress in 1897. William D. Anderson, a state senator from Tupelo, was little known outside his home county of Lee. Frank A. Critz had been defeated by Vardaman for governor in 1903. The candidates opposing Vardaman were known as conservatives, three of whom, Percy, Kyle, and Byrd, fifteen years earlier had been gold Democrats and opponents of free silver.[28] Not one of the six had a statewide following, and at the time of McLaurin's death it would have been difficult to imagine that they could defeat Vardaman in a popular primary.

Why did these candidates believe it their duty to make the fight against the ex-governor and to stick together until one of their number won? Their reasons, shared by anti-Vardaman men throughout the state, were many and varied. Some disliked Vardaman's constant harping on the Negro question. Convinced that Negroes could not gain social and political equality in Mississippi, they believed he used racism as a cheap political tool and in so doing encouraged lynch mobs and other forms of racial lawlessness.[29] In addition to believing that he unjustly caused trouble for innocent Negroes, another aspect of the problem frightened some even more: his harsh racial utterances might awaken the conscience of northern whites and result in actually strengthening the Negro's cause. The surest way to keep the Negro from voting and to keep him segregated was to soft-pedal the question and thus avoid rekindling sectional animosity.[30]

[28] Dunbar Rowland (ed.), *The Official and Statistical Register of the State of Mississippi, 1908* (n.p., 1908), 321, 323–24. Frank A. Critz to John C. Burrus, December 31, 1909, in John C. Burrus Papers. Macon *Beacon,* January 14, 1910.
[29] John Sharp Williams to William Tucker, March 26, 1910, in Williams Papers, Mississippi Department of Archives; Macon *Beacon,* February 11, 18, 25, 1910; *The Issue,* January 22, 1910.
[30] John Sharp Williams to LeRoy Percy, February 23, 1910, Williams to "Dear Pryor," February 15, 1910, in Williams Papers, Mississippi Department of Ar-

A charge frequently leveled at Vardaman was that he was a "radical" whose speeches and writings offended "sound thinkers" and "conservative citizens." Some considered the scathing language he had used in attacking such figures as President Roosevelt, Bishop Galloway, and Governor Noel improper and indecent. Unlike LeRoy Percy and Charlton H. Alexander, he lacked the background, education, and polish expected of one who hoped to win a senatorship formerly held by Jefferson Davis and L. Q. C. Lamar. In the Senate, Vardaman's colleagues would look upon him as a buffoon! [31] Yet, many opponents found more than his outspoken views and abusive language upsetting. Too many former Populists, such as state Senator Frank Burkitt, were working for his election. Not only had Vardaman come to endorse issues and causes formerly associated with Populism, he had by 1910 become a spokesman for advanced progressive legislation. As such, he alienated conservative Democrats who believed his sound defeat would only work for the good of Mississippi and the entire South. [32]

Of course, there were more superficial reasons for opposing Vardaman too. Some simply disliked him, believing he was a vain, overbearing, conceited egotist interested only in his own advancement. [33] Then, too, there was the reality that all politicians face—political enemies. Former friends and aides of the late Senator McLaurin, for example, could hardly be expected to support him.

By January 6, 1910, when the legislature met to consider the senatorial question, the quiet town of Jackson had become a buzzing center of political activity. Each candidate had established a headquarters where he held frequent meetings with friends and legislators. From throughout the state, trains brought hundreds of men to Jackson and soon every hotel room had been taken. Many who were unable to get

---

chives; H. L. Sutherland to John C. Burrus, January 1, 1910, in John C. Burrus Papers; Macon *Beacon,* February 25, 1910.

[31] John Sharp Williams to E. F. Noel, December 7, 1909, T. L. Wainwright to C. W. Thigpen, December 27, 1909, in Williams Papers, Mississippi Department of Archives; Macon *Beacon,* January 28, February 18, 25, 1910; Newton *Record,* February 17, 1910.

[32] John M. Inn to John Sharp Williams, January 24, 1910, in Williams Papers, Mississippi Department of Archives; Macon *Beacon,* January 21, 1910.

[33] Vicksburg *Herald,* January 16, 1910; Macon *Beacon,* January 14, 1910. For a general summary of anti-Vardaman views see: J. G. McGuire to A. S. Coody, February 28, 1910, in A. S. Coody Collection.

accommodations waited hours and days in hotel lobbies hoping that someone would check out. When actual meetings of the legislative caucus began, spectators so filled the hallways and galleries in the Capitol that legislators had to push their way through crowds to reach their seats and cast their ballots. Because so many Jackson lawyers were taken up with the senatorial contest, Chancery Judge Garland Lyell dismissed court. Men of means who had come to Jackson to work for various candidates saw to it that no legislator went thirsty. Other pleasures were also provided: women, "somewhat noticeable for their acceleration of the fashions," arrived on trains and quickly disappeared into hotels. And in the midst of it all were the candidates, with perpetual smiles plastered on their faces, rushing "into the thickest of the fray as fearlessly and good-naturedly as does the brawniest football player in the land." [34]

A number of problems confronted the legislature in deciding how to select the man to fill the last three years of McLaurin's unexpired term. At that time state legislatures still elected United States senators. In Mississippi, as in most southern states, all legislators were Democrats and whoever received that party's nomination for senator would automatically be elected by a joint session of the legislature. The real contest was in selecting a party nominee. In regular senatorial elections until 1903, Mississippi Democrats had used party conventions to select nominees; since that time—in 1903 and 1907—senatorial candidates had had to compete in popular primaries. For filling an unexpired senatorial term there was no established method. When the problem had last confronted the state in 1897, Governor McLaurin had simply appointed Hernando Money to fill the vacancy. In 1880 and 1894 legislative caucuses, using secret ballot, had selected nominees to fill unexpired senatorial terms. The caucus (a meeting of all Democratic legislators) afforded more freedom and protection than did a joint session in which all had to vote openly for a senator. In the caucus legislators could, if they so decided, use the secret ballot.

In 1910 Vardaman did not object to a legislative caucus, provided it

[34] Jackson *Daily Clarion-Ledger*, January 4, 5, 18, 1910; Batesville *Weekly Panolian*, February 3, 1910; Columbus *Commercial*, January 6, 9, 1910; George Creel, "The Carnival of Corruption in Mississippi," *Cosmopolitan*, LI (November, 1911), 729; H. H. Harrison to John Burrus, December 25, 1909, in John C. Burrus Papers.

selected the nominee by open ballot. Confident that he was the over-whelming choice of the electorate, he believed that with an open ballot a majority of the legislators would be forced by constituent pressure to vote for him.[35] Despite his appeals, or because of them, the majority of the legislators decided by a vote of 101 to 69 in favor of using the secret ballot.[36] It was the use of the secret ballot that caused the senatorial election of 1910 to be branded the "secret caucus," although actual meetings were open to the public. Anti-Vardaman men argued that the legislature only followed well-established tradition, for both Senators Money and McLaurin had been nominated by caucuses employing secret ballot. Vardaman himself, while a member of the legislature in 1894, had voted in the caucus that nominated McLaurin.[37] In defending the caucus and the secret ballot as the traditional method of selecting senators in Mississippi, however, the anti-Vardaman men ignored changes that had been wrought in the state's political system in the past decade, during which time public sentiment for popular primary elections had greatly expanded and, indeed, had become reality. The nineteenth century method of nominating senators by legislative caucus and secret ballot was no longer acceptable. Many politicians who supported the caucus and secret ballot in 1910 learned that fact too late.

On the evening of January 7, with House Speaker Hugh Street presiding, the caucus cast its first ballot. Vardaman led with 71 votes, but the majority needed to win the nomination was scattered among his six opponents, Alexander having 24, Percy 21, Anderson 21, Kyle 14, Byrd 12; former Supreme Court Judge Jeff Truly received 1 vote. For almost two months that pattern remained essentially unchanged. Sticking by Vardaman through ballot after ballot were 65 loyal supporters who could not be shaken from his cause. While on one ballot his vote rose to 78, it always fell short of the necessary majority of 86 votes. Some legislators had promised to vote for one man, such as Alexander, only as long as he remained in the race; should he drop

---

[35] Newton *Record,* December 30, 1909; Jackson *Daily Clarion-Ledger,* January 8, 1910; Macon *Beacon,* January 14, 1910; J. K. Vardaman to J. C. Burrus, December 27, 1909, in John C. Burrus Papers.

[36] Vicksburg *Herald,* January 7, 1910.

[37] Jackson *Daily Clarion-Ledger,* January 5, 1910; Macon *Beacon,* January 21, 1910; Tupelo *Journal,* January 21, 1910.

out of the contest, they would vote for whom they pleased and some of these eventually supported Vardaman.[38] The majority of legislators, however, refused to vote for the former governor under any conditions.

During the first week of the caucus, while Jackson was filled with visitors, many enjoyed the senatorial contest, some claiming there had not been such excitement since the days of the old state nominating conventions. As it became apparent that the caucus was deadlocked, dissatisfaction began to spread. The caucus consumed too much of the legislators' time which should have been devoted to the regular business of that session. In hopes of ending the contest, Vardaman's followers recommended everything from an open vote to a process of eliminating the lowest candidate after each ballot. Even some anti-Vardaman men urged that the opposition agree on one man and be done with it.[39] No one wanted the deadlock to end more than the legislators themselves, many of whom soon realized that they were embroiled in a determined fight that offered little possibility of a quick settlement. Although the six candidates opposing Vardaman had determined that the former governor would not be the new senator, each hoped that he himself would win the prize. With public dissatisfaction mounting and with the legislators aware of the growing unpopularity of their predicament, "there was a spirit of restlessness and nervous languor prevalent, as though the majority were tired of their job and devoutly wished that the thing was settled and out of the way." [40]

During the long weeks of the caucus the candidates and their aides fought hard to win. Friends of some candidates frequently took legislators to meals, bought them whiskey, and supplied automobiles to take them from their hotels to the Capitol. J. S. Hudson, a Kyle supporter, actually paid Representative W. H. King a hundred dollars to cover the expenses he incurred during the caucus. F. S. Cannon, a Percy aide, gave Representative Walter Robertson forty dollars with which to pay his property taxes.[41] Others tempted legislators with

[38] Vicksburg *Herald,* January 8, 1910; Macon *Beacon,* January 14, 21, 1910.

[39] Columbus *Commercial,* January 23, 1910; Yazoo City *Yazoo Sentinel,* January 27, February 3, 1910; Newton *Record,* February 10, 17, 1910; Jackson *Daily Clarion-Ledger,* February 15, 1910.

[40] Macon *Beacon,* January 21, 1910.

[41] *Investigation by the Senate of the State of Mississippi of the Charges of Bribery in the Election of a United States Senator* (Nashville, 1910), 309–11; House of Representatives, *Inquiry Into the Charge of Bribery,* 69–70, 379–81.

patronage, for at the time several county attorneys and six state judges had to be appointed.[42] Governor Noel had the authority to name the judges and attorneys, and there is no evidence that he promised an office to any legislator in return for his vote. Noel, however, strongly and openly opposed Vardaman's election; certainly a legislator known to support Vardaman could not expect favors from the governor.[43] Resorting to more direct means, some campaign workers warned that if legislators did not vote for their candidates, they could expect to be defeated in the next state election. Petitions and letters, all supposedly representing the sentiment of the home folks, were frequently sent to the legislators. Some enthusiastic aides even threatened uncooperative legislators with physical violence. The caucus ended many friendships.[44]

The Vardaman forces worked as hard, if not harder, than any other group in struggling for victory. Especially active in Vardaman's behalf were H. Vaughn Watkins, Swep J. Taylor, and John L. Hebron. Vardaman frequently met with his supporters, helped to plot strategy, and tried to persuade legislators to vote for him. Whenever a doubtful or wavering legislator was spotted by his lieutenants, he went "to perform the missionary work." Opposition legislators were frequently invited to his campaign headquarters, where the former governor sat talking to them for hours while he sipped sherry and saw to it that his guests always had a full glass.[45] Sometimes his followers staged mass meetings in various counties to help persuade local legislators for whom they should vote.[46] Throughout the contest the enthusiasm of his campaigners impressed visitors. Following an early meeting of the caucus Vardaman men filled the lobby of the Edwards House and when the former governor walked in, they burst into shouts that

[42] *Investigation by the Senate of . . . Charges of Bribery,* 213–15, 397–400.
[43] *Ibid.,* 469–72; *House Journal, 1910,* 1527–28; Newton *Record,* April 21, 1910; *The Issue,* February 19, 1910; House of Representatives, *Inquiry Into the Charge of Bribery,* 336.
[44] Macon *Beacon,* January 21, 1910; Newton *Record,* February 6, 1910.
[45] Columbus *Commercial,* January 13, 1910; House of Representatives, *Inquiry Into the Charge of Bribery,* 211–13, 247, 344, 354.
[46] Vicksburg *Herald,* January 2, 1910; Jackson *Daily Clarion-Ledger,* January 4, 1910; Newton *Record,* January 20, 1910.

"raised the roof." [47] A reporter from the New York *Times* described how Vardaman's followers raised money for his campaign.

When they said "money" at the caucus a small riot had started. One long tall fellow from the piney woods held his hat, a wide, tan felt headpiece. Money simply rained into that hat. Men struggled to reach it.

"There's a twenty" remarked one man, "and I'm good for another twenty if it's needed, and then some more twenties. By Gad, as long as I've got it, I'll shell out for Jim Vardaman." All that was needed was raised in ten minutes. Vardaman was not present. No list was kept of the contributions. They all just "chipped in." [48]

Believing their candidate the victim of ruthless politicians who would do anything to defeat him, newspaper editors supporting Vardaman strongly denounced the caucus and its use of the secret ballot. Why use a secret ballot? What did the legislators have to hide? Did not the secret ballot illustrate that a conspiracy existed to defeat the people's choice, Vardaman? Who, other than John Sharp Williams and the late Senator McLaurin, was so well known and so well liked by the people as Vardaman? Legislators were warned to heed the choices of the people or to suffer the consequences in the state elections of 1911.[49]

Anti-Vardaman legislators defeated four attempts to end the caucus, the first occurring on January 16 when state law required the legislature to meet jointly and elect a senator. Vardaman's friends had looked forward to the sixteenth, knowing that in joint session the legislators had to use open ballot and believing he would win when legislators were not protected by a secret vote. On the sixteenth, however, the Vardaman men suffered defeat. Senator Washington Gibbs, a leading anti-Vardamanite, introduced a resolution in the caucus providing that in the joint sessions no legislator would vote for any candidate who had received a vote in the caucus until the caucus had actually selected a nominee. In the joint session each legislator would

[47] Jackson *Daily Clarion-Ledger,* January 12, 1910.
[48] New York *Times,* January 9, 1910.
[49] *The Issue,* January 22, 1910; Yazoo City *Yazoo Sentinel,* December 30, 1909, January 13, February 3, 1910; Newton *Record,* December 30, 1909, January 6, 13, 20, February 6, 24, 1910; A. S. Coody to G. H. Alford, January 5, 17, 1910, Coody to C. H. Perkins, January 16, 1910, in A. S. Coody Collection.

vote for a man from his congressional district who was not an announced candidate for the Senate vacancy. The object of Gibbs's resolution was so to scatter the votes in the joint session that no one would have a majority and the caucus would continue its work of selecting a Democratic nominee. With Vardaman supporters strongly protesting, the Gibbs resolution passed in the caucus by the narrow vote of 86 to 80.[50] A few weeks later Representative Elder L. H. Bird introduced a resolution asking that the caucus be dissolved. When Senator Gibbs rose to fight the resolution, Vardaman partisans in the galleries loudly hissed him. Shouting that only "a snake, a fool, or a goose" hissed, Gibbs successfully rallied the opposing forces to defeat the Bird resolution. Two attempts by pro-Vardaman legislators to end the caucus by dropping the last-place candidate after each ballot also failed.[51]

From time to time the excitement of the caucus produced vigorous exchanges between the opposing sides, the first serious one occurring between Vardaman and LeRoy Percy. Through an editorial in *The Issue* Vardaman charged that railroad attorneys and lobbyists from the trusts were in Jackson fighting against his nomination.[52] Percy immediately published a reply in the Jackson *Daily News*. Admitting that he had been a railroad attorney, he unwisely boasted that, unlike his opponent, he had never been "a briefless barrister dependent upon the charity of . . . friends or the forebearance of . . . creditors." Accusing Vardaman of being a "reckless agitator and a demagogic strife-breeder," he challenged him to name the lobbyist working against him.[53] To the surprise of some, Vardaman issued a moderate reply to the bristling attack. Suggesting that Percy was over sensitive and perhaps had a guilty conscience because he was a railroad lawyer, Vardaman asserted it was unnecessary for him to name the agents working against him because every legislator knew who they were. He skillfully exploited Percy's charge that he was a poor man: "I have no desire to indulge in personalities, nor shall I stoop to notice Mr. Percy's

---

50 Vicksburg *Herald*, January 15, 16, 1910; Yazoo City *Yazoo Sentinel*, January 20, 1910; Jackson *Daily Clarion-Ledger*, January 15, 1910, Newton *Record*, January 20, 1910.

51 Vicksburg *Herald*, January 29, February 17, 1910; Jackson *Daily Clarion-Ledger*, January 29, February 17, 1910; Yazoo City *Yazoo Sentinel*, February 24, 1910.

52 *The Issue*, January 29, 1910.

53 Jackson *Daily News*, January 30, 1910; Macon *Beacon*, February 4, 1910.

thrust at my impecunious condition. If poverty is a crime, then I am guilty." This moderate reply to Percy's personal and bitter charge, widely hailed by the Vardaman press, probably worked to his advantage.[54]

On the same day Percy's attack appeared in the *News*, B. T. Hobbs, editor of the Brookhaven *Leader,* leveled the charge that early in the caucus some of Percy's friends had exploited Representative Walter W. Robertson's fondness for whiskey by getting him drunk and thereby persuading him to switch his vote to Percy. When he had found Robertson in the room of a Percy aide, Hobbs reported, the representative was on the verge of delirium tremens. Asserting he was not responsible for Robertson's condition, Percy had ignored Hobbs's appeals to help the drunken legislator. Robertson then suffered delirium tremens, Hobbs concluded, and was taken home by his wife.[55] Soon after Hobbs's story had appeared, Robertson published a rebuttal in which he admitted having suffered delirium tremens, not because he had accepted whiskey from a Percy aide, but because he had drunk rotgut whiskey in the Vardaman headquarters. Then, according to Robertson's version, some friends of Percy had taken him to a sanatorium where he had received proper medical attention. Admitting that he had switched his vote, Robertson promised to stand by Percy until the end of the caucus. In his rebuttal Hobbs speculated that someone had written Robertson's reply for him, for he charged the unfortunate legislator could "scarcely write a coherent article when sober." [56]

For almost two months the excitement and tension engendered by the caucus did not break. On ballot after ballot, it was Vardaman against the field. On the twenty-fourth ballot Senator Anderson withdrew from the race "in the interest of the common cause for which I have been fighting, on the success of which, in my judgment, depends

---

[54] *The Issue,* February 5, 1910; Newton *Record,* February 6, 1910; Yazoo City *Yazoo Sentinel,* February 3, 1910.

[55] Brookhaven *Leader,* January 30, 1910; House of Representatives, *Inquiry Into the Charge of Bribery,* 225–32.

[56] Newon *Record,* February 6, 1910; Columbus *Commercial,* February 3, 1910; Vicksburg *Herald,* February 1, 1910; *The Issue,* February 12, 1910; Yazoo City *Yazoo Sentinel,* February 3, 1910; House of Representatives, *Inquiry Into the Charge of Bribery,* 235–37.

the welfare of the state of Mississippi." [57] On the thirty-second ballot
Critz withdrew and Alexander followed on the forty-first, but, unlike
Anderson, neither openly admitted being part of the "common cause"
working against Vardaman.[58] As these men dropped from the race,
most of their votes were scattered among the remaining, opposing candidates. On the fiftieth ballot House Speaker Street, then seventy-six
years old, entered the contest and attracted a large number of anti-
Vardaman votes.[59]

The end came suddenly and, for some, unexpectedly. On February eighteenth Representative Van Buren Boddie, a Percy supporter,
moved that the caucus adjourn until the twenty-second. Perhaps the
adjournment was designed to give those opposing Vardaman an opportunity to pool their entire vote behind either Byrd, Kyle, Street, or
Percy, for Governor Noel had recently warned he would appoint Colonel Gordon for the full three-year term if the legislature failed to select
a senator before adjournment. During the recess the anti-Vardaman
steering committee selected S. L. McLaurin, a brother of the deceased
Senator, and Senators George J. Leftwich and William D. Anderson
to canvass the legislature and decide which candidate stood the best
chance of defeating Vardaman. In a long meeting on the afternoon of
the twenty-second the hard core Vardaman opposition agreed to support Percy in a final showdown that night.[60]

News of the decision spread quickly through Jackson, and, long before dark, anxious spectators, many carrying cold suppers, packed the
galleries of the house of representatives. Aware that the climax was
near, Vardaman led his supporters to the Capitol. As Representative
Malcomb P. Foy, a man who had made no secret of his opposition to
the former governor, was about to enter the house chamber, Vardaman seized him by the arm and "in a very excited and trembling
voice" said "he hoped to the Lord" Foy could see his "way clear to
get right." When the caucus assembled, Street announced his with-

[57] Vicksburg *Herald*, January 26, 1910; Newton *Record*, January 27, 1910;
Yazoo City *Yazoo Sentinel*, January 27, 1910.

[58] Vicksburg *Herald*, January 29, February 5, 1910; Jackson *Daily Clarion-
Ledger*, February 5, 1910; Macon *Beacon*, February 4, 1910.

[59] Yazoo City *Yazoo Sentinel*, February 17, 1910; Macon *Beacon*, February
11, 1910.

[60] House of Representatives, *Inquiry Into the Charge of Bribery*, 395; Vicksburg *Herald*, February 19, 1910.

drawal from the race, as did Byrd and Kyle. Then on the fifty-eighth ballot of the caucus, by a vote of 87 to 82, Percy won the nomination.[61]

Bedlam broke forth as two months of built-up tension exploded. Amid cheers of his partisans, Percy thanked the legislature for the victory. Vardaman men, most of whom had stood by him throughout the caucus, did not share in the festivities. Not until Vardaman thanked them for their loyalty and assured them that in the 1911 primary victory would not escape them did they applaud.

Percy's election, far from ending the strife and bitterness engendered during the caucus, only intensified political rivalry in Mississippi, for supporters of both men kept the issues alive. Many Vardaman adherents believed Percy had been elected unfairly. Not only had their candidate been the victim of a conspiracy and the secret ballot, they believed, but liquor and patronage had been used to corrupt legislators. Some even hinted that legislators had been bribed to vote against Vardaman.[62] Addressing a packed house of his ardent supporters in Jackson's Century Theatre two nights after the election, Vardaman himself implied that unfair methods had been used to defeat him.[63] All during March rumors of caucus corruption persisted.

His opponents retaliated by charging that, as governor, he had mishandled state funds entrusted to his care. Immediately after the caucus some anti-Vardaman men began to probe the financial records of the former governor's administration. Perhaps they realized that Percy's election by the caucus might create a strong wave of popular sentiment which would sweep Vardaman to victory in the 1911 primary. If they could prove that he had misused state funds, however, that feared wave of pro-Vardaman sentiment might never crest. Such motives may have caused Will Percy to visit Governor Noel's office near the end of the caucus and receive permission to investigate the back files of the executive contingent funds. Percy discovered that for Var-

[61] House of Representatives, *Inquiry Into the Charge of Bribery*, 216; Vicksburg *Herald*, February 23, 1910; Jackson *Daily Clarion-Ledger*, February 23, 1910; Yazoo City *Yazoo Sentinel*, February 24, 1910.
[62] Yazoo City *Yazoo Sentinel*, March 3, 10, 24, 1910; Newton *Record*, March 10, 1910; *The Issue*, March 5, 1910.
[63] Newton *Record*, March 3, 1910; Columbus *Commercial*, February 27, 1910; *The Issue*, February 26, 1910; Yazoo City *Yazoo Sentinel*, March 3, 1910.

daman's administration the records of some expenditures were missing.[64] Soon a number of newspapers began demanding that the former governor account for every dollar of his official expenditures. If Vardaman failed to give an exact accounting, they argued, it proved either he had stolen from the state or he was a poor businessman who could not keep accurate records. If either charge were true, they hoped, it should convince a majority of voters that he should not be a United States senator.[65]

Believing the charges that the former governor had mishandled state funds were nothing more than attempts to assassinate his character and to weaken him politically, Vardaman's followers reacted with anger. "The noise that has been recently made about Vardaman's contingent fund," the editor of the Ripley *Sentinel* asserted, "is all a lot of slimy rot." [66] Representative Polk Talbert, who had served on the committee which had investigated Vardaman's expenditures for 1904 and 1905, reported the records had been in perfect order. Even House Speaker Street, who had worked against him in the caucus, openly defended the honesty of the former executive. Vardaman ignored the charges against him and refused to comment on them.

In response to the mounting controversy over Vardaman's handling of contingent funds, a joint legislative committee held an investigation in late March. The investigation produced no evidence of corruption. A careful study by accountant Charles J. Moore revealed that the records for Vardaman's first two years in office, 1904 and 1905, were in order. The only problem was that for 1906 and 1907 some vouchers, which consisted of warrants and cancelled checks, were missing from the files in the governor's office. That was the sole issue. By law the governor had to present a report of his official expenditures to the legislature every two years. In accordance with that law Vardaman's secretaries had prepared such reports in 1906 and 1908. A legislative committee had checked the report in 1906, but two years later a similar committee had failed to check the report. Having left office early in 1908, he had not known of the legislature's failure to check the re-

[64] *House Journal, 1910,* 1489.
[65] Vicksburg *Herald,* February 22, March 12, 13, 20, 22, 1910; Jackson *Daily Clarion-Ledger,* March 9, 23, 1910; Tupelo *Journal,* April 1, 1910.
[66] Ripley *Sentinel,* quoted in Newton *Record,* April 7, 1910.

port until 1910, when the charge of mishandling funds was made against him. Nor did he know what had become of the missing vouchers since his administration had ended, for he had left them on file in the governor's office.

After investigating the governor's expenditures, the committee did not issue a report; it merely published the testimony of the witnesses. Of the six witnesses who had appeared before the committee, only John J. Henry, the former penitentiary warden whom Vardaman had fired, charged that the ex-governor had stolen from state funds. Because there was no evidence to support his charge, Henry's testimony was evidently that of an embittered political foe.[67] By failing to exonerate Vardaman from the charge of mishandling state funds and by publishing only the witnesses' testimony, especially that of Henry, the committee permitted the question raised by the missing vouchers to persist. That question caused trouble for Vardaman during the next two years. At the time of the investigation, however, it drew little attention, for public attention suddenly focused upon the charge that there had been bribery in the caucus.

While the contingent fund controversy had been receiving wide publicity during March, a few of Vardaman's closest supporters, such as Swep J. Taylor and H. Vaughn Watkins, had been quietly collecting evidence which they hoped would prove that in the caucus a Percy aide had bribed a legislator. By early March they had obtained enough evidence that Judge Samuel C. Cook of the Hinds County circuit court ordered the grand jury to investigate the charge of bribery. Exactly what evidence the grand jury was considering no one knew. While in Jackson shortly before leaving for Washington to assume his senatorial duties, LeRoy Percy, appearing thin and "very nervous," said he did not believe there had been any bribery in the caucus, but he promised to press charges should he discover votes had been bought.[68]

On March 28 the Mississippi public was electrified by the news that Lorraine Dulaney had paid Senator Theodore G. Bilbo to vote for Percy. The Hinds County grand jury had accordingly indicted the briber, a wealthy planter and levee contracter from Issaquena Coun-

---

[67] *House Journal, 1910,* 1455–57, 1484–95, 1495–1500.
[68] *Investigation by the Senate of . . . Charges of Bribery,* 78; Vicksburg *Herald,* March 8, 1910; Jackson *Daily Clarion-Ledger,* March 10, 1910.

ty. Bilbo, who a week earlier had announced that the next year he would run for lieutenant governor, had not been indicted because he had turned the bribe money over to the grand jury and had sworn that his sole purpose for accepting it had been to catch the briber. Believing it his duty to uncover corruption in the caucus, he had assumed the role of a detective.[69]

News of Dulaney's indictment engendered excitement surpassing even that of the recent caucus. Factional lines drew rigidly tight as Vardaman men demanded Dulaney be quickly convicted and as Percy men attempted to disprove the charge of corruption. Fistfights erupted and some men in Jackson armed themselves. General confusion further complicated the situation, for at first vague and conflicting reports ran rampant. Why had Bilbo waited so long to reveal the bribery? Would he not have helped Vardaman more by having told the caucus of Dulaney's activities? Was Bilbo just a Vardaman aide who was deliberately lying? Even men closely affected by the bribery charge were confused. LeRoy Percy, for example, could not understand why Dulaney, who for years had been his political enemy, would invest so much money in his candidacy. John Sharp Williams, realizing fully the consequences of Bilbo's charge, did not believe that Dulaney "could have been fool enough to endanger the whole cause of conservatism in Mississippi and by just that form of endangerment which kills a cause—corruption." [70]

The Mississippi legislature, especially the senate, reacted immediately and strongly to Bilbo's charge of bribery. For more than a month pro-Vardaman newspapers had denounced the legislature for having elected Percy; news of Dulaney's indictment drove the majority of legislators further onto the defensive. Failing to obtain a copy of all testimony given before the grand jury, the senate went into closed executive session, resolved itself into a committee of the whole and launched an investigation into Bilbo's charge of bribery. Governor Noel cooperated by extending the legislative session, thereby allowing

---

[69] Vicksburg *Herald,* March 29, 1910; Newton *Record,* March 31, 1910.
[70] LeRoy Percy to John Sharp Williams, March 30, 1910, Williams to "Dear LeRoy," March 30, 1910, in Williams Papers, Mississippi Department of Archives.

time for the investigation.[71] Vardaman supporters opposed the investigation, arguing that bribery was a criminal matter which should be left to the courts; they feared that the majority of senators were determined, if possible, to discredit Bilbo's story.[72] In that belief they were correct. From the beginning of the senate's investigation, the majority strove to prove Bilbo a liar and to impeach him. Even before the investigation began, a resolution had been introduced to expel Bilbo from the senate for having accepted a bribe, and that motion remained pending throughout the investigation. From its members the senate majority selected William D. Anderson and George J. Leftwich to prosecute, and Bilbo selected William F. Tucker and Will Tate McDonald to defend him.[73] Bilbo, not Dulaney, was on trial before the senate.

While the senate held its inquiry, the house of representatives appointed a committee to discover if during the caucus any of its members had sold their votes.[74] Of the two investigations the senate's was the most important and received the most attention. It was before the senate that the major witnesses, Bilbo and Dulaney, gave the most revealing accounts of the alleged bribery. The testimony given by them and other witnesses was upsetting to all classes and sections of Mississippi. Whether one believed Bilbo or Dulaney, the investigations revealed that, during the caucus, elected public officials had been tempted with promises of patronage and that others had indiscreetly accepted favors, drunk whiskey, and caroused with lewd women. Some, believing Bilbo had lied, denounced him for the charges he had brought against Dulaney and for the humiliation he had inflicted on Percy. Others believed Bilbo and resented the legislature's efforts to defend Dulaney and exonerate Percy's election. What most distressed many was that Bilbo's charge of bribery helped to uncover some of the more sordid aspects of the recent caucus and in so doing brought national disgrace to the state. Above all, the Bilbo-Dulaney bribery

[71] Grenada *Sentinel,* March 25, 1910; Vicksburg *Herald,* March 30, 31, 1910; *Investigation by the Senate . . . Charges of Bribery,* 16-28.

[72] Newton *Record,* March 31, April 7, 1910; Columbus *Commercial,* March 31, 1910.

[73] Macon *Beacon,* April 1, 1910; *Investigation by the Senate of . . . Charges of Bribery,* 28–29.

[74] House of Representatives, *Inquiry Into the Charge of Bribery, passim.*

scandal cut to the soul of Mississippi society and there were few people whom it failed to affect.[75]

The key witness to appear before the senate was Theodore G. Bilbo, then thirty-three and completing his first term in the state senate, where he had proved himself an advocate of progressive reforms and a spokesman for the interests of South Mississippi. A small man, he had a wide forehead and a strong, jutting jaw. His hair, parted in the middle and plastered down tightly, accentuated a sharp nose and a thin line of a mouth. Skin drawn tightly over hollow cheeks left his face neither wrinkled nor creased. Large, piercing eyes were his most impressive feature. Though small, he was wiry and tough and proved to be a man who thrived on combat and controversy. For Bilbo it was fortunate that he was so endowed, for otherwise he might not have survived the next two years.

Bilbo told the senate that early in the caucus he had heard rumors of lobbyists' paying legislators not to vote for Vardaman. After discussing the matter with a small group of Vardaman's aides and with three senate colleagues, he decided to try to uncover the corruption. He then led Mrs. Coral Johnson Neil, a guest at the Lemon Hotel, to believe that his vote could be bought and she soon sugested that it would be worth his time to meet Dulaney, who was in Jackson working for Percy's election. At first Bilbo hoped to have witnesses secretly hidden in Mary Stamps's assignation house to observe him as he received the bribe he expected Dulaney to offer. J. L. Raney, a Jackson policeman, arranged for such a meeting, but it was cancelled on the advice of Vardaman's aides. Later Bilbo met Dulaney in the Lemon Hotel, and after several conversations Dulaney offered him five hundred dollars to switch his vote from Vardaman to Percy and an additional five hundred dollars if Percy won. Although he accepted part of the money, Bilbo claimed he continued voting for Vardaman. During the remaining weeks of the caucus Dulaney had paid him installments on the thousand dollars from time to time, the final one coming the day after Percy's election; the total amount Bilbo received was $645. Bilbo explained that he had told no official of Dulaney's activities during the caucus for fear that such a revelation might appear to some legislators

[75] Newton *Record,* April 7, 13, 1910; Grenada *Sentinel,* April 1, 1910.

a trick to help Vardaman and thereby lead to his defeat in the caucus. He remained quiet until evidence had been collected which he believed sufficient to convict Dulaney. At no time, Bilbo concluded, did Dulaney say Percy had knowledge of the bribery.[76]

A number of witnesses confirmed parts of Bilbo's story. Those senators and Vardaman aides to whom he had early revealed his plan to uncover corruption remembered their conversations with Bilbo.[77] J. L. Raney testified that he had tried to help Bilbo catch the briber by setting a trap. On the final ballot of the caucus Representative Albert C. Anderson had seen Bilbo vote for Vardaman.[78] The major weakness in Bilbo's testimony was his failure to have spoken with reliable witnesses at the time he was being bribed or to have kept detailed records of each meeting with Dulaney and of the exact amounts of money that Dulaney had paid him from time to time. Once he had begun accepting payments from Dulaney, he told no one of the bribery except S. B. Culpepper, a Baptist minister from Newton County and the president of Clark Memorial College, who had spent several nights with him during the caucus. Culpepper recalled having seen some of the bribe money, but he could not remember if Bilbo had named the briber; Bilbo testified he had told Culpepper the Dulaney had given him the money.[79]

The witness who gave testimony most strongly collaborating Bilbo's story was Coral Johnson Neil, a woman of thirty-five, who had been largely on her own since leaving Abington, Virginia, at the age of nineteen. In less than a year after marriage her husband had died. Since then, while living in parts of Virginia, Tennessee, and Mississippi, she had supported herself in many ways, from working in real estate to selling patent medicine. She was a large woman who looked older than her age. In a rigorous cross examination before the senate, during which she was accused of being a liar and a prostitute, she proved a match for her interrogators. When asked if she did not know it was sometimes necessary to have people spied upon, she replied, "I was told that at the first Democratic caucus in Mississippi that I attend-

---

[76] *Investigation by the Senate of . . . Charges of Bribery,* 36–49, 74–75, 78–79.
[77] *Ibid.,* 29–35, 120–34, 151–58, 237–49, 297–301.
[78] *Ibid.,* 249–56, 296–97.
[79] *Ibid.,* 39, 100–112.

ed." Senator Leftwich asked why she had tried to bribe legislators, and she retorted: "What did Eve eat the apple for?" In describing how she had supported herself since the death of her husband, she explained that she had done so by "keeping books and working in real estate, and trying to buy Mississippi Legislators." [80] During the many hours of questioning by the senate she refused to be shaken from her basic story.

Mrs. Neil had moved to Jackson several weeks before Governor Noel ordered the legislature to elect a successor for McLaurin. She said that shortly after the caucus became deadlocked, Dulaney had employed her and Mrs. W. J. Hall, wife of the manager of the Lemon Hotel, to discover for him which legislators were "weak ones." She said, "I was working for Dulaney, to bribe anybody that I could get to take a bribe." [81] In accordance with instructions, she had sent Dulaney a list of legislators whom she considered "weak ones," and she had personally introduced Bilbo to Dulaney. She had never been paid a cent by Dulaney, however, for Bilbo refused to tell her if he had actually accepted a bribe. Two days after the caucus ended she left Jackson for Vicksburg and from there she later went to New Orleans and sold her story of the bribery affair to a newspaper, the *Item*. While in New Orleans, she said, R. S. Seay, an employee of Dulaney's brother-in-law, and several unidentified men had tried unsuccessfully to persuade her not to return to Jackson and testify before the senate.[82]

Representative Joseph Oliver Cowart revealed to the senate another method that had been used to swing votes away from Vardaman. Although Dulaney had talked to him about the possibility of being paid for his vote, he reported, the Issaquena planter only had been feeling him out and had not made a concrete offer. Cowart did charge, however, that R. N. Miller, a leading attorney from South Mississippi, had tried to persuade him to vote for Percy by suggesting it would improve his chances of obtaining a job with a prosperous law firm, or a position as county attorney, or even a judgeship. Miller had employed this means many times in attempting to persuade Cowart to vote for Percy,

[80] *Ibid.*, 274, 275, 287.
[81] *Ibid.*, 294.
[82] *Ibid.*, 259–96; House of Representatives, *Inquiry Into the Charge of Bribery*, 313–21.

once in the presence of Will Percy and once in the presence of former Congressman John Allen.[83] Miller later read a prepared statement to the senate in which he admitted having told Cowart a vote for Percy might help his chances of being appointed to office, but he denied anything improper had been offered.[84] The testimony of both Miller and Cowart made one thing clear: patronage had been pushed to the limits of legality, if not beyond. Cowart, however, had refused to be swayed by a general promise of reward; only the absolute assurance of a position would have tempted him to switch his vote.

The first witness to deny the charges that had been brought by Bilbo and Mrs. Neil was Mrs. Hall. Although she had earlier signed a statement in the presence of District Attorney M. S. McNeill that on the final night of the caucus Dulaney had given her twenty dollars "to hold him [Bilbo] in line," [85] she told the senate that she knew absolutely nothing about bribery during the caucus. She claimed McNeill had bullied her into signing the earlier statement by promising that it would keep her out of trouble. After the close of the caucus, she said, Bilbo once had asked for a $280 loan and later had offered her $1000 to tell all she knew to the grand jury. She did admit that she actively had supported Percy during the caucus and that on one occasion Dulaney had paid her $40 for a dinner which she had given for some legislators.[86]

After Bilbo, Mrs. Neil, Cowart, and Mrs. Hall had told their stories, Lorraine C. Dulaney came before the senate. He was a large, heavy man with a flourishing handlebar moustache. Because he had served in both the house and senate, he personally knew many legislators. For years Dulaney had been a leader of the McLaurin forces in the Delta, and during the governorship of Anselm McLaurin, he and Walter Sillers had led a savage fight against the faction with which both Percy and Vardaman had been aligned. Dulaney had once written Governor

[83] Investigation by the Senate of . . . Charges of Bribery, 207–32; House of Representatives, Inquiry Into the Charge of Bribery, 10–33, 49–50, 170–72.

[84] Investigation by the Senate of . . . Charges of Bribery, 397–400; House of Representatives, Inquiry Into the Charge of Bribery, 168, 187–89. Will Percy had also used federal patronage in attempting to win the senatorship for his brother. Through his friendship with Secretary of War J. M. Dickinson he had had the appointment of a United States attorney for Mississippi postponed until after the caucus.

[85] Investigation by the Senate of . . . Charges of Bribery, 186–207.

[86] Ibid., 169–86.

McLaurin to pay no attention to the "Percy gang." [87] With the death of McLaurin, Dulaney had chosen what he believed the least of evils and accordingly had gone to Jackson to work for Percy. He claimed that Vardaman's racial agitation had driven many Negroes from the Delta during his governorship, and he feared another Negro exodus should Vardaman become senator.[88]

Dulaney had other reasons, which he did not tell the senate, for so strongly opposing Vardaman. From 1896 to 1903, during the last years of the old convention system, Dulaney had enjoyed influence in the state government and had been one of the select group of Delta planters whose lands had been worked by state convicts.[89] Vardaman had contributed to the demise of the convention system and as governor had smashed the last remnants of the state's convict lease program. Dulaney had been part of that older order Vardaman had helped to destroy.

In testifying before the senate Dulaney never fully explained why he had been in Jackson lobbying for Percy. His only objective, he held, had been to defeat Vardaman. Whatever his full motives, he had proved himself a generous man who had not only given two months of his time to the Percy cause but had also spent between forty and fifty dollars a day taking legislators to meals, buying them cigars, and furnishing them with whiskey. He refused to reveal his total expenditures for the entire caucus.[90]

Dulaney completely denied the charges against him. Mrs. Neil, he said, had impressed him "as being a rather pitiful old creature that wanted to make a little money." She had once called him to the Lemon Hotel and had boasted that for two thousand dollars she could swing nine votes to any candidate. Dulaney claimed he had not taken her seriously. Although he admitted that during the caucus he had frequently seen Bilbo, he denied ever having offered him a bribe. He had usually seen the Pearl River senator, Dulaney explained, when Bilbo

[87] See Chapter III above.

[88] *Investigation by the Senate of ... Charges of Bribery,* 301–303.

[89] L. C. Dulaney to A. J. McLaurin, August 24, 1896, March 31, August 20, December 27, 1897, February 2, March 21, May 8, 21, August 9, 1898, December 20, 1899, in McLaurin Papers.

[90] *Investigation by the Senate of ... Charges of Bribery,* 309–311.

visited his room to quench his thirst: "He came to my room a number of times. He would often come in there and get two great big drinks and cast his eyes around a little, and when he came to leave he generally made some excuse about being out of whiskey, or booze—he called it booze most of the time—and he would usually go out with a whole quart. But that was all right. I was not making anybody mad." [91] Bilbo had once asked for a fifty-dollar loan, but Dulaney had refused to grant it. He did admit that along with Bell Hebron and George Alexander, two Percy aides, he had paid Mrs. Hall forty dollars to reimburse her for the dinner she had given.[92]

Many other witnesses appeared before the senate, some speaking in behalf of Bilbo and some testifying in behalf of Dulaney. The essential conflict, however, was represented by Bilbo and Mrs. Neil, on one side, and by Dulaney and Mrs. Hall, on the other. Bilbo and Mrs. Neil claimed that Dulaney had worked to bribe legislators; Dulaney and Mrs. Hall denied the charge. No others had been directly involved in the alleged bribery.

In an attempt to undermine the allegations made against Dulaney, the senate accepted the testimony of witnesses who claimed that neither Bilbo nor Mrs. Neil was trustworthy. When senators defending Bilbo tried to stop the admission of such evidence, the majority overruled them. Mrs. Neil was accused of being a prostitute,[93] and Bilbo was said to have cheated in school, to have seduced a female student when he had been a teacher, and to have accepted bribes at the legislative session of 1908.[94] No one offered a rebuttal in behalf of Mrs. Neil. Under cross examination, however, it became evident that much of the testimony given against Bilbo had been based on unfounded rumors.

[91] *Ibid.*, 305–306.

[92] *Ibid.*, 304–316; House of Representatives, *Inquiry Into the Charge of Bribery*, 175–80.

[93] *Investigation by the Senate of . . . Charges of Bribery*, 278–79, 407–10, 412–13. During the investigation conducted by the house of representatives, affidavits signed by police officials in Chattanooga, Tennessee, were introduced which alleged that Mrs. Neil had "the reputation of being a blackmailer, procuress and prostitute." Walker Percy had obtained the affidavits. House of Representatives, *Inquiry Into the Charge of Bribery*, 320–21.

[94] *Investigation by the Senate of . . . Charges of Bribery*, 94–96, 335–43, 348–54, 359–69, 375–90.

Bilbo himself returned to the witness stand and explained that each of the men who had testified against him had long been his personal enemy.[95]

During the two weeks required for the senate's investigation factional lines remained tightly drawn and tempers sometimes flared. While questioning Dulaney, Senator W. F. Tucker, a defender of Bilbo, asked if Percy had paid the expenses of all candidates who had opposed Vardaman in the caucus. So many senators were immediately on their feet protesting Tucker's question that it took several minutes to restore order. Then from the back of the chamber rose Senator George H. Banks, who shouted that anyone who made such a charge against his friend and former candidate Adam Byrd was "a liar and false as hell." Tucker immediately charged for Banks, but fellow senators intervened and kept them apart.[96]

After listening to the many witnesses, the senate majority attempted to defend its election of Percy and also to destroy Bilbo's charge of bribery. First, the pending resolution to expel Bilbo from the senate failed to obtain the necessary two-thirds majority by a single vote. When a minority of pro-Vardaman senators offered a resolution to protect Bilbo, the majority quickly voted to table it. Then Senator William Anderson's resolution, declaring "Bilbo as unfit to sit with honest, upright men in a respectable legislative body" and asking him to resign, passed by a vote of 25 to 1. Pro-Vardaman senators had refused to vote and had walked out. Without opposition, the majority finally passed a resolution declaring Percy's election had been free of all fraud and corruption.[97]

Like the senate, a majority of the house committee concluded its investigation of the caucus by passing a resolution announcing that Percy had been elected fairly and honestly. Unlike the senate, however, a minority of the house committee issued a separate report charging that unfair methods had been used to defeat Vardaman. During the entire caucus, the minority report pointed out, whiskey had been used excessively and it had helped persuade at least one house member, Representative Robertson, to change his vote from Varda-

[95] *Ibid.*, 390–96, 438–40, 479–86.
[96] Jackson *Daily Clarion-Ledger,* April 9, 1910.
[97] *Investigation by the Senate of . . . Charges of Bribery,* 6–10.

man to Percy. The minority report severely castigated the governor by noting that even though he had never offered any man an office in exchange for his vote, he had "conferred with and advised continually" with the Vardaman opposition and had urged legislators to switch their votes from Vardaman. Even federal patronage had been "brought into play," the minority report noted, although it had been without the knowledge of federal officials.[98]

Far from discrediting Bilbo and ending the charge of bribery, the legislative investigations, especially the senate's, deeply angered many Mississippians. By attempting to impeach Bilbo and by declaring him "unfit to sit with honest, upright men," the senate majority made him a martyr in the eyes of many and in so doing sealed its own doom. From the investigation he emerged as a new hero for those who followed Vardaman.[99] Bilbo refused to resign from the senate and charged that the entire investigation had been a "whitewash." He held that the real powers working to defeat him were the corporations of southern Mississippi he had dared to oppose in the interests of the people. Soon after the investigation he sounded the keynote for the Vardaman-Bilbo forces in the coming campaign: "People of Mississippi, the fight between the classes and the masses, between the corporate influences and the people is on, and it will be a fight to the finish." [100]

Vardaman played no part in the bribery scandal. The charge made by some that he had actually masterminded the whole case against Dulaney in order to help his chances of being elected in 1911 was groundless. Bilbo was his own man. Early in the caucus the former governor had been told by Senator J. O. Poindexter of Bilbo's plan to uncover bribery, and Vardaman had approved it with one stipulation: in the hope of removing all questions that might arise, he insisted that from the legislators opposing him in the caucus there be chosen a man, known for his honesty and integrity, to help catch the briber. After Senator Walter Price, a man who met Vardaman's requirements, refused to have anything to do with the scheme, Vardaman claimed he had been told nothing more of Bilbo's detective work until the time of

[98] *House Journal, 1910,* 1523, 1527–28.
[99] *The Issue,* April 16, 30, 1910; Newton *Record,* April 7, 28, 1910; Yazoo City *Yazoo Sentinel,* April 14, 28, 1910.
[100] *The Issue,* April 30, 1910.

Dulaney's indictment.[101] Probably Vardaman's lieutenants, such as Vaughn Watkins, believed it best that he not become involved in the bribery scandal, for it might backfire and hurt his chances of being elected in 1911. During most of the bribery investigation, Vardaman was conspicuously out of town; immediately after the inquiry into his handling of contingent funds, he had left for the Far West to present his lecture, *The Impending Crisis*. Through editorials in *The Issue* he did sympathize with Bilbo and defended him against the attacks by the senate.[102] Although Vardaman played no part in the bribery scandal, the affair bound him and Bilbo together in a close political alliance which in 1911 would help carry both to victory.

For two years the bribery issue refused to die. In late November and early December, 1910, after several delays and after a change of venue from Jackson to Yazoo City, Dulaney was tried for bribery and acquitted by the unanimous vote of a twelve-man jury, six of whom claimed to be Vardaman supporters.[103] The Percy press hailed Dulaney's acquittal and claimed that it should end once and for all the bribery controversy; Dulaney was innocent, Bilbo had lied.[104] Pro-Vardaman newspapers charged the entire trial had been conducted in a fashion partial to Dulaney.[105] Since an official transcript of the proceedings was not preserved and since newspaper accounts were so strongly biased for or against Dulaney, it is difficult to determine if the trial was conducted fairly or unfairly. The acquittal of Dulaney, however, did not change political developments already under way in Mississippi; if anything, it only strengthened factional lines that were already tightly drawn. While anti-Vardaman men now were more thoroughly convinced that there had been no bribery in the caucus, Vardaman followers considered the trial, like the senate's investigation, just another attempt to whitewash Dulaney and destroy Bilbo. It

101 *Investigation by the Senate of . . . Charges of Bribery,* 158–69, 233–37; House of Representatives, *Inquiry Into the Charge of Bribery,* 118–26; Vicksburg *Herald,* April 7, 1910.
102 *The Issue,* April 2, 16, 1910.
103 Jackson *Daily Clarion-Ledger,* November 22, December 3, 1910.
104 *Ibid.,* December 4, 30, 1910.
105 *The Issue,* December 9, 1910; Newton *Record,* January 5, 12, 1911; Yazoo City *Yazoo Sentinel,* January 12, 1911.

was this belief—that corruption had marred the caucus and that the legislature, the governor, and even the courts were trying to protect the guilty—that drove the electorate into a political uprising the likes of which Mississippi had never known before or has experienced since.

CHAPTER IX

POLITICAL UPHEAVAL

INSTEAD OF ENDING political controversy, LeRoy Percy's election in 1910 initiated a bitter power struggle that lasted almost two years and culminated in the Democratic primary of August 1, 1911. In that primary the most important contest was the senate race between Percy, Vardaman, and Charlton H. Alexander; that struggle affected every candidate running for office in Mississippi. In fact, the election represented a political uprising. It brought into the open a division of whites along class lines—small farmers and laborers rallied behind Vardaman and Bilbo, while most businessmen, lawyers, and planters supported Percy and Alexander. The political alignment that the Populists had tried unsuccessfully to achieve two decades earlier finally came to fruition.

This sudden explosion of class politics did not happen overnight. Economic conditions, educational opportunities, and a recognition of one's "place" in society had long divided Mississippi's whites into social classes, whether they were conscious of it or not. Also the adoption of primary elections in the first decade of the twentieth century had helped to kindle a new political awareness among the people. The caucus of 1910 and the Bilbo-Dulaney bribery scandal convinced many of the newly enfranchised voters that the most popular candidate, Vardaman, had been defeated by unfair means; they wanted to avenge the defeat. In the ensuing political campaign the people were made conscious of social class division, partly by design and partly by accident. Even though the political uprising was beyond the making or control of any one individual, the leading participants, Vardaman, Bilbo, and Percy, were well suited for the roles that history called on them to assume.

Disappointed and angered by Percy's election, many of Vardaman's

230

supporters immediately began to denounce the work of the "secret caucus." Not only had that assemblage used the secret ballot, they charged, but for two months in Jackson political leaders and "bosses" had held secret meetings and had swayed legislators by giving them whiskey and promising them rewards. At a time when the state had already begun to use primaries to elect public officials and when people throughout the country wanted senators popularly elected, the state legislature had resorted to an old-time caucus to elect Percy. The people had been robbed! The indictment of Dulaney for bribery only intensified the wide spread belief that Vardaman had been the victim of corrupt politics. The pro-Vardaman press warned that in 1911 many legislators would have to answer to the people.[1] As for Percy, at first many pitied him for the position he held and for the election he would have to face the following year.[2] The Raleigh *Reformer* well expressed that sentiment:

After a long drawn out contest in which the political wire pullers of the state working in double time, aided and abetted by whiskey, money and the concentrated influence and patronage of the commonwealth's chief executive, the practically unanimous choice of the people has been defeated by the narrow margin of five votes. Against Percy, the man, we have nothing to say, for in common with 90 per cent of the people of Mississippi we know nothing of him, save the fact that he has the appearance of a splendid gentleman. He will doubtless fill the vacancy of McLaurin with . . . satisfaction until March the 4th 1913 when the voters of Mississippi will ask him to get up and let Mr. Vardaman have his seat.[3]

This initial pity for Percy soon changed to anger. Immediately after the senate completed its investigation of the Bilbo-Dulaney bribery scandal, Percy returned to Jackson from Washington and in an address to a joint session of the legislature he denounced Bilbo as a liar and challenged Vardaman to meet him in an early primary election. Instead of waiting until August, 1911, Percy proposed, there should be a special primary in November, 1910, to decide who would fill the re-

[1] Yazoo City *Yazoo Sentinel,* March 3, 10, 24, 1910; Newton *Record,* March 31, May 5, 19, June 9, July 14, 1910; *The Issue,* March 5, 1910.
[2] Vicksburg *Herald,* February 26, 1910; Newton *Record,* April 3, July 21, 1910; Yazoo City *Yazoo Sentinel,* March 3, 10, 17, 1910.
[3] Raleigh *Reformer,* quoted in Newton *Record,* March 10, 1910.

mainder of his present senatorial term as well as the full term that began in March, 1913. Explaining that he did not want to be senator without the complete trust and confidence of the people, Percy promised that if defeated he would resign and he urged Vardaman to join with him in appealing to the state Democratic executive committee to arrange a special primary. Percy knew that an early election would be to his disadvantage because he was not widely known throughout the state. Many newspapers, therefore, hailed his proposal as a courageous act and a fair solution to the senatorial question.[4]

Vardaman quickly accepted Percy's challenge. At that point, however, Governor Noel announced that because he believed an early primary would be illegal, he opposed it. When the executive committee met in early May, 1910, Noel warned that even if it ordered a special primary, he would do everything possible to prevent it.[5] What the governor did not announce publicly, but what he may have told friends on the committee, was that an early primary would be too dangerous politically. The electorate was so aroused over the recent caucus that a November primary would inevitably result in Vardaman's victory. There had to be "a cooling spell" to allow time for the bitterness and excitement of the recent caucus to subside. Moreover, Noel knew that Vardaman's defeat could "only be insured by hard, persistent and well directed efforts." There had to be time to work up issues against him. The governor especially wanted to allow enough time so the charges that Vardaman had stolen from state funds could be more fully developed and thus produce a greater impact upon the voters.[6]

At first it appeared that the executive committee did not share Noel's qualms, because by a vote of 16 to 9 it ordered the special primary. There was only one hitch. The committee required all candidates entering the primary to engage in a series of joint debates; if the candidates refused to provide for such debates, then the committee would make the necessary arrangements for them. Charging that the

---

[4] Macon *Beacon,* April 22, 1910; Tupelo *Journal,* April 22, 1910; Columbus *Commercial,* May 5, 1910; Batesville *Weekly Panolian,* April 21, 1910; Columbus *Commercial,* April 28, 1910; Franklin L. Riley to LeRoy Percy, April 20, 1910, in Franklin L. Riley Papers.

[5] Newton *Record,* April 28, 1910; Jackson *Daily Clarion-Ledger,* April 22, 1910; Columbus *Commercial,* April 24, 1910.

[6] Edmund F. Noel to John Sharp Williams, May 3, 12, 1910, in Williams Papers, Mississippi Department of Archives.

committee had no more authority to order joint debates than it had to determine how many speeches he could make, Vardaman denounced the majority of the committee as men "whose souls are so shriveled with political hatred for me that they would do anything on earth to place me at a disadvantage before the voters of Mississippi." He explained that he believed joint debates between members of the same party only caused bitterness and endangered party unity. Because he refused to agree to joint debates, the committee canceled the special primary.[7]

Without doubt, the majority of the executive committee was against Vardaman and it had adopted a shrewd strategy designed to defeat the special primary and to put the blame for the defeat on him. Although many newspapers ridiculed him for being afraid to meet Percy in joint debate, the former governor probably emerged from the controversy stronger than ever. To many of his followers it appeared that their leader had again been the victim of a small group of politicians determined to offset the will of the people. Some even charged that Percy, Noel, and the committee had worked together; once Vardaman had accepted the challenge for an early primary, Noel and the committee had come to Percy's rescue and gotten him off the hook.[8] That charge had no validity: Percy wanted an early primary. Noel and a majority of the executive committee, however, feared Vardaman would win an early primary and so they skillfully offset it.

Immediately after the collapse of the special primary, Vardaman left Mississippi and resumed a lecture tour in the West. Because it was financially necessary for him to lecture, he did not begin his campaign for the Senate until the following year. While he was away, the senatorial campaign, as well as contests for state offices, got under way with such intensity that many people were alarmed at the spectre of political revolt.

By the late spring of 1910 the senatorial contest had broadened into a three-man fight after Charlton H. Alexander entered the race. Alexander's candidacy was a blow to the Percy forces. Anti-Vardaman leaders tried to make the best of the situation and strove to keep peace

[7] Newton *Record,* May 12, 1910; Jackson *Daily Clarion-Ledger,* May 1, 3, 7, 10, 1910.
[8] Yazoo City *Yazoo Sentinel,* June 2, 1910; Newton *Record,* May 19, 1910.

between Percy and Alexander; they hoped that Alexander would soon drop out of the race and that his votes would shift to Percy.[9] Because Percy had clashed with Noel in requesting the special primary, some feared the governor might throw his support to Alexander. To offset such a danger, Percy was urged to flatter Noel at every opportunity, for the governor "is as susceptible to it as a woman." [10] While Percy's aides tried to minimize the danger of Alexander's candidacy, the entry of the new candidate into the contest delighted the Vardaman forces, who dubbed Percy and Alexander the "gold dust twins." The Vardaman press reminded readers that Alexander had been part of the "common cause" against Vardaman in the caucus and predicted that in the primary, as in the caucus, Alexander would withdraw when Percy so ordered him.[11] But these attempts to alienate Percy and Alexander never succeeded.

As the two candidates canvassed the state during the summer and fall of 1910, they frequently shared platforms in addressing crowds gathered at county courthouses, at public parks, and at barbecues. Although Percy and Alexander opposed each other as strongly as they opposed Vardaman, their joint appearances probably worked to their disadvantage. In an effort to counteract Vardaman's popularity, they strongly attacked him, while treating one another with respect. This may have given many people the impression that the two had formed a combination to defeat Vardaman, for that was what pro-Vardaman newspapers charged.[12]

In one typical speech Percy devoted much time to explaining who he was and to defending himself against many of the charges leveled at him since the caucus. He had never held an elective office, but he had long been active in Delta politics. As a member of his county's Democratic executive committee, his chief job had been to convince

[9] LeRoy Percy to "My dear Williams," May 17, 27, 1910, Williams to Charlton H. Alexander, January 21, 1911, in Williams Papers, Mississippi Department of Archives.

[10] Frederick Sullens to "Dear Mr. Williams," May 24, 1910, in Williams Papers, Mississippi Department of Archives.

[11] Newton *Record*, June 16, 23, 1910; June 15, 1911; Yazoo City *Yazoo Sentinel*, July 21, 1910.

[12] Jackson *Daily Clarion-Ledger*, June 29, August 5, 23, 1910; Macon *Beacon*, July 22, 1910; Yazoo City *Yazoo Sentinel*, June 9, 1910, February 2, 1911; Newton *Record*, February 2, 9, May 4, 1911.

Republicans in Congress that the Negroes in the Delta, who greatly outnumbered the whites, always voted the Democratic ticket. The extent of his wealth and corporate law practice, he told his audiences, had been greatly exaggerated. Boll weevils infested his cotton fields! As a lawyer he had devoted most of his practice to serving the needs of friends and neighbors and only occasionally had represented railroads, banks, and utility companies. Since having been elected senator, moreover, he had abandoned his law practice. Then he turned to his election by the caucus and to Bilbo's charge of bribery. Not only had the caucus been the legal and traditional method for filling a senatorial vacancy, but Vardaman had not opposed it until he had realized he could not win. Vardaman was simply a poor loser. As to the question of bribery, had not the Mississippi senate's investigation disproved it? People who knew him, Percy asserted, knew that he would never accept an office tainted by bribery: "You must go back to my home where I have lived my life to find whether dishonor has ever touched me."

After a lengthy self-defense Percy launched into a detailed discussion of such deadly subjects as the workings of the agricultural department, the abolition of cotton futures, and the expansion of rural mail routes. In his discussion of these issues he repeated again and again his belief that an effective senator had to have a sound head for business and a detailed knowledge of law. During the short time he had served in the Senate he discovered that the chief business of the federal government was to collect revenue and then to disburse it among the states. He intended to see that Mississippi got its share.

Having explained that a senator must be a practical businessman, Percy read an article from *The Issue* in which Vardaman had urged southern congressmen to get off "their craven bellies" and to stop begging the Republican majority for favors. The man who would write such an article, Percy charged, would be of no value to Mississippi in the Senate. The days of extremism had passed; the nation had no respect for men who appealed to radicalism and emotionalism. He then pictured Vardaman as a senator trying to repeal the Fourteenth and Fifteenth amendments: "One can see Mr. Vardaman shake his locks and stride across the Halls of Congress and seize the Grand Old Republican Party and shake it like a terrier shakes a rat, and then kick it around the Halls of Congress and out of the door until it said 'Young man, desist; you are too many for me; take everything you want. Here is the Constitution; take it and fix it to suit yourself.' " In addition, Vardaman had even abused every Republican President since Mc-Kinley, his most recent attack having been directed against President Taft, whom he had described as "addicted to guff, golf and gab, and his smile is set in his face like the grin of a dead pig." Whenever Vardaman's attacks on Republicans and rival politicians had failed to help him, Percy concluded, he had always abused the Negro and had urged such schemes as the repeal of the Fifteenth Amendment. While admitting that he too favored its abolition, he warned that at the time Republicans would not stand for such action. Moreover, the race problem was under control! He maintained: "There was never a time since the war, when the relations between the whites and the blacks were more pleasant or better. Never was white supremacy surer or safer or more complete. No negro votes in Mississippi, nor sits on a jury. And this, without Federal aid, in fact, in spite of Federal opposition. We must not depend on Federal aid to maintain our station." Above all, responsible southern white men must continue to control the existing system of race relations; irresponsible agitators could only endanger it.[13]

In his frequent appearances on the same platform with Percy, Alexander gave speeches that closely resembled those of his rival. He, too, defended the legality of the caucus. Like Vardaman, he had been defeated by the caucus; unlike Vardaman, he had not whined but had taken his defeat like a man. He also agreed with Percy in believing that at the time the race problem should be left absolutely alone. Alexander differed from Percy by emphasizing the need for stricter regulation of corporate wealth; especially did he want the state to exercise greater power in limiting campaign contributions by corporations and in controlling the use of natural resources by industry and lumber companies. Actually, issues had little to do with the contest, Alexander argued, for all three candidates were Democrats and all supported the party's platform. The problem facing the voters was not that of considering issues, but of selecting the man they believed to have the

[13] Percy's entire speech was published in Macon *Beacon,* August 19, 1910. See also Jackson *Daily Clarion-Ledger,* August 31, November 1, 1910.

most character and ability for the job. With those criteria in mind, Alexander hoped a majority would vote for him.[14]

Neither Percy nor Alexander were gifted campaigners and their long, involved speeches were dull. Percy spent too much time explaining the intricacies of cotton futures, and Alexander must have lost the interest of many an audience in describing the complexities of corporate regulation. Neither man had experience in statewide campaigning, and consequently they lacked the rapport with their audiences that Vardaman had developed through years of practice. The summer of 1910 proved to be a difficult time for two such inexperienced candidates to begin a statewide canvass; for Percy it proved disastrous.

Percy's difficulties stemmed in part from the temper of the electorate. Many believed that Vardaman had been defeated in the recent caucus by corrupt methods and Percy came to bear much of the brunt of their dissatisfaction. Of the three candidates only Percy was heckled and hooted at by audiences: that was the price he had to pay for having been the victor in the caucus. Moreover, Percy's wealth, education, and social position separated him from the electorate by a gulf he could not bridge. In an age when men running for office had to be able to win the support and friendship of the voters, Percy proved to be a particularly inept campaigner. Years after the campaign his son William Alexander described a typical audience that candidates had to face in the summer of 1910, and his condescending description gives a valuable insight into his father's inability to communicate with the electorate. "I looked over the ill-dressed, surly audience, unintelligent and slinking, and heard him appeal to them for fair treatment of the Negro and explain to them the tariff and the Panama tolls situation. I studied them as they milled about. They were the sort of people that lynch Negroes, that mistake hoodlumism for wit, and cunning for intelligence, that attend revivals and fight and fornicate in the bushes afterwards. They were undiluted Anglo-Saxons. They were the sovereign voter. It was so horrible it seemed unreal." [15]

On July 4, 1910, Percy addressed such an audience at a political

[14] Jackson *Daily Clarion-Ledger*, June 29, August 25, 1910; Macon *Beacon*, September 23, 1910.
[15] Percy, *Lanterns on the Levee*, 149.

rally at Godbold's Wells, located in the pine woods of southern Mississippi. From miles around people flocked to that rally, many of them having come on trains from McComb and Summit. Although numerous candidates were to speak, what many people wanted most was to meet two famous visitors, Frank James and Kit Dalton, former outlaws whom some looked upon in awe. Compared to James and Dalton, the politicians probably seemed dull and colorless on that hot Fourth of July. When Percy rose to speak, the audience proved hostile and greeted him with shouts of "Hurrah for Vardaman!" and "Hurrah for Bilbo!" As he had to on many occasions during the campaign, Percy demonstrated his personal courage by standing quietly before his hecklers, awaiting silence and an opportunity to speak. The razzing did not stop. Then in anger Percy shouted back at his tormentors. He met "banter with banter and defiance with defiance," wrote one observer, and "a more thrilling encounter of wits was never witnessed." In the heat of that verbal battle Percy made a mistake. He shouted "Cattle!" [16]

Even before Percy's costly slip, many Vardaman followers had been sensitive to charges and insinuations that only hill billies, low brows, and rednecks supported the former governor.[17] Pro-Vardaman newspapers immediately seized upon Percy's denunciation of his Godbold Wells hecklers as cattle, and it became a rallying cry for their cause. Speakers sympathetic to Vardaman taunted their audiences by reminding them that they were cattle and rednecks.[18] Those terms came to symbolize the clash of class against class which the campaign brought into the open. J. A. Dicken, a Vardaman aide, described a trip that he, John Hebron, and Bilbo made to Kosciusko to "feed Vardaman's cattle": "Knowing how hungry they were, we devoted several days in the preparation of such food as we thought would be digestible. When we arrived, we found three or four thousand herded in the

---

[16] Magnolia *Gazette*, July 6, 1910; *The Issue*, July 22, 1910; Jackson *Daily Clarion-Ledger*, July 6, 1910.

[17] *The Issue*, May 14, 21, 1910; Newton *Record*, June 9, 1910.

[18] *The Issue*, October 21, 1910; Newton *Record*, May 4, 25, June 8, 1911. As the campaign progressed, even veteran politicians became rattled by the pro-Vardaman hecklers. Former Congressman "Private" John Allen once shouted to a hostile audience: "I don't believe in niggers voting, but there are lots of niggers superior to white men who have no idea of good citizenship and who yell for Vardaman." *The Issue*, July 14, 1911.

court house yard, and such bellowing and bleating would arouse the ire of LeRoy until he would surely want to put up another fight. . . . Senator Hebron was the first to scatter the feed around. He pitched in such arm fulls that those cattle raised such a noise that you could not have heard it thunder. They bellowed and pawed the dirt." Then Bilbo rose to feed the hungry herd:

Well sir, he is the most reckless feeder you ever saw. He pitched it in every direction by the bundle, and they would run over each other to get to it. As they ate they would bellow and bleat—even the yearlings would join in the chorus—and when Bilbo had pitched the last bundle, they hooked him up on their horns and ran all around the lot, followed by almost the entire herd, bellowing, pawing the dirt, and acting as if they were going to stampede. The secret caucus so starved out these cattle that they never intend to be herded in such another pen, and they are fattening and shedding off, and as sure as 1911 arrives they are certainly going to stampede.[19]

It was Bilbo, in fact, more than any other man, who whipped the white masses into fury and excitement. While Vardaman was away during the summer of 1910, Bilbo became the most exciting speaker in the campaign. Probably a more controversial character has never burst forth so suddenly on the political scene of any state. When he began campaigning for lieutenant governor, people wanted to see and hear him because he had charged Dulaney with bribery. Early in the campaign Bilbo appeared nervous at the beginning of his appearances but as he warmed to his subject and as his listeners encouraged him by shouting "Go on, Bilbo," "Eat 'em up, boy," "We believe you, old man," his uneasiness vanished and he launched into his speech with enthusiasm.[20] Speaking two and three times a day, he discovered that a certain gesture, expression, or inflection of his voice evoked a favorable response and he then would use it again and again. As the summer advanced, his method became more polished and he frequently brought his audiences to their feet shouting. Never hesitating in his delivery, Bilbo used the idiom of the people, and so directly and forcefully did he speak that there was "none of that moving out or rest-

[19] Newton *Record,* August 11, 1910; *The Issue,* August 19, 1910.
[20] Yazoo City *Yazoo Sentinel,* June 2, 9, 1910; Newton *Record,* June 9, 23, 30, 1910; Magnolia *Gazette,* September 21, 1910.

lessness that shows weariness or inattention." [21] Above all, he convinced many people that he told the truth. Men who came to jeer, stayed to cheer. Bilbo was political dynamite.

Bilbo entitled his speech "Jim Vardaman, the Radical; LeRoy Percy, the Conservative; Grandma Noel, the Sissy; Senator Bilbo, the Liar." After first describing the attempts that had been made to slander and discredit him since having testified against Dulaney, Bilbo gave his version of how Percy had been elected senator. The caucus had been an organization—"a hell of an organization"—which had had the sole objective of defeating Vardaman. Legislators had no right to elect United States senators by secret ballot. Any man who believed that was either a liar or insane! Bilbo did not hesitate to name the men who had worked to defeat Vardaman. Many a legislator he had seen going and coming from the private railroad car of Jim Neville, an official of the Gulf and Ship Island Railroad, who generously gave cigars, whiskey, and advice on how to vote. Then there was the leader of the anti-Vardaman forces in the legislature, Senator Washington Gibbs, who Bilbo described as an "old renegade Confederate." Bilbo reserved his most savage attacks for Governor Noel, whom he denounced for having used the powers vested in him by the people for the dastardly purpose of defeating Vardaman. He maintained that Noel had promised to appoint legislators and their friends to judgeships and county attorneyships if they would not vote for Vardaman! Finally he described how Dulaney had paid him $645 to vote for Percy and how his fellow senators had tried to destroy him for his subsequent efforts to defend the people's interests by uncovering corruption.[22]

Early in the summer Percy announced that he would not speak from the same platform with Bilbo and he accordingly rejected an invitation to attend a political rally scheduled for July 1 at Lauderdale Springs. The Vardaman press harshly criticized Percy's refusal to speak, and some newspapers published a telegram sent by Bilbo to the chairman of the rally in which he taunted Percy: "Your telegram announcing the flight of the enemy on first approach, just received. I am very sorry, indeed, but presume the Hon. LeRoy Percy was afraid

---

[21] Macon *Beacon,* October 14, 1910.
[22] Newton *Record,* June 30, 1910.

that he would not have his secret caucus legislature along to 'applaud' when he cussed Bilbo." [23] In response to Bilbo's challenge Percy agreed to the engagement, and as a result hundreds of people attended, hoping perhaps to witness a confrontation between Percy and Bilbo. Knowing that Bilbo was going to tell his story of the caucus, Percy's brother, Walker, tried unsuccessfully on the morning of the rally to kill him. At six o'clock on the morning of the rally Bilbo sat in a "dreary dining-room eating breakfast." A few tables away sat Walker Percy, who suddenly rose, pointed at Bilbo, and "boomed out the epithet which makes an American fight if he's a man." Bilbo ignored Percy and continued eating his oatmeal.[24]

Later from the front porch of an old hotel he gave his speech to a wildly enthusiastic crowd. At the conclusion of his speech several followers hoisted him onto their shoulders and the people cheered and cheered. It was no easy task for LeRoy Percy to follow such a demonstration. The audience, now openly hostile to Percy, jeered and howled when he rose to speak. Fearlessly facing the crowd, Percy eventually silenced his hecklers with stinging insults and then launched into a scathing denunciation of Bilbo, who sat nearby quietly rocking on the hotel porch. In cold fury Percy denounced Bilbo as a "vile degenerate" and a "consorter with lewd women," and he warned that before the campaign ended Vardaman "will be praying to his God: Oh God! deliver me from this body of death." Although the crowd cheered Percy's speech, Bilbo had carried the day.[25] In the future Percy avoided addressing gatherings on days Bilbo was scheduled to speak.

From the beginning of the campaign anti-Vardaman leaders tried to stop Bilbo from speaking. Any man who slandered the governor and the legislature as did Bilbo, they argued, should not be allowed to speak in public, and accordingly they frequently refused to let him speak in schoolhouses, in courtrooms, and at political rallies. The attempts to silence Bilbo rarely worked, and they even convinced some that he was being persecuted by the same forces that had been responsible for Vardaman's defeat in the caucus. People wanted to hear

23 *Ibid.*, June 16, 1910; *The Issue*, June 24, 1910.
24 Percy, *Lanterns on the Levee*, 149–50.
25 Newton *Record*, July 7, 1910; Natchez *Daily Democrat*, July 2, 1910; Jackson *Daily Clarion-Ledger*, July 2, 3, 1910.

Bilbo and hear him they did, because he spoke in fields, on street corners, along railroad rights-of-way, and anywhere else a crowd could gather. The attempts to silence him only enhanced his popularity, as was so well illustrated at a rally in the little town of Newton. Although he had not been invited to speak, he was present and sat quietly in the audience. Many demanded that he be given a chance to speak, but the officials in charge of the rally refused. Several men then pulled a wagon into a nearby field and just as Charlton Alexander began to deliver his address, Bilbo mounted the wagon and began speaking. Most of the crowd then flocked to the wagon, only a few remained around the platform listening to Alexander.[26]

Some were able to stand up to Bilbo and answer him in front of wildly partisan crowds. Representative T. O. Yewell and Senator James A. Cunningham, for example, met Bilbo on the stump where they denounced him as a liar and charged that he had committed various sex crimes.[27] Others who attempted to meet him were not so fortunate. In his own home town of Bay Springs, Senator C. W. Thigpen tried to answer Bilbo's charges against the caucus, but he became nervous and rattled by Bilbo's stinging rebukes and by the crowd's thundering applause. In desperation he shouted to his listeners, "Will you allow a man who abuses your governor and the courts to come into my own town and crucify me?" [28] They did. On another occasion Bilbo shared the platform with Representative Van Buren Boddie. In the midst of a warm exchange Boddie struck Bilbo in the face and then Bilbo threw him to the floor, jerked off Boddie's wig, and slapped him.[29]

By the end of the summer Bilbo had become a phenomenon in state politics. What explains it? It was more than his ability to hold a crowd's attention, more than his sensational disclosures about the caucus, and more than the attempts to silence him or to answer him. Of greater importance in explaining Bilbo's appeal to the people was the belief expressed by the *Jones County News*: "There is some indescribable something in the demeanor of the young senator which carries

[26] Newton *Record,* July 28, August 4, 1910.
[27] Macon *Beacon,* August 26, 1910.
[28] Newton *Record,* August 11, 1910.
[29] *Ibid.,* September 15, 1910; Jackson *Daily Clarion-Ledger,* September 9, 1910.

conviction, and we are forced against our own will to the conclusion that he is telling the truth. . . . Senator Bilbo is telling the truth about the 'secret' caucus. The whole miserable affair was so rotten and the temper of Mississippians is manifested in the demonstrations recently made against the beneficiary of such rottenness." The Crystal Springs *Meteor* expressed a similar view: "At first blush, we attributed the drawing powers of the man to idle curiosity—a desire to see the person who caused the most tremendous political sensation in the annals of the state—but there is something more deep seated, more impelling than curiosity—a wide-spread conviction that there was 'something rotten in Denmark' pending the sitting of the late and lamented caucus." [30]

As Bilbo's speeches helped to convince thousands of people that Percy had been elected corruptly, the caucus became a leading issue during the summer of 1910 in the state's congressional elections. Nowhere was the issue more clearly drawn than in the fifth congressional district where Samuel A. Witherspoon, a strong Vardaman man, challenged the incumbent, Adam M. Byrd. Because Byrd had been a senatorial candidate before the caucus and because Witherspoon so strongly denounced the "secret caucus," the election proved a test of strength between Vardaman supporters and enemies. John Sharp Williams, for example, considered Witherspoon's candidacy as a "tail to the Bilbo-Vardaman kite and hence the importance in the cause of political decency of defeating him." [31] The Byrd-Witherspoon race proved to be a hard-fought contest in which the two men frequently engaged in joint debates. Witherspoon attacked his opponent for having abandoned his congressional duties during the caucus in order to join the "conspiracy" against Vardaman. In defending himself against that charge, Byrd argued that he had never joined a combination against Vardaman—he had run for the Senate to win, not to help Percy.[32]

Byrd was already on the defensive when, late in the campaign, Bilbo began to tell his story of the caucus to huge crowds throughout

[30] *Jones County News,* quoted in Newton *Record,* July 28, 1910; Crystal Springs *Meteor,* quoted in Newton *Record,* July 21, 1910.
[31] Williams to "My Dear Mr. Foster," August 18, 1910, in Williams Papers, Mississippi Department of Archives.
[32] Newton *Record,* June–August, 1910.

the fifth congressional district. Perhaps by himself, Witherspoon would have beaten Byrd, but without doubt Bilbo contributed to the incumbent's defeat. Both sides clearly understood the significance of Witherspoon's victory. LeRoy Percy even admitted the Vardaman forces had "a right to feel elated over it." [33] Vardaman backers did indeed rejoice at the outcome; some warned that Witherspoon's victory only previewed the magnitude of Vardaman's victory over Percy and Alexander the next year.

Although the Byrd-Witherspoon race received the most attention and although factional lines were most clearly drawn in that contest, pro-Vardaman candidates also won in the second, fourth, and sixth congressional districts. Three incumbent congressmen, those in the first, third, and eighth districts, had no opposition in their bids for reelection. Only in the seventh congressional district did incumbent William A. Dickson defeat a pro-Vardaman candidate, Percy Quinn. Dickson, however, had wisely avoided taking a stand on the caucus. With victories by Vardaman men in four out of five congressional races, especially Witherspoon's triumph, by the fall of 1910 the prospect of a Percy or Alexander victory was not bright.[34]

Like the congressional elections, Vardaman's lone public appearance in Mississippi during the fall of 1910 must have dimmed the hopes of his opponents. After he had completed his lecture tour, his aides arranged for a rally on October 29 at the state fair. On that day followers of the former governor from throughout the state descended on Jackson and more than five thousand people flooded the fairgrounds. At eleven in the morning Vardaman began speaking to the cheering multitude. Never once did he mention his opponents, Percy and Alexander, who for four solid months had been campaigning. He did not have to mention them, because Bilbo and other anti-

[33] LeRoy Percy to John Sharp Williams, August 29, 1910, in Williams Papers, Mississippi Department of Archives. Williams believed Byrd had conducted a weak campaign, for he had not admitted that he had joined a "combination" during the caucus of 1910 to defeat Vardaman. Williams believed Byrd should have openly admitted that he opposed "Vardaman and Bilbo because of what they meant to the state, the south and the nation." Williams to Percy, September 1, 1910, Williams to V. F. Cameron, September 12, 1910, in Williams Papers, Mississippi Department of Archives.

[34] Magnolia *Gazette,* August 31, September 7, 24, 1910; Jackson *Daily Clarion-Ledger,* September 1, 1910; Newton *Record,* September 29, 1910.

caucus candidates had already dramatized the issues and personalities of the campaign. So he entertained the crowd with a brief discussion of national issues along with well-chosen excerpts from his lecture, *The Impending Crisis,* which he had given daily during the past five months. When he stopped speaking at one o'clock, hundreds of his impassioned followers charged the small platform on which he stood, and only the frantic efforts of his aides prevented him from being pulled bodily into the crowd. Then someone from the mob jumped onto the platform and jerked off his wide-brimmed hat and in no time men cut it into pieces and distributed them as souvenirs. After almost an hour of handshaking, Vardaman tried to descend the platform, but at once several men seized him, hoisted him to their shoulders and then carried him through the cheering crowd to a waiting automobile. Jackson had never known such a demonstration.

Although the candidates stopped giving speeches in the fall of 1910, the state newspapers carried on the campaign. From the caucus of 1910 through the primary of August, 1911, in fact, the campaign dominated the attention of the press. Because Percy was attacked far more frequently than Alexander, anti-Vardaman editors devoted much attention to defending him. Accordingly, they pictured Percy as a man standing against the wave of radicalism that had swept the South for the past twenty years. While no one defined radicalism, it was said to be associated with "demagogues" like Ben Tillman of South Carolina, with needless racial agitation, and with attempts to discourage capital from coming into the South. As governor, they charged, Vardaman's reckless agitation had driven Negroes and capital from Mississippi, and the abuse and vilification with which he had filled his newspapers only stirred strife among the people. Percy could be counted on to curb such dangerous policies.[35] Then in hopes of ending the outcry against the caucus, the anti-Vardaman press charged that the issue should be dropped because a Mississippi jury, as well as both houses of the state legislature, had ruled that Dulaney had not bribed Bilbo.[36] Finally, they explained that on the unfortunate day at Godbold's Wells,

[35] Macon *Beacon,* April 29, May 6, 13, 27, July 15, August 12, 1910; Columbus *Commercial,* May 8, 1910.
[36] Macon *Beacon,* May 6, 27, July 1, 27, September 9, 1910; May 12, July 21, 1911.

Percy had not called the crowd cattle; he had shouted only at those hoodlums who had lacked the decency to let him speak.[37]

As the campaign progressed, the attacks upon Vardaman by the opposition press became rougher and rougher. At first he was accused of shouting "nigger" solely to win office, of having adopted the platform of the Populist Party, and of being afraid to meet Percy and Alexander in joint debates.[38] Then hostile newspapers began hammering away at his personal honesty. Was not the "evil Bilbo" actually Vardaman's hired henchman? Why had it taken the jury in Yazoo City only eighteen minutes to acquit Dulaney? The answer was simple. When Bilbo had testified in court, every member of the jury had concluded that he was lying. Yet Vardaman still believed Bilbo! [39] Not only did he employ a "self-confessed bribe-taker," Vardaman himself was personally dishonest. As governor he had stolen money from the state. Although the legislative investigation of 1910 had found no evidence that he had mishandled state funds, the opposition press charged that such evidence did exist and in an effort to convince readers, it sometimes published detailed statistics which supposedly proved that Vardaman was a thief.[40]

Frederick Sullens, who as editor of the Jackson *Daily News* had become one of Vardaman's most persistent and caustic critics, gave what he hoped would be both a sensational and deadly blow. Soon after the caucus, Sullens claimed that despite Vardaman's pretense of being a foe of railroads and other corporations, he actually was a hypocrite and a tool of the railroads, because as governor he had used a free pass. At first Sullens offered no proof and for almost a year he taunted Vardaman for having used the pass. In January, 1911, Vardaman finally demanded that Sullens prove that he had used a pass or stand branded a liar. The latter quickly complied. On the front page of the *News* he published the Gulf and Ship Island pass number 834 bearing

[37] *Ibid.,* November 4, 1910, July 28, 1911; Jackson *Daily Clarion-Ledger,* October 4, 1910.

[38] Macon *Beacon,* June 3, 17, July 8, August 26, October 14, 1910; Jackson *Daily Clarion-Ledger,* November 20, 1910, February 12, April 25, 1911.

[39] Macon *Beacon,* June 10, September 16, 1910, February 3, April 21, July 28, 1911.

[40] Jackson *Daily Clarion-Ledger,* May 13, August 9, 11, October 11, 1910, May 9, July 2, 1911; Macon *Beacon,* April 22, May 13, 1910, March 4, 17, May 26, June 2, July 7, 1911.

Vardaman's signature and dated March 21, 1904. Vardaman had used the pass in traveling from Jackson to the Gulf Coast to inspect Beauvoir, Jefferson Davis' former home which the state then had been in the process of taking over and turning into a home for Confederate veterans. Immediately after the governor had made the trip, officials for the Gulf and Ship Island Railroad had obtained a notarized statement by the train's conductor swearing that Vardaman had used the free pass. Sullens published the conductor's statement along with an article which Vardaman earlier had written on the evils of railroad companies influencing public officials.[41] Although Vardaman never admitted that he had used the pass, it seems clear from the evidence that he did. Yet, except for creating momentary excitement, Sullens' disclosure had little effect on the campaign. He made such an issue of the pass that he overplayed his hand. Some wondered why the railroad officials had so carefully collected and saved the evidence against Vardaman. Did it not prove that the railroads considered him a dangerous foe? The governor, moreover, had used the pass in connection with a worthy cause—a home for Confederate veterans.[42]

In retaliation for the attacks by the opposition, the Vardaman press never ceased piling abuse upon Percy. Alexander was immune from such criticism, perhaps because Percy had won the caucus and perhaps because Percy provided such an easy target: his corporate law practice, his inability as a campaigner, and his unfortunate mistake of having shouted "cattle" all combined to make him a sitting duck for the Vardamanites. On two counts they most frequently hit Percy. First, he was described as a wealthy aristocrat who had no sympathy for the people.

Mr. Percy is a man of affairs, of large affairs. In his business dealings he comes in contact with the great of the earth, his practice being largely with and for the railroads. Inborn dignity so peculiar to the air of quaint Greenville, coupled with constant association with nobility of

---

[41] Jackson *Daily News,* quoted in Macon *Beacon,* February 10, 1911. The railroad officials had offered to let John Sharp Williams use the pass against Vardaman in the senatorial campaign of 1907, but Williams had rejected it. By 1910, however, he urged that the pass be so used. Williams to James H. Neville, January 15, April 30, 1910, Neville to Williams, February 22, 1910, in Williams Papers, Mississippi Department of Archives.
[42] Newton *Record,* February 9, March 2, 16, 23, 30, 1910.

the country, may have had a tendency to develop that spirit of haughti-
ness which is so attractive in our betters. For, if the wealthy and powerful did not have that air of distinction and distance, the poor would be
constantly pulling their leg, if we may be permitted to use a common
slang expression in connection with the new senator.[43]

Second, more than any other man, Percy bore the stigma of the secret
caucus, for he alone had emerged from the struggle victorious. Many
demanded that he resign.[44] Editors friendly to Vardaman frequently
compared Percy with William Lorimer of Illinois, who allegedly had
been elected to the Senate after state legislators had been bribed to vote
for him. Both Percy and Lorimer, they charged, had been elected with
the support of large corporations. Both had been elected in defiance of
popular sentiment. Both bore the taint of corruption.

Early in 1911 Percy and Alexander resumed their canvass and
until the August primary they delivered speeches similar to the ones
they had given the previous year, the major difference being that now
each attacked Vardaman more harshly by pointing to his use of the
railroad pass and by ridiculing him for not meeting them in joint debate. Alexander conducted a quiet campaign. Traveling from county
to county, he addressed small, unenthusiastic audiences which listened
to him respectfully. Although the state press gave Alexander little
attention, he proved to be a better campaigner than Percy and in the
August primary he received the larger share of the anti-Vardaman
votes.

By the spring of 1911 some of Percy's friends and supporters organized a central campaign committee to work in his behalf, and the
committee even arranged for Senator John Sharp Williams and former
Congressman John Allen to give speeches in behalf of Percy.[45] The
committee's efforts to bolster Percy's cause, however, proved futile.
Because Congress remained in session during much of 1911, Percy
returned to Mississippi only for brief intervals of campaigning.
Throughout his canvass hecklers continued to jeer and taunt as he

43 Yazoo City *Yazoo Sentinel,* March 10, 1910.
44 *The Issue,* July 7, 1911; Newton *Record,* July 6, 1911.
45 William Crump to John Sharp Williams, March 27, 1911, Williams to F. W.
Williams, July 1, 1911, Williams to T. O. Yowell, March 30, 1911, Williams to
Thomas P. Gore, May 2, 1911, in Williams Papers, Mississippi Department of
Archives.

spoke. Sometimes men from the audience asked questions designed to embarrass him. Was it true that Percy hunted on Sunday? Did he gamble? Did he drink? Had he paid the expenses of any legislators during the senatorial caucus? [46] Although Percy never flinched in standing up to the abuse, he was fighting a hopeless cause and he knew it.[47]

When Vardaman began his canvass in 1911, he had working for him an energetic and well-organized campaign committee. Swep J. Taylor, a Jackson businessman who would later serve as that town's mayor, and H. Vaughn Watkins, an attorney and Vardaman's long-time friend, headed the central campaign committee. That organization kept abreast of developments in each county, it raised campaign contributions, and it arranged the dates and places for Vardaman's appearances.[48] From time to time the central campaign committee warned that Governor Noel was appointing anti-Vardaman men as election commissioners in the hope that they would disfranchise as many voters as possible. All Vardaman men, therefore, should register to vote immediately and see to it that no one stopped them from casting their ballots.[49] Beginning early in 1911 the committee urged that clubs be formed in every county and as the campaign built up momentum many appeared. The Vardaman club in Jackson was the first to be organized and had an initial membership of over five hundred. Although the other groups were neither as large nor as active as the one in Jackson, they all sponsored rallies at which their candidate or one of his aides spoke, they frequently donated railroad tickets to help Vardaman in making his canvass, and on election day they saw to it that all Vardaman men got to the polls.

For weeks after Percy and Alexander had begun actively campaigning in 1911, Vardaman remained quiet. Confident of victory, he rested in preparation for the grueling canvass. So strongly had the caucus and the bribery scandal aroused the electorate, he believed, most people

---

[46] Newton *Record,* June 15, July 13, 1911; Macon *Beacon,* June 23, 1911.

[47] Percy, *Lanterns on the Levee,* 151.

[48] H. Vaughn Watkins to A. S. Coody, March 29, June 5, 1911, Coody to Watkins, May 12, 1911, in A. S. Coody Collection.

[49] *The Issue,* January 6, 1911; Newton *Record,* February 2, April 20, 27, May 11, 1911.

had already decided to vote for him.[50] The task ahead would be to arouse the electorate once again to such a pitch that on August 1, 1911, it would bury Percy and Alexander beneath an avalanche of Vardaman votes. The opening of his campaign on the evening of February 24 in Jackson indicated that his objective was within easy reach. On that cold winter night the Canton, Mississippi, band led thousands of people in a torchlight parade from the depot to the city coliseum, where every seat was taken and standing men lined the walls and aisles. When Vardaman walked onto the stage, the crowd broke into a deafening roar that even drowned out the band's playing of "Dixie." After order had been restored, he gave the speech that he would give time and time again during the next six months.

Mississippi needed a senator, he urged, who would help small farmers, laborers, and merchants. The tariff must be lowered, railroads must be more strictly regulated, all subsidies to shipping companies must be abolished. The graduated income tax offered the fairest method of raising revenue, for it collected from the rich and the poor in accord with their actual ability to pay. Why shouldn't the government collect the largest share of revenue from men of great wealth? Did not the wealthy enjoy more benefits from society? Along with an income tax, the country needed a stronger banking system, one in which the federal government would issue all money. For too long, Wall Street bankers had controlled the nation's money supply. Other reforms were needed to preserve the nation's moral fiber. A national prohibition law would help to eliminate one of the greatest curses known to man. In foreign affairs America should never again expend its money and energy by following the imperialistic example of European nations which had so ruthlessly acquired foreign possessions. Rather America should cling to its traditional policy of isolationism and shun such anti republican institutions as large armies and navies. Such institutions threatened the people's very liberty, and they absorbed money that could be used for domestic reforms.

How could the nation achieve the reforms it needed? Vardaman recommended a number of steps. The masses of people—the poorer members of society—should have a greater voice in the government.

[50] Newton *Record,* January 12, 1911.

The government had for too long reflected the wishes of wealthy men. Government should be made more directly responsible to the voters by instituting such reforms as the direct election of senators and the popular election of federal judges. The judiciary especially needed change because the courts had become citadels of conservatism that defended corporations and propertied interests against honest attempts to reform them. The Supreme Court had even ruled the income tax unconstitutional! Above all, the people could gain a greater voice in government by electing men who would defend their interests, men like himself.[51]

In his speeches Vardaman gave little attention to racism, although he still advocated abolishing the Fifteenth Amendment and he warned that Negro crime was steadily increasing. The emotional appeal that he had engendered in past campaigns by riding the Negro issue he nurtured now by discussing the caucus of 1910 and the attacks that had been made upon him. In describing how the caucus had perpetrated a crime upon the people of Mississippi, he refrained from naming the men responsible, but he did refer to Percy as a man "spawned in the cesspool of the secret caucus." [52] Turning to campaign attacks, he charged that someone must have forged his name on the railroad pass which Frederick Sullens had published in the *Daily News*. Those who charged that he had ever stolen a cent while governor were liars and knew that they were liars. In every speech he pointed with pride to his achievements as governor and promised that in the Senate he would continue to work in behalf of the people.

In the campaign of 1911 Vardaman's popularity climaxed. He reached his fiftieth year in sound health. He still brushed his black hair straight back from his forehead and let it fall to his shoulders. While campaigning he continued to wear only white and it was in this campaign that he became widely known as the "White Chief." Because he had spent much of the previous three years lecturing, he had become a more polished speaker. Then, too, the caucus, the bribery scandal, and the speeches that Bilbo had given in 1910 all prepared the people of Mississippi to receive Vardaman as they never had before. Far more important than what he said to his followers during

51 *The Issue,* March 3, 1911; Newton *Record,* July 6, 1911.
52 Newton *Record,* March 2, 1911.

the campaign was what he represented to them—the victim of the caucus and bribery. Although the campaign had unleashed the issue of the elite of society versus the masses of small farmers and laborers, the caucus had also aroused public indignation that cut across class lines. Men from all stations believed corrupt methods had been used to defeat Vardaman in 1910. As a correspondent of John Sharp Williams so well expressed: "I have received letters from friends who were your staunchest supporters in your race [1907], charging Mr. Percy and his friends with every crime on the calendar, and holding up Mr. Vardaman as the representative of every virtue. These men are no triflers, but are substantial citizens, and influential." [53]

So many were the demands to see Vardaman and to hear him that he could not possibly comply with all of them. Everywhere he went large, enthusiastic crowds greeted him. In the little town of McComb, for example, he had been scheduled to speak in the Opera House, but so great was the gathering that at the last minute the speech was shifted to the town park. Because Vardaman was late arriving, the master of ceremonies invited a candidate for the state legislature to address the crowd. Just as he began speaking, Vardaman arrived at the park and as he walked onto the platform bedlam broke forth and shouts of "Vardaman, Vardaman, Vardaman" filled the air. Wisely the legislative candidate immediately sat down and the master of ceremonies quickly introduced Vardaman.[54]

The most celebrated demonstration of the campaign occurred at Meridian on the evening of July 4 when more than two thousand men participated in a Vardaman parade. Bands from nearby towns supplied music for the march, as hundreds of men rode on horseback and other hundreds walked. Many carried flaming torches and others bore signs with such inscriptions as "Cattle," "Rednecks," "Hillbillies," "Low Brows," and "The White Chief." Behind the marchers, mounted high on a long, flat wagon pulled by eighty oxen, rode Vardaman. Men struggled for the honor of leading the oxen, and the crowd along the parade route pushed forward to touch the wagon and, if

[53] Carl H. Shaifee to John Sharp Williams, July 13, 1910, in Williams Papers, Mississippi Department of Archives.
[54] Magnolia *Gazette,* April 26, 1911.

possible, to touch Vardaman.[55] The intensity of the Meridian demonstration not only worried Vardaman's opponents, it baffled them. John Sharp Williams wrote: "I hope the News is right about it taking more than eighty steers to pull Vardaman out, but there was a fanaticism about the fool performance that rather frightened me. When men get to fighting about who shall touch the stupid car, upon which a man almost as stupid is riding, there enters into it a factor of fanaticism that I don't understand and am not capable of measuring." [56]

As in the previous year, Bilbo's campaign in 1911 created great excitement and further enhanced Vardaman's cause. As Bilbo continued to tell the story of the secret caucus, he drew large, enthusiastic crowds. Several incidents in the campaign added to his popularity, the most important occurring a month before the August primary. In a speech at Blue Mountain early in the summer, Bilbo had described John J. Henry as "a cross between a hyena and a mongrel; he was begotten in a nigger graveyard at midnight, sucked by a sow and educated by a fool." [57] Henry, the former penitentiary warden whom Vardaman had dismissed from office, had been circulating unsigned statements charging that, as governor, Vardaman had embezzled state funds. Angered by Bilbo's remark, Henry confronted him on a train while traveling from Starkville to Sturgis and while a friend held the other passengers back at gunpoint, he brutally pistol-whipped Bilbo, fracturing his skull and badly bruising his face and arms. Bilbo was rushed to Jackson aboard a special train, and he spent a week in the hospital recovering from his wounds. Many anti-Vardaman men hailed Henry's action and claimed he had given Bilbo what he deserved. Vardaman's followers, however, denounced Henry's attack as a cowardly act, and some groups held indignation meetings and adopted resolutions praising Bilbo. With the primary less than a month away, Henry's attack greatly increased the excitement of the campaign and it strengthened the Vardaman-Bilbo cause.

[55] Newton *Record,* June 29, July 13, 1911. Several weeks after the Meridian demonstration there was another oxen parade at Louisville, Mississippi, in which Vardaman participated. Macon *Beacon,* July 14, 1911.

[56] John Sharp Williams to Dunbar Rowland, July 10, 1911, in Williams Papers, Mississippi Department of Archives.

[57] Jackson *Daily Clarion-Ledger,* July 8, 1911.

Without doubt Bilbo contributed greatly to Vardaman's success in 1911, for by giving his version of the caucus he helped to create the intense upsurge of favorable sentiment. "He talked to the country people all over the state," one anti-Vardaman writer observed, "and the strange thing is that the people believed him. . . . The people believed that Bilbo is a sadly abused man." [58] Although Bilbo definitely helped Vardaman, it does not appear that the two men were ever close. Each enhanced the political strength of the other. Bilbo's remarks sometimes proved embarrassing to Vardaman, as when on one occasion he publicly denounced a man as a "dirty sheeny Jew." Through *The Issue,* Vardaman explained that he had no control over Bilbo, but maintained that he himself harbored no anti-Semitic sentiments.[59] During the campaign neither eulogized the other. It could well be that they, both of whom enjoyed such great popularity, were jealous of one another. Being a vain man, Vardaman must have disliked having to share the leadership of his faction with a younger man who had risen so quickly to political prominence. Regardless of the personal relations between the two, they formed a political alliance which at the time dominated the politics of Mississippi.

On August 1 the voters elected Vardaman and Bilbo by overwhelming majorities. Vardaman carried seventy-four of the state's seventy-nine counties, his total vote coming to 79,380 compared to Alexander's 31,500 and Percy's 21,521. By receiving 76,240 votes, Bilbo gained a victory over two opponents in the lieutenant governor's race that almost equalled the magnitude of Vardaman's triumph. In most other state elections where candidates had openly campaigned as Vardaman-Bilbo men, they won. The one major exception was the gubernatorial election in which Earl Brewer of Coahoma County had run without opposition. Brewer had skillfully walked a tightrope between the factions. In the state legislative races pro-Vardaman candidates won a majority of seats and thereby insured their control over the legislative session of 1912. Many were surprised that Ross Collins, a Vardamanite who had been little known in the state prior to the campaign, won an upset victory over the incumbent Attorney Gen-

58 W. L. Pryor to John Sharp Williams, August 2, 1911, in Williams Papers, Mississippi Department of Archives.
59 *The Issue,* November 11, 1910, March 3, 1911.

eral S. S. Hudson. So overwhelming was the victory that no one could dispute its decisiveness. Vardaman had reached the apex of his career. He had become the dominant power in Mississippi politics.

Shortly after the election the Vardaman forces staged a huge victory celebration in Jackson. Hundreds of men wore red neckties and red bandannas in celebration of the "redneck" victory. Many newly elected officials, including Bilbo, addressed the cheering crowd and the last to speak was Vardaman. The past campaign, he said, had been marked by bitterness and hatred, but he hoped that ill-feeling would quickly die. He wanted to be senator for all the people and he hoped that in the future he might win the support of many who had voted against him. To those who had voted for him he would be forever thankful, and in the Senate he would do his best to serve them.[60]

The magnitude of the victory shocked many people throughout the nation. Some believed Mississippians had been "imposed upon by the arts of the demagogue," and they were convinced that the state had stepped back into the Dark Ages.[61] The Indianapolis *News* erroneously described Vardaman as a cheap showman who had won the election by riding up and down the state on ox carts shouting "nigger" to all who would listen.[62] Granted he had made an exciting campaign, but he had made little use of racism in it and he had always conducted himself with dignity. Only twice during the campaign had he ridden on ox carts. He was no buffoon, but a proud man who always maintained self-respect.

Early in the campaign R. H. Henry, editor of the *Daily Clarion-Ledger,* provided a valuable insight into the secret of Vardaman's strength.

Vardaman's hold upon his followers is extraordinary and hard to understand, his power over people inexplicable, for he defies all rules of conventionality, and while posing as a commoner, looks and acts the part of the aristocrat. There is nothing about the man that would appear to fascinate or attract what is known as the common people, those who work with their hands, earning their bread in the sweat of their face, for he is always dressed like a dandy, and moves

[60] *Ibid.,* August 11, 1911; Newton *Record,* August 10, 1911.
[61] Justin H. Smith to Dunbar Rowland, September 19, 1911, in Dunbar Rowland Papers.
[62] Indianapolis *News,* quoted in Newton *Record,* August 17, 1911.

around with a stilted imperious air, a kind of look at me style, convey-ing the idea, "if I am not the whole show I am the biggest part of the menagerie, and I don't want you to forget it."

No other man could dress and do as Vardaman does and receive much consideration at the hands of the people. . . .

He is an odd man, a dilettante who seems able to say what he pleases, abuse any body he dislikes, curse out those who oppose him, and still hold his following, to grapple them to him with hooks of steel.[63]

There was much truth in Henry's observation. Far from being "com-mon" in his dress, speech, and personal manner, Vardaman was a sensationalist who stood out from those about him. His dignified car-riage, long hair, and eccentric dress all helped to create the image that he was no ordinary man. But he could talk to people, could understand them, could stir them with his oratory. His disciples, in turn, believed that he understood their needs, and they followed him with an intense devotion.

His victory cannot be attributed solely to his personal magnetism, his appearance, and his ability to speak, for those qualities had been present in 1907 when Williams had defeated him. In 1911 the per-sonalities and issues combined to make conditions right for Vardaman as they had never been before and never would be again. In the first place he faced weak opponents, for Percy and Alexander were in-experienced campaigners, neither of whom excited the electorate. The most decisive influence was the widespread belief that Percy had been unfairly elected, that the "secret caucus" had ignored the will of the people. Then the campaign divided class against class. Percy's costly mistake of having once shouted "cattle" at his audience had been pounced upon by the Vardaman forces and exploited to the hilt. Percy's very presence in the campaign added to the issue of class appeal, because in many ways he was a model of the old southern aristocrat, "polished, reserved, cultured, . . . but poor 'gladhander' and not gifted in the art of popular appeal." Many considered Alexander only a "less pronounced example of the class of which Percy is the archetype." [64] Thus on August 1, 1911, Vardaman's ability as a cam-

63 Jackson *Daily Clarion-Ledger*, February 25, 1911.
64 Baton Rouge *News Advocate*, quoted in Macon *Beacon*, August 18, 1911; John M. Mecklin, "Vardamanism," *The Independent*, LXXI (August 31, 1911), 461–63.

paigner, the weakness of his opposition, the arousal of class feeling and the conviction that the caucus had been corrupt all combined to carry him to his most decisive victory.

The indisputable results of the 1911 primary did not deter Vardaman's and Bilbo's political enemies from making a last-ditch effort to undermine the power of the victors before they had a chance to use it. Governor Noel and a small group of men worked secretly during the fall of 1911 until November, when Noel called a special session of the legislature just sixty days before the next regularly scheduled session would convene. He knew that he had to act quickly, for as one friend noted, once the newly elected state officials took office in 1912, "the dominance of Vardaman in Mississippi is going to be something fierce." [65] He alleged that a special session was needed to defray costs that the state had recently incurred. Not many were fooled by this feeble excuse, and the popular press immediately charged Noel with wanting to give the outgoing legislature of "secret caucus fame" a final chance to slur the Vardaman faction.[66]

The suspicions of Noel's opponents proved true. After the legislature had quickly made the special appropriations that Noel had requested, it then went after Bilbo by changing the state law on bribery. In response to recommendations by the governor, the legislature passed an act empowering circuit judges in cases of bribery to require witnesses to testify even if their testimony incriminated them. To protect such witnesses, the judge at his own discretion could grant them im-

[65] Frederick Sullens to John Sharp Williams, August 11, 1911, in Williams Papers, Mississippi Department of Archives.

[66] Jackson *Daily Clarion-Ledger,* October 20, 1911; Columbus *Commercial,* October 22, 1911; *The Issue,* November 3, 17, 1911; Jackson *Daily News,* November 2, 1911; Magnolia *Gazette,* October 25, 1911. Noel gave two reasons for the special session. First, an appropriation was needed to cover the costs of state troops which had been used to maintain order during railroad strikes at McComb and Water Valley. Second, between July and December, 1910, Noel had sold state bonds on the understanding that interest on all bonds would accrue from July 1, 1910. State Treasurer George Edwards, a strong Vardaman partisan, argued that interest began only at the actual date of the sales and accordingly he refused to pay the accrued interest that came to a total of $10,500. The state supreme court upheld Edwards and, as a result, Noel asked the legislature to make a special appropriation to cover the disputed interest. Throughout the special session, factional lines strongly divided the Vardaman forces and the anti-Vardaman forces.

munity from self-incrimination.[67] The bill was designed to send Bilbo to prison, for during the Dulaney trial in 1910, T. R. James had refused to testify about a report that he had bribed Bilbo, explaining that his testimony might be self-incriminating. Many legislators who voted for the "immunity bill" hoped it would enable James to present evidence which would convict Bilbo.[68]

In the only speech that he delivered during the special session, Senator Bilbo gave a clear and damning analysis of the law. Believing it was designed to prevent him from taking office as lieutenant governor, he considered the law just another attempt to discredit him. Even though the bill was intended to hurt him, he would vote for it. He had nothing to hide. He was "ready for the fray." He wondered, however, if the legislative majority realized what the bill would permit? By empowering judges to grant immunity as they wished, it would endanger many innocent men:

But understand, if you leave immunity solely to the discretion of the judge, I, or any other man, would take $10,000 and go into the slums of this city, or into almost any county in this state, and get evidence to convict any member of this body of any crime in the calendar. And especially is this true in a bribery case, for there is always a question of politics—political motive and political influences—involved in it. And this is why this legislation is so vicious, and every senator on this floor knows it. For, with money, and such influences at work, you can get any kind of evidence and as much as you want when you give the lying criminal immunity from his crime.[69]

Even though the legislature quickly passed the "immunity bill," it was never employed against Bilbo. The reason is unknown. Perhaps someone convinced Noel that the act violated the Fifth Amendment and would probably be ruled unconstitutional if tested in court. A more likely explanation is that James actually had no evidence that Bilbo had ever accepted a bribe. By passing the "immunity bill," however, the anti-Vardaman majority of legislators clearly revealed the extremes to which they would go in attempting to destroy Bilbo.

[67] Jackson *Daily Clarion-Ledger,* November 7, 12, 1911; Magnolia *Gazette,* November 18, 1911; *Mississippi Laws, 1911,* 11–13.
[68] *The Issue,* November 17, 1911.
[69] Newton *Record,* November 23, 1911; *Senate Journal, 1911,* 84–91.

Noel led a stronger fight to keep Vardaman out of the Senate. Immediately after the August primary, Noel and a small group of Vardaman's most resolute enemies, one of whom was Frederick Sullens, began secretly working to prove the old charge that the former governor had stolen from state funds. They covered the same ground as had the legislative investigation of 1910: again the only questionable matter was that some of the vouchers for Vardaman's expenditures were missing from the governor's office. Noel hoped to convince a majority of the United States Senate that Vardaman had been a corrupt governor and therefore should not be seated.[70] John Sharp Williams tried to stop the scheme, arguing that it would establish a dangerous precedent to bar Vardaman from the Senate after he had been legally elected.[71] Noel ignored Williams' advice and immediately after the special legislative session in November, he had Attorney General S. S. Hudson file suit against Vardaman demanding an exact accounting of his expenditures as governor. Hudson also filed suit against two Jackson banks to compel them to turn over their records relating to Vardaman's financial activities while he had been in office. Noel employed two private attornies, Lex Brame and Sergeant Prentiss Knut, to assist Hudson in prosecuting the case.[72]

Through his attorneys Vardaman filed a demurrer, asking that the suit be dropped on the ground that the legislature had already investigated the question of his missing vouchers.[73] While the court was still considering the appeal for dismissal, the newly elected legislature

[70] One of Noel's aides wrote to John Sharp Williams: "Vardaman and Bilbo are both going to be indicted and enough matter will be furnished to keep Vardaman out of the Senate. Nothing is being said, but the work is going on all the same." Sergeant Prentiss Knut to Williams, August 11, 1911, in Williams Papers, Mississippi Department of Archives. Frederick Sullens wrote Williams on the same day: "Don't you think that, if we can convict him of grafting, even though no criminal proceedings are instituted, that we can prevent him from taking his seat in the Senate?" Sullens to Williams, August 11, 1911, and Noel to Williams, August 18, 1911, in Williams Papers, Mississippi Department of Archives.

[71] John Sharp Williams to E. D. DeLap, August 19, 1911, in Williams Papers, Mississippi Department of Archives.

[72] Jackson *Daily Clarion-Ledger*, November 19, December 24, 27, 28, 1911; Newton *Record*, November 23, 1911; *The Issue*, November 24, 1911. Sergeant Prentiss Knut to John Sharp Williams, January 4, 15, 1912, Williams to Knut, January 6, 1912, W. H. Miller to Williams, January 14, 1912, in Williams Papers, Mississippi Department of Archives.

[73] Jackson *Daily News,* January 6, 1912.

convened in early January, 1912. After the majority of Vardaman followers had quickly established control over the assemblage,[74] the senator-elect asked Frank Burkitt, chairman of the joint committee on executive contingent funds, to have the question of his official expenditures thoroughly investigated. Burkitt immediately complied with Vardaman's request, and in less than a week the legislature adopted a report that exonerated Vardaman.[75] Accountant Charles J. Moore, who had been employed by Noel to investigate the ex-governor's financial records, published a statement denouncing Burkitt and his committee for having "whitewashed" the former governor. Moore was especially angered because while he had been testifying before the committee all of the records he had collected about Vardaman's expenditures had been "accidentally" dumped into the Capitol furnace by a porter. As soon as the Jackson newspapers had published Moore's protest, Burkitt's committee resummoned the accountant and fired him on the spot.[76] Soon after the legislature had issued its report, Ross Collins, the new attorney general, withdrew the suit against Vardaman. Only one incident marred Vardaman's victory over his accusers: Williams refused to comply with the legislature's instructions to enter the contingent fund report in the *Congressional Record*.[77]

Just as the anti-Vardaman majority of legislators had run roughshod over the minority in 1910 and 1911, so the supportive majority of 1912 initiated a "steamroller" of its own. Noel became one of its victims. Soon after Burkitt's committee had issued its report exonerating Vardaman, it investigated Noel's expenditures. Like Vardaman, Noel had been an honest governor. The committee, however, reported that Noel had lavishly spent state funds to indulge his pleasures, to

[74] Jackson *Daily Clarion-Ledger*, January 3, 1912; Newton *Record*, January 4, 1912; John W. Webb to John Sharp Williams, January 3, 1912, in Williams Papers, Mississippi Department of Archives.

[75] *Senate Journal, 1912*, 96–102; Jackson *Daily Clarion-Ledger*, January 7, 10, 13, 1912; Magnolia *Gazette*, January 17, 1912; Newton *Record*, February 4, 8, 1912.

[76] Jackson *Daily Clarion-Ledger*, January 16, 1912; Magnolia *Gazette*, January 10, 1912; Jackson *Daily News*, January 7, 8, 12, 14, 1912.

[77] John Sharp Williams to J. W. T. Falkner, January 29, 1912, Williams to Stokes V. Robertson, January 29, 1912, Edmund F. Noel to Williams, February 1, 1912, in Williams Papers, Mississippi Department of Archives.

defray his campaign expenses, and to cover the costs he had incurred while lobbying for his own interests in Washington. Although the two governors had received identical contingent fund appropriations, the committee concluded, Noel's expenditures had substantially exceeded Vardaman's.[78] The Jackson *Daily News* immediately denounced the report as the work of Frank Burkitt, "the hoary-headed hellion whose political knavery and malevolent machinations, have made him the acknowledged leader of the Vardaman forces in the senate at this session." [79] In response to the attack on Burkitt, the legislature barred *News* reporters from attending its proceedings for the remainder of the session.

The pro-Vardaman majority also inflicted its wrath upon LeRoy Percy, who in the wake of his crushing defeat in 1911 had announced that at the next regular legislative session he would resign from the Senate.[80] Later Percy changed his mind and decided to complete his term. *Cosmopolitan Magazine* had published an article which sharply criticized Percy's 1910 election by the caucus, and he decided that he could not resign honorably.[81] The pro-Vardaman members of the legislature, therefore, passed a resolution instructing him to resign. When the senator rejected the instructions, the legislature then passed a series of strongly critical resolutions.[82]

Despite its attacks upon Noel, Percy, and a number of lesser state officials, the legislature of 1912 failed to initiate the radical era of "socialist" and "anarchist" rule that some anti-Vardaman newspapers had predicted. Far from attempting changes in the existing social and economic systems, it failed even to produce a record of progressive reforms as had earlier state legislatures in 1906 and 1908. Perhaps the pro-Vardaman majority expended too much energy inflicting revenge upon Noel and Percy. Weak executive leadership also account-

[78] *Senate Journal, 1912,* 655–60.
[79] Jackson *Daily News,* February 26, 1912.
[80] Jackson *Daily Clarion-Ledger,* August 5, 8, 1911; Macon *Beacon,* August 4, 11, 1911.
[81] Columbus *Commercial,* October 29, 1911; Jackson *Daily Clarion-Ledger,* December 13, 1911; John Sharp Williams to LeRoy Percy, October 26, 1911, Percy to Williams, November 2, 1911, in Williams Papers, Mississippi Department of Archives.
[82] Jackson *Daily News,* March 5, 10, 1912; Jackson *Daily Clarion-Ledger,* March 14, 1912; Newton *Record,* March 7, 14, 21, 1914.

ed for the legislature's failure to achieve an impressive record of reform. Governor Brewer failed to pursue a carefully planned legislative
program and devoted most of his attention to trying to establish peace
between the warring factions.

Although 1912 was an election year, the Mississippi public expressed little interest in the struggle—between Woodrow Wilson,
Champ Clark, and Oscar Underwood—for the Democratic presidential nomination. The hard-fought political campaigns of the past two
years had convinced many that they had had enough of politics. The
state's political leaders, however, did take a keen interest in the nomination fight, and they followed a strange and baffling course in supporting the candidates. Brewer, Percy, Vardaman, and a majority of
state officials supported Underwood, a conservative Democratic congressman from Alabama. Senator Williams and Lieutenant Governor
Bilbo backed Wilson, who had so recently risen to national prominence as a reform governor of New Jersey. Attorney General Ross
Collins supported Clark, the speaker of the state house of representatives and a man of mediocre ability.[83]

This strange choice of political bedfellows can certainly not be explained on the basis of issues. The most conservative of the three
candidates, Underwood, had the support of Percy, a conservative, and
Vardaman, a "radical" progressive. Even Williams thought Underwood would make an able president, although he supported Wilson
because he thought that only the New Jersey governor could beat the
Republicans. Underwood cut across the factional lines drawn among
the Mississippi politicians and appealed instead to their sectional pride.
He was, after all, the first resident southerner to be a candidate for
the presidency since 1860.

In accord with an appeal made by Vardaman, the state Democratic
executive committee met on April 18, 1912, and ordered a party
primary on May 7 to determine the state's preference for presidential
nominee and to elect delegates for the Democratic national convention. Also on that date the state's Democrats would gather in precinct

[83] Newton *Record,* April 25, 1912; John Sharp Williams to C. C. Elliot, April
17, 1912, in Williams Papers, Mississippi Department of Archives; Walker W.
Vick to A. S. Burleson, in Albert Sidney Burleson Papers, Library of Congress;
Arthur S. Link, "The Underwood Presidential Movement in 1912," *Journal of
Southern History,* XI (1945), 231–45.

meetings to select delegates for the state convention which would meet on May 15 in Jackson and canvass the vote of the primary. The hastily called primary attracted little interest, for scarcely a third of the electorate bothered to vote. Because of a $50 filing fee, only the names of Underwood and Wilson appeared on the ballot, and the Alabaman won by a vote of 38,343 to 20,482. Vardaman followers dominated the precinct elections and thereby insured their control over the state convention.[84]

The state convention proved to be a "Vardaman day from start to finish." The newly elected senator saw to it that his friends dominated the new state executive committee, and he personally supervised the writing of the party platform, which advocated such reforms as a low tariff, an elective federal judiciary, abolition of the Fifteenth Amendment, stricter regulation of railroads, restriction of corporate land holdings, direct election of senators, national prohibition, and federal support for flood control and road construction. Twice during the convention Vardaman and Charlton Alexander engaged in harsh verbal clashes. The first occurred when Alexander asked the convention to adopt a resolution commending the state legislature for not having followed Vardaman's campaign plan to repeal the Fifteenth Amendment. Vardaman immediately arose and castigated his critic. With a "defiant toss of his head" and a finger pointed at his opponent, Alexander began to reply, but he was loudly booed and the chairman ruled him out of order. Later Alexander argued against a resolution instructing the Mississippi delegation to vote as a unit at the national convention. Alexander, who had been elected a delegate and who supported Woodrow Wilson, believed unit rule should apply only as long as Underwood remained in the contest. Before Alexander could say anything more he was again booed and forced to take his seat. No one came to his aid. Then Vardaman rose and in "an impassioned speech which fairly blazed" denounced Alexander for threatening to disobey the instructions of the convention.[85]

After Alexander had been booed from the convention floor and

[84] Jackson *Daily Clarion-Ledger,* May 14, 15, 1912; Magnolia *Gazette,* May 11, 1912; Arthur S. Link, "The South and the Democratic Campaign of 1912" (Ph.D. dissertation, University of North Carolina, 1945), 317–19.
[85] Jackson *Daily Clarion-Ledger,* May 16, 1912; Magnolia *Gazette,* May 18, 1912; Newton *Record,* May 23, 1912.

was walking to his home, he suddenly reeled and fell to the ground—
the victim of a stroke that killed him instantly. This disconcerting turn
of events certainly dimmed the luster of Vardaman's victory in the
convention, but it did not eliminate the indisputable fact of the existence of a Vardaman "steamroller" in Mississippi politics.

When the Democratic national convention met on June 25 in Baltimore, Vardaman was able to play a role of moderate importance
because of his long-time friendship with William Jennings Bryan. Since
the presidential campaign of 1896 Vardaman had greatly admired
Bryan. After that election, while visiting in Mississippi on two occasions, the Nebraskan had been a guest in Vardaman's home. In Baltimore Bryan had declared himself in open opposition to the choice
of the majority of leaders for temporary chairmanship of the convention. He wanted a progressive Democrat for the position and announced he would fight the nomination of conservative Judge Alton B.
Parker. In an effort to avoid an open battle within the convention, a
group of party leaders persuaded Vardaman to offer Bryan the permanent chairmanship of the convention in return for dropping his opposition to Parker. When Bryan heard the offer, he became so "frigid"
that Vardaman picked up his hat and while making his way to the
door explained, "I thought our personal and political relations were
intimate enough to permit me to talk about the matter to you." Then
putting his hand on Vardaman's shoulder, Bryan explained that he
had not intended to offend him, but he could not accept the offer. Despite Bryan's opposition, Parker won the temporary chairmanship.[86]

Bryan then caused an uproar in the convention by introducing a
resolution pledging the party not to nominate any candidate subservient
to "J. P. Morgan, Thomas Fortune Ryan, August Belmont, or any
other member of the privilege-hunting and favor-seeking class" and demanding the withdrawal of delegates representing Wall Street interests.
Because Belmont and Ryan were delegates to the convention, Bryan's
resolution posed a serious problem. Southerners especially disliked
the resolution, because it interfered with a state's election of its dele-

---

[86] New York *World,* June 24, 1912, quoted in Arthur S. Link, *Wilson: The
Road to the White House* (Princeton, 1947), 435; Magnolia *Gazette,* June 26,
1912; Newton *Record,* July 25, 1912.

gates. Vardaman shared the sentiment of his fellow southerners and he therefore asked Bryan to withdraw that part of his resolution demanding the expulsion of Ryan and Belmont. Vardaman's second attempt to mediate with his old friend proved more successful. Bryan agreed to the request, and the resolution, then in harmless form, easily passed.[87]

For forty-five ballots the Mississippi delegation stuck with Underwood. But many of the Mississippi delegates were being swayed by the pro-Wilson sentiment that steadily increased as the convention remained deadlocked. After all, Wilson was a man of proven ability and his Virginia birth and Georgia boyhood was a source of pride for all southerners. Only the insistence of Governor Brewer that the delegation follow their instructions kept Mississippi in Underwood's camp for as long as it was there. Vardaman originally had favored Champ Clark as his second choice, but after a majority of his fellow Mississippi delegates said they wanted Wilson, he, too, switched his support to the New Jersey governor and did it "very gracefully." [88] On the forty-sixth ballot the Mississippi delegation, along with those of Alabama, Georgia, and Florida, went to Wilson and thereby helped him to win the nomination.

Many hailed Wilson's nomination as a personal victory for John Sharp Williams, since he had openly supported the nominee throughout the preconvention contest.[89] In a way it was, for eventually Wilson and Williams became intimate friends, while Vardaman remained outside the circle of the future President's close friends and aides. Shortly after the convention Vardaman volunteered to campaign anywhere in behalf of the Democratic ticket, but Wilson ignored his offer.[90] Vardaman's offer was ignored, perhaps, because during the campaign of 1912

[87] Link, *Wilson: The Road to the White House,* 444; Urey Woodson (ed.), *Official Report of the Proceedings of the Democratic National Convention of 1912* (Chicago, 1912), 132; Memphis *Commercial Appeal,* quoted in Newton *Record,* July 11, 1912.

[88] Williams to Edmund F. Noel, July 9, 1912, in Williams Papers, Mississippi Department of Archives.

[89] M. G. Campbell to Williams, July 3, 1912, Thomas Springth to Williams, July 3, 1912, H. C. Herring to Williams, July 3, 1912, in Williams Papers, Mississippi Department of Archives.

[90] Vardaman to Wilson, July 8, 1912, in Woodrow Wilson Papers.

Wilson tried to lure the Negro vote away from the Republicans. Undaunted, Vardaman warmly congratulated Wilson following the Democratic victory in November and predicted he would "be the first really American president we have had since the war between the states." [91] Events of the next six years shattered his great expectations.

[91] Vardaman to Wilson, December 14, 1912, in Woodrow Wilson Papers.

CHAPTER X

PROGRESSIVE
SENATOR

BY LATE FEBRUARY, 1913, Vardaman was ready to move to Washington, for he wanted to be there in time for Wilson's inauguration on March 4. Earlier he had severed his connections with *The Issue*, which had been purchased by three of his friends, John L. Hebron, H. M. Quinn, and Swep J. Taylor. Two days before Vardaman left for Washington, some of his supporters arranged for a final demonstration in Jackson, and on the evening of February 27 more than two thousand people marched in a torchlight parade that culminated in a rally at the Century Theatre. So many of his friends honored him with tributes and eulogies that it was late in the evening before he was able to speak. He was visibly moved and his voice trembled as he thanked the crowd for "the most thrilling thing he had ever experienced." He promised that as a senator he would work to fulfill his campaign pledges. His brief farewell address even moved one of his avowed opponents, R. H. Henry, editor of the *Daily Clarion-Ledger*, who wished him well and predicted that in the Senate Vardaman would bring honor on himself and his state.[1]

Vardaman and Wilson assumed their new duties at a time when the progressive movement stood at the crossroads. During the presidential campaign of 1912 Wilson and Roosevelt had utilized different approaches in the quest to solve the nation's social and economic problems. Through his program of the New Freedom, Wilson had urged the restoration of free competition in business by destroying special privileges and artificial barriers. Specifically, he advocated a stronger antitrust law to abolish monopolies, a sharp reduction in the protective tariff, and a new banking and currency system. He did not believe government should intervene directly in attempting to cope with the

[1] Jackson *Daily Clarion-Ledger*, February 21, 27, 28, 1913.

267

problems of laborers and farmers; rather, government should simply play the role of an impartial policeman.

In outlining his program of the New Nationalism, Roosevelt, the Progressive Party candidate, called on Americans to abandon their old laissez-faire ideas and to replace them with a new approach in which government would assume an active role in attacking economic and social problems by directly intervening to control large corporations, protect laborers, and improve the lot of oppressed groups. He expounded his programs in bolder terms as the campaign advanced and advocated a national child labor law, a workman's compensation act for federal employees, and a minimum wage for women workers. Despite widespread support for his program, Roosevelt bore the burden of having split the Republican Party, and Wilson—with the backing of a united Democratic Party—won the election.

Between the time he became President in 1913 and won reelection in 1916, Wilson came to espouse practically all of the programs of Roosevelt's New Nationalism. The experiences of his early years in office caused Wilson to change and expand his views of what was needed to solve some of America's social and economic problems. Besides, he faced a difficult fight for reelection in 1916, for by that time Roosevelt had rejoined the Republican Party. To win again Wilson knew he would have to capture the votes of many Progressives who had supported Roosevelt in 1912, and the surest way to win their allegiance was by adopting the reforms of the New Nationalism.

Other influences that prodded Wilson to move to the left are more difficult to discern. Persistent congressional pressure may have had a bearing on his change because, from the beginning of his administration, a number of congressmen consistently urged that the government adopt bolder reform programs. Most of the strong progressive congressmen were not hampered by a laissez-faire philosophy nor were they dedicated to only one specific reform. They wanted positive programs that called for the government to act directly in meeting the needs of such wide-ranging groups as farmers, industrial laborers, urban dwellers, businessmen, and bankers. Sometimes described as "radical" progressives, they cut across party and sectional lines in Congress, for they drew strength from such midwesterners as Robert La Follette of Wisconsin and George W. Norris of Nebraska, southerners such as Morris Sheppard of Texas and Luke Lee of Tennessee, and westerners such as Harry Lane of Oregon. While Wilson fought for his New Freedom reforms, the "radicals" supported him, although they urged him to go further; when the President finally moved to the left in 1916, the "radicals" were awaiting him and gave valuable support to his new programs.[2]

One of the few southern "radicals" in the Senate was Vardaman.[3] When describing his own political philosophy, he usually claimed to be a Jeffersonian Democrat. In a limited sense he was, for he wanted simplicity in government, the ending of wasteful federal expenditures, and the concentration of political power directly in the hands of the white voters.[4] Consequently, Vardaman favored the popular election of all public officials and came to fear that under Wilson the presidency had usurped too much authority from that branch of the government which directly represented the people—Congress. Because he so stoutly believed in popular government, he found it difficult, for example, to support federal regulatory commissions, fearing that they would undermine popular government by seizing legislative authority.[5]

Coupled with his "Jeffersonian ideals" was a most enlightened progressivism. Representing a rural constituency, he had come to adopt those reforms which the Populists had advocated two decades ear-

[2] Arthur S. Link, "The South and the 'New Freedom': An Interpretation," *American Scholar,* XX (1951), 314–24; Howard W. Allen, "Geography and Politics: Voting on Reform Issues in the United States Senate, 1911–1916," *Journal of Southern History,* XXVII (1961), 216–28; Richard M. Abrams, "Woodrow Wilson and the Southern Congressmen, 1913–1916," *Journal of Southern History,* XXII (1956), 417–37; James Holt, *Congressional Insurgents and the Party System, 1909–1916* (Cambridge, Mass., 1967), 8–15.

[3] Although there is controversy over the influence exerted by southern congressmen on shaping progressive legislation, most students agree that Vardaman was one of the South's strongest progressives during the Wilson era. Link, "The South and the 'New Freedom,' " 319; Abrams, "Woodrow Wilson and the Southern Congressmen," 426; Allen, "Geography and Politics," 228; Anne Firor Scott, "Southern Progressives in National Politics," 184, 219–30; John W. Davidson, "The Response of the South to Woodrow Wilson's New Freedom, 1912–1914" (Ph.D. dissertation, Yale University, 1954), *passim*; George Brown Tindall, *The Emergence of the New South, 1913–1945* (Baton Rouge, 1967), 10.

[4] *Congressional Record,* 63 Cong., 1st Sess., 3321–22, 3328–29, 4814–15, 2 Sess., 10394, 10406; 64 Cong., 1st Sess., 7960, 8048–49, 11805, 13113–15; Vicksburg *Post,* August 15, 1914; Washington *Star,* August 9, 1914, in Vardaman Scrapbook.

[5] *Congressional Record,* 64 Cong., 1st Sess., 9695–96.

lier: government ownership of utilities; an elastic currency; long-term credit for farmers; a strong graduated income tax; postal savings banks and the expansion of parcel post; the initiative, referendum, and recall; and the ending of speculation in agricultural commodities.[6] Vardaman's progressivism went beyond agrarian "radicalism." He considered himself a defender of the "great, silent, slow-thinking, toiling multitude," by which he meant not only small farmers who worked the land, but also laborers who toiled for the nation's industries; as a senator he consistently voted in behalf of labor's interest. Moreover, he supported most of the objectives of the social justice movement, as was evidenced by his votes for child labor laws, immigration restriction, and woman suffrage. Above all, he believed in the need for a dynamic federal government, and he scorned the arguments that some of the Wilsonian reforms were unconstitutional. Insisting that government's chief purpose was to make life better for as many people as possible, he held that twentieth century America should not be strictly —but loosely—bound by a constitution written in the eighteenth century.[7]

To view Vardaman only as an advanced liberal would be a grave distortion, for he added open racism to his Jeffersonian and progressive convictions, resulting in an unusual political *menage à trois*. Like many southern congressmen he advocated segregating Negro employees in all federal agencies and nothing would have pleased him more than to have seen blacks disfranchised throughout the United States. There were other national politicians such as Hiram Johnson of California, who appealed to the prevailing racist sentiment of this era, but none was quite so rabid as was Vardaman in expressing his prejudice.

Throughout his six years in the Senate an uneasy truce existed between Vardaman and his fellow Mississippi senator, John Sharp Williams. Soon after Vardaman's election Williams asked every Democratic member of the Senate Judiciary Committee to appoint his colleague the first time a vacancy occurred. Believing the committee would have the authority to initiate the work of abolishing the Fifteenth Amendment, Williams wanted Vardaman to have no excuse for failing to fulfill his campaign pledge. After Senator James P. Clarke of Arkan-

[6] *Ibid.*, 63 Cong., 2d Sess., 2159.
[7] *Ibid.*, 64 Cong., 1st Sess., 12220–23.

sas advised him that any attempt to repeal the Fifteenth Amendment would probably be referred to the Committee on Privileges and Elections, Williams may well have worked to secure that appointment for his colleague.[8] Vardaman was, in fact, named to that committee, as well as to the Committees on Commerce, Conservation of National Resources, Expenditures in the Post Office Department, Military Affairs, Post Offices and Post Roads, Transportation Routes to the Seaboard, and Additional Accommodations for the Library of Congress. Following the death of Senator Joseph F. Johnston in August, 1913, he became chairman of the Committee on Conservation of National Resources.[9]

Vardaman and Williams usually gave the impression of being outwardly cordial, but the two men harbored an acute dislike for one another, as is well illustrated by an incident which occurred during Vardaman's first year in the Senate. Soon after arriving in Washington, Vardaman tried to meet every Mississippian living in the capital who worked for the federal government. Not only did he go out of his way to be friendly, but he also worked to secure promotions and salary raises for some by personally visiting the departments in which they worked. At the time many of the more well-to-do Mississippians in Washington had formed a society which met from time to time for social functions and to hear addresses by congressmen and other government officials. Vardaman had been informed before arriving in Washington that the Mississippi Society was a snobbish organization whose leaders intended to snub him by ignoring his arrival at the Capitol. Because some members of the society demanded that Vardaman be officially welcomed and because the officers learned that the new senator had been warned to avoid its activities, the Mississippi Society held a reception to welcome Vardaman and he, in turn, accepted an invitation to give an address. The society's display of cordiality for Vardaman so deeply angered Williams that Charlton M. Clark, the president of the society, apologized to the senior senator

8 John Sharp Williams to D. U. Fletcher, James P. Clarke, J. H. Bankhead, John W. Kern, Thomas S. Martin, September 22, 1911, James P. Clarke to Williams, October 17, 1911, in Williams Papers, Mississippi Department of Archives.

9 *Congressional Record,* 63 Cong., 1st Sess., 20–26, 3351.

and explained that circumstances had forced him and the other officers to recognize Vardaman.[10]

A squabble over patronage in 1913 also added to the estrangement of the two Mississippi senators. Although Williams had openly supported Wilson for the presidential nomination while Vardaman had endorsed Underwood, the administration was determined to divide patronage equally between Democratic congressmen in each state, regardless of whom they had backed in the preconvention fight. Such a policy was necessary because Wilson needed every possible Democratic vote in his efforts to achieve tariff and banking reforms. Vardaman and Williams realized they would have to divide patronage equally, but for ten months they were unable to reach an agreement.

The nub of their dispute involved the two United States attorneyships for Mississippi. Williams wanted his close friend Robert C. Lee to remain attorney for the Southern District. He was even more determined that another friend, Wilson Shedric Hill, be appointed attorney for North Mississippi. Having formerly represented a strong pro-Vardaman district in Congress, Hill had openly supported Williams in the senatorial election of 1907, and the following year that support had led to Hill's defeat for reelection. Williams, therefore, would not compromise on Hill's appointment.[11] Vardaman would have willingly given Williams the attorneyships if, in turn, he could name the two United States marshals to which Mississippi was entitled. To that Williams refused to agree. Because Lee's current term as attorney did not expire until 1915, Williams argued that he should be entitled to name one of the marshals.

During the summer and fall of 1913, public pressure in Mississippi mounted steadily for the two senators to reach an understanding, because most of the disputed positions continued to be occupied by Re-

10 Charlton M. Clark, "Autobiography of Charlton Moore Clark" (MS in Charlton M. Clark Papers, Mississippi Department of Archives and History); Clifton P. Clark to John Sharp Williams, November 25, 1913, Charlton M. Clark to Williams, November 26, 1913, Williams to Charlton M. Clark, November 28, 1913, in Williams Papers, Mississippi Department of Archives; Vicksburg *Post*, August 23, 1913, in Vardaman Scrapbook.
11 John Sharp Williams to William Howard Taft, September 13, 1912, Williams to W. S. Hill, April 10, 15, 1913, Williams to George L. Donald, May 20, 1913, J. C. McReynolds to Williams, May 1, 1913, in Williams Papers, Mississippi Department of Archives.

publicans. President Wilson also urged them to end the deadlock. Not until late December did they finally reach an agreement whereby Williams picked the two attorneys and Vardaman chose the two marshals. They agreed without problem on the division of several other federal offices.[12]

Vardaman later wondered if his appointments did not hurt him as much as they helped him, for many of his followers were disappointed that they had not been rewarded.[13] For two of the positions Vardaman selected newspaper editors who had supported him in his race for the Senate: John G. Cashman of the Vicksburg *Post* became marshal for the Southern District, and Percy W. Maer of the Columbus *Dispatch* became collector for the port of Mobile. Both of the selections were wise, because Cashman and Maer continued to boost the senator's cause through their editorials. His other two appointments were less fortunate. He named W. F. Cummings, a close friend, as registrar of the land office and appointed his own brother Will as marshal for the Northern District; neither of these appointments strengthened Vardaman politically.[14] Will Vardaman, by refusing to appoint John W. T. Falkner of Oxford as his deputy marshal, alienated a family that had given generous financial support to Vardaman's past campaigns.[15]

One reason, perhaps, why Vardaman and Williams took so long to divide patronage was that during 1913 official duties consumed much of their time. On April 7 President Wilson called Congress into special session, and from that time until March, 1915, the Sixty-third Con-

[12] Material on the patronage deadlock was drawn from the following sources: J. K. Vardaman to John Sharp Williams, April 21, June 13, November 15, 21, December 11, 1913, Williams to Vardaman, April 24, May 29, June 6, October 8, 9, November 12, 17, 19, 22, December 12, 1913, Williams to Woodrow Wilson, September 30, 1913, Williams to George L. Donald, June 16, July 10, October 15, November 3, 8, 1913, in Williams Papers, Mississippi Department of Archives; Woodrow Wilson to Williams, September 18, 1913, in Woodrow Wilson Papers; Jackson *Daily Clarion-Ledger,* April 3, June 22, July 2, 9, 1913; *The Issue,* August 21, 1913; Magnolia *Gazette,* September 27, 1913, Hattiesburg *News,* n.d., McComb City *Journal,* September 26, 1913, in Vardaman Scrapbook.

[13] *Vardaman's Weekly,* August 21, 1919.

[14] Jackson *Daily Clarion-Ledger,* January 23, 1914; Columbus *Dispatch,* February 8, 1914, Pascagoula *Chronicle,* February 14, 1914, New Albany *Gazette,* February 12, 1914, in Vardaman Scrapbook; John Sharp Williams to C. H. Williams, December 20, 1913, in Williams Papers, Mississippi Department of Archives.

[15] Interview with James K. Vardaman, Jr., May 1, 1968.

gress remained almost continuously in session. Only for a month and a half during the fall of 1914 was there a lengthy recess. Vardaman gave careful attention to his official duties and rarely left Washington while Congress was in session. As was customary for first term senators, he made no long speeches nor did he engage extensively in debates during his first session in the Senate. During 1913 he spent most of his time in committee work and in learning customs and procedures; not until 1914 did he become active as a debater and a speaker. Even then he never indulged in excessively long addresses; he carefully prepared his speeches and in comparison to those of many senators, his were short.

Although maintaining an official silence in 1913, Vardaman exerted decisive influence on the Senate's action on one occasion in that year. At the time President Wilson was fighting for the passage of the Underwood Tariff Act, the first genuine reduction in tariff duties in over half a century. Vardaman supported tariff reform and throughout the many roll call votes on the Underwood bill, he consistently voted for reducing tariff duties. He regretted only that the Underwood Act had not gone further toward establishing free trade.[16] To offset a reduction in federal revenue that would result from lowering the tariff, the Underwood Act provided for a graduated income tax, the first since the Sixteenth Amendment had been ratified on February 25, 1913. Like many progressives, he favored such a tax, believing it would assess men in accord with their ability to pay and in so doing would hopefully shift much of the tax burden from lower to upper income groups. More conservative congressmen, however, were determined to keep the tax as modest as possible. During the hot days of July the Senate Democratic caucus debated the income tax provision of the tariff bill, and finally a majority agreed on a mild proposal that, among other things, provided a maximum surtax of only 3 percent on incomes over $100,000. A majority of Senate Democrats initially endorsed the income tax amendment, but Vardaman and five others announced they

---

[16] United States Senate, *Underwood-Simmons Tariff Bill, Yea and Nay Votes in the United States Senate on All Amendments to the Bill (H.R. 3321) to Reduce Tariff Duties and to Provide Revenue for the Government, and for Other Purposes, Approved October 3, 1913.* Senate Document, 63 Cong., 2d Sess., No. 556 (Washington, 1914), *passim; Congressional Record,* 63 Cong., 1st Sess., 4617; Jackson *Daily Clarion-Ledger,* October 25, 1914.

would not be bound by the caucus ruling, for they wanted higher surtaxes on upper incomes.[17]

As members of the Senate Finance Committee, John Sharp Williams and William Hughes of New Jersey were assigned the task of defending the income tax amendment when the Senate took it up in debate. The issue clearly cut across party lines. Conservative Republicans such as Henry Cabot Lodge were as determined as Williams that the income tax provision should be as weak as possible, while strong progressives like La Follette joined with Democrats like Vardaman in fighting for a stronger tax. During the first two days of debate the Democratic majority maintained party discipline and successfully defeated amendments to raise the income tax. Rebellion broke on August 28, when Vardaman bolted from the ruling of the caucus and voted for an amendment offered by La Follette that provided a maximum surtax of 10 percent in place of the 3 percent provided in the administration bill.[18] Although Vardaman was the lone Democrat to vote for the La Follette amendment and although it was easily defeated by a vote of 43 to 17, three other Democratic senators said they had not voted for the amendment only because they had assurance that the Finance Committee would recommend an increase in the surtax. Williams denied that any such assurance had been given and warned that if the Democratic Party adopted a policy of strongly taxing large incomes, it would become "the communist party, or quasicommunist party of the United States." Despite the opposition of Williams, enough Democrats made known their intention to follow Vardaman's lead in bolting their party that the income tax provision was resubmitted to the Democratic caucus. Soon the finance committee offered a compromise whereby the surtax was increased to a maximum of 6 percent on incomes over $500,000. After President Wilson endorsed the compromise, it became part of the Underwood bill and successfully passed the Senate.[19]

Some observers believed Vardaman had bolted his party and led

[17] Sidney Ratner, *American Taxation: Its History As a Social Force in Democracy* (New York, 1942), 330–31.

[18] *Congressional Record*, 63 Cong., 1st Sess., 3819, 3830.

[19] New York *Times,* August 29, 1913; Washington *Post,* August 29, 30, 1913; *The Issue,* September 4, 11, 1913; Ratner, *American Taxation,* 331–32; Link, *Wilson: The New Freedom,* 191–93.

the fight for a higher income tax to spite Williams and to undermine him politically in Mississippi, a state where large incomes were a rarity.[20] Perhaps those motives did influence Vardaman. Of greater importance was the principle that divided the two Mississippi men: Williams viewed the graduated income tax as making "war upon great fortunes," whereas Vardaman saw it as a major advance in social welfare.[21]

In addition to tariff and tax reform Congress devoted much attention in 1913 to creating the Federal Reserve Banking System, the most far-reaching reform of the Wilson administration. The fight for banking and currency reform caused sharp conflicts between conservatives who favored a banking system free of government regulation and under control of the banking community, and progressives who wanted strong federal control of the nation's currency and banking systems. The Wilson administration had originally backed a highly conservative bill sponsored by Representative Carter Glass of Virginia which would have created a decentralized banking system exclusively under private control, but in response to the urgings of William Jennings Bryan and Louis D. Brandeis, the bill had been modified in the House of Representatives to provide for some federal regulation and for short-term agricultural credit. Once it reached the Senate, only minor modifications were made and the Democratic majority in the upper chamber marshaled its strength to insure the bill's passage. The one threat to the bill came from Senator Gilbert M. Hitchcock of Nebraska, who introduced an amendment that would not only have given member banks greater freedom in subscribing to the stock of the Federal Reserve banks, but which also would have provided greater federal control over the entire system. Apparently Hitchcock designed his amendment to undermine the administration bill, for it won the support of a strange coalition of progressive and conservative Republicans.[22] Vardaman wanted the new banking system to have the strongest possible federal regulation, but he consistently supported the Glass bill and voted against every attempt to amend it. He believed

[20] Philadelphia *Inquirer,* September 15, 1913, in Vardaman Scrapbook.
[21] Vardaman himself claimed that his relations with Williams had no influence on his fight for higher taxes. *Vardaman's Weekly,* May 29, 1919.
[22] Link, *Wilson: The New Freedom,* 199–240; Davidson, "The Response of the South," 143–80.

that, at the time, it was the best bill that could be obtained and accordingly he gave his full support to the administration forces in the struggle to secure its passage.[23]

Having achieved tariff and banking reforms in 1913, the next year the Wilson administration turned to the third major objective of the New Freedom—the destruction of monopoly and the restoration of free competition. Among those progressives who wanted more effective antitrust legislation, there were differing views on how best to achieve it. In the presidential campaign of 1912 Theodore Roosevelt had advocated a strong federal commission to regulate business mergers in accord with public interest. Wilson opposed such direct government intervention in the economy, preferring instead the enactment of laws that would lead to the destruction of trusts. Accordingly, early in 1914 Wilson endorsed the Clayton bill which prohibited a number of unfair trade practices, outlawed interlocking directorates and stockholdings, and made company officials criminally liable for violating antitrust statutes. As it originally passed the House, the Clayton bill was strong. The House also passed a second, but much weaker measure, the Covington bill, providing for the creation of an interstate trade commission to serve as a fact-finding agency for the justice department in antitrust matters.

After the Clayton and Covington bills had passed the House and had gone to the Senate, President Wilson made a sudden change in his antitrust program by endorsing a bill prepared by Louis Brandeis and George Rublee embodying the plan advocated earlier by Theodore Roosevelt. Instead of trying to enumerate all forseeable antitrust violations—an impossible task—the Brandeis-Rublee plan provided for a Federal Trade Commission which would have the broad authority to outlaw unfair methods of competition as they arose and to prevent them by issuing cease and desist orders. After Wilson gave his full support to the measure, the Senate incorporated it into the Covington bill and it was successfully enacted into law. The administration dropped its support for the Clayton bill, however, and it emerged from the Senate in an emaciated form.

Vardaman supported the administration's antitrust legislation, but

[23] *Congressional Record,* 63 Cong., 2d Sess., 885, 906, 965, 1051, 1063, 1077, 1116–21, 1126, 1128, 1230.

he did so grudgingly and with reservations. As did many strong progressives, he opposed federal commissions' being anything more than investigative agencies for Congress, believing "one of the real dangers to the future of this Government and the permanency of our institutions is the delegation of legislative authority to bureaus and commissions." Such an agency was too far removed from the people, he feared, and it might therefore become a tool of big business.[24] Because he distrusted federal regulatory commissions, Vardaman broke from the ruling of his party caucus and voted for a motion by Senator James A. Reed of Missouri proposing that the new measure specifically define "unfair competition." An avowed opponent of the proposed commission, Reed wanted to weaken the agency, but administration forces successfully defeated his motion.[25] Then, in spite of his distrust, Vardaman voted for the establishment of the Federal Trade Commission in the hope that it might curb business mergers.[26]

Although the commission initially disappointed many who had expected it to eliminate unfair competition, Vardaman continued to hope that it would become a strong and effective antitrust institution. In 1916 he joined with a small group of progressives who tried unsuccessfully to increase the efficiency of the commission by enlarging its membership and by boosting the commissioners' salaries.[27] At that time, for some unexplained reason, Vardaman voted against the confirmation of Rublee to the commission, an appointment that most progressives favored. In the light of Vardaman's support of the commission, his vote against Rublee must have been on personal grounds.[28] Two years later he was still defending the commission while the

[24] *Congressional Record,* 64 Cong., 1st Sess., 9696. A number of strong progressives in Congress shared Vardaman's distrust of federal regulatory commissions. Gabriel Kolko, *The Triumph of Conservatism: A Reinterpretation of American History, 1900–1916* (New York, 1963), 260.

[25] *Congressional Record,* 63 Cong., 2d Sess., 13234–35; Davidson, "Response of the South," 212; Abrams, "Woodrow Wilson and the Southern Congressmen," 427.

[26] *Congressional Record,* 63 Cong., 2d Sess., 14802.

[27] *Ibid.,* 64 Cong., 1st Sess., 10050, 10062.

[28] *Ibid.,* 7962, 8510. Senator Jacob H. Gallinger of New Hampshire opposed Rublee's nomination on grounds that it was "personally obnoxious" to him. Perhaps Vardaman voted against Rublee out of respect for Gallinger. Jackson *Daily Clarion-Ledger,* May 16, 1916; Scott, "Southern Progressives in National Politics," 218.

Chamber of Commerce protested against its activities. If the business community was complaining, he concluded, the commission must be on the right track.[29]

While Vardaman swallowed his reservations about commissions and voted for the Covington bill, he vehemently fought against the movement led by Senator Charles A. Culberson, chairman of the Judiciary Committee, to weaken the Clayton bill. Vardaman strongly favored the House version of the bill, especially the provisions that company officials could be criminally prosecuted for antitrust violations. For such a law to be effective, he believed, it had to have teeth of a "fear-inspiring kind." [30] Consequently, he fought to salvage the original Clayton bill by attempting to restore a provision for criminal prosecution of antitrust violations, a provision outlawing interlocking directorates, and one making corporations more liable in personal damage suits.[31] He also supported an amendment which would have exempted labor unions from antitrust suits.[32] On nearly all of the Senate amendments to the Clayton bill, Vardaman consistently voted against the administration forces. His efforts were of no avail, for a coalition of conservative Republicans and administration Democrats defeated all attempts to make the bill a strong antitrust measure. So dissatisfied was he with the Senate version of the bill that he abstained from voting for or against its final passage. During the debates on the joint House-Senate conference report he tried unsuccessfully to have the bill re-submitted to committee in a final attempt to put muscle into the flabby piece of legislation.[33]

His stand on the Wilson administration's antitrust legislation revealed his agrarian radicalism more clearly than any issue that had come before the Senate since he had assumed office. He wanted the strongest possible laws to prevent business mergers which he feared would reduce free competition and hurt the public interest. One of the

[29] *Congressional Record,* 65 Cong., 2d Sess., 10074–75.

[30] *Ibid.,* 63 Cong., 2d Sess., 14318, 14514–17; New Orleans *Times-Picayune,* August 29, 1914, in Vardaman Scrapbook.

[31] *Congressional Record,* 63 Cong., 2d Sess., 14271–72, 14273, 14274, 14319, 14420–21, 14462.

[32] *Congressional Record,* 63 Cong., 2d Sess., 14331, 14588–89; Vicksburg *Post,* September 8, 1914, in Vardaman Scrapbook.

[33] Davidson, "Response of the South," 256; *Congressional Record,* 63 Cong. 2d Sess., 14610, 16170.

surest ways to achieve that objective, he believed, was to make company officials subject to criminal liability for antitrust violations. On the other hand, he was equally convinced that man's labor "is not a commodity or article of commerce" and therefore did not want labor unions subject to antitrust suits. Likewise, his skepticism concerning the Federal Trade Commission was not based on opposition to strong federal regulation of business, but stemmed from his fear that such bureaus might succumb to the influence of corporate wealth.

Vardaman's progressive convictions continued to make him follow an on-again-off-again course in cooperating with the administration. As the 1914 legislative session continued, he expressed his wholehearted support of the administration in its bill empowering the President to have a government-owned and -operated railroad constructed across the far northern frontier of Alaska. In explaining why he favored the bill that was meant to develop the resources of Alaska, the new senator said he had absolutely no fear of government ownership of railroads, telephone, and telegraph lines; in fact, he favored it because he had come to accept those principles that twenty years earlier had been expounded by the Populist Party.[34]

He also shared the deep distrust that Populists had held for business and financial leaders, and for that reason he now opposed President Wilson's attempt to win the favor of the business community by selecting well-known corporation and banking executives to man the Federal Reserve Board. Wilson's most controversial nominee was Thomas D. Jones, a director of the International Harvester Company, an enterprise that many farmers considered a trust. Vardaman vehemently denounced Jones's nomination: "I would as soon think of men of that school of thought doing anything in the interest of the toiling masses as I would expect protection for the lamb at the hands of the wolf or the coyote."[35] So widespread was the opposition to Jones's appointment that the Senate refused to confirm the nomination, despite intense pressure by the administration. This issue clearly spotlighted the split that existed between the President and the unwavering progressives in the Senate.

34 *Congressional Record,* 63 Cong., 2d Sess., 2159; Vicksburg *Post,* January 24, 1914, Kosciusko *Herald,* February 6, 1914, in Vardaman Scrapbook.
35 Washington *Evening Star,* quoted in Jackson *Daily Clarion-Ledger,* July 25, 1914; Oxford *Lafayette County Press,* July 29, 1914, in Vardaman Scrapbook.

Considering himself a defender of the "toiling masses"—dirt farmers of his constituency as well as laborers employed by corporations —Vardaman consistently supported labor legislation that came before the Congress. In 1913 and 1914 he voted for riders to the sundry civil appropriations bills which forbade the use of federal funds for prosecuting antitrust suits against labor unions and farm organizations.[36] He also supported a resolution by Senator John W. Kern of Indiana calling for the Senate to investigate reports that the rights of laborers had been violated in West Virginia coal fields.[37] Although it is doubtful if either of the above measures actually helped labor, the Sixty-Third Congress did enact one major labor reform, the La Follette Seaman Act, which set careful standards to regulate the hours and living conditions of American seamen and also abolished imprisonment of sailors who broke their labor contracts. In 1913, while the struggles for tariff and banking reform dominated the Senate's attention, Vardaman urged his colleagues to pass the Seaman bill, which he believed was one of the most important measures before Congress. In 1915 he served as a conferee in arranging the final version of the bill, and he pleaded eloquently for its successful passage: "I can not for the life of me see how any man who loves his fellow man can object to securing to the sailor those rights, those privileges, those immunities which are provided in this bill. It is only doing scant justice to a long-suffering class of patient toilers. It can not hurt business. No business is entitled to prosper that has to prosper upon injustice and wrong." [38]

In 1916 Vardaman was one of the few southern senators who worked for the passage of the Child Labor Act, under which the federal government invoked its authority over interstate commerce to curb the practice of employing children to work in factories and mines. Earlier, President Wilson had withheld his endorsement of such a measure for fear it exceeded the government's authority over interstate commerce. For more than two years before Wilson decided to support the measure, Vardaman had been urging the passage of laws

[36] *Congressional Record*, 63 Cong., 1st Sess., 1292, 2d Sess., 11805.
[37] *Ibid.*, 63 Cong., 1st Sess., 1178.
[38] *Ibid.*, 5516–17, 5721, 5790–91; *Ibid.*, 63 Cong., 3d Sess., 4807–4808, 4817; *The Issue*, March 11, 1915.

to abolish child labor on both the state and national levels. Nothing was more important, he believed, than for society to provide proper care and protection for children, nothing more important than to offer them every opportunity to develop their full potential. As he said: "Excessive work in childhood universally results in mental and physical paralysis—it stunts the physique—empties the heart of passion and drives poetry from the brain. It results in general deterioration, which in the course of time, will bring its victim on the dead level with the ox." Vardaman did not agree with those who argued that the bill was unconstitutional, for too often conservatives had used the Constitution as a shield in opposing progressive legislation. When the President began to fight for a child labor act, the measure easily passed the Senate. Believing the government should curb child labor and that Congress must use its authority for the welfare of the people, Vardaman enthusiastically welcomed the passage of the Act.[39]

On the heels of that Act in 1916 came another reform for labor, the Adamson Act, which provided an eight-hour work day for railroad employees engaged in interstate commerce. Considering it only a stopgap measure to offset an impending railway strike, Vardaman reluctantly voted for the Act. As it was, it was suitable, for he sympathized with the workers and feared that during a strike they, not the company officials, would suffer. But he regretted that Congress had not devoted more time to devising a broader program that could eliminate the danger of future railroad strikes. Believing that all enterprises which supplied communities with water, electricity, gas, and transportation were utilities that should be publicly owned, he wanted the government to nationalize the railroads. Whatever profits utilities made should be divided between the managers and workers. Should the railroads remain privately owned, however, then the workers should receive a larger share of the profits than the stockholders. To insure that the railroad's earnings were properly divided, Congress should establish a commission to guard the interests of workers.[40] Thus, while Vardaman voted for the Adamson Act with reservations, it was only

[39] *Congressional Record,* 64 Cong., 1st Sess., 12220–23, 12313; Jackson *Daily Clarion-Ledger,* February 18, 1914; Philadelphia *Philadelphian,* May 4, 1914, Gulfport *Gulf Coast Advocate,* August 19, 1916 in Vardaman Scrapbook.
[40] *Congressional Record,* 64 Cong., 1st Sess., 13481–83, 13640, 13655; Jackson *Monday Morning Leader,* September 25, 1916, in Vardaman Scrapbook.

because he hoped it foreshadowed a more thorough program of reform for the nation's railroads.

Another measure strongly backed by organized labor—as well as by various nativist groups and also by welfare workers concerned with the problems of urban slums—was the restriction of immigration into the United States. During the past two decades Congress had tried to halt the flow of immigrants by passing bills to bar all foreigners who could not pass a literacy test, but Presidents Cleveland, Taft, and Wilson had vetoed those bills which had been designed chiefly to reduce immigration from southern and eastern Europe where illiteracy was common. Vardaman supported immigration restriction. In 1915 he voted for the Burnett bill which employed the literacy test, and the next year he and ten fellow Democrats rebelled against the ruling of the Senate Democratic caucus in an unsuccessful attempt to force a vote on the measure. Finally in 1917 he joined with a two-thirds majority of Congress which passed the literacy test bill over President Wilson's veto.[41]

In voting for the immigration bill Vardaman had reasons other than his sympathy for organized labor. Of greater importance to him was the threat of the city to American society. Because for the past half century most immigrants had settled in cities, he knew that immigration had helped the population of urban areas to exceed that of rural America. For Vardaman the rise of an urban nation caused foreboding. Having spent his entire life in states where most people made their living by farming, he believed an agrarian society superior to all others. Not only did farmers provide the basic substratum for American economic life by producing food and other raw materials, but the men and women who grew up in a rural environment were better people than those who lived in cities. Being the products of "fresh air and free sunshine," farmers exceeded in honesty and patriotism those who came from the "soulless city."[42] How much of his agrarian boasting was for home consumption is impossible to determine; that he did believe agrarian life superior to urban life there can be no doubt.

[41] *Congressional Record*, 63 Cong., 3d Sess., 638; 64 Cong., 1st Sess., 12940–48, 64 Cong., 2d Sess., 157, 159, 217–18, 2629; Vicksburg *Post*, August 28, 1916, in Vardaman Scrapbook.

[42] *Congressional Record*, 63 Cong., 2d Sess., 8897–98, 3d Sess., 638, 64 Cong., 1st Sess., 10793.

Being a spokesman for agrarian virtues and the representative of an overwhelmingly rural state, he frequently argued for larger agricultural appropriations, the expansion of the parcel post system, and the establishment of more postal savings banks.[43] During his years in the Senate he believed the most important farm reform considered by that body to be the Federal Farm Loan Act of 1916, a measure which provided farmers long-term, low interest credit. "It is the first time in the history of the Government," he noted, "that an effective scheme has been provided under Government control by which the man who tills the soil shall be enabled to get cheap money with which to develop his farm, improve his home, and make farm life more tolerable." [44] In that same year he voted for the Good Roads Act which provided federal funds to states in the building of highways. Not only would improved roads help farmers to get their crops to market more easily, but they would enable rural people to have access to better schools.[45] Congress passed two other agricultural bills in 1916. The Warehouse Act authorized bonded warehouses to issue receipts against certain agricultural commodities and those receipts could serve as collateral for loans from national banks. The Smith-Hughes Act provided federal grants to improve vocational education in rural high schools. Although both the Warehouse and Smith-Hughes acts passed the Senate without roll call votes, it is safe to assume that Vardaman supported them.

A measure which Vardaman thought would help many of his farmer constituents in the Delta and for which he fought hard in 1917 was the Flood Control Act. It provided for a continuous program of building and maintaining levees in the Lower Mississippi Valley and was intended to be more effective than the older system that had depended upon the renewal of yearly contracts. Because Senator Joseph E. Ransdell of Louisiana was ill at the time, Vardaman assumed the responsibility of steering the bill successfully through the Commerce Commit-

43 Ibid., 63 Cong., 2d Sess., 3832, 3944, 4012–13, 4020, 4022, 4392, 7674–77, 7684–85, 15199–15200, 64 Cong., 1st Sess., 9633, 64 Cong., 2d Sess., 1533–42, 2480–83, 2549, 65 Cong., 1st Sess., 2921–22, 65 Cong., 2d Sess., 751, 2992, 3468–73, 6543, 9937.

44 Ibid., 64 Cong., 1st Sess., 4017, 7412, 2d Sess., 1533–36, 1540, 1542.

45 Ibid., 64 Cong., 1st Sess., 2053–55, 6568, 6784–85, 7461–62, 7516; Jackson Daily Clarion-Ledger, April 22, 1916; The Issue, May 18, 1916.

tee. Even then there was danger that the Senate Democratic caucus might not allow the bill to be considered before Congress adjourned. But Vardaman and a number of southern senators from the Mississippi Valley threatened to bolt the caucus should it not give priority to the Flood Control bill. The strategy worked and, following a brief debate, the bill successfully passed Congress.[46] Vardaman's joy over the bill's passage was short lived, for before Congress could appropriate funds for it, the United States entered World War I. As a result the Flood Control Act was never adequately funded.[47]

Another measure designed to help rural America was the Smith-Lever Act of 1914 that provided federal funds to land grant colleges to encourage farm demonstration work.[48] It was during the debates on that measure that Vardaman first discussed in the Senate his version of the race problem. He injected the issue after Senator Albert B. Cummins of Iowa offered an amendment to distribute funds in accord with the acres of improved farm land in each state, rather than on the basis of rural population as the Smith bill provided. Although the Midwest had far more improved acres than the South, under the Smith bill the southern states would get the largest share of appropriations. In response to Cummins' amendment, Vardaman argued that the South trailed the North in improved farm land because of its large proportion of Negro farmers; because Negroes were inferior to whites and because they retarded economic growth, the South deserved the largest share of appropriations. Cummins then conceded that the funds should go to the neediest groups, but he believed Negro farmers should get their fair share. In an ensuing exchange with the southern senator, he clearly demonstrated the strength of his position, as time and again he asked how much Mississippi spent on the education of Negro farmers in comparison to white farmers. Vardaman claimed that Negroes had the same educational opportunities as did whites, but he shied away from producing the exact figures that the Iowan demanded. Although Cummins clearly revealed the inconsistency of the Mississip-

46 Yazoo City *Yazoo Sentinel,* March 3, 1917, New Orleans *Times-Picayune,* December 16, 1916, January 24, 25, 1917, in Vardaman Scrapbook; *Congressional Record,* 64 Cong., 2d Sess., 2987–88, 4287–88, 4301–4302.
47 *Congressional Record,* 65 Cong., 1st Sess., 596–97.
48 For a discussion of this act, see Dewey W. Grantham, Jr., *Hoke Smith and the Politics of the New South* (Baton Rouge, 1958), 256–64.

pian's claim, southern senators marshaled enough strength to defeat the Iowan's amendment.[49]

Vardaman again took up the race issue when Senator Wesley L. Jones of Washington introduced an amendment providing that in the South funds from the Smith-Lever bill be divided equally between white and Negro colleges. Vardaman then quoted from numerous writers, including Jefferson and Lincoln, in an effort to prove the Negro innately inferior and able to prosper only under the strict supervision of whites. As in his exchange with Cummins, he asserted that southern Negroes and whites enjoyed equal educational opportunities. His encounter with Jones proved more successful, however, for in the course of their sparring he led his opponent to admit his own racism—Jones voiced his hope that Japanese residents of the West Coast would never become American citizens and also implied that he did not believe Negroes should ever have been given citizenship. After other southern senators joined Vardaman in denouncing Jones's amendment, it was defeated.[50] Throughout the debates on the Smith bill, Vardaman conducted himself with moderation and while sharply disagreeing with his opponents, he treated them politely. He did not use the outspoken approach that Ben Tillman had used during his early years in the Senate.

Although Vardaman waited until the Smith-Lever bill debates officially to voice his racist views in the Senate, he had been actively working in behalf of white supremacy since his arrival in Washington. During 1913 he helped to pressure the Wilson administration to adopt anti-Negro policies by establishing racial segregation in such agencies as the post office, the treasury, the bureau of printing and engraving, and the bureau of the census. During that year, while addressing various groups in Washington, he had launched into racial diatribes that rivaled the campaign speeches he had given earlier to backwoods audiences in Mississippi. He gave his most blistering speech in August to the National Democratic Fair Play Association, an organization then pushing for the immediate segregation of Negro employees in all federal agencies. On that occasion Vardaman skillfully manipulated the emotions of his listeners, arousing their sympathy when describing the "old

[49] *Congressional Record*, 63 Cong., 2d Sess., 2649–53.
[50] *Ibid.*, 2929–39, 2947–48, 3036–42.

colored mammy" who had cared for him as a boy and in the next moment firing his audience to indignation when describing attacks by black rapists on southern white women. In the course of his address he advocated the disfranchisement of every nonwhite voter in the country, urged the abolition of all Negro education, and justified, without reservation, the lynching of Negro rapists.[51]

Without doubt Vardaman was as extreme a racist as lived at the time; yet in America of the early twentieth century even his rabid views were not markedly out of place. Anti-Negro thought was then strong, not only in the South but throughout the nation, and its strength was felt by the Wilson administration. Despite the President's appeal for Negro votes in the campaign of 1912, the following year his administration capitulated to the strong racist sentiment of the time by condoning the Jim Crow policies within various federal agencies and by drastically reducing the number of Negroes appointed to federal office.[52]

Vardaman first openly clashed with the administration on the race question during the summer of 1913, when the President nominated Adam E. Patterson, a Negro lawyer from Oklahoma, to be registrar of the treasury. Patterson had the support of the National Colored Democratic League and of Senator Thomas P. Gore of Oklahoma. On receiving word of Patterson's nomination, Vardaman immediately began working to defeat it. Ignoring Gore's appeal not to marshal southern opposition, Vardaman contended he felt "a great deal more interested in defeating Patterson's confirmation than I do in the passage

[51] Washington *Herald*, October 23, 1913, in Vardaman Scrapbook; *The Issue*, August 21, 1913.
[52] Kathleen L. Wolgemuth, "Woodrow Wilson and Federal Segregation," *Journal of Negro History*, XLIV (1959), 158–73; Wolgemuth, "Woodrow Wilson's Appointment Policy and the Negro," *Journal of Southern History*, XXIV (1958), 457–71; Link, *Wilson: The New Freedom*, 243–54. In writing to President Wilson, John Sharp Williams described the depth of racist sentiment in the South at the time: "Of course, there are some Senators upon the floor who will be more loud-mouthed and exclamatory in opposition to the negro's confirmation than anybody else but who really are at heart perhaps glad that you sent the name in; it gives them an opportunity to roar through the press and otherwise for home consumption. It is grist come to their mill, while for conservative men who have been and want to remain friends of the Administration it is most embarrassing, in fact, either hurtful to them here or suicidal to them at home, depending upon what course they take." Williams to Wilson, March 31, 1914, in Williams Papers, Library of Congress.

of either the tariff or the currency bill." [53] Because Vardaman succeeded in arousing enough southern senators to oppose the nomination, Patterson asked Wilson to withdraw his name. The President
knew he would need the votes of every possible Democratic senator
in the fights for tariff and banking reform, thus he readily complied
with Patterson's request.[54]

A year later Vardaman suffered defeat in attempting to block the
reappointment of Robert R. Terrell, a Negro, as a municipal judge
for Washington, D.C. Although Wilson initially wavered and considered withdrawing Terrell's nomination, in the end he stood firm and
the Senate approved the appointment.[55] So deeply did Terrell's victory disappoint Vardaman, that in August, 1914, he was the only
Democrat who voted against the appointment of Attorney General
James C. McReynolds as Supreme Court justice. McReynolds had
supported Terrell's reappointment.[56]

Vardaman's racism strongly affected his views on foreign policy and
partly explained why he favored a bill to grant the Philippines independence beginning in 1921. Having been a foe of imperialism since
the Spanish-American War, he charged that only the influence of selfish interests, who exploited the timber and mineral resources of the
islands, had earlier prevented the United States from granting independence to the Philippines. Already America had committed "a
crime against humanity" by ruthlessly killing thousands of Filipinos

[53] J. K. Vardaman to William H. Murray, August 18, 1913, quoted in cam-
paign circular of 1914 election, in Thomas P. Gore Papers, as cited in Monroe
Lee Billington, *Thomas P. Gore: The Blind Senator from Oklahoma* (Lawrence,
Kansas, 1967), 56.

[54] *The Issue*, July 31, August 14, 1913; Hattiesburg *News*, July 29, 1913,
Vicksburg *Herald*, August 31, 1913, Aberdeen *Weekly*, January 30, 1914, in
Vardaman Scrapbook.

[55] Wolgemuth, "Wilson's Appointment Policy," 465–66; Washington *Herald*,
January 22, April 17, 1914, Washington *Times*, February 7, 1914, Washington
Star, February 24, April 29, 1914, Washington *Post*, April 17, 1914, in Varda-
man Scrapbook.

[56] Ripley *Sentinel*, September 3, 1914, Forest *Scott County News*, September
4, 1914, in Vardaman Scrapbook. Opposition to Vardaman's racist policies was
strong among Negro leaders. Bishop Alexander Walters to Woodrow Wilson,
January 30, 1914, Robert S. Hudspeth to Wilson, May 6, 1913, in Wilson
Papers; Cincinnati *Tribune*, August 8, 1913, Kansas City *Central Christian Advocate*, August 20, 1913, Chicago *Broadax*, March 1914, Portland *Oregonian*,
April 18, 1914, in Vardaman Scrapbook; *The Nation*, XCVII (August 7, 1913),
114.

in suppressing insurrections in the islands. No nation had the right to rule a foreign people who wanted independence. Moreover, he feared America's imperialistic experiment might lead to more serious problems, for the occupation of the Philippines had required the maintenance of a larger army than in the past and thereby posed a threat of militarism undermining free government. Also the millions of dollars spent in the Philippines could have been used to reduce poverty at home. In addition to his humanitarian reasons for opposing imperialism, Vardaman also wanted America to free the Filipinos because he considered them an inferior race who someday might endanger white supremacy in America. It was hypocritical and unjust to talk of educating and uplifting the Filipinos, he argued, when American whites had no intention of ever granting them social and political equality. To Vardaman's disappointment, the House failed to follow the Senate's lead in enacting legislation to free the Philippines from American control.[57]

Because he believed in the inferiority of all nonwhites, Vardaman fought against granting Puerto Rico territorial status. The acquisition of the island would only increase the danger of mongrelization in America, and for him there could be no more serious threat. Having read widely in racist literature, he was convinced that race played the most important role in explaining the entire development of a people. In those countries where whites predominated and where they had maintained their racial purity, there was progress; where whites and nonwhites had intermarried, civilization had declined. It would be far better, therefore, to leave the Puerto Ricans to themselves. As with the Philippine question, he believed the sole reason America wanted Puerto Rico was to protect investments there; America had no intention of granting the islanders citizenship. As much as he detested the infusion of more nonwhites into American society, he believed that the Puerto Ricans should be granted full citizenship if the island became a territory of the United States. Any other policy would be hypocritical.[58]

Sometimes Vardaman's racist views clashed with his desire for pro-

[57] *Congressional Record*, 64 Cong., 1st Sess., 771–73, 1074–75, 1152, 1252–53, 1497–1501, 1558, 2060, 10957–58, 12713–14.
[58] *Ibid.*, 64 Cong., 2d Sess., 2250–51.

gressive reforms, as was well illustrated in the dilemma he experienced on the question of woman suffrage. Throughout his adult life he had never shared the belief that women were inferior to men; on the contrary, he had long believed women excelled men in intellect, morality, and endurance. Believing as he did, he favored granting suffrage to women. There was only one hitch: a constitutional amendment on woman suffrage would enfranchise both Negroes and whites. For that reason he refused in 1914 to vote for any measure that would enfranchise Negro women, explaining that "a decent white woman will not put herself in a position where she is to be elbowed, pushed around, and insulted by a vulgar, vicious, and ignorant Negro woman who has no more conception of the importance or the significance of the elective franchise than a chimpanzee is capable of comprehending or understanding the nebular hypothesis." By 1918 Vardaman relented and announced that he would vote for woman suffrage, regardless of the enfranchisement of Negro women. At the time when America was fighting a war to make the world safe for democracy, it would be an injustice to deny suffrage to women. The good would offset the bad, he concluded, because there were far more white than black women in the United States. Once white women began voting, he expected them to elevate the moral tone of American politics and to assume a leading role in abolishing all Negro suffrage.[59]

His conviction that the Negro was an inferior being explained in part why Vardaman strongly advocated national prohibition. Negroes were far too likely to succumb to the evil effects of alcohol. Yet he wanted prohibition imposed on both blacks and whites, for like many progressives he believed that the need to outlaw alcohol was one of the most pressing in the nation. As a young man he had worked for local option, but as the movement to abolish the demon rum intensified, he moved with it and by the time he entered the Senate he strongly advocated national prohibition. Warning that liquor had ruined the lives of more people than any single evil, he described its terrible work:

I once had a young friend who was almost as great a genius as Byron or [S. S.] Prentiss. I knew him in the morning of life; the pulses of

[59] *Ibid.,* 63 Cong., 2d Sess., 4338–39, 5096–98; *ibid.,* 65 Cong., 2d Sess., 10770–73, 10984.

youthful spring bounded in his veins; hope sprang eternal in his breast. Life to him was a glorious prospect. He lived in a world of promise. At an unguarded moment he entered the saloon, drawn there by the siren song of temptation. The first drop of the seductive drug that passed his lips fired the latent appetite, which probably was the uncoveted legacy from indiscreet ancestors. He went back again, and again, and again until the love for the accursed stuff had become a gnawing disease against which his imperious will was absolutely helpless. . . . Anything that encourages excessive drinking and leads to this unhappy end is the enemy to society and ought to be exterminated.[60]

With such intense views, Vardaman consistently voted for measures to encourage prohibition. He was especially pleased when in December, 1917, Congress passed and submitted to the states for ratification a constitutional amendment establishing national prohibition. His one regret was that the amendment would not go into effect until a year after ratification: if prohibition would help to eradicate an evil, it should be enforced as soon as enough voters approved it.[61]

As a senator, Vardaman directed his racist views chiefly against Negroes, although he also favored disfranchising Orientals. For several minority groups in America, however, he displayed concern and respect. Throughout his years in the Senate he worked in behalf of those Choctaws who had remained in Mississippi after the majority of their fellow tribesmen had moved to Oklahoma almost a century earlier. Whenever the Senate considered appropriations for the Choctaws, the Oklahoma senators argued that the funds should go only to those who had moved to their state, while Vardaman and Williams argued persistently but unsuccessfully that the descendents of those Choctaws who had chosen to remain in Mississippi also deserved a share of the funds.[62]

In accord with views he had expressed since his early days as a newspaper editor, he denounced anti-Semitism. In 1913 he urged the

[60] Ibid., 63 Cong., 3d Sess., 1615.

[61] Vardaman's views on prohibition are presented in following: Congressional Record, 63 Cong., 3d Sess., 1504, 1612–15, 1618–19, 64 Cong., 1st Sess., 10137, 11862, 64 Cong., 2d Sess., 140–41, 144, 326–32, 478, 482–83, 1050–52, 1065, 1166–67, 3326–27, 3339, 65 Cong., 1st Sess., 2172, 3096, 4585, 4713, 4724–27, 65 Cong., 2d Sess., 704–705, 8974–75, 9649–50, 10085–86, 65 Cong., 3d Sess., 790.

[62] Ibid., 63 Cong., 1st Sess., 2088–89, 63 Cong., 2d Sess., 11013, 63 Cong., 3d Sess., 5143–56, 64 Cong., 2d Sess., 2121–22.

State Department to use every possible means to persuade the Russian government to stop its persecution of Mendel Beilis who had been accused of killing a young Christian boy and using his blood for a religious ceremony. "The persecution of the Jews by the Russian government," Vardaman asserted, "is the most indefensible thing in the history of nations." [63] In 1916 President Wilson's nomination of Louis Brandeis to the Supreme Court aroused the opposition of many anti-Semites, especially in the South where the writings of Tom Watson were widely read. The nomination also alarmed many conservatives, because Brandeis had long been at the forefront of American economic and social reform. Vardaman shared neither the views of the anti-Semites nor those of the conservatives. He had long seen the Court as dominated by reactionary justices, and he therefore welcomed the nomination of a man with Brandeis' views. He had another reason for supporting the nominee, as he explained to a constituent: "He represents that wonderful people who have made the greatest fight against great odds that any race on earth has ever made. It affords me great pleasure to be able to have the race of which he is a member recognized in this way." [64]

Vardaman's stands on domestic legislation during his Senate years demonstrated a political journey far from the point at which he had started his career. Since having entered public life as a Bourbon Democrat in the 1890's, he had become a proponent of advanced progressive legislation. His journey to progressivism resulted in part from changes in his own convictions: he had come to believe that many of America's social and economic problems could be solved only if the federal government adopted dynamic, positive programs. His keen political awareness also accounted for his move to the left. Earlier, as a state legislator and governor, he had demonstrated an ability to perceive popular trends, to follow and even develop them. Because he had been so adept at measuring the political climate in Mississippi, he had always abided by the tenets of the state Democratic Party. In Washington, Vardaman found it far more difficult to judge popular trends within the national Democratic Party than it had been within

[63] Havana (Cuba), *Post*, February 17, 1913, in Vardaman Scrapbook.
[64] *Congressional Record,* 64 Cong., 1st Sess., 9032; Jackson *Daily Clarion-Ledger,* June 6, 1916.

his state party. He therefore turned to his inner convictions for direction. After all, had not his overwhelming victory in 1911 demonstrated that he had the support of his constituents? By this time, however, he found his convictions more in accord with those of such strong Midwestern progressives as La Follette and Norris, neither of whom were Democrats. Thus he bucked his party's caucus on a number of occasions—something that brought down on him his own anathemas which he had voiced as a state legislator against "traitors" who refused cooperation with the Democratic Party. The terrible political consequences of the gulf that was beginning to emerge between Vardaman and the national Democratic Party would indeed seem to be the result of those dire maledictions.

CHAPTER XI

OPPONENT
OF WAR

VARDAMAN GENERALLY SUPPORTED Woodrow Wilson's reform programs. True, he balked on several measures, such as the income tax, but not in opposition so much as in disappointment at their conservative weakness. Though his pleas for a stronger antitrust law and for nationalizing the railroads probably irritated Wilson, they did not estrange the two men. It was their clashes over foreign policy that produced far more serious consequences for the Mississippi Senator. In fact, soon after Vardaman entered the Senate he fought against Wilson's attempt to revise the Panama Canal Act of 1912, a measure which exempted American coastal shipping from paying tolls.

The Democratic platform of 1912 endorsed the tolls exemption policy, and Wilson, without giving the matter careful consideration, strongly supported it in campaign speeches. By the time of his election the British began criticizing the tolls exemption policy, arguing that it violated the Hay-Pauncefote Treaty of 1901 in which the United States had pledged that the canal would be open to ships of all nations on terms of complete equality. The British argument soon persuaded Wilson that America's tolls exemption policy was unfair and a blot on the nation's honor. During 1913 only the knowledge that some Democratic senators, such as Vardaman and James O'Gorman of New York, strongly opposed any change in the existing tolls policy convinced the President to delay confronting Congress with the issue until the tariff and banking acts had safely passed.[1]

When Wilson finally turned to the tolls question, he discovered congressional opposition was greater than he had anticipated. He

[1] Link, *Wilson: The New Freedom*, 304–307; William Jennings Bryan to Woodrow Wilson, June 12, 1913, in William Jennings Bryan Papers, Library of Congress; Wilson to Bryan, June 13, 1913, in Woodrow Wilson Papers.

therefore threw his entire weight into the fight and on March 5, 1914, informed a joint session of Congress that if America was to maintain its self-respect among nations, it must not discriminate in favor of its own ships. During the next three months, while the fight for repeal raged, Wilson used every weapon at his command to insure the success of his cause. In the end the administration forces prevailed and the Canal Act of 1912 was amended.

From the outset Vardaman fought against changing the existing tolls policy, and throughout the Senate's heated debates he never wavered in opposing the President's request. Despite his long-standing opposition to imperialism, he believed America's sovereignty over the Panama Canal was as absolute as its control over the Mississippi River. Moreover, because the United States had paid for the canal's construction, its ships deserved reduced rates which hopefully would result in lower consumer prices at home. An isolationist at heart, Vardaman did not want America to humiliate itself by giving in to England's demands; he preferred to enjoy the respect of his own nation to that of any foreign country. The issue that he stressed again and again was that the President had asked Democratic congressmen to break their party platform. Having served on the platform committee at the Baltimore convention, Vardaman insisted that the plank endorsing the Panama Canal Act had been as carefully considered as those promising tariff and banking reforms.[2] He caustically ridiculed Wilson for violating the party's platform: "I have no more respect for the integrity of a man who will violate a pledge made in the performance of a public function than I have for a man who accepts a bribe to control his official conduct." [3]

In an effort to block the President's demand for an immediate repeal of the exemption policy, Vardaman proposed a solution asking that Congress suspend the existing policy for a year, during which time all tolls collected from American ships would be kept in a separate fund. In the meantime the United States and Great Britain would hold a "diplomatic conference" to determine if the exemption of American shipping violated the Hay-Pauncefote Treaty; if the conference de-

[2] *Congressional Record,* 63 Cong., 2d Sess., 10158, 10160, 10167, 10170–71, 9723–29.
[3] Washington *Post,* March 30, 1914, in Vardaman Scrapbook.

termined that the treaty had not been violated, all tolls collected from American ships would be returned. What weakened his plan was that the findings of the conference would not be binding; after a year the problem might not be one step nearer solution. It is easy to understand, therefore, why the Senate rejected his proposal.[4]

Vardaman was one of eleven Democratic senators who voted against the President's demand to abolish tolls exemptions for American ships.[5] Yet he alone was so outspoken in his opposition to the measure that he even managed to anger a number of his fellow Democrats. Tempers had become so riled when the Senate finally voted to abolish the exemptions, that Vardaman and Senator William Stanley West of Georgia almost fought. Having just been taunted by several senators for voting against the administration, Vardaman was already angry when West arose and asked how many thousands of dollars the shipping trust had spent to maintain the toll exemptions. Believing West implied that he had been bribed by shipping interests, Vardaman sprang to his feet and charged him. Senator Henry F. Ashurst kept the two apart and the sergeant at arms quickly seated them. Then, for the first time since they had been in the Senate together, John Sharp Williams ripped into Vardaman for having opposed President Wilson on the tolls question. Describing him as "a very excitable man with great intemperance of thought and of expression," Williams read an article from the Washington *Post* in which Vardaman had severely criticized Wilson. While reading the article he dared Vardaman to deny the report. Although fuming with anger, Vardaman sat quietly during the attack. After curbing his temper, he apologized to West, then said he preferred Williams' disapproval, believing it the surest indication that he had been correct.[6]

The fight over the tolls question further alienated the two Mississippi senators, for Vardaman did not forgive Williams for having

[4] *Congressional Record,* 63 Cong., 2d Sess., 8823–24; Washington *Herald,* May 20, 1914, Washington *Post,* May 20, 1914, New York *American,* May 20, 1914, in Vardaman Scrapbook; Jackson *Daily Clarion-Ledger,* May 20, 1914; *The Issue,* June 4, 11, 1914.

[5] *Congressional Record,* 63 Cong., 2d Sess., 10247–48.

[6] *Ibid.,* 10235–38; Washington *Herald,* June 12, 1914, in Vardaman Scrapbook; *Congressional Record,* 63 Cong., 2d Sess., 10238–40.

criticized him.[7] More important, the clash marked the beginning of a long list of occasions on which Vardaman found it necessary violently to oppose the President's foreign policy. In fact, between 1914 and 1917, the Mississippian so consistently opposed Wilson that by the time the United States declared war on Germany, Vardaman had burned all his bridges with the administration. At this time, however, the tolls issue did not permanently impair his relations with other senators nor with his constituents. Many Mississippians admired him for having the courage to vote according to his convictions, although some regretted the scathing attacks he had levelled at the President.[8]

Fortunately the tolls question was settled in June, 1914, for by the end of that summer the nation faced far graver problems in foreign affairs following the outbreak of World War I. More than any other issue, the war eventually wrecked Vardaman's political career, as it repeatedly brought him into conflict with the Wilson administration and isolated him from the leadership of his party and a majority of his constituents. From the outset he believed America should avoid being dragged into the holocaust and during the next three years he became an outspoken advocate of neutrality. Like other strong progressives, he felt that wars resulted from the greed of munition makers and bankers. His own experiences in the Spanish-American War had led him to believe that while many men had then supported war for the humanitarian reason of freeing Cuba from Spain's despotic rule, greedy investors and businessmen had turned the conflict into an imperialistic conquest. He did not want his country to make a similar mistake by entering a new war. Moreover, along with many fellow progressives, he wanted America to continue devoting its attention to domestic reform and thereby set an example for the nations of Europe to follow. Once the war ended, Europe could look to the United States and discover the strength of a peaceful, progressive democracy.[9]

[7] John Sharp Williams to C. H. Williams, July 7, 1914, in Williams Papers, Library of Congress.

[8] Jackson *Daily Clarion-Ledger*, June 9, 16, 21, 1914; Memphis *Commercial Appeal*, June 4, 1914, Laurel *Daily Argus*, May 21, 1914, Crystal Springs *Monitor*, June 12, 1914, Purvis *Booster*, June 21, 1914, Oxford *Press*, June 13, 1914, in Vardaman Scrapbook. For strong denunciation of Vardaman's opposition to tolls repeal, see Vicksburg *Herald*, June 9, 15, 17, 1914.

[9] Meridian *Dispatch*, November 4, 1915, in Vardaman Scrapbook; *Congres-*

Because the Wilson administration adopted a policy of strict neutrality at the beginning of the war, Vardaman did not then fear that America would be drawn into the fray. At that time he was more concerned about an economic crisis in the South which resulted from the sudden collapse of the international cotton market. An oversupply of domestic cotton and the disruption of European trade by the war led the major American and English cotton exchanges to close in early August, 1914, and by October the price of cotton plunged from twelve and a half cents a pound to between six and seven cents a pound. As cotton was still the Deep South's leading crop, the section suffered a financial loss that contemporaries estimated at $500,000,000. Southern spokesmen did not wait long to begin demanding that the federal government take direct action to relieve the economic crisis. Still clinging to a laissez-faire philosophy, the administration denounced any plans for direct relief as "perfectly wild and ridiculous." On August 27, Treasury Secretary William G. McAdoo announced that in accord with the Aldrich-Vreeland Act of 1908 he would issue emergency currency to national banks in the South in the hope of producing enough short-term credit to help farmers through the crisis. Then in an attempt to revive international commerce, the administration got through Congress a bill altering the ship registry law, thereby encouraging foreign vessels to travel under the neutral flag of the United States.

The administration's halfhearted efforts to relieve the cotton crisis sorely irritated Vardaman. Hoping the new registry law might encourage the shipment of more cotton, he voted for it pessimistically, as he did for a bill creating the Bureau of War Risk Insurance which offered protection to American ships going into war zones when private companies refused to give coverage at reasonable rates.[10] His skepticism was well founded: neither measure relieved the cotton crisis. When by September it became evident that the Aldrich-Vreeland Act was failing to help cotton farmers, Vardaman supported an amendment to the act that would have permitted state banks, as well as national

sional Record, 64 Cong., 1st Sess., 11167–70. For a discussion of the opposition of rural people and progressives to the war, see Arthur S. Link, Woodrow Wilson and the Progressive Era, 1910–1917 (New York, Harper Torchbook Edition, 1963), 180–81; Link, Wilson: Confusions and Crises, 22–30; Tindall, The Emergence of the New South, 1913–1945, 40–43.
[10] Congressional Record, 63 Cong., 2d Sess., 13840, 14085.

banks, to receive emergency currency. In Mississippi, he knew, there were 326 state banks compared to only 32 national banks. The amendment passed the Senate; it failed to pass the House.[11]

In October the South's economic plight had become so pressing that Vardaman joined nine fellow senators in an effort to force the administration to grant direct relief to cotton farmers. At that time Congress was nearing adjournment and the Senate was considering the administration's revenue bill which contained a series of special internal taxes to offset loss of tariff revenue resulting from the war's disruption of foreign trade. Georgia's Senator Hoke Smith led the movement for direct federal aid to cotton farmers by offering an amendment to the revenue bill calling for the issuance of $250,000,000 in bonds to buy five million bales of cotton. President Wilson opposed the measure and threatened to veto the revenue bill if it passed with the Smith amendment; Vardaman believed that only such a massive program of direct federal relief could save the South from economic ruin, and he therefore gave the Smith plan his full support. Much to his regret, administration forces prevailed, and a vote of 40 to 21 defeated the amendment.[12]

The defeat of the Smith plan so angered Vardaman that he threatened to bolt the ruling of the Democratic caucus and vote against the revenue bill. Earlier he had argued against putting new taxes on the southern people at a time of such economic want and had even suggested a plan for raising additional revenue by taxing only federal employees.[13] Following the defeat of the Smith amendment, he proposed that the Senate delay voting on the revenue bill until the administration did something to relieve the cotton crisis. Again he experienced

11 *Ibid.,* 14891–95, 14979, 14986–88; Grantham, *Hoke Smith,* 277–78.
12 *Congressional Record,* 63 Cong., 2d Sess., 16301–302, 16644–46, 16724, 16772–73, 16784–85, 16917–18; Washington *Times,* October 18, 1914, Ripley *Sentinel,* October 22, 29, 1914, Laurel *Jones County News,* November 12, 1914, Vicksburg *Herald,* October 30, 1914, in Vardaman Scrapbook; *The Issue,* November 5, 1914; Jackson *Daily Clarion-Ledger,* October 25, 1914; Arthur S. Link, "The Cotton Crisis, The South and Anglo-American Diplomacy, 1914–1915," in J. Carlyle Sitterson (ed.), *Studies in Southern History in Memory of Albert Ray Newsome, 1894–1951* (Chapel Hill, 1957), 126–28.
13 *Congressional Record,* 63 Cong., 2d Sess., 16101–102; St. Louis *Globe-Democrat,* September 9, 1914, New Orleans *Times-Picayune,* September 10, 1914, Washington *Post,* October 4, 1914, *Civil Service Magazine,* October 9, 1914, in Vardaman Scrapbook.

defeat as his motion to delay was beaten by the vote of 32 to 25. The Senate quickly passed the revenue bill and adjourned. Realizing the bill would pass, Vardaman paired his vote and thereby avoided actually violating the ruling of his party's caucus.[14] The failure of the Wilson administration to support a program of direct federal relief for cotton farmers not only added to the growing alienation of Vardaman and the President, it also served further to illustrate the differences between the conservative executive and the strongly progressive senator.

Before adjourning, the Senate adopted a resolution introduced by Hoke Smith which called for the appointment of five senators to investigate the seizure of cotton shipments. Vardaman served on the committee which met with Robert Lansing, the State Department counselor, on October 24, 1914. The senators reported that although cotton was not contraband, cotton exports to Europe had been detained, and they urged Lansing to obtain assurance from the Allied powers that they would stop harassing cotton shipments. As a result of the meeting Lansing took up the question with British officials, and he received the assurance of Foreign Minister Sir Edward Grey that England had not declared cotton contraband.[15]

Despite Grey's assurances, Britain soon restricted the shipment of cotton. In response to Germany's use of submarine warfare, she tightened her blockade and announced that after March 1, 1915, no merchant vessel would be allowed into Germany. At that time England agreed to buy whatever American cotton its ships might seize. Technological change further complicated the problem, because cotton was then being used in the manufacture of some explosives. For that reason Britain declared cotton contraband in August. Aware of the South's economic plight, the British strove to avoid further alienating the region by buying cotton in such huge quantities that by the fall of 1915 the cotton prices had begun to rise and the economic crisis eased.

Britain's policies of restricting the shipment of American cotton deeply angered Vardaman and affected his subsequent views on the war. Congress was not in session during the spring and summer of

[14] *Congressional Record,* 63 Cong., 2d Sess., 16801, 16806–807.
[15] *Ibid.,* 16904–905; New York *Times,* October 25, 1914; Vicksburg *Herald,* October 24, 1914; Grantham, *Hoke Smith,* 281.

1915, but he publicly denounced England's violations of American neutrality rights:

It is well known that Great Britain has, in contemptuous violation of international law, well nigh destroyed the business interests of the Southern states. By her present unwarranted interference with commerce between neutral countries, the European cotton market has about been destroyed and in consequence disaster confronts the cotton growers of the South, and the worst feature about it is she continues to do so, treating the protests which the Administration has made with an indifference amounting to contempt. To my mind, the conduct of Germany is not half so reprehensible and offensive to the American people as that of Great Britain.[16]

When England declared cotton contraband, he interrupted a lecture tour and went to Washington, where he urged the President to impose an arms embargo against Great Britain until she rescinded her cotton orders.[17] Only one other senator, Hoke Smith, advocated an embargo. Neither man could understand why cotton had been declared contraband, despite the fact that it had become an ingredient in the manufacture of explosives. On that matter they were simply behind the times. Furthermore, neither realized that an arms embargo could have been disastrous to the South, because it might have prompted Britain to drop her price control policy for cotton and the South would have suffered even more. Apparently most southern congressmen appreciated the possible consequences of an embargo, for they did not join Vardaman and Smith in advancing such a policy.[18]

Even after the South began to enjoy prosperity in 1916, Vardaman remembered the suffering of the two previous years. He blamed England and the Wilson administration and forgave neither. The hard

16 New York *Times,* July 26, 1915; Vicksburg *Herald,* August 29, 1915.
17 Greenwood *Enterprise,* October 1, 1915, New Orleans *Times-Picayune,* September 23, October 18, 1915, in Vardaman Scrapbook. One anti-Vardaman paper reported that he had urged President Wilson to use the Army and Navy to get southern cotton through the British blockade. In view of Vardaman's determination for America to remain at peace, the validity of that report is highly doubtful. Vicksburg *Herald,* September 29, October 13, 1915.
18 Timothy G. McDonald, "Southern Democratic Congressmen and the First World War, August 1914–April 1917: The Public Record of Their Support for or Opposition to Wilson's Policies" (Ph.D. dissertation, University of Washington, 1961), 77–83; Grantham, *Hoke Smith,* 287–90.

times of 1914 and 1915 caused him to join other southern congressmen to fight against imposing price controls on cotton after America
had entered the war. The southerners succeeded and, as a result of
the inflated wartime prices, cotton farmers enjoyed a rare period of
prosperity in 1917 and 1918.[19]

The failure of the Wilson administration to relieve the cotton crisis
partly explains why Vardaman fought against the ship purchase bill
in 1915. From the outbreak of the war American foreign trade suffered because of an inadequate merchant marine. To relieve the shipping shortage, some urged the government to buy German vessels
trapped in American ports at the beginning of the war. Ignoring Allied protests against such a move, President Wilson in August, 1914,
endorsed a bill calling for the creation of a government shipping board
authorized to spend $30,000,000 to purchase and operate a shipping
line. Had the bill not died in the House at that session, German ships
undoubtedly would have been purchased.

Still convinced that America needed a government-owned shipping
line, Wilson made it the main item of his legislative program for the
lame duck session of Congress that convened in December, 1914. Administration officials expected strong opposition to the measure, for
they knew that conservatives considered it socialistic and that pro-
Allied congressmen feared Britain would look upon it as an unneutral
act. Despite opposition to the bill, the President hoped the Democratic
majority in Congress would pass the measure. After Senator William J.
Stone of Missouri introduced the ship purchase bill into the Senate, it
quickly passed the Commerce Committee where only one Democrat
voted against it—Vardaman.[20]

Unlike many of the bill's opponents, Vardaman did not fear government ownership of railroads, ships, or other transportation facilities. On the contrary, he strongly favored such programs, provided they
were permanent and would benefit the masses of people. The shipping
bill would be only a temporary measure, however, and even the Presi-

[19] *The Issue*, April 25, June 6, September 15, 27, December 12, 1918; John
Sharp Williams to Woodrow Wilson, October 16, 1918, in Woodrow Wilson
Papers; *Congressional Record*, 65 Cong., 1st Sess., 4888–89, 6224–25; Tindall,
The Emergence of the New South, 60–61.
[20] Washington *Post*, January 10, 1915, in Vardaman Scrapbook.

dent admitted that as soon as the war ended, the board would be abolished and the ships resold, probably at a loss to the government. Even more alarming to Vardaman was his fear that the ships would help only industrialists and financiers, and he warned that the vessels would become "business missionaries." He was especially irritated by Wilson's willingness to endorse a program of direct aid for the business community, while he had refused to respond in a similar fashion to the South's economic plight. Recalling that the administration had branded as socialistic the attempts to secure direct federal relief for cotton farmers, Vardaman charged that the administration in supporting the shipping bill assumed "it is orthodox democracy, sound political economy, and the flower of justice now to take the money contributed for the support of the Government by the suffering laborer and spend it to maintain a line of boats to carry cotton to foreign markets for the speculator and the broker." [21] The ship purchase bill he branded as "class legislation."

In the hopes of insuring the bill's passage, administration leaders in the Senate secured for it the endorsement of the Democratic caucus. Even then there were signs that party discipline would not hold, for fifteen Democratic senators, one of whom was Vardaman, refused to attend the caucus. During almost two weeks of debate the Republicans managed to block the Democrats from voting on the bill. Then on February 1, 1915, rebellion broke out within the Democratic ranks, when Senator James P. Clarke of Arkansas moved to recommit the bill to committee. Immediately Senator Stone tried to have Clarke's motion tabled, but Vardaman and six other Democrats joined the Republicans in defeating the attempt to table. All efforts to discipline the seven rebellious Democrats failed.

More than the other insurgents, Vardaman forcefully denounced the ruling of the caucus. He realized the necessity of party discipline, but he believed it more important to remain loyal to his own principles. In addition, he denounced the Wilson administration for again violating the party platform, just as it had the previous year on the Panama Canal tolls issue; the shipping bill was more serious since it

21 *Congressional Record,* 63 Cong., 3d Sess., 1921–37, 3096–3100.

offered a direct subsidy to business interests, a scheme that for many years the Democratic Party had denounced.[22]

Before Congress adjourned, Wilson tried again to secure the bill's passage. In response to strong pleas by the administration, House Democrats on February 17 passed the bill, but the following day all hope was abandoned of getting it through the Senate. Vardaman and the other rebellious Democrats stuck to their guns and refused to bow to administration pressure. At that time the Senate considered two amendments to the bill which gave more insight into Vardaman's avowed opposition to the measure. New York Senator O'Gorman's amendment forbade the United States to purchase ships from any belligerent power and therefore would have stripped the bill of its effectiveness. By supporting O'Gorman's amendment, which was tabled, Vardaman displayed his opposition to the purchase of ships which would have endangered American neutrality.[23] Senator Gilbert Hitchcock of Nebraska offered a more important amendment, which, had it passed, would have outlawed the sale of all arms to the belligerent powers. By voting for the Hitchcock amendment the Mississippian gave approval for an arms embargo, a measure that he believed would remove the danger of munition makers leading the nation into war.[24]

In failing to pass the ship purchase bill the Senate handed the President his first major legislative defeat. Wilson's disappointment was exceeded only by his anger over the insurgency of the seven Democratic senators. He even prepared a statement for the press blaming the rebellious Democrats for the nation's shortage of shipping facilities, but decided not to issue it. By the close of the Sixty-Third Congress, he was well aware that Vardaman had become one of his most persistent and outspoken critics within the Democratic Party.

After Congress adjourned in March, 1915, America first confronted the challenge posed by Germany's use of submarine warfare. One of the most serious incidents occurred in May when a German submarine sank the British liner *Lusitania,* resulting in the death of almost 1,200 civilians, 128 of them Americans. Although he regretted the incident,

[22] *Ibid.,* 2787, 3841, 3844–45; Jackson *Daily Clarion-Ledger,* January 26, February 2, 3, 9, 11, 1915.
[23] *Congressional Record,* 63 Cong., 3d Sess., 4016; McDonald, "Southern Democratic Congressmen," 68–69.
[24] *Ibid.,* 61–62; *Congressional Record,* 63 Cong., 2d Sess., 4016.

Vardaman did not condemn Germany, for he believed she was only retaliating against England's blockade. There was absolutely no cause for the United States to act against Germany, he asserted: not only had the *Lusitania* been in a war zone when sunk, but the German government had advertised in British and American newspapers warning prospective passengers not to risk travelling on the ship.[25] At first he applauded the administration's restrained reaction to the crisis, but he soon became alarmed when the President issued a note sternly warning Germany to abandon unrestricted submarine warfare against unarmed passenger ships. So strong was Wilson's stand that just before he issued a second *Lusitania* note, Secretary of State Bryan resigned in protest. Vardaman praised Bryan's resignation as an act of courage and believed it would "do more to curb the rampant war spirit in America than any recent event." Like Bryan, he feared Wilson demanded too much of Germany and therefore might force the United States into war.[26]

For Vardaman the most disastrous result of the *Lusitania* crisis was the conversion of Wilson to an advocate of military preparedness. Since the beginning of the war a minority had been urging that America sharply increase its Army and Navy as the surest means of protecting its neutral rights and to be ready should it ever become necessary to join the fighting. Until the summer of 1915 Wilson had resisted the demands of the preparedness advocates, but after the *Lusitania's* destruction he became convinced that America must expand its armed forces. By late summer, it became known that the administration was formulating a preparedness program, but the President did not officially outline his plans until November. In accord with the recommendations of Secretary of War Lindley M. Garrison, he proposed a substantial increase in the regular Army and the virtual replacement of the National Guard by a continental Army of 400,000 men. For the Navy he urged that during the next five years the nation spend $500,

[25] Columbus *Dispatch,* May 12, 1915, Asheville *Citizen,* June 4, 1915, in Vardaman Scrapbook; New York *Times,* May 10, 1915.

[26] Jackson *Daily Clarion-Ledger,* July 4, 1915; J. K. Vardaman to William Jennings Bryan, June 9, 1915, in William Jennings Bryan Papers; Columbus *Dispatch,* July 14, 1914, Muscatine *Daily Tribune,* June 17, 1915, in Vardaman Scrapbook. Vardaman opposed Wilson's third *Lusitania* note, as he had the second. New York *Times,* July 24, 25, 26, 1915.

000,000 on the construction of battleships, cruisers, destroyers, and submarines.

From the time Vardaman learned of Wilson's new position, he fought against preparedness and urged others to do the same. "You are dead right on the question of 'preparedness,'" he wrote to Claude Kitchin, the leader of the anti-preparedness forces in the House, "and I hope and pray to Almighty God that you may let your light so shine that others seeing your good work and the correctness of your position on this question may be constrained to follow you and save the farmers and wealth producers of this Republic from being plundered in the interest of the manufacturers of munitions of war." [27] What especially disgusted him was the certainty that a majority of congressmen would approve Wilson's plans for expanding the Army and Navy. During a newspaper interview in November, he lashed out at the President and those congressmen who supported preparedness:

Now I read an admirable paper [one outlining the administration's preparedness program] by the President last night and let me tell you, that man is the most wonderful writer in the world today, the most potential man who has ever occupied the White House. Why the way he handles Congress is a revelation. The average Congressman is as pliable as putty in his fingers, as squashy as slush. The little fools go up there to see him and soon they are down on their stomachs before him like pointer pups. . . . I believe in team work with each man playing his part of the game properly. But I don't believe in the kind of team work you have when a man sits upon a high seat and drives a brace of mules ahead of him with a whip.[28]

Vardaman reacted so vehemently against preparedness from fear that it endangered the very existence of a Democratic republic. Why, he asked, had the demand arisen for preparedness? With Europe absorbed in war there was less danger of the United States being attacked than at any time during the past century. Certainly preparedness had not kept the European powers from going to war! Should America build a huge Army and Navy, it would mark an unfortunate

27 Vardaman to Claude Kitchin, October 22, 1915, in Claude Kitchin Papers, Southern Historical Collection. In the same collection, see also Vardaman to Kitchin, August 28, September 24, 1915, Kitchin to Vardaman, September 10, October 27, 1915.
28 Vicksburg Herald, November 26, 1915.

turning point in the nation's history: not only would the people be burdened with staggering taxes, but the country might fall under the control of a military despotism. Republican institutions had never long survived in nations addicted to militarism.

If there was no need for preparedness and if it actually posed a danger, who then had whipped the country into a military craze? For Vardaman the answer was simple: greedy businessmen and financiers who expected to make money from the programs. Rather than give in to the advocates of preparedness, America should set a living example for the world of the benefits of disarmament. Once the war ended (Vardaman hoped it would finish in a stalemate) the exhausted powers could turn to America to see the benefits of a peaceful society. The United States would never be able to demonstrate the wisdom of disarmament, however, if it yielded to the proponents of preparedness.[29]

During 1916 Congress devoted much attention to the President's preparedness program. Until then Vardaman had been a member of the Military Affairs Committee, but perhaps because of his views on preparedness, he was not reassigned to it.[30] Although no longer on the committee, he fought against practically every piece of preparedness legislation that came before the Senate, the first being the National Defense Act that provided for expanding the Army. Believing that a volunteer army composed of state militias was adequate for the nation's needs, Vardaman criticized the administration's plan to scrap the National Guard and replace it with a continental Army. He also opposed the establishment of volunteer summer training camps, because he charged Negroes might flock to them and thereby pose a threat to the South. His arguments were of no avail, for Congress included in the National Defense Act a provision for volunteer camps. Even more distressing to him, the act almost doubled the size of the regular Army.

[29] *Congressional Record*, 64 Cong., 1st Sess., 147–48, 10259–60; Vicksburg *Herald*, November 10, 19, December 3, 10, 1915, February 3, 1916; Jackson *Daily Clarion-Ledger*, December 14, 1915; Meridian *Dispatch*, November 4, 1915, Bay St. Louis *Echo*, November 13, 1915, Washington *Post*, September 19, 1915, Washington *Star*, December 10, 1915, in Vardaman Scrapbook.
[30] *Congressional Record*, 64 Cong., 1st Sess., 232–33. While a member of the Military Affairs Committee, Vardaman had publicly announced his determined opposition to a large standing army. Washington *Post*, October 7, 1913, in Vardaman Scrapbook.

The National Guard was not abandoned, but it was expanded and thoroughly integrated into the federal defense structure.[31]

Only one section of the National Defense Act received Vardaman's approval—that providing for the construction of a dam and nitrate plant at Muscle Shoals, Alabama, on the Tennessee River. The nitrate would be used in the production of munitions. He believed that if the government would produce all the nation's arms and munitions, it would knock the bottom out of the preparedness craze by removing the possibility that businessmen and bankers might profit from it. In addition, he hoped that once the war ended, the facilities at Muscle Shoals would produce more positive benefits by improving transportation on the Tennessee River and by supplying the region with electric power and nitrate fertilizer at low costs. With such bright hopes for the future, Vardaman joined with fellow progressive senators to defeat an amendment which would have directed the government at the close of the war to sell the facilities at Muscle Shoals to private business. Because the government would build the dam and nitrate plant, he argued, the people—not private interests—should be allowed to enjoy the profits derived from the enterprise.[32]

After having enlarged the Army by passing the National Defense Act, Congress turned its attention to the administration's naval program. The House passed a bill providing less than the President had requested, but the Senate went much further by providing that the program be completed in three years instead of five as the administration had recommended. After much wrangling the House capitulated and accepted the Senate version. Throughout the debates on the bill Vardaman consistently joined a small minority which opposed any expansion in the country's naval forces. Warning that "commercial pirates" and "power hungry politicians" had led the nation into the preparedness craze, he charged there was absolutely no excuse for spending millions of dollars to expand the Navy. Only steel magnates and ship building companies would profit from such expenditures. Even as he presented his arguments, he knew the Senate was determined to provide for a sharp increase in the Navy, so he consistently voted for

[31] *Congressional Record,* 64 Cong., 1st Sess., 4012–13, 4017, 5359, 5417–18, 5571, 5587, 6217–18, 6338, 6357, 6359, 6368, 6374, 6376, 11476.
[32] *Ibid.,* 6106–107, 8135, 10070–72.

amendments designed to make the increase as slight as possible. All such amendments were soundly defeated, and the naval bill finally passed the Senate by a vote of 71 to 8. One of the eight was Vardaman.[33]

A final part of the preparedness program was a shipping bill that empowered the government to spend fifty million dollars to expand the nation's merchant marine. Actually it was a revised version of the ship purchase bill that Vardaman had helped to defeat the previous year. The new measure contained a number of important provisions the earlier one lacked. For one thing, the shipping board became a strong agency which could regulate the rates and services of all vessels engaged in American domestic and foreign trade. The new bill also prohibited the shipping board from purchasing vessels under the registry of any belligerent power and thereby reduced the possibility of endangering America's neutrality. The modifications pleased Vardaman, especially the regulatory powers given the board. Moreover, by the time the bill came up for final vote, the Democratic Party had endorsed the measure in its 1916 platform. Because of the modifications and because it had been incorporated into the Democratic platform, he voted for the bill's passage, although he did not believe it would produce broad benefits. The chief beneficiaries, he feared, would be businessmen who shipped goods to Europe.[34]

The opponents of preparedness failed to block the administration's programs, but they obtained some satisfaction by pushing through a progressive revenue bill to pay for the expansion of military resources. Not only did the revenue bill of 1916 double the normal income tax from 1 to 2 percent and increase the maximum surtax from 6 to 13 percent, it also imposed new taxes on the munitions industry, on surplus corporation capital, and on individual profits. The progressives designed the bill to hit hardest the upper income groups, especially those profiting from the war.

Although Vardaman had long been an exponent of such tax schemes and although he hoped the new bill might reduce the enthusiasm of the wealthy classes for preparedness, he determinedly opposed

[33] *Ibid.*, 11043, 11161–70, 11367, 11372–73, 11375, 11378, 11379, 11384.
[34] *Congressional Record,* 64 Cong., 1st Sess., 12435–36, 12825; New Orleans *Times-Picayune,* July 12, 1916, in Vardaman Scrapbook.

two amendments to it. One created the Federal Tariff Commission, an agency to supervise tariff rates and advise the President and Congress on changes that should be made in existing schedules. The business community strongly endorsed the commission and some hailed it as a reform that would remove the tariff from the arena of partisan politics and place it on a more scientific basis. Vardaman did not trust the new commission. Even though he had come to support some regulatory agencies, like the Federal Trade Commission, he remained generally leary of them, especially those enthusiastically supported by businessmen.[35] Another amendment provided protection to the chemical industry by imposing high tariff rates on dyestuffs, medicines, and synthetics. Believing the amendment represented a surrender to high tariff principles, Vardaman joined six other senators in voting against it. The fact that the Senate passed both amendments which he considered unjustified concession to the business community probably explains why he withheld his vote on the final passage of the revenue bill.[36]

New crises stemming from Germany's use of submarine warfare during the spring of 1916 helped to attract strong congressional support for Wilson's preparedness programs. In the previous summer Germany had promised to abandon unrestricted submarine warfare against unarmed passenger liners, but that pledge applied neither to armed nor unarmed merchant ships. Not only did the State Department recognize the right of Americans to travel on merchant ships, but it expected submarines to surface and give warning before attacking such vessels so that passengers and crew could be evacuated. Until the fall of 1915 no serious problem had arisen, but by that time the British had armed most of their merchant ships. Because a single shot could easily sink a submarine, Secretary of State Lansing believed it unfair to expect Germans to surface and give warning to armed ships. In the hope of avoiding future confrontations with Germany over the submarine issue, Lansing proposed early in 1916 that the Allies disarm all their merchant ships and in return Germany would be expected to observe the rules of cruiser warfare. Germany immediately endorsed the American suggestion and announced that unless England also complied, she

[35] *Congressional Record,* 64 Cong., 1st Sess., 13859; Link, *Wilson: Confusions and Crises,* 341–45.
[36] *Congressional Record,* 64 Cong., 1st Sess., 13768, 13873.

would attack armed merchant ships without warning. The Allies, however, rejected the American proposal, for they knew that such a change would hurt them.

To the surprise of many, Lansing announced on February 15, 1916, that the United States would not insist upon a change in the conventional rules nor warn its citizens against traveling on armed merchant ships. There were several reasons for this about-face. President Wilson did not want to alienate the Allies and thereby weaken his position as a possible mediator. More important, at that time Wilson's close aide, Colonel Edward M. House, was secretly working to arrange mediation between the warring powers, and he had warned that Lansing's proposal might undermine his efforts.

Unaware fully of why the administration had apparently reversed its policy, many Americans were baffled by Lansing's announcement of February 15. Some congressmen suspected the administration was deliberately working to bring the country into the war on the side of the Allies. To offset such a danger, Representative Jeff McLemore of Texas and Senator Thomas P. Gore of Oklahoma introduced resolutions declaring that Americans should not travel on armed ships. Because the resolutions directly challenged his leadership of foreign policy, the President demanded that they be brought quickly to a vote. To preserve Wilson's control of foreign policy, Senate Democratic leaders marshaled a substantial majority of votes and tabled the Gore resolution; a week later the House defeated the McLemore resolution.[37]

Vardaman favored the Gore resolution. Admitting that Americans had the right to travel on armed merchant ships, he believed it would be wiser for Congress to warn people to travel at their own risk. Far better for America to remain at peace than to quibble over international law. Germany's submarine policies posed no threat to America, he pointed out. Those demanding strict adherence to international law were the

---

[37] Link, *Wilson: Confusions and Crises,* 163–64, 167–78, 186–94; Ernest R. May, *The World War and American Isolation, 1914–1917* (Cambridge, Mass., 1959), 187–89; Billington, *Thomas P. Gore,* 69–77. Actually the Senate did not vote on the original Gore resolution. Just before the measure came up for vote, Gore amended it so as to warn Germany that a surprise attack on an armed merchant ship would be cause for war between the United States and Germany. Why Gore changed his resolution is unknown. Perhaps he wanted to embarrass the President because his amended resolution expressed the view that Wilson supported and it was known that the Senate would table his resolution.

profit-hungry speculators who were enriching themselves by wartime trade. Such men wanted American passengers on merchant ships in the hopes that their presence would guard against German submarine attacks. So strongly did Vardaman believe in the righteousness of his cause that he sharply criticized his fellow congressmen who had voted to uphold the President's power of foreign policy; to guard America against being drawn into war, Congress should have wrested control of foreign policy from the executive. Should the United States go to war because Germany sank a merchant ship, he concluded, the responsibility would rest with Congress for having failed to pass the Gore and Mc-Lemore resolutions.[38]

Despite congressional support for the President's insistence that Germany respect America's neutral rights, the nation faced a new crisis on March 24, 1916, when a submarine sank the French steamer *Sussex,* killing eighty people. On April 18 President Wilson warned Berlin that the United States would break diplomatic relations if Germany did not abandon its attacks on all merchant and passenger ships. The following day he told Congress of his ultimatum. While the nation waited for Germany's reply, Vardaman denounced Wilson's demand as ridiculous and unfair: "The President, obeying the 'dictates of humanity,' would involve the United States in the bloody conflict now being waged in Europe in order that British and French commerce might not be interfered with. Think of it—sacrificing thousands of American boys and squandering millions, probably billions of dollars, to force the belligerent powers engaged in a death grapple to respect scrupulously international law." He did not doubt that the President's message "sent thrills of joy into the hearts" of munition manufacturers, the holders of British and French bonds, and all others who expected to reap profits from an Allied victory.[39] Much to his surprise and relief, Germany conceded to Wilson's demands on May 1 by announcing that in the future submarines would respect the rules of visit and search before attacking merchant ships.

Wilson's policy of demanding that Germany adhere strictly to inter-

---

[38] *Congressional Record,* 64 Cong., 1st Sess., 3846–50. Vardaman voted to table the amended Gore resolution, explaining that if he had had the opportunity, he would have voted for the original resolution. Jackson *Daily Clarion-Ledger,* March 5, 1916.
[39] Vicksburg *Herald,* April 22, 1916.

national law, Vardaman believed, was unfair in the light of the administration's lenient policy toward Great Britain. He remembered that during 1914 and 1915 the British blockade had cost the South millions of dollars and yet the administration had failed to demand a rigid adherence to international law. Then in the summer of 1916 Britain announced a blacklisting of American firms suspected of trading with the Central Powers, and again the administration failed to take a strong stand with England. Vardaman suspected the reason for the dichotomy in dealing with England and Germany was simple: American businessmen had made far more trading with the Allies than with the Central Powers and wanted to continue enjoying the handsome profits. While he urged the administration to pursue a tougher course in demanding that England respect American neutral rights, he did not want to risk war with her any more than with Germany. He continued to believe that Britain could be forced to respect American rights simply by the threat of an arms embargo.[40]

Following the settlement of the *Sussex* crisis, Germany's use of submarine warfare did not threaten America's neutrality during the remainder of 1916. After his reelection that year President Wilson began his last major effort to bring the warring nations to the conference table for peace talks. He proposed to both Germany and the Allies that he would use his influence as an arbitrator to arrange a just peace. While still pursuing his efforts for arbitration, the President addressed Congress on January 22, 1917, and described his hopes for a settlement. Neither the Allies nor the Central Powers should suffer a crushing defeat, for to avoid future wars there must be a "peace without victory." The peace must respect the right of all people to self-determination and freedom of the seas. Large standing armies must be abolished and all nations must work together as equals in order to maintain peace. Like most senators, Vardaman praised Wilson's appeal for a true and lasting peace. Describing the speech as "full of human sympathy and concern for mankind," he predicted it would mark "a turning point in the policy of the governments of the world in their relations to each other." [41]

Vardaman's enthusiasm for such a peaceful settlement to the war

[40] *Congressional Record,* 64 Cong., 1st Sess., 1311; New York *American,* July 22, 1916, in Vardaman Scrapbook; Vicksburg *Herald,* July 28, 1916.
[41] Link, *Wilson and the Progressive Era,* 252–66; *The Issue,* June 27, 1918.

quickly died. On January 31, 1917, Germany rebuked the President's appeal for arbitration and announced that she would immediately resume unrestricted submarine warfare. The end of American neutrality was near. On February 2 the State Department broke diplomatic relations with Germany and on the following day Wilson informed Congress of the break. The majority of Congressmen applauded the President's action, but Vardaman did not share their sentiment. Accordingly, when on February 7 the Senate considered a resolution endorsing the administration's action, Vardaman argued against the motion. He believed Wilson had made a mistake in breaking diplomatic relations with Germany, for the President had brought the United States to the brink of war. Congress could insure peace by taking the step it had failed to take a year earlier: warn all citizens to travel in the war zones solely at their own risks. Vardaman's appeal went unheeded, for by a vote of 78 to 5 the Senate adopted the resolution endorsing the President. Only Robert La Follette, William F. Kirby, Asle J. Gronna, John D. Works, and Vardaman voted against the resolution.[42]

During the remainder of February, Germany's submarine policy forced more and more ships to remain in port and as foreign commerce lagged, demands arose to arm American vessels. In response, the President went before Congress on February 26 and asked for the authority to arm merchant ships and to employ whatever additional powers he might deem necessary to protect American life and property. Wilson's request for such sweeping authority caused feverish excitement in the nation, but three days later the American public received an additional jolt—the publication of the Zimmermann telegram in which the German foreign secretary proposed an alliance with Mexico and Japan in the event that the United States declared war on Germany. With the publication of the telegram a wave of fierce anti-German sentiment swept the country. On the very day of its publica-

[42] *Congressional Record,* 64 Cong., 2d Sess., 2734, 2749–50. Before deciding to break relations with Germany, Wilson went to the Capitol and conferred with a group of fifteen senators, one of whom was Vardaman. The President asked for their views on the subject. Of the fifteen, only Vardaman did not respond; he left early, explaining he had another engagement. On leaving, he wished Wilson luck and told him to "sit straight in the boat and keep looking ahead." New York *Times,* February 3, 1917, quoted in McDonald, "Southern Democratic Congressmen," 210.

tion, March 1, the House of Representatives voted overwhelmingly to authorize the President to arm merchant ships, although it did not grant the broad general powers that he had requested.

The next day the Senate took up an armed ship bill, which, had it passed, would have given Wilson power to take whatever steps he believed necessary to protect American life and property. Because Congress was scheduled to adjourn within two days, the Senate discussed the bill until well into the night. It was at that time—shortly before midnight on March 2—that Vardaman delivered his one address on the armed ship bill, an address that lasted sixteen minutes. He denounced the selfish forces that were capitalizing on the hysteria of the moment in the hopes of leading the nation to war. At such a critical time Congress should exert its full authority to curb the President's reckless policies, and it should not give him unlimited power that he might use to draw the nation into war. So strongly did Vardaman want to avoid war that he urged the government to halt all trade between the United States and Europe and to repay those Americans to whom the Allies were financially indebted.[43]

When the Senate resumed its consideration of the armed ship bill the following day, Republicans La Follette, Norris, Gronna, and Albert B. Cummins blocked every attempt to vote on the measure. Throughout the night of March 3 and into the next day the Senate discussion droned on and the four obstructionists refused to allow a vote on the bill. In the midst of that Senate marathon three Republican leaders drafted a statement explaining that they would vote for the bill if they had an opportunity. Seventy-five senators endorsed the statement, but eleven, including Vardaman, refused to sign. Their refusal to sign did not block a vote on the bill; it only indicated they opposed the measure. Despite the many senators supporting the armed ship bill, they were not able to obtain unanimous support to limit debate and, at noon on March 4, the Sixty-Fourth Congress adjourned without granting Wilson the broad authority he wanted.

The defeat of the armed ship bill so angered the President that he immediately issued a hastily prepared statement, charging that in a time of national crisis the government had been paralyzed by a "little

---

[43] *Congressional Record,* 64 Cong., 2d Sess., 4777–79.

group of willful men," who had abused the Senate's rule of unlimited discussion to talk the bill to death. The only way to guard against the recurrence of such a filibuster, he concluded, was to change the rule of unlimited discussion. Wilson's blanket accusation was neither true nor fair, for he implied that all eleven senators who had refused to sign the round-robin had filibustered the bill.[44] Certainly Vardaman had not blocked the vote: he had made his short speech on March 2 and had not even participated in the debates on the third and fourth.

In reply to the President's charge, Vardaman said he was proud to be associated with the "little group of willful men" and furthermore he was delighted that the armed ship bill had not passed. As to the charge of having joined a filibuster, he denied it. He had always opposed such tactics, for he believed in majority rule.[45]

He proved true to his word. At a special session of the Senate on March 8 he voted with the majority to change the rule of unlimited debate which had been in effect for over a century. The Senate adopted a rule of cloture by which a two-thirds majority of the members present could vote to limit each senator to speak no more than one hour on the question at hand.[46]

Vardaman had not filibustered the armed ship bill, but he suffered because of his opposition to it and because of the President's rash statement. When news of Wilson's accusation reached Mississippi, Vardaman was bitterly denounced by the state's press. The *Daily Clarion-Ledger,* which earlier had been an ardent advocate of peace, well represented the patriotic fervor that the President's message excited:

The American republic was betrayed in the Senate of the United States yesterday in the dying hours of the sixty-fourth Congress.

The liberty of the American republic was jeopardized by a small group of men.

It is useless to discuss their motives. Their personality is not worth

44 Link, *Wilson: Campaigns for Progressivism and Peace,* 361–67. The eleven senators who refused to sign the round-robin were Vardaman, La Follette, Norris, Cummins, Gronna, William J. Stone of Missouri, James O'Gorman of New York, Moses E. Clapp of Minnesota, John D. Works of California, William F. Kirby of Arkansas, and Harry Lane of Oregon.
45 *Congressional Record,* 65 Cong., Special Sess., 5–6.
46 *Ibid.,* 31.

the attention. They will permit Germany to draw an erroneous conclusion that the American republic is divided. . . . Our kaiser bund is already formed.[47]

Irate people in Clarksdale hung Vardaman in effigy, and some of his former supporters wrote letters to their local newspapers repudiating him. Thomas Collins, a Biloxi blacksmith, forged a huge iron cross for the senator. Groups of citizens in Gulfport, Wiggins, and Cleveland adopted resolutions condemning him. Twenty voters in Red Bank signed a statement declaring "to the world, as well as KAISER VARDAMAN, we are not hankering for a fight but we are not for this peace propaganda. We think Kaiser James should be given a shearing and bath, and put to bed with an old-fashioned sugar teat." [48]

Vardaman did not flinch in face of the criticism heaped upon him. He announced that he was proud of his stand against the armed ship bill and asserted that should the issue again confront the Senate, he would still fight it. He predicted that the President would soon ask Congress to declare war against Germany, but he would not vote for it because such a war would be fought to protect the interests of wealthy shippers, manufacturers, and munition makers. "Now these are my views; if it be treason, make the most of it." [49]

As Vardaman had predicted, Congress was called into special session on April 2 to declare war against Germany. The Mississippian realized that if he continued to oppose the President it might end his political career. Shortly before Congress convened he had gone to New Orleans and while there was visited by friends from Jackson, who warned that patriotic sentiment was so strong in Mississippi a vote against the war might cost him reelection the next year. For a few moments the senator did not reply, but silently stood before a window overlooking the Baronne Street entrance to the Roosevelt Hotel. Then he turned and thanked his visitors for coming but explained that even "if it should cost me my life I cannot do what you now think you want me to do." [50]

[47] Jackson *Daily Clarion-Ledger,* March 6, 1917.
[48] *Ibid.,* March 8, 10, 21, 1917; petition by citizens of Red Bank, Mississippi, to John Sharp Williams, April 4, 1917, in Williams Papers, Library of Congress.
[49] Jackson *Daily Clarion-Ledger,* March 13, 1917; *The Issue,* March 15, 1917.
[50] Henry V. Watkins, "Address at Presentation of Portrait of Senator James K.

When Wilson asked Congress for a declaration of war, Vardaman remained loyal to his convictions. He wished that he could follow the majority of his colleagues, for he knew they believed America had to go to war. He doubted only their wisdom, saying: "I only wish I could believe that the thing the Senate is about to do will redound to the interests of the American people, but for the life of me I can not bring myself to believe it will contribute to the welfare of the great mass of American people and to the happiness of the world, and elevate and render more permanent the civilization of mankind." Because Germany had violated its neutral rights, he admitted, America had legal cause to declare war. The Allies, however, also had violated American rights and had committed atrocities the equal of Germany's. The brutalizing influence of war had driven all belligerent powers to commit acts which in calmer times would shame them. That alone was reason enough for America to "keep out of this slaughter pen." He recalled what Wilson had earlier described as a "peace without victory," a just peace in which neither side crushed the other. American entry into the war would prevent such an amicable settlement, for it would insure Germany's defeat. Confident that the American people did not want war, he ridiculed the administration for not maintaining peace as it had promised during the election of the past year. If the "plain, honest people, the masses who are to bear the burden of taxation and fight the Nation's battles" were consulted, there would be no fighting.[51]

Vardaman knew he was in a hopeless minority. On April 4, 1917, by a vote of 82 to 6 the Senate declared war on Germany. As had happened so many times, he voted with the minority.[52] For three years he had unwaveringly struggled to keep the United States out of a war that he believed did not affect her security. Convinced that selfish interests had aroused the war sentiment, he had wanted his country instead to set an example for the world of the benefits derived from a peaceful, progressive democracy. Too frequently, he believed, the Wilson administration had pursued an unneutral course in its dealings with the

---

Vardaman to the Mississippi Hall of Fame," May 17, 1936 (MS in Henry V. Watkins Collection, Mississippi Department of Archives and History).

[51] *Congressional Record*, 65 Cong., 1st Sess., 208–210.

[52] *Ibid.*, 261. Those who joined Vardaman in voting against war were Gronna, La Follette, Lane, Norris, and Stone.

belligerent powers—it had set harsher demands on Germany than on England. If it would preserve peace, Vardaman would have had America suspend all trade with the warring nations. Few congressmen had been more consistent than the Mississippian in struggling to preserve American neutrality. Few demonstrated more courage in pursuing the lonely course that ultimately led to political demise.

Once America entered the war, Congress turned its attention to mobilizing the nation's resources. Not only did a large Army and Navy have to be raised as quickly as possible, but new federal agencies had to be created to insure that American industry and transportation facilities operated at peak efficiency.

Vardaman supported many of the administration's requests. He voted to grant huge war loans to England and France, consistently supported military appropriations bills, and endorsed the declaration of war against Austria-Hungary.[53] He even voted for some acts, such as the Overman bill, despite his fears that the measures were unwise and unnecessary. Yet he did not give blanket approval to all wartime legislation. On some issues he opposed measures which he believed would endanger free institutions in America or would concede too much to wealthy interests. Although Vardaman supported most of the measures recommended by Wilson and his aides, his opposition to some administration policies gave the clearest insight into his thought and action during the war years.

The nation's immediate problem was to raise an Army and get it to the European front. The administration maintained that the Army would have to be conscripted, and accordingly Congress began considering a bill to provide for a selective service system. On that issue Vardaman balked. The Army, he believed, should consist solely of volunteers, men who were willing to fight for sheer love of country. Anything less would be an affront to the American people, for the conscript and the convict were too much alike. Only if the country failed to raise a strong army voluntarily would he be willing to vote for conscription.

The draft, he feared, would create a permanent standing Army, but a volunteer Army would give the most assurance of quickly disband-

53 *Ibid.*, 761, 3790–91, 4794, 6268–70, 7737–38, 65 Cong., 2d Sess., 66, 8351.

ing. Throughout history, large armies had frequently overthrown republican governments because soldiers, he warned, did not respect civil authority.[54] Vardaman's fear of a permanent standing Army thus led him to oppose measures to increase the salaries of officers, because he wanted to avoid all inducements that might make an Army career attractive.[55] He also believed Negroes would be drafted, and that would pose the greatest danger to the South since the enactment of the Fourteenth and Fifteenth amendments, because "it will mean there will be arrogant strutting representatives of the black soldiery in every community." [56]

Though opposition to the draft was widespread, only a handful of congressmen actually voted against the Selective Service Act. Vardaman enjoyed more success in supporting several amendments to it than he did in defeating the bill. He wholeheartedly endorsed prohibiting the sale of alcoholic beverages at all military installations and the sale of liquor anywhere to men in uniform, and he also approved setting the draft age at twenty-one instead of nineteen. Since men under twenty-one could not vote, they should not be drafted.[57] When Congress lowered the draft age to eighteen the following year, he bitterly opposed the change, arguing that it would be better to take older men than to draft boys during their most formative years.[58]

As the war progressed, Vardaman's opposition to conscription never slackened. When President Wilson asked for legislation authorizing the creation of an Air Force, Vardaman opposed the request because it provided for drafting men.[59] He also pleaded on several occasions to exempt farmers and laborers, for they could render more valuable service at home.[60] Although opposed to conscription and all measures that would attract men to an Army career, he favored increasing the pay of enlisted men.[61] He supported an amendment to the War Risk

[54] *Ibid.*, 932–33, 1085–87, 1483, 1322.
[55] *Ibid.*, 490; Forest *Scott County News*, April 20, 1917, in Vardaman Scrapbook.
[56] Vicksburg *Herald*, April 7, 1917.
[57] *Congressional Record*, 65 Cong., 1st Sess., 1453, 1464, 1471.
[58] *Ibid.*, 65 Cong., 2d Sess., 4067–68, 8237–38, 8478, 9338, 9352, 9476–77; *The Issue*, May 16, 1918.
[59] *Congressional Record*, 65 Cong., 1st Sess., 5210–11, 5369, 5372.
[60] *Ibid.*, 65 Cong., 2d Sess., 2905, 2908–909, 65 Cong., 3d Sess., 1399; *The Issue*, March 14, 1918.
[61] *Congressional Record*, 65 Cong., 1st Sess., 6856; Forest *Scott County News*,

Insurance Act providing compensation for dependent wives, children, and parents of military personnel. It was one of the few wartime acts, he believed, which recognized the human being.[62]

A difficult problem confronting Congress was that of paying for the staggering costs of war. Conservatives favored the issuance of government bonds that could be paid off gradually in the future, but strong progressives wanted sharp tax increases on upper income groups, especially those reaping profits from the war. Vardaman favored the progressive tax schemes, arguing that they afforded the fairest means of raising revenue and also put the major burden on those whom he believed had led the nation into war.

I think if Senators will consult their memories and indulge in a little retrospection, they will find that it is that peculiar type of gentleman known for the last three years as the patriotic advocate of "preparedness," the man who paid for the bunting that decorated the houses, who paid the bills for the bands that furnished the music for the preparedness parades, who bought the flags that were flaunted in the air by the hired claquers along with the real patriots who marched in the parade, who rented the screens in the moving-picture theaters to show the necessity for organizing a great army and a great navy and to demonstrate our utter unpreparedness for defense. [sic] That class of men who capitalize their pretended patriotism and who have made fabulous fortunes out of war contracts are the men who are now protesting against enactment of [taxes on excess war profits].[63]

The 1917 Revenue Act embodied some of the principles that Vardaman favored, for not only did it reduce all tax exemptions, it also increased the surtax on upper income groups to a maximum of 63 percent, imposed a graduated excess profits tax ranging from 20 to 60 percent, and raised the estates tax to a maximum of 25 percent. He only regretted it had not done more to tax war profits. If the government could conscript young men to give their lives in the war, he argued, then it could conscript every cent of excess profits.[64] The 1917

September 14, 1917, Yazoo City *Yazoo Sentinel,* September 12, 1917, in Vardaman Scrapbook.

[62] *Congressional Record,* 65 Cong., 1st Sess., 7737–39.

[63] *Ibid.,* 6269.

[64] During the Senate debates on the revenue bill, Vardaman joined with a small liberal block in voting consistently for amendments offered by Robert M.

Revenue Act fell far short of what Vardaman wanted, but the following year Congress adopted a measure more to his liking. The Revenue Act of 1918 greatly increased the nation's over-all tax burden and put four-fifths of the new load on large incomes, war profits, and inherited estates.

Though the war wrought changes in the nation's tax structure, it also led the government to exert more control over the economy. New agencies were formed to control food and fuel supplies, coordinate production among various industries, encourage shipbuilding, and improve the operation of all major communication facilities. Vardaman voted for the establishment of all such agencies, but he had reservations about the powers and operations of some of them.[65] He felt, for example, that Director of the Food Administration Herbert Hoover had exceeded his authority in fixing the prices of sugar and wheat.[66] Perhaps for that reason he came to dislike Hoover intensely and when the food director appeared before the Committee on Manufactures to testify about a national sugar shortage, Vardaman exceeded the bounds of common decency in grilling him. Not only did he imply that Hoover was more partial to England than to America and was unfit for his present position, but he even charged Hoover had employed men in the administration "whose private pecuniary interests conflict necessarily with the public service." By his vitriolic attacks on Hoover, he brought upon himself the wrath of newspapers throughout the country, many of whom greatly admired the food administrator.[67]

La Follette, Thomas Hardwick, and Henry F. Hollis, all of which aimed to put more of the tax burden on upper income groups and on those industries profiting from the war. *Congressional Record,* 65 Cong., 1st Sess., 6155, 6162, 6288, 6383, 6503, 6542, 6549, 6561, 6619, 6620, 6621, 6623, 6727, 6732, 6740–41, 6854, 6861, 6865–70, 6879, 6883, 6884, 6886. Although Vardaman regretted that the bill did not go farther in taxing excess profits, he voted for its final passage. *Congressional Record,* 65 Cong., 1st Sess., 6886. *The Issue,* September 13, 18, 1917; Magnolia *Gazette,* September 8, 1917, in Vardaman Scrapbook.

[65] *Congressional Record,* 65 Cong., 1st Sess., 1637, 4453–54, 4477–78, 5367, 5908–909, 65 Cong., 2d Sess., 5766, 9091, 9093–94.

[66] Although Vardaman voted for the establishment of the Food Administration, he feared from the outset that it was vested with too much power. He wanted the entire food program on a voluntary basis, arguing that if the people were asked to restrict food consumption, they would do it. *Congressional Record,* 65 Cong., 1st Sess., 3919–20, 4216, 4453–54, 4477–78; Newton *Record,* June 28, 1917, Vicksburg *Post,* June 22, 1917, in Vardaman Scrapbook.

[67] *Shortage of Sugar. Hearings Before the Subcommittee on the Committee on*

While criticizing the Food Administration, he applauded the government's performance in other areas of the economy and in a few instances believed it should exert even greater control. When the Emergency Fleet Corporation confronted the problem of having to pay exorbitantly high prices for steel, Vardaman charged that the manufacturers were exploiting the war to enrich themselves and urged that the government nationalize the steel companies.[68] Although the steel industry remained free of government control, much to his delight the Railroad Administration came to direct the operation of every railway in the country. He supported that agency, his only objection being that it permitted the stockholders to enjoy the average profits for 1915–17, the most lucrative years in the railroads' history. He preferred limiting stockholders to lower returns and applying excess profits to improving railroad tracks and equipment. So successful was the Railroad Administration that Vardaman hoped the government would permanently nationalize the railroads.[69]

Despite strong reservations, he voted for the Overman Act which gave the President almost unlimited power to improve the nation's war efforts by reorganizing executive departments and administrative agencies. He did not question Wilson's motives, but he feared the powers conferred by the measure would have to be delegated to subordinates, some of whom might seriously abuse their positions. If the President wanted more authority, Congress should delegate specific powers as needed. Even as the bill had been introduced in the Senate, the senator argued, it unnecessarily usurped authority by giving the executive control over the Interstate Commerce Committee and the Federal Reserve Board, agencies that did not relate directly to the war effort. Although amendments to exempt those bureaus from the Overman bill failed, Vardaman voted for the measure's final passage, explaining that it would not increase the difficulty of reducing executive authority and reestablishing free government once the war ended.[70]

Manufactures, United States Senate (Washington, 1918), 689–91; New York *Times,* January 3, 4, 1918; Vicksburg *Herald,* January 5, 20, May 31, 1918.

[68] *Congressional Record,* 65 Cong., 1st Sess., 3841, 4059–60.

[69] *Ibid.,* 65 Cong., 2d Sess., 2428–30, 2502; *The Issue,* December 13, 1917, March 7, 1918.

[70] *Congressional Record,* 65 Cong., 2d Sess., 4968–69, 5699, 5703, 5747, 5753–55, 5757, 5761, 5766.

What most displeased him about America's war mobilization was the active role played by businessmen in directing the new federal agencies. Just as he believed they had led the nation into war, so he suspected that many of those directing wartime agencies were enriching themselves by allowing the government to pay unjust prices and by awarding contracts to companies in which they had investments. A government shipyard at Hog Island, near Philadelphia, helped to confirm his suspicions. Organized soon after America declared war, the Hog Island yard did not produce a single ship until the fighting had ended. The Senate Commerce Committee, of which Vardaman was a member, and the Justice Department investigated the Hog Island operation, and both found that it had been miserably managed. Neither report disclosed any evidence of corruption.[71] Vardaman, however, charged that the committee had not dug deep enough, for he was convinced that the men in charge at Hog Island had perpetrated "the most shameful scheme to rob the Public Treasury." [72] So sure was he that there had been corruption at the shipyard that until the day he left the Senate he worked to "perpetuate the memory of that notorious transaction." [73]

Next to profiteering, Vardaman vehemently deplored the bridling of free expression. The Espionage Act of 1917 imposed stiff penalties on anyone who obstructed the war effort and gave the Postmaster General sweeping authority to ban from the mails any publication which he considered seditious. In one of his finest Senate speeches Vardaman urged that America needed freedom of expression more during the war than at any previous time. Not only did a free press inform the people, but it also kept government officials abreast of public opinion. By giving the Postmaster General the authority to abridge free expression, Congress ran the risk of concentrating dangerous authority in the hands of one man. It could be a step toward tyranny. Certainly it was ironic, he noted, for the United States to be fighting

[71] United States Shipping Board Emergency Fleet Corporation. Hearings Before the Committee on Commerce, United States Senate . . . on S[enate] Res-[olution] 170. . . . (Washington, 1918), passim; Frederick L. Paxson, America at War, 1917–1918 (Boston, 1939), II, 73–74.

[72] Congressional Record, 65 Cong., 2d Sess., 1853, 1932–33, 4903, 7290–91.

[73] Ibid., 65 Cong., 3d Sess., 248–49, 435–37, 4852–55; James K. Vardaman to T. W. Gregory, December 14, 1918, Gregory to Vardaman, December 16, 1918, in Justice Department Records, File No. 189836, National Archives.

against an autocracy in Europe, while building one of its own at home. Knowing that only the unsettled conditions of the times had enabled the government to censor the press, he denounced the war for what it was doing to the country:

> There never has been a war waged among civilized peoples that could not have been avoided or settled without bloodshed, with honor, if the masses had been wise, provident, and prudent and the leaders, the officeholders, those in authority, had been brave, patriotic, and unselfish.
> War is the game of the men in power, and those who profit pecuniarily thereby—a bloody game in which the ignorant and subservient masses are merely the pawns.[74]

His pleading went for nought, because the Espionage bill passed the Senate by a vote of 77 to 6, with only William E. Borah, Joseph I. France, Asle Gronna, Lawrence Y. Sherman, La Follette, and Vardaman voting against it.[75]

In order to strengthen government censorship over international publications and the foreign language press, Congress also passed the Tradings With The Enemy Act. Because Vardaman believed it did not confer any powers that had not earlier been granted by the Espionage Act, he signed the conference committee report and voted for its passage. He still opposed any abridgment of free speech and hoped that the actual enforcement of the new Act would lead to its hasty repeal.[76]

In 1918 he continued to fight for freedom of speech by opposing the harsh Sedition Act that imposed penalties on those who made remarks that were considered disloyal. While debating the measure Vardaman, to his surprise, found himself defending the right of Theodore Roosevelt to criticize Congress for blindly following President Wilson's conduct of the war. Though Roosevelt had served as a whipping boy for him in the gubernatorial primary of 1903, Vardaman observed that "from the gush of this human Vesuvius has fallen, perhaps accidently, some jewels of truth." He then turned to the broader dangers posed by the sedition bill and warned his fellow senators not to make

---

[74] *Congressional Record,* 65 Cong., 1st Sess., 1873, 2001–2004.
[75] *Ibid.,* 2270–71.
[76] *Ibid.,* 6952–56, 7021–22, 7340–41, 7345–46, 7353.

a mistake during the excitement of war by enacting a law the people would never tolerate once peace had been restored.[77]

When La Follette became the victim of the wartime sedition phobia, the senator from Mississippi defended him against a demand by the Minnesota Commission on Public Safety that he be expelled from the Senate for allegedly having made a treasonous speech at St. Paul in September, 1917. The case was referred to the Senate Committee on Privileges and Elections, of which Vardaman was a member. To protect La Follette by allowing time for public opinion to cool, Vardaman and Senator James Reed delayed committee action until they were assured a majority would vote in his favor.[78] When the issue finally came before the Senate in 1919, Vardaman joined with the majority in dismissing the charges against La Follette.[79]

As happened so frequently in his career, while striving to guard the rights and expand the welfare of whites, he worked equally hard to suppress the Negro. Following a race riot in East St. Louis, Illinois, in the summer of 1917, he warned that because the government was foolishly permitting Negroes to serve in the Army, the nation faced grave danger. The black veterans would demand equality as the price for having served their country. Whites had created the problem by permitting them to join the armed forces; now the danger would be met only by segregating the returning Negro soldiers. Like all nonwhites, they must be relegated to a menial position. He warned of the consequences should Negroes ever obtain social and political equality in the United States:

We are threatened in America with the deleterious effects of the "melting pot" of war, the merging of the races, and the enforced equality and solidarity of citizenship. The suggestion is monstrous and shows how brutalizing is war and stupefying its influences. Let it not be forgotten Mr. President, that political equality in a country where the races are practically equal in number means ultimately social equality;

77 *Ibid.*, 65 Cong., 2d Sess., 4709–712. On the final passage of the Sedition Act, Vardaman was "detained on official business" and did not vote. *Congressional Record,* 65 Cong., 2d Sess., 6057.
78 James A. Reed to Fola M. La Follette, April 28, 1938, cited in Bell C. and Fola M. La Follette, *Robert M. La Follette, 1855–1925* (2 vols.: New York, 1953), II, 815–16; Record of the United States Senate Committee on Privileges and Election, 65 Congress, re La Follette Investigation, National Archives.
79 *Congressional Record,* 65 Cong., 3d Sess., 1527.

social equality is universally followed by race amalgamation; race amalgamation means race deterioration, and with race deterioration will come the final disaster, the blighting touch of disintegration, downfall and death of our civilization.

The East St. Louis riot might prove a blessing to the nation, he concluded, should it awaken the whites to the racial problems that would confront the country once the war ended.[80]

Some observers found Vardaman's opposition to President Wilson's foreign policy baffling, for they had long assumed that he was only a cheap demagogue. Yet the unpopular course the Mississippian insisted on taking during the war years was not surprising to those who knew the man. He based every stand on advanced progressive sentiment that he had come to advocate by the time he entered the Senate. What made him differ from many of his fellow congressmen was that he did not subordinate his convictions to bow to the war hysteria that gripped the majority of the voting public. Convinced that large businessmen had duped the country into a needless and costly war for their own selfish interests, he feared that free government at home was being endangered and undermined by war legislation. The master politician, so astute at measuring and utilizing the dominant sentiments of his constituency to gain political office, could no longer listen to a world "gone mad." Thus, the country editor who once fought a gun battle to stick by what he had written, now went to battle with prevailing wartime forces to stick by what he believed to be the only "sane" course. Vardaman lost the battle and his political life to the war.

[80] *Ibid.,* 65 Cong., 1st Sess., 6061–67.

CHAPTER XII

POLITICAL DEMISE

WHEN VARDAMAN LEFT for the Senate in 1913, he was without doubt the strongest man in Mississippi politics. Anti-Vardaman forces were by no means dispirited, however, nor inactive in their efforts to topple their opponents. When Governor Earl Brewer skillfully managed to straddle a neutral fence between the two warring factions during the 1912 state legislative session, the leaders of the anti-Vardaman camp took special pains to avoid alienating the governor and thereby drive him into the opposition camp.[1] Their strategy succeeded, because Brewer had not long been in office before he began to irritate Vardaman and Bilbo followers who complained that he had become too proud of his new position, that he had begun to enjoy such frills as riding in an automobile, and that he had threatened to veto legislation favored by the Farmers' Union. Others rumored that Brewer did not want to associate "with the hill billies but with the swell crowd, the well-to-do and society people. He wanted to be the champion of the [John Sharp] Williams kind of people and not the Vardaman bunch." [2]

Such pro-Vardaman static helped to drive Brewer little by little into the opposition's camp, until in 1913 an open rupture alienated Brewer and the Vardaman faction. At the time, a financial scandal was uncovered in the state prison board when the treasurer, Lawrence Yerger, confessed to having embezzled thirty thousand dollars. Governor Brewer immediately began an investigation of the penitentiary system, but as soon as it became known that he intended to press charges against some officials who had been appointed by Vardaman, he met

[1] John Sharp Williams to Frederick Sullens, September 4, 1911, in Williams Papers, Mississippi Department of Archives.

[2] E. R. Holmes to John Sharp Williams, March 1, 1912, Henry Minor to Williams, June 4, 1912, in Williams Papers, Mississippi Department of Archives.

opposition. Newspapers favoring Vardaman sharply criticized the investigation, charging it was politically motivated and directed against innocent men. At a special session of the Mississippi legislature in June, 1913, the senate, acting in response to Lieutenant Governor Bilbo's leadership, successfully defeated Brewer's request for a legislative investigation of the penitentiary system. Despite the senate's opposition, the governor had five prison officials indicted, three of whom were eventually convicted. Only Yerger was guilty of a serious crime.³ What angered many Vardamanites was a five-year sentence imposed on board president Charles C. Smith for having overcharged the state several hundred dollars for a secondhand automobile. While Vardaman never publicly criticized the investigation, he appealed privately to the governor to suspend Smith's sentence because of the prisoner's wretched health. Brewer complied with the request.⁴

Developments stemming from the penitentiary scandal completely estranged Bilbo and Brewer. Deeply angered by Bilbo's opposition to him, Brewer soon told an acquaintance that he had "but one ambition in life, politically, and that is to put that s-of-a-b- Bilbo where he belongs." ⁵ Bilbo had similar designs. In the fall of 1913 a Texas publication, *The Pitchfork,* created a mild sensation in Mississippi when it reported that, because of the penitentiary affair, state Senator George A. Hobbs and Lieutenant Governor Bilbo were plotting to ruin Brewer by spreading reports that he had had illicit sexual affairs.⁶ Whether there was such a plot is unknown, but *The Pitchfork's* reports may have persuaded Brewer to destroy Bilbo and Hobbs before they had a chance to do the same to him. Whatever his motives, the governor did furnish evidence to the Warren County grand jury, which on December 1, 1913, indicted Bilbo and Hobbs for having allegedly taken bribes in 1912 to get a bill through the state legislature to create a new Delta county. Brewer claimed that he and Steve Castleman, a wealthy Delta planter, had assumed the role of detectives and secured incrim-

³ Kirwan, *Revolt of the Rednecks,* 236–39; Jackson *Daily Clarion-Ledger,* August 3, 10, 26, 1913; *The Issue,* September 11, 1913; W. A. Percy to John Sharp Williams, August 29, 1913, R. C. Lee to Williams, September 6, 1913, in Williams Papers, Mississippi Department of Archives.
⁴ Columbus *Dispatch,* March 15, 1914, in Vardaman Scrapbook.
⁵ Frederick Sullens to John Sharp Williams, August 25, 1913, in Williams Papers, Mississippi Department of Archives.
⁶ Jackson *Daily Clarion-Ledger,* October 16, 21, 1913.

inating evidence against Bilbo and Hobbs. The indicted officials retaliated by charging that Brewer was attempting to frame them; moreover they, too, claimed to have been playing detective to get evidence against Castleman, whom they accused of having bribed legislators.[7]

The indictment of Bilbo and Hobbs created a furor throughout the state. The anti-Vardaman press denounced the accused bribe takers and demanded that they be quickly convicted and sent to prison.[8] From the outset, however, many people—both friends and foes of Bilbo—believed Brewer was attempting to frame his enemies, and they realized that such an overt effort might backfire. Had not a similar attempt to destroy Bilbo during the Dulaney bribery scandal only resulted in enhancing his political strength, thereby paving his way to election as Lieutenant Governor? The actions of Judge Pat Henry, a longtime foe of both Vardaman and Bilbo, revealed the suspicions that many had of Brewer's efforts to send Bilbo and Hobbs to prison. Being one of Mississippi's most able lawyers, Henry was asked to assist the prosecution in trying the accused. Not only did Henry reject the state's request, but he represented Bilbo and Hobbs as defense attorney, for like so many others he believed Brewer's charges were false. In the end the governor lost, for at separate trials the two men were declared innocent. Bilbo enjoyed renewed political strength as a result of his acquittal and celebrated by announcing he would run for governor in 1915. [9]

In Washington at the time, Vardaman carefully avoided becoming involved in the dispute between Bilbo and Brewer. During a brief visit to Mississippi in the fall of 1913 he refused to comment on *The Pitchfork's* reports that Bilbo and Hobbs were trying to destroy the governor.[10] Then, soon after the bribery scandal broke, Hobbs tried to win the senator's support by charging that Brewer had slandered Vardaman and his followers. Being fully aware of Vardaman's strength, Brewer immediately denied Hobbs's charge. Actually the governor did not have to fear that Vardaman would come to the rescue of either Hobbs or Bilbo, for the senator wanted no part of the nasty affair.

[7] *The Issue,* December 4, 1913.
[8] Jackson *Daily Clarion-Ledger,* December 7, 9, 10, 13, 15, 20, 1913.
[9] *Ibid.,* January 2, July 10, 1914.
[10] Magnolia *Gazette,* November 1, 1913, in Vardaman Scrapbook.

He accordingly rejected a summons to testify as a character witness at the Hobbs trial, explaining he could not leave Washington while Congress was in session.[11]

His refusal to become involved in the bribery case led many to speculate that all was not well between him and Bilbo.[12] Although anti-Vardaman newspapers overemphasized the reports of such a rift, there was truth in the accusations. Circumstances had brought Vardaman and Bilbo into a political alliance in 1910, but the two had never been close personal friends. Anna Vardaman, in fact, had never forgiven Bilbo for not disclosing Dulaney's bribery during the senatorial caucus, thereby swinging the election to her husband; as a result, she had adamantly refused to invite him into her home.[13] Bilbo's increasing political strength in the state legislature also probably helped to abort the development of a personal intimacy between the two politicians. Vardaman was too much the star of a one-man political show to appreciate being "upstaged" by his understudy. On at least one occasion he intervened to quash a Bilbo-sponsored measure providing that state and national elections in Mississippi be held in the same year. Many opposed the change, fearing it would lead to too much political swapping at election time. To defeat Bilbo's plan, Vardaman conferred with two close friends in the state legislature, Albert C. Anderson and Frank Burkitt, and under their leadership the system of electing state and federal officials in separate years remained unchanged.[14]

The gubernatorial election of 1915 further strained the Vardaman-Bilbo alliance. More than two years before the election, it was generally known that Bilbo intended to run for governor along with three other Vardaman men: W. Marion Reily, Hilary M. Quinn, and John R. Tally. Only one anti-Vardaman candidate, P. S. Stovall, entered the race, but he was never a serious threat. Believing that Var-

[11] Jackson *Daily Clarion-Ledger,* December 5, 17, 1913; *The Issue,* December 11, 1913; Shreveport *Times,* n.d., in Vardaman Scrapbook.
[12] Poplarville *Free Press,* September 25, 1913, Vicksburg *Post,* March 23, 1914, in Vardaman Scrapbook; *The Issue,* April 9, 1914.
[13] Macon *Beacon,* February 6, 1914, in Vardaman Scrapbook.
[14] D. M. Quinn to John Sharp Williams, January 10, 1914, Williams to J. K. Vardaman, January 12, 1914, in Williams Papers, Mississippi Department of Archives; Vardaman to Williams, January 16, 1914, in Williams Papers, Library of Congress.

daman's political influence was so great that he could name the next
governor, some newspaper editors appealed to him not to inflict Bilbo
on the state. If he could not endorse someone other than the lieutenant
governor, they pleaded for him to remain neutral.[15] At the same time,
however, some of Vardaman's closest supporters, H. Vaughn Watkins,
Swep Taylor, and John Hebron, were working for Bilbo's election,
and they urged the senator to help their cause.

Again Vardaman tried to remain neutral. When he returned to Jackson in October, 1913, to speak at the state fair, he rejected a request
by Bilbo's aides to allow the lieutenant governor to introduce him.
Then as he was speaking to the huge assemblage of his stanch partisans,
a man shouted from the crowd asking whom he had selected to be
the state's next governor. Some urged him to ignore the question, but
he answered it: Because he did not want to be a "political boss," he
would not attempt to name the governor. Moreover, since four men
from his faction were in the race, he would not give an advantage to
anyone with an endorsement. Only if an anti-Vardaman candidate
threatened to win would he intervene.[16]

Despite his determination to remain on the sidelines, on several
occasions he was drawn into the tussle. In September, 1914, Governor
Brewer charged that Bilbo was a crook and that Vardaman knew it.
Vardaman immediately issued a statement denouncing Brewer as a
liar. Then after admitting that Bilbo was not perfect, he asserted that
he had as much faith in his integrity and "devotion to duty" as he had
in Brewer's. Although pro-Bilbo newspapers praised the senator's letter and hailed it as an endorsement of the lieutenant governor, it
appears that by equating Bilbo's ability with Brewer's, Vardaman had
damned his old ally with faint praise.[17]

A costly slip while speaking at Pontotoc, Mississippi, in May, 1915,
brought Vardaman closer to direct involvement in the campaign. On

[15] Osyka *Herald,* October 31, 1913, in Vardaman Scrapbook; Jackson *Daily
Clarion-Ledger,* June 24, 1914.
[16] Ripley *Enterprise,* November 8, 1913, Magnolia *Gazette,* November 5, 1913,
in Vardaman Scrapbook; *The Issue,* November 6, 1913; Jackson *Daily Clarion-
Ledger,* August 12, 1914.
[17] Jackson *Daily Clarion-Ledger,* October 4, 6, 1914; Yazoo City *Yazoo
Sentinel,* October 8, 1914, Woodville *Republican,* October 10, 1914, Kosciusko
Herald, October 9, 1914, in Vardaman Scrapbook.

that occasion he had condemned corruption in government and warned that a "man who would accept a bribe while in the discharge of an official duty is a worse enemy to society that Benedict Arnold or Judas Iscariot and a man who votes for one of this kind lends an endorsement." Immediately newspapers throughout the state asked if he had not been speaking of Bilbo? Some did not ask. They charged that Vardaman must have meant Bilbo, for bribery had been unknown in Mississippi until he had appeared on the scene.[18] So intensely did the anti-Bilbo press play upon the Pontotoc speech, that Vardaman addressed a letter "To the People of Mississippi," flatly denying that his denunciation of bribe takers had been intended as a condemnation of Bilbo. He then praised Bilbo for having uncovered corruption in the caucus of 1910 and asserted that Bilbo's ability equalled that of the other candidates running for governor.[19] Though he had not gone so far as some Bilbo supporters wanted, he had come close to open endorsement of the lieutenant governor. Soon after having issued his statement, he left Mississippi and spent the summer of 1915 on the Chautauqua circuit in the Midwest, giving his standard lecture on "The Impending Crisis."

With Vardaman too far away for further involvement in the gubernatorial contest, Bilbo conducted a masterful campaign by appealing to the issues that had brought him and Vardaman to power in 1911. He again presented himself as the foe of predatory wealth, as the champion of the common people, and as the victim of the old "secret caucus" forces.[20] Bilbo won a decisive victory over his four opponents in the first primary, demonstrating that his faction was still powerful in Mississippi politics. What is most significant about the event is that in no way did he owe his success directly to Vardaman. In fact, Bilbo's stunning victory probably made him the leader of their group.

Waning strength within his own faction was the least of Vardaman's political problems by 1915. During his first two years in the Senate

[18] Jackson *Daily Clarion-Ledger*, May 8, 1915; Vicksburg *Herald*, May 19, 23, 30, June 6, 1915.
[19] *The Issue*, May 20, 27, June 3, 1915.
[20] *The Issue*, June–August, 1915; Vicksburg *Herald*, June–August, 1915; Jackson *Daily Clarion-Ledger*, June–August, 1915; A. J. Hackett to John J. Coman, July 19, 1915, in John J. Coman Papers, Mississippi Department of Archives and History.

his support for the Underwood Tariff Act, his fight for a higher tax on upper income groups, his opposition to Negro appointments and advocacy of Jim Crow policies for federal agencies, all served to strengthen him with his constituents. Even his fight with the Wilson administration over the Panama Canal tolls questions did not lessen his popularity at home. Not until he opposed the ship purchase bill in 1915 did he begin to lose strength. Anti-Vardaman newspapers charged that by joining with the Republicans he had helped to defeat a bill that might have relieved the South's economic plight by furnishing more ships to transport cotton to foreign markets. What especially irked many people was his caustic criticisms of Wilson for advocating the measure.[21] While it would be a mistake to believe that Vardaman's opposition to the ship purchase bill did him irreparable harm, it certainly marked a turning point in his career.

Nevertheless, his opposition to the administration's preparedness program during the fall of 1915 and his anti-Wilson tirades made him more and more unpopular in Mississippi. This fact was made all too clear by the experiences of Samuel A. Witherspoon, the only Mississippi politician of consequence who joined Vardaman in opposing both the ship purchase bill and the preparedness program. He had first won election to Congress in 1910, when in the wake of the "secret caucus" he had run as a pro-Vardaman candidate and defeated incumbent Adam Byrd. During his years in Congress he and Vardaman became close friends. By 1915 there were reports that the following year Witherspoon would run for the Senate against John Sharp Williams and that the chief issue would be the ship bill.[22] At first, Witherspoon did not fear making that the issue, and shortly after Congress adjourned in the spring of 1915 he accepted an invitation to debate the question with Williams. Since Witherspoon had not officially announced as a candidate for the Senate, Williams refused to meet him.[23]

[21] Jackson *Daily Clarion-Ledger,* January 26, 1915; Vicksburg *Herald,* March 7, 14, 19, 25, 28, 30, 31, 1915. Although Vardaman was sharply criticized for opposing the ship purchase bill, many supported him. *The Issue,* February 11, 18, 25, 1915; Kosciusko *Star Ledger,* February 12, 1915, Aberdeen *Weekly,* February 11, 1915, Brookhaven *Leader,* March 3, 1915, Newton *Record,* February 18, 1915, Clarksdale *Mississippian,* February 12, 1915, in Vardaman Scrapbook.

[22] Vicksburg *Herald,* March 30, April 1, 1915.

[23] Elnathan Tartt to John Sharp Williams, July 21, 1915, Williams to Tartt,

By the fall of 1915 the Mississippi political climate altered the impending contest between Williams and Witherspoon. Public support for preparedness had then increased in Mississippi, as it had throughout the nation and as a result, Williams, an advocate of preparedness, found his political fortunes sharply increasing. So discouraged was Witherspoon by the sudden shift in public opinion that he abandoned all plans to oppose Williams for the Senate.[24]

The preparedness question received a political testing sooner than had been expected, for on November 24, 1915, Witherspoon died. To select his successor, a special primary election was set for early the next year. During December, 1915, there ensued a fierce political fight. Judge William Webb Venable ran as an administration candidate, promising to support preparedness and any other measures that the President believed necessary to safeguard the nation's security. Because Wilson was greatly admired in Mississippi, Venable staked his hope for election on the President's popularity. W. H. Joyner, Witherspoon's former secretary, opposed Venable and denounced preparedness as "a scheme of a certain class of millionaires to get their hands in the public till." [25]

When Congress reconvened in December, Vardaman was away from Mississippi during the Venable-Joyner contest, and he did not actively participate in the campaign. He did, of course, support Joyner, for he wanted someone to carry on Witherspoon's work and to stand with him in opposing preparedness. He and Witherspoon had shared so many beliefs that Vardaman closely identified with his deceased friend. Like himself, Witherspoon had been so devoted to the interests of the "great, silent, slow-thinking, toiling multitude," that he had refused to surrender to the predatory interests advocating preparedness.[26] Shortly before the special election Vardaman attempted to help Joyner by issuing a "New Year Greeting to the People of Missis-

---

July 24, 1916, in Williams Papers, Mississippi Department of Archives; Magnolia *Gazette,* July 31, 1915; Columbus *Dispatch,* August 15, 1915, Jones County *News,* August 26, 1915, in Vardaman Scrapbook.

[24] G. W. George to John Sharp Williams, October 15, 1915, in Williams Papers, Mississippi Department of Archives.

[25] Vicksburg *Post,* December 16, 1915, in Vardaman Scrapbook; Vicksburg *Herald,* December, 1915.

[26] *Congressional Record,* 64 Cong., 1st Sess., 4836–37.

sippi," in which he warned that preparedness would only burden the
working man with new taxes and would increase the danger of America's being drawn into the war.[27] Much to Vardaman's disappointment,
Venable defeated Joyner in the special election. There could be no
missing the significance of Venable's election, for the issues had been
too clearly drawn. Joyner's defeat gave the first clear sign that Vardaman's political strength had begun to ebb.[28]

During 1915 and 1916 Vardaman's opposition to the Wilson administration's war policies caused other changes in the Mississippi
Democracy. Since he had inflicted his crushing defeat on LeRoy Percy
and Charlton Alexander, it had been rumored that in 1916 a candidate
from the Vardaman-Bilbo faction would win John Sharp Williams'
seat in the Senate. The list of possible candidates included Bilbo,
Witherspoon, Congressman Thomas U. Sisson and state Senator John
L. Hebron. Until 1915 any of the prospective candidates might have
run Williams a close race. Following the defeat of the ship purchase
bill, however, Williams realized that his support of that measure was
enabling him to regain political strength that he had lost in 1911 by
supporting Percy. At the same time, Vardaman's opposition to the
measure and his sharp criticism of President Wilson had caused some
of his followers to abandon him. "Little straws show which way the
wind is blowing," Williams wrote a trusted friend, "and maybe this
is an indicator of a revolt among Vardaman's friends against his egotism and vain glory, all of which makes him imagine now and then
that he is the Democratic party or something bigger than the Democratic party." [29]

In addition to boosting Williams' own strength, the shipping bill
caused dissension within the Vardaman-Bilbo faction. In the hope of
insuring his own victory in the gubernatorial race of 1915, Bilbo proposed a deal to Vardaman's old friend, Dr. B. F. Ward: If Ward
would use his influence to get Vardaman and Congressman Sisson to
support him for governor, Bilbo would endorse Sisson for the Senate
in 1916 and back Ward's son Will for the congressional seat that

27 *Ibid.,* 147–48; Jackson *Daily Clarion-Ledger,* January 1, 1916.
28 Vicksburg *Herald,* January 18, 1916.
29 John Sharp Williams to H. Clay Sharkey, July 25, 1915, in Williams Papers,
Library of Congress.

Sisson would vacate. Ward accepted the proposal and the following day endorsed Bilbo. There was only one hitch—Vardaman refused to go along. Not only had he earlier announced his determination to remain neutral in the gubernatorial race, but he would not endorse Sisson because he had voted for the ship purchase bill.[30] Thus, by the spring of 1915 issues stemming from the war first produced serious ruptures in the faction that had united so solidly behind Vardaman in 1911.

The strain that Vardaman's stand on foreign policy was causing within his own faction was further revealed in the gubernatorial primary in August. Many men who supported Bilbo in that contest announced their intention to vote for Williams in the senatorial election the following year. Just as they were attracted by Bilbo's appeal on the state level, they applauded Williams for having stood by the Wilson administration on the shipping bill.[31] At that time Williams carefully avoided becoming involved in the gubernatorial contest and did not, as some had expected, openly oppose Bilbo.

By 1916 the shifts in Mississippi politics had become even more pronounced. Williams' complete support for Wilson's preparedness program added momentum to his reviving strength, whereas Vardaman's outspoken opposition to preparedness caused him to become more and more isolated in Mississippi politics. Witherspoon's death the previous year had removed the man whom Vardaman would have preferred to replace Williams in the Senate. Bilbo and Sisson had abandoned all plans to run for the Senate that year, for neither would risk running against Williams' surging strength. Only John Hebron remained as a possible candidate from the Vardaman-Bilbo clique. Fearing that Hebron did not have a chance to win, Bilbo warned him not to expect his help should he take on Williams. Hebron heeded the warning and never announced his candidacy.[32] The Vardaman-Bilbo faction, which had dominated Mississippi politics from 1911 to 1915,

---

[30] Vicksburg *Herald,* April 10, 1915; Jackson *Daily Clarion-Ledger,* April 11, 1915.

[31] T. L. Wainwright to John Sharp Williams, February 18, 1916, in Williams Papers, Library of Congress.

[32] T. M. Scanlan to John Sharp Williams, November 29, 1915, January 2, 1916, T. L. Wainwright to Williams, March 22, 1915, J. W. George to Williams, February 11, March 28, 1916, Williams to Scanlan, January 6, 1916, in Williams Papers, Library of Congress; Vicksburg *Herald,* May 2, 1916.

had become so weakened that it could not even put forth a candidate to run against Williams, the man generally recognized as the leader of the opposition faction.

Vardaman's political death knell began to toll during the state Democratic convention of 1916. Four years earlier he had literally dictated the proceedings of the convention and his forces had ridden rough shod over the opposition. By 1916 he no longer had things his way. Three weeks prior to the convention the state Democratic executive committee asked Congressman Pat Harrison to serve as chairman and to give the keynote address. At the time, Harrison was completing his third term in Congress to which he had been elected in 1910, when he had campaigned against the work of the "secret caucus" and had ridden into office on the surging pro-Vardaman wave. Harrison had never been an avid Vardamanite, for John Sharp Williams had noted that "Pat is a Vardaman man in a sort of way, but he is not one of the men who hate me." [33] In Congress Harrison had loyally supported the Wilson administration on every issue except the Panama Canal tolls question and the Child Labor Act. Until 1915 relations between him and Vardaman had remained cordial, but the two men became alienated after Harrison backed the ship purchase bill and the preparedness program.[34]

Shortly before the convention Vardaman announced that he wanted Dr. Ward to serve as temporary chairman and to be the keynote speaker. Since no man was closer to Vardaman than Ward, the doctor could be counted on to uphold the senator's views on preparedness. Vardaman also wanted another friend, John Hebron, whom Bilbo had earlier turned down cold in his bid to run for the Senate, to be elected a delegate to the national convention.[35] On both requests Vardaman lost. After a series of caucuses between leaders of the rival groups, they agreed to divide every honor at the convention between the two camps. Mike S. Conner, a Vardaman-Bilbo man who was then the speaker of the state house of representatives, became temporary chairman. Pat

[33] John Sharp Williams to F. W. Foote, August 26, 1912, in Williams Papers, Mississippi Department of Archives.
[34] William Sidney Coker, "Pat Harrison: The Formative Years, 1911–1919" (M.A. thesis, University of Southern Mississippi, 1962), 4–20, 95; Scott, "Southern Progressives in National Politics," 190.
[35] Vicksburg *Herald*, May 14, 1916.

Harrison served as permanent chairman and gave the keynote address. John W. T. Falkner, a longtime Vardaman supporter, became secretary, and Walker Wood, a Vardaman opponent, became assistant secretary. Of the eight delegates selected from the state at large, four were from the Vardaman-Bilbo team and four from the opposition team.[36]

The convention represented a defeat for Vardaman. Although he had known that it would endorse Wilson's administration, it did much more than he wanted. In his keynote address Harrison so lavishly praised the administration that Wilson personally thanked him for the glowing tribute.[37] Temporary chairman Conner, moreoever, went out of his way enthusiastically to endorse the President and in so doing clearly revealed the rift the war was making among the Vardaman-Bilbo followers. Still the faction remained a force to reckon with in state politics, for it succeeded in defeating a move to elect Harrison as a delegate to the national Democratic convention. Yet its remaining strength would continue to wane during the next two years and no individual would be more responsible than Vardaman.

Vardaman played little part in the presidential campaign of 1916, because only in Missouri did he deliver a few speeches in behalf of the Democratic ticket.[38] He spent the fall at home and avoided public discussion of the war. The following year, 1917, he suffered irreparable political harm, first by opposing the armed ship bill and then by voting against declaring war on Germany. Because he opposed the armed ship bill, President Wilson branded him one of the "little group of willful men" and as a result he was denounced throughout Mississippi. Once he voted against war, the criticism became more widespread and cut more sharply across sectional and factional lines, as a constituent expressed in a letter to John Sharp Williams: "I tell you Senator these fellow[s] who are spying and sympathize with the Kaiser be he 'red neck' or millionare [sic] they had better keep mighty quiet, is my

[36] The account of the convention's proceedings is taken from: Jackson *Daily Clarion-Ledger,* May 18, 19, 1916; Vicksburg *Herald,* May 19, 21, 1916; Magnolia *Gazette,* May 20, 1916; McComb *City Enterprise,* May 25, 1916; *The Issue,* May 25, 1916; Kosciusko *Herald,* May 26, 1916, in Vardaman Scrapbook; Coker, "Pat Harrison," 68–72.
[37] Woodrow Wilson to Patrick Harrison, May 29, 1916, in Woodrow Wilson Papers, Library of Congress.
[38] *The Issue,* November 9, 1916.

opinion, for the people is being [sic] wrought up over this thing of treason and are not going to stand a bit of it, the first thing they know if they get too fresh a lot of them will be treated like you know Henry Dixon treated niggers back in the '70's." [39]

Once America was at war and the Committee on Public Information and various patriotic organizations began to inundate the country with propaganda on the horrors of German warfare and the righteousness of the Allied cause, the entire nation became increasingly intolerant of anything that bordered on dissent or obstructed the war effort. As a result, Vardaman received even sharper criticism than before during the remainder of 1917, for he then opposed such war measures as the Selective Service Act, the Aviation Act, and the Espionage Act. Some charged he was a German sympathizer, while others accused him of opposing President Wilson for pure spite. Why could not Vardaman, some asked, give his full support to the war effort as did Senator John Sharp Williams and Representative Pat Harrison? The avalanche of criticism sweeping at him had a telling effect, as he described in a letter of May, 1917: "I am well physically but I have been more distressed and suffered more heartaches in the past two months than all the balance of my life put together. It seems to me that the world has gone crazy. Where it will all end God only knows." [40]

Although Vardaman's opposition to the Wilson administration's war measures seriously undermined his political strength in 1917, many of his followers continued to stand loyally by him. Some who had voted against him in his past campaigns now believed that the senator was correct, and they admired his courage in opposing the war.[41] Especially active in his defense was a hard core of editors who published country newspapers throughout Mississippi. The Kemper Herald-Star typified those that rallied to his defense at the time Wilson accused the "willful men" of having obstructed the passage of the armed ship bill: "If you are simple enough to believe that the people of Kemper county have deserted Jim Vardaman because he was man enough to vote against a measure leading directly towards a declara-

[39] O. C. Stubberfield to John Sharp Williams, April 13, 1917, in Williams Papers, Library of Congress.
[40] Vardaman to Mary B. Bryan, May 18, 1917, in William Jennings Bryan Papers.
[41] Ed [Burrus] to John C. Burrus, March 20, 1917, in John C. Burrus Papers.

tion of war, then put your ears to the ground and hear the 'God bless you, Jim,' coming from hundreds of happy firesides of honest hard working farmers who are firm in their belief that we need no war and that 'Jim' is right. These are the people whom Jim Vardaman is representing in the United States Senate, and they want no war and ask for no war." [42] Even after he had voted against the declaration of war, many of those country editors continued to stand by him and some predicted that time would vindicate his vote against the war. "Our junior Senator has lost votes, he may lose his seat on account of his action," wrote the editor of the Greenwood *Enterprise*, "but that is a small matter. He did his duty as he saw it, and who knows, but that after our fair land has been baptized in the blood of her stalwart men, and washed in the tears of her spotless women, we may come to see that he was right." [43]

Vardaman's 1917 stand against war gave added momentum to political developments that had been under way in Mississippi for the past two years. For one thing it openly broke the Vardaman-Bilbo alliance. His persistent opposition to the current administration had already accounted for a slight that Bilbo suffered at the Democratic national convention in 1916. The governor did not share Vardaman's opposition to preparedness, but he must have realized that should he announce support for the President's program he might further weaken the faction of which he and Vardaman were still co-leaders. He tried, therefore, to straddle the issue by explaining that he had not made up his mind on preparedness.[44] His stand angered many of the Mississippi delegates, for some believed he actually shared Vardaman's opposition to the President's program. As a result they elected as chairman of the state delegation Ben Wells, a member of the anti-Vardaman-Bilbo faction. This was an honorary position that in the past had always been bestowed on the governor.[45]

But with the declaration of war Bilbo threw his full support behind the administration and instructed the state's teachers to read Wilson's war message to every school child. Not only did the governor

[42] Kemper *Herald Star,* quoted in *The Issue,* March 15, 1917.
[43] Greenwood *Enterprise,* April 20, 1917, in Vardaman Scrapbook.
[44] Vicksburg *Herald,* May 30, 1916.
[45] Frederick Sullens to John Sharp Williams, June 21, 1916, Williams to Sullens, June 23, 1916, in Williams Papers, Library of Congress.

urge Mississippians to give their total support to the war effort, but as he became swept up in the passions of the time he warned that German spies were at work in the state trying to sabotage sawmills.[46]

As the war sharply divided Vardaman and Bilbo by the spring of 1917, reports spread that the next year the two men would be rival candidates for the Senate. Astute anti-Vardaman leaders dismissed the possibility of such a contest, for they did not believe Bilbo would dare risk such a dramatic confrontation because they had always drawn strength from the same sources.[47] Although there was little possibility that Bilbo would run for the Senate in 1918, Vardaman's stand against war had so seriously weakened him that many did believe he would be defeated in his bid for reelection. By summer, speculation centered more and more on Congressman Pat Harrison as the man who would oppose Vardaman. In July, Harrison returned to Mississippi from Washington to sample public opinion before making his decision to take on Vardaman.[48]

After Harrison had decided to run, but before he had officially announced his candidacy, the anti-Vardaman forces received an unexpected jolt when former Governor Edmund Noel revealed that he would definitely make the race. Some feared that Noel's announcement would force Harrison to stay out, because the two would only split the anti-Vardaman vote and thereby enable the senator to win reelection. Convinced that Noel did not have a chance to win, Harrison's supporters urged the former governor to withdraw, but Noel ignored all such appeals for he was determined to inflict revenge on his old enemy Vardaman.[49] Actually the Harrison forces had little to fear from Noel. In addition to being a weak campaigner, he still bore the stigma of having played a major role in the "secret caucus"

[46] Vicksburg *Herald,* April 17, May 16, 1917; Jackson *Daily Clarion-Ledger,* March 27, October 18, 1917; Magnolia *Gazette,* April 21, 1917.

[47] Jackson *Daily Clarion-Ledger,* April 13, 1917; *The Issue,* May 3, 1917; John Sharp Williams to Clay Sharkey, September 6, 1917, Sharkey to Williams, September 18, 1917, in Williams Papers, Library of Congress.

[48] Magnolia *Gazette,* March 24, 1917; *The Issue,* July 5, 1917; Vicksburg *Herald,* July 20, 1917; Ripley *Southern Sentinel,* June 7, 1917, Brookhaven *Leader,* July 1, 1917, in Vardaman Scrapbook.

[49] Jackson *Daily Clarion-Ledger,* August 12, 16, 1917; Vicksburg *Herald,* August 14, September 7, 1917.

of 1910. Despite an intense canvass, Noel exerted no influence on the election.

Shortly after Noel had muddied the Mississippi senatorial waters, Harrison announced that he, too, would be a candidate. In a speech at the Neshoba County Fair on August 21, 1917, Harrison set the tone for his campaign. The issue was Vardaman versus President Wilson. The voters would have to choose between the two, for there could be no middle ground. The Democratic victory of 1912, Harrison recalled, had given the nation high hopes for constructive reform after so many years of Republican rule. President Wilson had not betrayed those hopes, for under his leadership Congress had lowered the tariff, reformed the banking and currency systems, and provided long-term credit for farmers. Certainly such achievements entitled Wilson to be ranked as the greatest statesman of his age. In working for those reforms, Mississippi's senators and representatives had backed the President, but trouble had arisen with the outbreak of war in Europe. At that time Wilson had seen that the nation would need additional ships to boost America's foreign trade and had called on Congress to pass the ship purchase bill. The measure would have become law in 1915, Harrison charged, except for the opposition of seven Democratic senators, one of whom was Vardaman. By failing to support the bill he had not only hurt the farmers and businessmen of his state, but he had greatly pleased the shipping trust. His vote against the bill had revealed for the first time his hatred for the President and his contempt for the many Mississippians who in 1911 had voted for him so overwhelmingly.

Harrison then recalled the need for preparedness legislation in 1916 and told how the President had fought for the nation's interest by urging an expansion of the Army and Navy:

But in congress opposition again lifted its head against the manifest needs of the nation. One of the most determined attacks was organized and fostered in the Senate of the United States, and no man worked harder, more bitterly and more persistently against the progress of preparedness than did the Junior Senator from Mississippi. Not satisfied with opposing the program with his voice and vote in the senate, he gave to the press a statement that challenged the President's patriotism. Among other things, he said, "whatever may be the President's motive, the effect of the position taken by him yesterday is an unfortunate surrender to predatory interests."

He proceeded to describe in similar fashion how Vardaman had supported the Gore resolution and how he had opposed the armed ship bill. Not only had the senator voted against the declaration of war, but since the nation began fighting on the side of the Allies, he had also opposed the administration on such key issues as the Selective Service Act, the Espionage Act, and the Food Administration.

What had Vardaman achieved by his record of persistent opposition to the administration? Harrison outlined the results. The vote against the ship bill had cost farmers and businessmen millions of dollars. His stands on preparedness, the Gore resolution, and the ship bill had encouraged Germany to violate American rights, believing the country would never go to war. Since entering the fight, his votes had frequently obstructed the war effort. It was because Vardaman had become such a bitter opponent of President Wilson, Harrison explained, that he had decided to try to unseat the senator in 1918. Although he had supported Vardaman in the past, he could do so no longer, adding: "If you are a supporter of the peerless president of this great republic you cannot consistently support the junior senator from Mississippi. If you love your country, which was born in the womb of war and nurtured and protected by the blood of your heroic ancestors, his reeking record cannot command your suffrage. If you love liberty and freedom the blood-bought legacy of every free-born American, you cannot reward the man who gives aid and comfort to the enemies of the government that insures liberty and freedom." If elected, Harrison promised, he would uphold Wilsonian Democracy and "simon-pure Americanism." [50]

The huge crowd at the fair frequently interrupted with applause and cheering, and many newspapers published his entire address. Some declared Vardaman had destroyed himself and Harrison would be the state's next senator. One longtime Vardaman foe, Frederick Sullens, was more cautious. He admitted that Harrison had launched his campaign "amid wonderful enthusiasm," and he noted that a

[50] Vicksburg *Herald,* August 24, 1917.

number of former Vardaman leaders had come over to Harrison. "But Vardaman is never an easy man to whip. I have taken part in five fights against him, and know where of I speak." [51]

Shortly before Harrison announced he would oppose Vardaman, Bilbo revealed his plans to run for the congressional seat that Harrison would vacate. When Lieutenant Governor Lee Russell, a strong Bilbo partisan, announced his intention to run for governor in 1919, rumors were rampant that these men were in a conspiracy to defeat Vardaman. A new dimension was added to the "plot" rumors when Harrison opened his campaign at the Neshoba Fair accompanied on the speakers' platform by the rather unlikely political bedfellows, Bilbo, Frederick Sullens, and Earl Brewer! [52]

Though the announcements of Harrison and Bilbo could understandably lead some to suspect they were working together, there is little likelihood that they reached any such agreement. Each had formerly supported Vardaman and could not risk alienating his supporters by such an alliance. In fact, Bilbo was running for Congress in a district where both Vardaman and Harrison had been strong, making it politically imperative that he remain neutral and out of the senatorial contest.

The coincidence of their political announcements was merely the result of the changes that had been wrought in Mississippi politics. Vardaman's opposition to Wilson and the war had made him highly vulnerable to defeat by an electorate caught up in the general war hysteria. Being a shrewd politician, Harrison had seized upon the situation in hopes of obtaining a higher office. No less astute as a politician and openly alienated from Vardaman, Bilbo, too, saw a chance to advance his own career by seeking a new office.

While the state press continued to debate the possibility of a plot to defeat Vardaman, Harrison began an intensive canvass that lasted through the fall of 1917. He spoke frequently at county fairs and at courthouses in the hills of the northeast and in the piney woods of

[51] Frederick Sullens to John Sharp Williams, August 24, 1917, in Williams Papers, Library of Congress.
[52] Mobile *Register*, August 3, 1917, Pass Christian *Coast Beacon*, n.d., Calhoun *Monitor*, August 30, 1917, Senatobia *Democrat*, September 6, 1917, in Vardaman Scrapbook; Jackson *Daily Clarion-Ledger*, August 2, 1917; Vicksburg *Herald*, August 28, 1917.

the south, the two greatest centers of Vardaman strength. Only thirty-six years old, Harrison was a vigorous and seasoned campaigner who entertained his listeners by describing in speech after speech how Vardaman had betrayed the President. Denying that he and Bilbo had formed an alliance, he explained that he had never opposed Varda-man until the senator had betrayed the Democratic Party and the President. As his canvass progressed, Harrison directed sharper at-tacks at his opponent. Because Vardaman had not begun to campaign, he accused him of being afraid to go before the people and discuss the record he had made in Congress.[53] Frequently he arranged for former Vardaman campaign workers to introduce him and in so doing to denounce the senator. At Tupelo, for example, Judge J. Q. Robbins explained that he could no longer support Vardaman because the senator had refused to participate in the Wilson administration's team-work: "Because he [Vardaman] is not allowed to make all the rules of the game and be pitcher, manager, captain and umpire, all at the same time, he curses the rules, knocks the team, and roots for the enemy." [54]

As Harrison campaigned during the fall of 1917, he was assisted by an upsurge of anti-Vardaman sentiment. Just as Mississippi had re-acted so vehemently to the "secret caucus" of 1910 and thereby made possible Vardaman's victory the following year, so in 1917 the state reacted with similar intensity to the war and thereby paved the way for his defeat. Vardaman's critics ranged from those who had honest disagreements with his Senate votes to those, like Frederick Sullens, who had always opposed him. Sullens now described the senator as the "arch traitor and super-demagogue," who was deliberately working to undermine the nation's war effort.[55] A former Vardaman appointee, Judge R. F. Cochran, suggested that every member of the "little group of willful men" be shot for treason. Wiley N. Sanders resigned as deputy United States marshal, explaining he had been appointed by Vardaman for whom he would never vote again.[56]

[53] Vicksburg *Herald*, September 19, 20, 25, November 3, 16, 1917; Jackson *Daily Clarion-Ledger*, October 30, November 29, 1917; Magnolia *Gazette*, September 29, October 6, 1917.
[54] Tupelo *Journal*, October 5, 1917.
[55] Jackson *Daily News*, quoted in Forest *Scott County News*, n.d., in Varda-man Scrapbook.
[56] Vicksburg *Herald*, August 9, 1917; Jackson *Daily Clarion-Ledger*, Novem-

Several prominent state politicians made speeches during the fall of 1917 in behalf of Harrison, the most effective being John Sharp Williams. During the past three decades Williams had been one of the most popular men in the state; since the outbreak of the war, his pronounced support of the administration and his close friendship with President Wilson had helped to bring his personal popularity to a new height. For two weeks in October, Williams delivered speeches in Mississippi supposedly to arouse public support for the war effort, but he worked equally hard to undermine Vardaman and to boost Harrison. Williams described in detail the events that had led the United States into war—obstruction of American commerce, outrageous submarine attacks, the murdering of innocent women and children, and the Zimmermann note. Why America could no more have remained at peace than could a man avoid fighting a thief who would enter his home and begin slapping his wife! Now that the United States was fighting for its life, there was a serious problem confronting the nation, Williams warned, and it should be clearly understood by everyone. "The case that is being tried in America today is the case of the President of the United States against a small disloyal element, . . . led by a little group of willful men in the Congress of the United States. The thing to determine is whether you are going to respect the opinion of your elected representatives and of your elected chief magistrate or whether you are going to pay a sort of sacred attention to the so-called sacred convictions of a little group of egotistical and willful men who set themselves upon a high pedestal and prate about the sacredness of their convictions." [57] Williams helped Harrison not only by giving speeches, he also worked quietly behind the scenes organizing support for the man whom he hoped would soon sit with him in the Senate.[58]

For more than a month after Harrison had begun campaigning,

---

ber 20, 1917. Throughout 1917 and 1918 the *Herald* and the *Clarion-Ledger* are filled with intense attacks upon Vardaman.

[57] Vicksburg *Herald,* October 13, 1917. See also Jackson *Daily Clarion-Ledger,* October 17, 1917; Tupelo *Journal,* October 19, 1917; John M. Dabney to Woodrow Wilson, October 17, 1917, in Wilson Papers; Madeleine [Dickson] to Harris Dickson, October 22, 1917, in Harris Dickson Collection.

[58] John Sharp Williams to Frederick Sullens, November 7, 1917, Sullens to Williams, n.d., in Williams Papers, Library of Congress.

Vardaman remained in Washington until Congress adjourned in early October. Although he did not take to the stump until the middle of November, a number of his former supporters rallied to his cause, especially the country editors who had always remained loyal to him. They urged their readers not to become so swept up in the excitement of the war that they could be led to oppose the man who had always worked in their behalf. They denounced the charges that Vardaman had been disloyal in opposing the war, and they pointed to his work as governor and senator in behalf of constructive social and economic reform.[59]

Besides defending Vardaman, they tried to put Harrison on the defensive. Why was Harrison campaigning in home territory while Congress was still in session? Why was a thirty-six-year-old man not serving in the Army? At thirty-seven Vardaman had volunteered for duty in the Spanish-American War! Was Harrison not basing his entire campaign on criticism of Vardaman? Did he have anything positive to offer? It would be better to stick with Vardaman, a man who had the courage to do his own thinking. Harrison, moreover, had become just another tool of the "secret caucus" faction.

This gang wrapped themselves in the American flag, flouted their patriotism and denounced Vardaman, the peerless leader of Democracy and the common people, as a traitor, while he was at his post of duty in Washington defending the people's rights whom he had sworn to serve.

It must be remembered that this same gang has been denouncing Vardaman ever since he has been in public life, the only difference being in a new leader who is ambitious to enhance his own political fortunes at whatever cost and who has accepted the position as commanding general of this political army.[60]

The Vardaman press even tried to use tricks that had worked so well against Percy in 1911, for some charged that Harrison had in-

[59] Among the weekly papers that supported Vardaman were the McComb City *Enterprise*, Aberdeen *Weekly*, Columbus *Commercial*, Magnolia *Gazette*, Hattiesburg *News*, Wiggins *Stone County Enterprise*, Cleveland *Enterprise*, Ripley *Southern Sentinel*, Water Valley *Herald*, Brookhaven *Leader*, and *Yazoo Sentinel*. The Vicksburg *Post* was the lone daily paper that defended Vardaman. *The Issue* was devoted almost entirely to defending Vardaman. Articles from all of the above papers are in Vardaman Scrapbook.

[60] *The Issue*, November 15, 1917.

sulted the Vardaman following by labeling it "redneck." In 1917 the charge fell flat. The war had partially obliterated the strength of the class appeal, and Harrison was too experienced a politician to make the mistake that had cost LeRoy Percy so dearly.

Only once while he was in Washington did Vardaman issue a public statement denouncing Harrison and other politicians who were attempting to exploit his opposition to the war: "My attention has been called of late to a peculiar species of embryonic statesman, the spawn and product of the slime covered pools of war, the evolution from the human microbe, which found its origin in the troubled womb of abnormality. There are found on every hand these days robust specimens of this runty genus, which I mentioned only because such as they present a problem with which the people must deal, men with ambition but without the slightest capacity of independent thought or independent action, fit only to follow and fawn at the feet of power." [61] He also wrote letters to his old paper, *The Issue,* promising that he would soon return to Mississippi and defend himself. Proud of his senatorial record, he asked only to be given a chance to explain why he had pursued such an unpopular course in opposition to the Wilson administration's war measures.[62]

Vardaman returned to Jackson on October 10, but unlike many of his earlier homecomings his reception was tepid. At that time, the state legislature was in special session and the senator went to the Capitol to visit old friends. When he entered the house of representatives, the legislators received him politely, but they did not cheer and applaud as in the past. The Jackson newspapers reported they even snubbed the senator. In response to those reports the house asked Vardaman to address it and he accepted the invitation. In a short speech he urged the lawmakers to give their complete support to the American war effort, but he warned that they should guard against one thing: while fighting a war in Europe, the American people should constantly strive to preserve free institutions at home. Already it had become difficult to express a dissenting opinion, he warned, and such measures as the Espionage Act threatened free speech. In

[61] Yazoo City *Yazoo Sentinel,* August 22, 1917, Brookhaven *Leader,* August 22, 1917, in Vardaman Scrapbook; Vicksburg *Herald,* October 14, 1917.
[62] *The Issue,* September 13, October 2, 1917.

the past, wars had destroyed free governments in other republics; that must not happen in America.[63]

Shortly after addressing the legislature Vardaman announced that he would not begin campaigning until the following year, explaining that active politicking might detract from the war effort. Because the past session of Congress had been the most trying time he had ever experienced, he needed a rest: "The ordeal was simply horrible." What he did not reveal was that his health had begun to deteriorate. For at least three years he had suffered from high blood pressure which had begun to sap the strength and vigor that in the past had enabled him to conduct strenuous campaigns. By 1917, in fact, it is probable that he had suffered one or more strokes.[64] Moreover, he realized the time was not right to go before the people; he had been so frequently misrepresented in the past year, and the nation had become so wrought up by war propaganda that at the time he could do little to help his cause. Perhaps by the next year the war would have ended and he might then stand a better chance of winning back the support of many of his former followers. So while Harrison continued to campaign, Vardaman spent the early fall quietly visiting with his family and friends in Jackson, Sidon, and Greenwood.

Because the rest enabled him to regain strength, and perhaps because he feared Harrison was making too much headway, Vardaman took to the stump during the last two weeks of November. Never apologizing for his Senate votes, he declared that if he could relive the past five years he would not change his record on a single issue, not even to altering "the dotting of an 'i' or the crossing of a 't.' " He explained why he had opposed American entry into the war and why he had voted against the Selective Service Act and the Espionage Act. His stand on the present conflict, he asserted, resembled Robert E. Lee's stand on the Civil War: each had opposed war, but once the fighting began each supported the effort. Any man who doubted his loyalty had only to recall that during the Spanish-American War he had volunteered and served for almost a year in Cuba. He pointed

---

[63] Jackson *Daily Clarion-Ledger*, October 11, 12, 1917; Magnolia *Gazette,* October 17, 1917; Vicksburg *Post,* October 12, 1917, in Vardaman Scrapbook.

[64] *The Issue,* October 18, 1917; Pontotoc *Sentinel,* October 25, 1917; interview with James K. Vardaman, Jr., May 1, 1968.

out that immediately after America had declared war on Germany he had again volunteered for the Army, but the Secretary of War had rejected his offer. His son was serving, however, and was then preparing to go to the battlefront. Turning to Harrison's assertion that he had always supported President Wilson, Vardaman charged that his opponent had opposed the administration on the Panama Canal tolls issue and on the Alaskan Railroad Act. More important, he observed, Harrison had voted against the Child Labor Act, one of the most constructive reforms of the Wilson era. What kind of man, he asked, would oppose a measure to protect children from the greed of conscienceless manufacturers? [65]

At the beginning of his brief canvass he spoke so vigorously and entertainingly that he sometimes drew large, enthusiastic crowds. Yet he did not always enjoy the affection that he had known in the past; sometimes he was heckled and ridiculed because of his opposition to the war. Moreover, the strain of travel and constant speaking began to take its toll and at Thanksgiving he left Mississippi to spend the holiday with his oldest daughter, Aletha, who was then living in Birmingham, Alabama. From there he returned to Washington. While he had roused many of his listeners, he had been unable to withstand the rigors of campaigning.

Because Congress remained in session from December, 1917, through the following summer, neither Vardaman nor Harrison returned to Mississippi the next year for extended canvassing. While they remained in Washington, their supporters carried on the fight at home. President Wilson was persuaded to intervene and help Harrison's cause by stripping Vardaman of all federal patronage. Since Harrison had announced his candidacy, John Sharp Williams had urged Wilson to remove Vardaman's appointees from office. He once sent Wilson a copy of John G. Cashman's Vicksburg *Post* containing an article in which Vardaman had charged that Wall Street bankers and the munition manufacturers had led the nation into war. Williams urged that Cashman, who had been appointed United States marshal for the Southern District upon Vardaman's recommendation,

[65] *The Issue,* November 15, 22, 1917; Jackson *Daily Clarion-Ledger,* November 16, 1922; Purvis *Booster,* November 22, 1917, in Vardaman Scrapbook; Magnolia *Gazette,* December 12, 1917.

be replaced by someone supporting Harrison. "How long you and the Attorney General want to encourage disloyalty in the State of Mississippi," he wrote the President, "in the person of the Marshall [sic] and his deputies, all of whom are Vardaman and anti-Administration employees, is a question for you to consider." [66]

Williams' efforts to persuade Wilson to remove Vardaman's appointees failed until Frederick Sullens took up the same cause. Writing to Williams in January, 1918, the Jackson editor explained why all Vardaman appointees should be turned out of office:

Down here his followers are boasting that, in spite of his hostility to the Administration, Vardaman can get anything he wants in the way of patronage; that he is having his friends appointed to office every few days, and the administration is actually afraid of him.

Of course, you know, and I know, and most intelligent people know, that this is a damed [sic] lie, but nevertheless it is being used, and with excellent effect.

In fact, it is crippling our chances to elect Pat Harrison. If it can come out of Washington, in this official form, that Vardaman is 100 per cent persona non grata with the administration, and cannot get recognition in anything, it will have a most excellent effect.

Percy Maer, John G. Cashman, Thos. P. Barr, Will Vardaman and every other person who holds Federal office through Vardaman favor, ought to be unceremoniously tossed out, and I believe President Wilson has the nerve to do anything you might suggest to him in this regard.

Let it become known far and wide that only the pure in heart can hold office in Mississippi by presidential appointment. [67]

Sullens' letter did the trick. Soon after Williams had forwarded it to the chief executive, Wilson informed Attorney General Thomas W. Gregory that no Vardaman appointees would be renamed to office when their terms expired. [68]

[66] John Sharp Williams to Woodrow Wilson, August 16, 1917, in Williams Papers, Library of Congress. See also Williams to Wilson, August 20, 1917, Woodrow Wilson Papers.
[67] Frederick Sullens to John Sharp Williams, January 21, 1918, in Williams Papers, Library of Congress.
[68] Woodrow Wilson to John Sharp Williams, January 26, 1918, in Wilson Papers; Wilson to T. W. Gregory, January 26, 1918, in Thomas Watt Gregory Papers, Library of Congress. See also Williams to Frederick Sullens, January 29, 1918, Williams to W. S. Hill, March 22, 1918, in Williams Papers, Library

News of the administration's decision became public in March, when it was officially announced that Will Vardaman and John Cashman would not be reappointed as marshals. Instead the administration nominated Bruce Alexander and Floyd Loper, both of whom had been Vardaman supporters but who by then were working for Harrison's election.[69] Percy Maer, Vardaman's appointee as collector of the port of Mobile, realized that he had no chance of being reappointed and resigned when his term expired.[70] The patronage shake-up in Mississippi apparently enhanced Harrison's candidacy. It signified clearly that Vardaman had lost all influence with the administration, and it may well have convinced some former supporters to get aboard the Harrison bandwagon.

In addition to help from the President, Harrison had a well-organized campaign committee working in his behalf. In March, 1918, Harrison leaders held a statewide campaign meeting in Jackson and among the many in attendance were some who had formerly been known as Vardaman supporters. The group adopted a resolution that reiterated the campaign theme set by Harrison the past summer, loyalty to President Wilson: "Loyalty, absolute, unconditional and unmodified, is the supreme test to be applied in this hour to those asking official trust." [71] Through pamphlets, broadsides, and editorials the Harrison forces reiterated time and again how badly Mississippi needed a senator who would uphold Wilson's efforts to win the war: "Vardaman vs. Wilson; Disloyalty vs. Loyalty; Prussianism vs. Americanism." [72] Even the Mississippi legislature reflected the upswell of

---

of Congress; Williams to William G. McAdoo, March 9, 1918, in William G. McAdoo Papers, Library of Congress; Wilson to Albert S. Burleson, March 30, 1918, in Albert Sidney Burleson Papers.

[69] Jackson *Daily Clarion-Ledger,* March 16, 1918; Grenada *Sentinel,* March 22, 1918.

[70] Jackson *Daily Clarion-Ledger,* April 2, 1918. Vardaman did protest to the Senate Judiciary Committee about the new appointments. He charged they were intended solely to undermine him politically and as long as he remained in the Senate he succeeded in blocking their confirmation. Albert B. Cummins to John Sharp Williams, March 21, 1918; John McBeath to Williams, March 22, 1918, in Williams Papers, Library of Congress; Samuel J. Graham to J. P. Tumulty, March 10, 1919, in Wilson Papers.

[71] Grenada *Sentinel,* March 29, April 5, 1918; Vicksburg *Herald,* March 20, April 2, 1917.

[72] Grenada *Sentinel,* May 10, 1918.

pro-Wilson and pro-Harrison sentiment when it unanimously adopted a resolution endorsing the administration's handling of the war. Two years earlier a resolution commending Wilson's preparedness program had been defeated because it was considered a condemnation of Vardaman. By 1918 no legislator dared vote against the pro-Wilson resolution, for Representative Emmett D. Cavett demanded a roll call vote, charging that he wanted to know if there were any "damned traitors" in the assemblage.[73]

A device used more and more by the pro-Harrison press in 1918 was that of publishing letters from some of Vardaman's former supporters. The writers ranged from those who honestly could not agree with Vardaman's opposition to the war to those who charged he was a treasonous German sympathizer. Those letters that leveled the strongest emotional impact came from parents whose sons were in the Army. One that was published widely in the anti-Vardaman press was written by J. H. McDermit:

Senator, one of my boys, proud, brave, patriotic son, has just fallen in this great battle. He was buried a few days ago on the shell-torn fields of bleeding France. I do not feel that he died in an unholy cause, on account of the interference on the part of Germany with the commerce between New York and London. I feel that he died fighting for freedom, in a just and righteous cause, and that he fills a patriotic grave. I have another whom the government has selected to die for his country and freedom's holy cause, if need be, and I do not feel that when he is called to march away in khaki that he will resemble a convict.[74]

Unlike earlier primaries in which Vardaman had been a candidate, in 1918 he did not have an efficient committee working in his behalf. In all of his campaigns since 1903, Vardaman clubs had sprung up in many counties to boost his cause, but in his fight against Harrison none was organized. Many of his former campaign workers went over to Harrison, or as one anti-Vardaman critic described it, "they are deserting him like rats on a sinking ship." [75] Only a few of the senator's

[73] Vicksburg *Herald*, March 2, 1918.
[74] *Ibid.*, July 17, 1918.
[75] John B. Robinson to John Sharp Williams, January 3, 1918, in Williams Papers, Library of Congress.

loyal followers, men such as Watkins and Taylor, actively worked for him and yet not until a month before the August primary did they organize a statewide campaign committee.[76] Those who continued to do the most to uphold the Vardaman cause were the country editors, many of whom had been writing in his behalf for almost two decades.

Through pamphlets and editorials the Vardaman men tried to play down the issue of loyalty to Wilson which the Harrison forces were exploiting so adroitly. Had the President not already attempted to exert far too much authority by removing Vardaman's appointees from office and thereby interfering in a state election? Mississippians should not allow the Chief Executive to intimidate their representatives. Voters should elect senators to serve them, not to give blind allegiance to the President. While Harrison was basing his entire campaign on a promise to uphold the President, the people should remember that Wilson would leave office in less than two years. To whom would Harrison then look for leadership? Should a Republican win the presidency in 1920, would he blindly follow him? [77]

Pat Harrison returned from Washington and officially opened his campaign on July 4, 1918, in Meridian, the town where seven years earlier Vardaman had triumphantly ridden through the streets on a lumber wagon pulled by forty yoke of oxen. Now Harrison enjoyed a similar spectacle. Judge R. F. Cochran, who had organized the Vardaman parade in 1911, performed the same task for Harrison. Admitting that his earlier support for Vardaman had been a serious mistake, Cochran boasted, "We pulled him in—we'll pull him out again." [78] The parade of 1918 resembled its predecessor, for thousands of men carried flaming torches and eighty lumbering oxen pulled the cart from which Harrison waved to cheering crowds along the way. American flags draped the oxen and many of the marchers carried banners with such inscriptions as: "Germany has been more observant of international law than the Allies," and "All Vardaman men are not disloyal, but every disloyal man is for Vardaman." [79] Cochran

---

[76] *The Issue,* July 18, 25, 1918; Memphis *Commercial Appeal,* July 12, 1918, in Vardaman Scrapbook.
[77] *The Issue,* May–August, 1918; Vardaman Scrapbook, *passim.*
[78] Vicksburg *Herald,* May 18, 1918.
[79] Jackson *Daily Clarion-Ledger,* July 5, 1918.

assumed the duties of introducing Harrison and he explained why he would no longer support Vardaman:

We do not want in Washington a senator who believes that we are stabbing Germany in the back while France and England have her down. We do not want in Washington a senator who believes that Germany made every possible concession to avoid war. We do not want in Washington a senator who believes that Germany was more observant of international laws than France or England. We do not want in Washington a senator who believes that the cause of the war was pecuniary profit. We do not want in Washington a senator who believes that the millions of women and Red Cross workers and our boys who are offering up their lives on the battle fields of France and are doing it for pecuniary profit.

We want a senator in Washington to represent Mississippi, who believes that Woodrow Wilson's policies are the clearest expressions of God's will on earth to mankind.[80]

Harrison's speeches in 1918 resembled the ones he gave the previous year. The question he urged Mississippians to decide was whether he or Vardaman had most consistently supported the policies of the President. While avoiding all mention of domestic legislation, he insisted that the war constituted the only important issue. To strengthen his cause, Harrison frequently read articles in which Vardaman had severely criticized the President, and then he produced affidavits from various newspapers to prove he had quoted his opponent correctly. Could anyone, he asked, vote for a man who had so criticized President Wilson? [81]

For almost two weeks after Harrison had begun campaigning, Vardaman remained in Washington attending to senatorial duties. When he finally returned to Mississippi, he spoke only in those areas where he had traditionally been strong—the northeastern hills and various southern counties—and avoided larger towns such as Jackson, Meridian, Vicksburg, and Natchez. He may have feared hostile crowds in the larger towns, for he knew his greatest support was in the rural areas. In all his speeches he hammered away at a few essential points. He had compiled a constructive record in the Senate, one that demon-

80 Grenada *Sentinel,* July 12, 1918.
81 Vicksburg *Herald,* July 21, 26, 28, 30, 31, 1918.

strated concern and understanding for the needs of his people. True, he had not voted for war, but he had stood for what he honestly believed. It would have been far easier to have followed the administration's lead than to have taken the lonely course that he had pursued for the past three years. At a time when America was passing through one of the most crucial periods in her history, the nation needed congressmen with the courage to stand by their convictions. "A vacant chair in the Senate," he warned, "is preferable to a vacuous echo." [82]

The pro-Vardaman press reported that such large crowds came to hear the senator that frequently he had to speak in public parks and fields so that everyone could hear him. Despite those glowing reports, Vardaman frequently had to go before hostile audiences. Sometimes as he spoke he was heckled with shouts of "von Vardaman," and on several occasions he was handed lists of embarrassing questions with the demand that he answer them. In towns such as Ackerman, Amory, and Charleston he spoke from platforms painted bright yellow. Sometimes on the nights before he was to speak in small hill towns the front doors of his leading supporters were splashed with yellow paint. For a man who had earlier been almost idolized by his followers, such vindictive treatment must have been well-nigh unbearable and did as much as his high blood pressure to drain the vigor he had always displayed in earlier campaigns. Vardaman was not well. He had visibly aged since his last campaign; his massive body had begun to shrink, and deep creases lined his face. After only a few days of campaigning, his voice had become terribly hoarse and the summer heat and strain of the canvass exhausted him.

The change caused by his physical decline and by the hostile crowds was well revealed by his attempts to incite Negrophobia. He warned that the war had created new dangers for the South because Negroes had been allowed to serve in the army; soon the black veterans would return home and demand equality with the whites. In France they had even known white women! [83] In the past the crowds had enjoyed his racial harangues and that appeal might have alarmed his listeners and have brought them to their feet cheering when he urged that Negroes

[82] *The Issue,* June 6, July 25, August 1, 18, 1918.
[83] Vicksburg *Herald,* July 26, 1918.

must be kept in their place, if necessary by force. In 1918 this appeal to racism had no punch. He had used it too many times. And now a more pressing emotional issue—the war—consumed the public's attention.

Despite this attempt to incite racism and to call attention to his constructive voting record, he failed to offset the issue on which Harrison based his campaign—complete loyalty to the President. In fact, a week before the primary Wilson gave an added boost to Harrison's campaign by urging Mississippians not to reelect Vardaman. In reply to an inquiry concerning Vardaman's support for his administration, the President wrote: "Senator Vardaman has been conspicuous among the Democrats in the Senate for his opposition to the administration. If the voters of Mississippi should again choose him to represent them, I not only have no right in any way to criticize them, but I should be obliged to accept their action as a condemnation of my administration, and it is only right that they should know this before they act." [84] Newspapers throughout Mississippi published the President's letter, and undoubtedly it hurt the senator's cause.

Vardaman accused Wilson of butting into the affairs of Mississippi and of trying to destroy him because he had not blindly followed the administration's lead. The Vardaman forces also published letters from Senators Hiram W. Johnson of California and George E. Chamberlain of Oregon, both of whom praised the Mississippian for his work in the Senate.[85] Such letters had little chance of offsetting the damage inflicted by Wilson's letter.

The primary on August 19 resulted in a Harrison victory; he received 56,715 votes to Vardaman's 44,154 and Noel's 6,730. Of Mississippi's eighty-two counties Harrison carried fifty-seven, Vardaman twenty-four, and Noel one. Vardaman ran strong only in the hills of the northeast, although he picked up a few counties in the central and southern parts of the state. Harrison swept the entire Delta and the Gulf Coast; he carried most of the counties in the southern piney woods, and the Black Belt of east-central Mississippi; he even won a number of counties in the hills.

[84] Woodrow Wilson to M. S. McNeil, August 5, 1918, quoted in Magnolia Gazette, August 14, 1918, in Vardaman Scrapbook.
[85] The Issue, August 15, 1918; Hiram W. Johnson to A. S. Coody, March 13, 1918, in A. S. Coody Collection.

Vardaman's defeat was the signal for rejoicing among many of his hardened enemies, and an editorial in the Grenada *Sentinel* expressed the glee that many experienced when they learned of Harrison's victory.

> Mississippi takes her first step in her political redemption. Vardaman, the strife breeder, the objector, the obstructor, the great "I" am and the little "you" are, the one who never sees his errors, the one who would not change the dotting of his "i's" or the crossing of his "t's", the one who has little use for friends who disagree with him, has been beaten in a square stand up fight before the people of the grand old state of Mississippi. . . . There was no chance for the Senator to tie his kite to martyrdom. Poor old Sambo had been ridden by him until Sambo's knees were sore. . . . Not constructive by nature, never a builder, he is what it takes little talent to do, an iconoclast, and a critic of what somebody else does. The harness never fits him when he must pull with somebody else. He wants to be the whole show, ring master, clown, the lion, the tiger, the giant and all other things that people gaze at and sometimes wonder at.[86]

Many of the anti-Vardaman men soon had further cause for celebration, because in a runoff primary for Harrison's old congressional seat, Paul Johnson decisively defeated Bilbo. Thus the two men who had won smashing victories in 1911 went down to defeat seven years later.

Some of Vardaman's followers could not understand why he had been defeated. How could the people have failed to appreciate his consistent work in behalf of their interests? Vardaman had worked harder for progressive reforms during his one term in the Senate, some argued, than had John Sharp Williams during his entire career in Congress. They offered a number of reasons for his defeat: rains on election day had muddied the roads and prevented many country people from getting to the polls; some of Vardaman's followers had been intimidated by wartime patriots and had been too frightened to vote.[87] Those excuses probably had little validity. Far more important was the influence of the war. So caught up were the people by the conflict and the barrage of propaganda that accompanied it that many were led to believe Vardaman had betrayed his President

[86] Grenada *Sentinel,* August 23, 1918.
[87] *The Issue,* August 22, 29, 1918.

and his country. The demise of the Vardaman-Bilbo faction also affected the outcome; in 1911 the two leaders had been bound together
against a common enemy, but by 1918 they had become divided and
no longer had common issues to which they could appeal. Finally,
Vardaman's ill health weakened his ability to campaign as of old.

An era had ended. The powerful faction that Vardaman and Bilbo
had forged seven years earlier in their fight against the "secret caucus"
had been divided and conquered. Still a young man, Bilbo promised to
return to public life and he kept that promise. Vardaman left for
Washington immediately after the election and did not issue a statement until the end of August. Then he thanked those who had voted
for him and promised that after the war they would overcome the
defeat of the past primary—a defeat that had been wrought by the
lies and unfair methods of his enemies. He hoped that in the future
he would be able to lead his followers once more to victory.[88] He never
did.

[88] *Ibid.*, September 12, 1918.

CHAPTER XIII

THE LAST YEARS

AFTER HIS DEFEAT in 1918, Vardaman returned to Washington for the last session of the Sixty-Fifth Congress. With President Wilson away at the Paris peace conference, little was accomplished at that lame duck session. Not until Vardaman's term expired in March, 1919, did the Senate begin to consider the peace treaty. Though his last session was colorless compared to previous ones, he continued to follow the course which he had unwaveringly traveled since the beginning of his Senate career.

As in the past, he mistrusted Wilson's handling of foreign policy. He believed Wilson had made a mistake in going to the Paris peace conference where he would be subjected to intense pressures that he might be unable to withstand.[1] After the conference began its deliberations, Vardaman feared it was not pursuing policies that would insure a lasting peace: Germany should be treated as charitably as possible and should not be subjected to harsh terms; all nations should eliminate the "Prussian System" of conscription and disband their armies; except to stop an invasion of its territory, no nation should ever go to war without first submitting the question to its people for a vote; to guard against countries being led into wars by profit-hungry businessmen and bankers, all future wars should be on a strict cash basis.[2]

Especially upsetting to Vardaman was the President's determination to include the covenant of the League of Nations in the peace treaty and his request for the Senate to refrain from discussing the matter until the conference had completed its work. The question of Ameri-

---

[1] *The Issue,* December 5, 1918.
[2] Vardaman interview, January 1, 1919, unidentified source, in Vardaman Scrapbook.

ca's joining the League was one of the most serious that had ever confronted the nation and should be discussed thoroughly and openly. So important was the issue, Vardaman charged, that Wilson would commit a grave wrong if he tried to have the Senate approve America's entry into the League without first submitting the issue to the national electorate.[3]

Because the Senate heeded Wilson's advice and refrained from discussing the treaty, Vardaman found his attention directed almost exclusively toward domestic issues. Having long been an isolationist, and sick at heart over his country's participation in the war, he was eager for the United States to end totally its involvement with Europe and devote attention first to its own needs and second to developing the western hemisphere.[4] It is not surprising, therefore, that he opposed granting aid to the war-torn countries of Europe. America should obliterate her own poverty problems and then, if such foreign aid could be afforded without putting new burdens on the American people, he would consider voting for it.

The government should immediately rectify mistakes made during the war, the most oppressive of which, in Vardaman's opinion, were the Espionage and Sedition Acts. The repeal of those acts and the restoration of free speech was as imperative as was the pressing need to demobilize the American armed forces as quickly as possible.[5] He had opposed conscription, fearing that it would threaten free government by creating a large, permanent Army. Now that the fighting had ended, the government could eliminate that danger by quickly discharging the soldiers.

Yet he realized the sudden return of thousands of ex-servicemen might create serious problems of unemployment and social unrest. To facilitate demobilization he introduced a bill providing that for six months after discharge all veterans would continue to receive their full salaries. In pleading for his bill, which failed to pass, he argued that the Bolshevik Revolution of 1917 had resulted largely from the poverty and exploitation that the Russian people had long experienced.

[3] *Congressional Record,* 65 Cong., 3d. Sess., 3656–58.
[4] *Ibid.,* 1792, 1996, 2514–15; *The Issue,* December 19, 1918.
[5] *Congressional Record.,* 65 Cong., 3d. Sess., 874–75, 1399, 2117, 2938.

The United States should learn from the upheaval in Russia and strive to guard its own citizens from having to contend with such conditions.

Six months of extra pay to the soldier will stimulate production, give encouragement and hope. It will not be a donation of charity, but rather an acknowledgement of the Nation's gratitude, and the best investment the American people could make through their Government for the good of all. . . . These men have shown their love and devotion to the flag, and it is as little as the country can afford to do to tax the great substantially untaxed war made fortunes for the consolation and comfort of the soldier and his family. If in America permanent peace shall follow this war, we must provide against the wolf of want howling at the door, especially of the men who bared their heroic breasts to the storm of war. Bolshevism is not a contagious social disease, but, like scurvy and pellagra, the result of lack of nutrition, or malnutrition. . . . The panacea for this disease and all other similar social disorders will be found in giving the laboring people of the world an equal chance in the race of life with the capitalists. Give them good wages, enough of the products of their own toil to furnish comfortable homes, to educate their children, and otherwise improve their manner of living, and then there will be no more Bolshevism or conflicts between capital and labor.[6]

Besides devoting attention to problems of demobilization, Vardaman continued to advocate progressive reforms. He favored expanding federal aid for highway construction not only because it would provide jobs for returning soldiers but also because it would help relieve the isolation of rural America.[7] He recommended, too, the establishment of a national old-age pension program. When the Senate considered a retirement plan for federal employees, the Mississippian objected on grounds that such a program should be extended to the entire citizenry; it would be unfair to discriminate in favor of one group. Taxing people to make them put something aside for old age would be "a little bit socialistic in principle," but it would serve a valuable and necessary purpose.[8]

During the lame duck session Vardaman worked hard on his

[6] *Ibid.*, 1312–13, 1813, 3545.
[7] *Ibid.*, 2881–82, 2887–88.
[8] *Ibid.*, 41–42, 139.

committee assignments. As the new chairman of the Committee on Manufactures he inaugerated an investigation of the anthracite coal industry.[9] The committee was unable to publish its findings before Congress adjourned, but he presented a summary of the work to the upper chamber and urged the next Congress to take appropriate action. Eight transportation companies so controlled the production of anthracite coal found exclusively in four Pennsylvania counties that independent operators could not compete because they had to pay excessively high transportation costs. In addition, these eight companies had gobbled up leases for practically all coal lands in the four counties, even though they had facilities to work only a small portion of their leases. Vardaman charged they had established a monopoly and forced consumers to pay unduly high prices. The Pennsylvania constitution outlawed monopolies, but state officials had failed to enforce it. He therefore recommended that the federal government invoke its authority over interstate commerce to break up the monopoly.[10]

After completing the anthracite coal investigation Vardaman left Washington and returned to Mississippi. The close of his senate term marked the end of his political career. Never again would the flamboyant "White Chief" rally the white masses of Mississippi as he had in past campaigns. It was a disillusioned old man, broken in health and spirit, who returned to Jackson in 1919 and resumed editorship of his newspaper, *The Issue,* newly renamed *Vardaman's Weekly.* The publication had survived solely because of the financial backing of his faithful and more affluent friends—men such as Watkins, Hebron, and Taylor—who continued to back it even after it became *Vardaman's Weekly.*

During the years Vardaman edited the *Weekly,* 1919 to 1922, it was never more than a pale shadow compared to his Greenwood papers, *The Enterprise* and the *Commonwealth. Vardaman's Weekly* consisted chiefly of nationally syndicated articles and of pieces written by the editor's friends. Though more and more slowed by ill health,

[9] *Ibid.,* 73. When Vardaman became chairman of the committee on manufactures at the third session of the Sixty-Fifth Congress, he was relieved of his duties as chairman of the committee on conservation of natural resources.
[10] *Congressional Record,* 65 Cong., 3d. Sess., 4830–40; Philadelphia *American,* March 3, 1919, in Vardaman Scrapbook.

he wrote many editorials, but they rarely displayed the fire of old. The readers of the *Commonwealth* at the turn of the century often relished with good reason the scathing satire and blistering attacks Vardaman levelled against political and religious leaders. As vigorous as the man who wrote them, those editorials, even at their extremes of harshness—trying to dehide Roosevelt for his commerce with Negroes, for example—always stayed within the bounds of legitimate satire. Because their outspoken sentiments never stooped to malevolent backbiting they provided lively and entertaining reading whether one agreed with the opinions expressed or not. After leaving the Senate, Vardaman was a bitter man and all too frequently his editorials in *Vardaman's Weekly* were petty and mean.

Vardaman had always been a man of strong likes and dislikes, ever ready to praise his friends and damn his enemies. Because by 1919 he had come to hate Wilson, it is not surprising that *Vardaman's Weekly* constantly hurled vitriolic attacks at the President. Wilson had allowed greedy munition makers and bankers to lead the nation into war, and now the President was again trying to betray the country by having the Senate ratify an unjust treaty. Vardaman's editorials flogged Wilson for having bungled America's splendid opportunities to arrange a true peace, because he had not been a match for the European leaders at the Paris conference. During the negotiations he had been forced to make concession after concession until the final treaty made a mockery of the fourteen points: through huge indemnities a terrible penalty had been imposed on Germany; territories had been taken from weak powers to satisfy the greed of mighty nations. In an effort to bolster opposition to the President, Vardaman frequently published articles by other critics of the Treaty, the most notable being Robert Lansing, William C. Bullitt, Walter Weyl, Tom Watson, La Follette, and others.[11]

Even more alarming to the editor was Wilson's desire for America to join the League of Nations. Had he still been in the Senate there can be little doubt he would have joined with the Republican "irreconcilables" who fought Wilson every step of the way in the battle over the League. He believed the League dangerous because he considered it a threat to America's sovereignty and independence. While sur-

[11] *Vardaman's Weekly,* May–September, 1919.

rendering its authority to an international assemblage, the United States would gain little in comparison to France, Belgium, and Japan, all of which received mandates from the League giving them control over new territories. Should America join the League it would surrender its influence in the Western Hemisphere by abandoning the Monroe Doctrine, thus leaving Latin America to the ambitions of imperialistic powers. Not only would the League undermine American authority, Vardaman argued, it would also serve the interests of Great Britain, the nation that he believed partly responsible for drawing America into the war. In the League each country of the British Empire would have a vote and thereby enable England to dominate the organization. Racist convictions strengthened his opposition, for he feared the League would coerce the Caucasian nations into accepting black and yellow people as equals. For the first time he warned of a Catholic conspiracy, charging that, because Catholicism was the state religion in many nations, the Pope would enjoy too much influence in the League.[12]

When President Wilson attempted to rally support for the League in September, 1919, by giving speeches across the nation, Vardaman asserted that the people already knew they did not want it. He feared, however, that Wilson might deceive some into supporting the League. After the President was stricken and forced to abandon his tour, Vardaman urged that Congress relieve him of his duties, and he even reported that Wilson had suffered a mental breakdown. "I have believed for some time that the President was suffering from a serious mental disorder. His refusal to counsel with the Senators and his apparent determination to run the whole thing himself indicated that if he was not mentally deranged, he was a dangerous man to exercise the wonderful power with which the President is clothed." When the Senate at last refused to ratify the Versailles treaty and thereby vetoed America's entry into the League, Vardaman hailed it as a victory for the country.[13]

In addition to Wilson's advocacy of the treaty and the League,

12 *Ibid.* From May, 1919, through March, 1920, the *Weekly* carried many articles opposing American entry into the League. In the issue of January 29, 1920, Vardaman summarized many of his reasons for opposing the League.

13 *Vardaman's Weekly,* August 28, September 11, October 15, November 20, 1919, March 18, 1920.

Vardaman criticized the administration's direction of demobilization. Soldiers were not being discharged fast enough, he felt, and he accused career army men of deliberately working to maintain large fighting forces to enhance their power and maintain their wartime ranks. Stories frequently appeared in the *Weekly* charging that officers subjected enlisted men to beatings and sexual perversions; they even drove weaker ones to suicides.[14] Not only were the soldiers mistreated in the Army, Vardaman reported, but the government was taking no steps to ease their return to civilian life by creating jobs through public works programs in highway construction and soil conservation. During the war the government had contributed to the prosperity of the business community by granting lavish contracts and by directly subsidizing ship building. Why should it not also extend help to those who had sacrificed the most—the returning servicemen?[15]

The Wilson administration's failure to push for programs to help discharged soldiers only strengthened Vardaman's conviction that the President had become a tool of business and banking interests. "No man ever occupied an important office in this country whose sympathies with the wealthy were more profound and complete than his [Wilson's]." Without reliable information and with deliberate distortion, he described how only a select group had benefited from the war: "Isn't it horrible to contemplate the fact that thirty thousand millionaires should have grown up in America out of the profits of the war? Fifty thousand of our boys killed, 400,000 maimed for life and 30,000 millionaires are the fruits of this war that will make the world safe for democracy."[16]

The President was not the only dupe of the selfish business leaders who had led this country into war, according to the former senator. When the Supreme Court ruled the Child Labor Act of 1916 to be unconstitutional, that decision proved the extent of the business community's hold on the entire United States government.[17] Labor unions, he believed, offered the best hope of guarding the country against the unjust and dangerous threat that the industrialists posed and would

[14] *Ibid.*, July 24, September 4, 1919.
[15] *Ibid.*, July 3, 10, October 16, 1919, February 5, March 11, 1920.
[16] *Ibid.*, September 11, 1919. *See also* July 3, 24, August 14, 28, September 4, 1919.
[17] *Ibid.*, May 1, 1919, May 18, 1922.

guard workers against exploitation by the moneyed interests.[18] Consequently Vardaman became more and more vocal about the problems of the industrial workers. The Bolshevik Revolution had demonstrated the stupidity of allowing people to suffer from low wages, poor housing, and inadequate medical care. The government should promote the welfare of the working people, he maintained, by fighting for permanent government ownership of railroads, shipping companies, and telephone and telegraph lines; for nationalization of coal mines; and for the continued public operation of the hydroelectric dam and nitrate plant at Muscle Shoals, Alabama. Such programs could help America alleviate some of her more serious domestic problems and, hopefully, reduce the danger of conflicts between capital and labor.[19]

Vardaman's antipathy toward the business community had come to border on psychosis by this time. In 1919, when the nation became swept up in an inordinate fear that an international Communist conspiracy was trying to seize control of the country, he believed the hysterical fear of Communism resulted largely from ignorance and was probably the work of businessmen trying to undermine the cause of labor unions and Socialists. Wealthy men were using the Red Scare to foster a "deceitful, damnable scheme . . . to convert this republic into a plutocracy." [20] He especially denounced the attempts of Attorney General A. Mitchell Palmer to capitalize on the hysteria of the Red Scare by deporting aliens. Palmer should spend his time prosecuting the wealthy businessmen who had led the nation into the war and who had plundered the public treasury during the conflict. "The most contemptible flannel-mouth anarchist in America is not as great an enemy to the republic as the high-collared son-of-a-gun who under the guise of patriotism stole millions from the soldiers and the laboring people who stayed at home." Rather than worry about imaginary Communist plots, Vardaman suggested, it would be far better for the government to consider tax reforms that would tap the wealth of millionaires.[21]

18 *Ibid.*, December 1, 1921.
19 *Ibid.*, May 15, 22, August 14, 1919, March 4, 1920, July 28, 1921.
20 *Ibid.*, April 1, 1920.
21 *Ibid.*, January 29, February 12, 1920.

As in his earlier career, he frequently combined demands for domestic reforms with appeals to racism and, as a result, his writings sometimes followed strange courses. Nowhere was that better revealed than in his editorials on Henry Ford. Though Vardaman wanted the government to continue operating its dam and nitrate plant at Muscle Shoals, Alabama, it became evident by 1921 that the facilities would be leased to private interests. He then wanted them turned over to Henry Ford, for he believed the automobile manufacturer, more than most businessmen, would use the facilities for the benefit of the people in the Tennessee Valley.[22] Yet at the very time Vardaman commended him as an "altruist as well as a pretty sensible car-builder," he denounced the anti-Semitic tirades that appeared in Ford's *Dearborn Independent.* "Henry Ford persists in his slanderous ignorant persecution of the Jews. The last number of his paper contains a very derogatory and abusive article on the Jewish element of our people for bootlegging. . . . Ford has no ability, but his slander of the Jews is one of the most disgraceful things in journalism in the history of America. The man is as ignorant as an ass, and his ignorance is only equalled by his moral obtundity. The Jews will not be injured by Henry—the poor creature only hurts himself."[23] While damning Ford for his anti-Semitism, Vardaman in the next breath praised him for warning the country that Negroes and Orientals must never be given equality with whites. "If Ford shall direct the influence of his paper to an effort to solve the Japanese and Chinese problem of the Pacific Coast and the negro problem in the south, how very much better it will be for the world than his foolish, ignorant, vicious fight against the Jews, who have blessed every country in which they have lived."[24]

As could be expected, anti-Negro writings frequently appeared in *Vardaman's Weekly,* although not as often as in his earlier papers; by 1919 he devoted more attention to attacking Wilson's foreign policy, to denouncing predatory interests, and to demanding greater justice for labor. His racist views were the same ones he had been expounding since the 1890's. He sometimes republished articles that his old friend Dr. Ward had written in the 1890's on the necessity of lynch-

[22] *Ibid.,* July 28, December 8, 1921.
[23] *Ibid.,* January 5, 1922.
[24] *Ibid.,* January 26, 1922.

ing. As it had for the past quarter century, racist thought remained strong in America and Vardaman thus had many sources on which he could draw to support his views. He often recommended that his readers study contemporary racist works like Lathrop Stoddard's *The Rising Tide of Color* and Madison Grant's *The Passing of a Great Race.*[25]

As editor of the *Weekly,* Vardaman rarely tried to hide how he felt about the men whom he had known while in the Senate. He frequently praised Republican progressives Hiram Johnson of California and William E. Borah of Idaho. James A. Reed of Missouri, he believed, was the most able Democrat remaining in the Senate. North Carolina Congressman Claude Kitchin, who had been a leading opponent of preparedness and the war, received glowing tributes in *Vardaman's Weekly,* as did the former Georgia Populist Tom Watson. The man whom Vardaman had learned to respect above all others was Wisconsin Senator Robert M. La Follette, and well he should since they had so frequently stood together on both domestic and foreign policy: La Follette, too, believed that selfish businessmen had led America into the war and he had tried to retaliate by fighting for a revenue bill in 1917 that would have scraped off excess war profits. Like Vardaman, La Follette had suffered personal injustices because of his opposition to the war.[26]

Outnumbering his friends were those whom he despised. After President Wilson, Postmaster General Albert S. Burleson and Treasury Secretary William G. McAdoo ranked high on his hate list. Under the Espionage Act Burleson had served as press censor during the war, and McAdoo had refused to endorse a direct program of federal relief for the South during the cotton crisis of 1914 and 1915. Moreover, Vardaman believed that both men had assisted Wilson in stripping him of patronage in 1918.[27] Former Food Director Herbert Hoover was another administration official upon whom the editor heaped scorn: "I think beyond a doubt Hoover the most successful

[25] The article by Ward appeared in *Vardaman's Weekly,* July 3, 1919. For the references to Stoddard and Grant, see issues of February 3, April 7, May 5, 1921.

[26] *Vardaman's Weekly,* May 22, 1919, April 15, 29, May 27, September 9, November 18, 1920.

[27] *Ibid.,* March 11, May 6, September 16, 1920.

fraud since the days of John Law of 'Mississippi Bubble' fame." [28]
He accused Senator Pat Harrison of having sold out to the railroad
and banking interests. Harrison had proved himself a liar, he charged,
because he had campaigned in 1918 on the promise always to support
the President, but in 1920 he voted against the administration's Esch-
Cummings bill. "The charming young statesman, Honorable Pin-
Headed Pat Harrison, during the campaign promised that he would
cross hell on a raw cotton string to follow the President, opposed this
Railroad Bill notwithstanding that it was Wilson's pet measure."
Vardaman reserved his most vicious attacks for John Sharp Williams,
whom he accused of having sided with the conservative Republicans
throughout his years in Congress and of having wrecked himself by
excessive drinking: "He is like an old, worn-out race horse—you
have to use a lot of cocaine and ginger to make him 'step up.' " [29]

Vardaman attacked Williams and Harrison, in part, to pave the
way for his own reelection to the Senate in 1922; the voters could
count on him not to follow the weak, hypocritical course that the two
incumbent senators pursued. While making plans to run for the Senate,
Vardaman watched state politics and in the primary of 1919 tried to
revive some of the influence he had once commanded. In that year
four men ran for governor: Oscar Johnson, a successful Delta lawyer;
former governor Andrew H. Longino; State Attorney General Ross
Collins; and Lieutenant Governor Lee Russell. The key issue of the
campaign was the newly created state tax commission. For more than
half a century Mississippi had an archaic tax system under which the
legislature determined the tax rate, but the boards of supervisors as-
sessed property values thereby largely determining the proportion of
revenue their respective counties would pay. Because many counties
deliberately lowered their property evaluations, the state had long
suffered from a revenue deficit. In 1916 Governor Bilbo had succeeded in getting the legislature to create a state tax commission with the
authority to assess property values for the entire state.[30] The new
agency had aroused much controversy, especially in the Delta where

[28] *Ibid.*, September 18, 1919.
[29] *Ibid.*, June 26, July 10, 24, August 7, 14, September 11, 1919, April 22, 1920.
[30] Kirwan, *Revolt of the Rednecks*, 260–61. During the summer of 1919 A.S.
Coody, a Vardaman aide, wrote a series of articles for *Vardaman's Weekly*,
describing the workings and merits of the tax commission.

it immediately had increased assessments on rich cotton lands. Many accused the commission of exercising arbitrary power and of making unfair rulings. Three of the gubernatorial candidates, Collins, Johnson, and Longino, openly opposed the commission, while only Russell defended it.

Vardaman opposed both Johnson and Longino. He accused Johnson of having always been a conservative in the state legislature where he had been a spokesman for the large Delta planters. Johnson, moreover, was a law partner of former governor Earl Brewer, a leading opponent of both Vardaman and Bilbo. Describing Longino as the last governor to have been elected by the old convention system, the editor ridiculed him for having appointed Negroes to minor state offices.[31]

Surprisingly, during the first primary Vardaman supported both Russell and Collins. He praised Russell for defending the tax commission, which he believed the state badly needed and which he declared only "tax dodgers" opposed. Russell also called for many of the reforms that Vardaman had long advocated: more road construction, better public health facilities, a department of labor, the initiative and the recall, and expanded educational opportunities for whites.[32] Ross Collins, on the other hand, was an old friend who had stood by him in the elections of 1911 and 1918, and Vardaman would not oppose so loyal a comrade.

His support for Collins revealed how the old Vardaman-Bilbo faction had split: Collins and Bilbo also had once been political allies, but they had fallen out in 1916. In his campaign for governor, Collins accused Russell of having promised to appoint Bilbo to the presidency of the state women's college in return for his support. Both Russell and Bilbo denied ever having made such a deal.[33]

The first primary eliminated both Collins and Longino from the race, and Russell and Johnson then met in a runoff. No longer having to walk a line between two friends, Vardaman enthusiastically supported Russell: "Coming from the humbler walks of life—one of the

[31] *Vardaman's Weekly,* June 19, 26, July 3, 17, 24, 31, 1919.
[32] *Ibid.,* June 26, July 24, 1919.
[33] *Ibid.,* June–July 24, 1919.

common people—he understands the trials and tribulations of the poor and, therefore, he is capable of sympathizing with them. He will see that they are given a square deal." [34] He accused Johnson of having the solid support of the vested interests and of spending enormous sums in behalf of his candidacy, while Russell had to depend on meager contributions from friends. Bilbo also supported Russell, who defeated Johnson by a vote of 77,427 to 69,565. His victory represented a feeble revival of the old Vardaman-Bilbo clique, but it would be a mistake to assume that the faction had reunited. It had not. Ross Collins' candidacy had revealed how it was irreparably split: Collins had bitterly opposed both Russell and Bilbo, but he still enjoyed Vardaman's support. In his editorials the ex-senator had avoided any mention of the old Alliance; it just happened that both he and Bilbo favored Russell over Johnson.[35] Russell's election did illustrate that the appeal of the old faction still lived, for he had directed his campaign to the country people on a platform containing progressive reforms much like those Vardaman and Bilbo had used in their gubernatorial campaigns. He had, moreover, run against a conservative.

By the time Russell won the governorship, the breach between Vardaman and Bilbo was even more pronounced because of conflicting views over foreign policy. While Vardaman opposed the peace treaty and the League of Nations, Bilbo endorsed President Wilson's stand. In his final address to the state legislature in January, 1920, the departing governor warned that selfish and ambitious men were working to undermine the treaty and the League.

Like vultures of the air, they are gnawing at the heart strings of our civilization, undermining the hope of the world, piling up inflamable materials for the torch of terrorism and anarchy, but before it is too late in this hour of the world's opportunity for a brighter and better day, the dawning of the millennium, let us fervently pray that the God of righteousness shall move the hearts and minds of our representatives in the American senate to promptly ratify the Treaty of Peace and adopt with or without amendments and reservations, which ever seems best in their judgment, the League of Nations, which is

[34] *Ibid.,* August 7, 1919.
[35] *Ibid.,* August 7, 14, 1919.

built upon the tears and blood of the teeming millions who died for
the sake of humanity and let us dedicate and consecrate it to the peace
of the world, the brotherhood of mankind and the freedom of all the
people of the earth.[36]

Just as Bilbo was lashing out at the President's opponents in his message, Vardaman entered the legislative chamber, but as soon as he got
the "drift" of what the governor was saying, he beat a hasty retreat.
Later in an editorial he charged, Bilbo "may know something about
state matters, but his discussion of international affairs was sophomor-
ic and of the echo variety." [37]

After Bilbo left the governorship there were reports that he would
run for the Senate against Vardaman in 1922 for the seat that John
Sharp Williams had announced he would vacate. Bilbo dismissed all
such rumors, explaining that he intended to devote his time to practicing law. Once, while denying that he would be a candidate, Bilbo
reportedly ridiculed Vardaman and declared that no man "who works
for a living" should vote for the ex-Senator: "Vardaman is like the
lilies of the field—he toils not, neither does he spin. Seemingly he
has not thought of bread or meat for tomorrow, yet Solomon in all
his glory was never arrayed like Jim. Why he even surpasses the Queen
of Sheba with the talcum on his face and toilet water on his hair." [38]

Any hope that Governor Russell might permanently revive the
strength of the Vardaman-Bilbo group vanished soon after he took
office. The new governor failed to win the support of a majority of
the state legislators and therefore failed to secure the reforms for
which he had campaigned. Russell, moreover, soon split with Bilbo
and the two became hardened enemies.[39] At the state Democratic
convention in 1920 Russell attempted to join his forces in an alliance
with the remnants of Vardaman's old following, but the new coalition
proved no match for the wing of the party that looked to Pat Harrison
and John Sharp Williams for leadership. The Vardaman-Russell men
tried to have the convention adopt a resolution that praised the domestic reforms of the Wilson administration but that refrained from

[36] *Senate Journal, 1920,* 19–23.
[37] *Vardaman's Weekly,* January 22, 1920.
[38] Jackson *Daily News,* March 21, 1921.
[39] Kirwan, *Revolt of the Rednecks,* 296–98.

endorsing its foreign policy. The resolution was quickly squelched. The Harrison-Williams faction further demonstrated its strength by refusing to select Russell as a delegate to the national convention, an honor that former governors had always received.[40]

Even though his old junta had split and had lost most of its power, Vardaman was determined to run for the Senate in 1922. From the time of his return to private life he tried to prepare for a political comeback by expounding his views in the *Weekly* and by giving speeches throughout the state. During the summers of 1919, 1920, and 1921 the *Weekly* frequently reported that Vardaman spoke to enthusiastic crowds numbering in the thousands.[41] It is difficult to determine the accuracy of those reports, because other newspapers did not mention his speeches. Moreover, he always spoke at out-of-the-way places of which few Mississippians probably had ever heard— places such as Lingle, Enon, and Richton. He may have been making speeches during the summers, but it is significant that he avoided towns of any size. By that time his health was steadily declining and he had lost his dazzling speaking ability. He may well have avoided going before audiences in larger towns for fear of having the issues of the 1918 campaign thrown at him and for fear that he would be ridiculed. A vain man, his physical decline must have affected him acutely.

Because of his ill health, Vardaman should never have made the senatorial race in 1922. That he did was due to his own stubbornness and to the ambition of relatives and friends. His two brothers Will and John were determined that he should run, as were some of his former aides.[42]

In his last campaign he faced two opponents. Belle Kearney was the first woman in Mississippi history to run for the Senate, and her sex eliminated her from all serious consideration as a candidate.[43] Hubert D. Stephens resigned his seat in the House of Representatives to make the race. Like Pat Harrison, Stephens had first won election to the House in 1910 when he had campaigned as a foe of the "secret caucus"; until Vardaman had burned his bridges with the Wilson ad-

[40] *Vardaman's Weekly,* June 17, 24, 1920.
[41] *Ibid.,* June 26, July 3, August 7, 1919, July 15, 22, August 5, 1920.
[42] Interview with James K. Vardaman, Jr., May 1, 1968.
[43] Jackson *Daily Clarion-Ledger,* July 19, 1922.

ministration over the war, Stephens had been considered a member of the Vardaman faction. In his campaign for the Senate, Stephens used the strategy that in 1918 had worked successfully for Harrison: he campaigned as a Woodrow Wilson Democrat who had loyally upheld the President throughout the World War. In his campaign speeches he read excerpts from Vardaman's addresses and writings about Wilson and accused the former senator of having betrayed his President. Typical of Stephens' campaign literature was a broadside entitled *Hate*, consisting of quotes extracted from the *Weekly*, all denouncing Wilson.[44]

A bland and colorless man, Stephens failed to win the admiration of many who voted for him. Some anti-Vardamanites, in fact, regretted there was no one else whom they could support: "It is a shame that anti-Vardamanism could not find a leader," one dissatisfied voter complained, "and we had to go into the Vardaman Bilbo Russell camp to get a second class politician to fill the place that had been occupied by men like Lamar, George, Walthall and Williams." Senator John Sharp Williams admitted that Stephens had "never set anybody's rivers afire," but he preferred him to Vardaman. Still, Stephens was too much even for some long-time Vardaman opponents to swallow. "Lord have mercy upon the miserable sinners," wrote Florence W. Sillers after the election, "I could not vote for him!" [45]

With Vardaman a sick man and his two opponents devoid of color and dynamism, the campaign of 1922 was dull. He had announced early that since he had neither the money nor the time to canvass the entire state, he would campaign chiefly through his newspaper. He accordingly reduced the subscription price of his paper from two dollars to one dollar a year.[46] His campaign officially began in September, 1921, when many of his old followers honored him with a barbecue in Jackson. They had predicted that upwards of fifteen thousand peo-

[44] *Ibid.*, July 16, 19, 20, 1922; *Hate*, issued by Hubert D. Stephens Headquarters, Jackson Mississippi, n.d.; copy in Mississippi Department of Archives and History.

[45] Clay Sharkey to John Sharp Williams, August 27, 1922, Williams to Florence W. Sillers, December 23, 1922, Sillers to Williams, December 19, 1922, in Williams Papers, Library of Congress.

[46] *Vardaman's Weekly*, May 26, November 17, 1921.

ple would attend, but the crowd was less than five thousand. During the day many long-time Vardaman supporters, Governor Lee Russell, Ross Collins, John L. Hebron, Tom Brady, and Albert C. Anderson, gave glowing tributes to the former senator. Although present at the rally, Vardaman did not speak.[47]

When the campaign actually got under way in the following spring, he remained inactive. By that time *Vardaman's Weekly* was largely under the direction of his former secretary, Mrs. Mary Dinkins, and she devoted the paper entirely to election propaganda in Vardaman's behalf. A. S. Coody, another former aide, wrote a campaign biography in the hope of rallying support for Vardaman.[48] Judge Luther Burch became Vardaman's campaign manager and gave speeches throughout the state in defense of his record as governor and senator. Frequently Burch hounded Stephens and challenged him to joint debates, but Stephens ignored him.[49] When asked why Vardaman was not speaking for himself, Burch explained that he had had his teeth pulled and had not become accustomed to his dentures. He promised that Vardaman would soon begin his own canvass.[50]

The extended silence inspired the opposition to report that he suffered from a fatal disease, and some charged he had gone insane. In May, he published an explanation: denying all charges of physical or mental illness, he explained that bad teeth had poisoned his system and that he had not fully recovered. In accord with his doctor's instructions he had agreed to rest until July, but at that time he promised to begin campaigning.[51] He never kept that promise. True, he had been unable to find a satisfactory pair of false teeth, but by that time high blood pressure, which had afflicted him for almost ten years, had broken his health. He did not look well, and he had aged so that many of his old followers might not have recognized him. No longer a man of fine physique, he was shriveled and bent. The flowing black hair, so long his trademark, was streaked with white, and he could see only when wearing glasses. Far more alarming, high blood pressure had begun to affect his mind. Although certainly not insane, he

[47] *Ibid.*, September 15, October 6, 1921.
[48] Coody, *Biographical Sketches of James Kimble Vardaman*.
[49] *Vardaman's Weekly*, April 20, 27, May 11, June 15, July 27, 1922.
[50] *Ibid.*, May 18, 1922.
[51] *Ibid.*, May 25, 1922.

could not always carry on a rational conversation. Under such conditions it would have been dangerous for him to have risked public speaking. Though his sons tried to persuade him to abandon the struggle, his two brothers encouraged him to remain a candidate.[52]

The dull campaign dragged on through the summer and attracted little attention. Some newspapers that had always fought Vardaman were so confident he would be defeated that they rarely devoted an editorial to the Senate race. The contest was devoid of live issues, for Stephens continued to hammer away at the question of Vardaman versus Wilson—a question that should have died four years earlier. As he had in 1918, Wilson wrote a letter warning the Mississippi electorate not to make the mistake of selecting Vardaman.[53] Those running the Vardaman campaign also failed to put forth meaningful issues. In fact, they dug into Reconstruction history and discovered that as a state legislator Stephen's father had voted for Blanche K. Bruce, a Negro, to represent Mississippi in the Senate.[54] In the closing weeks of the campaign Vardaman received unexpected help: Bilbo took to the stump and began to campaign for him.[55]

The results of the first primary surprised many. Vardaman led with 74,573 votes to Stephens's 65,980 and Kearney's 18,285. He led Stephens by more than eight thousand votes! The results shocked the anti-Vardaman forces out of their lethargy, and they immediately began working in earnest for Stephens. The Jackson *Daily News* displayed the alarm of the anti-Vardamanites and illustrated the strategy that would be used in the second primary.

The returns from the Senatorial primary of Tuesday show conclusively that Bolshevism and party treason are far from being dead in Mississippi, and that vigorous warfare must be waged on a hydra-headed monster.

[52] Interview with James K. Vardaman, Jr., April 30, 1968. See also James K. Vardaman, Company A, 5th Regiment, United States Volunteer Infantry, Spanish American War, Pension Number XC2633522, National Archives.
[53] Woodrow Wilson to James McCaleb, July 8, 1922, in Jackson *Daily Clarion-Ledger*, July 26, 1922.
[54] *Vardaman's Weekly*, June 1, 15, 1922; Jackson *Daily Clarion-Ledger*, July 16, 1922.
[55] *Vardaman's Weekly*, July 27, August 3, 1922; Jackson *Daily Clarion-Ledger*, July 29, 1922.

The real issue in the second stage of the campaign is whether or not James K. Vardaman is a Democrat who had been true to his party and loyal to his people . . . . There can be no middle ground in a matter of this kind. A man is either a Democrat or he isn't and Vardaman, both by words and action, has proven himself a traitor to the party.[56]

The Vardamanites also intensified their efforts. Bilbo now stumped hard in behalf of his old ally, as did many others. Vardaman actually made a few public appearances by riding in an automobile through several counties in South Mississippi, but he made no speeches.[57]

The end came on September 5, when Stephens defeated Vardaman by a vote of 95,351 to 86,753. More than twenty-three thousand more people had voted in the second primary than had voted in the first. In both the first and second primaries Vardaman's strength came chiefly from those areas where it had been concentrated since his race against Williams in 1907—the hills of the northeast and some of the poorer counties of the south. He also had carried a few counties of east-central Mississippi. Stephens carried the Delta, the Gulf Coast, and a block of counties stretching from the center of the state into the southwest corner. In the second primary he managed to take some counties from Vardaman in the northeast. As throughout his political career, Vardaman appealed most strongly to counties where white small farmers predominated and where rural inhabitants outnumbered town dwellers. Earlier in his career he had always campaigned vigorously, canvassing the state for months in advance of the primaries and relying upon his moving oratory to rally the people to his cause. Had he still enjoyed sound health in 1922, he might again have known victory.

Two days after the primary he left Mississippi with his older brother John for a vacation on the West Coast. Before leaving he issued a statement thanking those who had worked so hard for him and those who had voted for him. He promised not to forget them during his "wanderings through the West," and he hoped that after returning he might again serve them.[58] That hope he never realized.

Because of his seriously impaired health, he could not provide for himself financially. During his last years a Spanish-American War

[56] Jackson *Daily News,* August 16, 1922.
[57] Jackson *Daily Clarion-Ledger,* September 3, 1922.
[58] *Vardaman's Weekly,* September 7, 1922.

pension constituted his only income. Late in 1922 he and his wife moved to Birmingham, Alabama, where they lived in the home of their oldest daughter Aletha whose husband was a successful businessman. The Vardamans' youngest daughter Minnie was also married and lived in Birmingham. Both daughters tried to make life as pleasant as possible for their parents: for hours on end they entertained their ailing father by reading aloud to him from his favorite volumes of prose and poetry. The Vardamans returned to Mississippi several times each year for visits with relatives and friends, but as time passed, the "White Chief" increasingly lapsed into senility. After a sound night's sleep under heavy sedation he awakened bright and alert, but by afternoon his mind sometimes wandered and he imagined himself again in Winona or Sidon or Greenwood. By 1928 he was a complete invalid. "He has been almost entirely helpless nearly all of this year," his wife wrote in November, 1928. "We have to keep a man to stay with him, he cannot move from one chair to another without help, nor use himself at all. Can hardly use his right arm at all. Scarcely ever says any thing, takes not interest in any thing, but is always glad to see his old friends. It is very sad to see him so helpless. He does not suffer any pain, sleeps well, and eats everything." [59] For more than a year and a half he lingered in that state. On June 25, 1930, at the age of sixty-nine, he died peacefully in his sleep.

His body was returned to Jackson for burial. It lay in state at the Capitol, where long lines of mourners filed past the casket. Though more than a decade had elapsed since he had last held public office, thousands still remembered the man they had followed many years before. Frederick Sullens, editor of the Jackson *Daily News* and Vardaman's long-time foe, presented the most meaningful eulogy.

James K. Vardaman is dead.

No leader ever lived in this commonwealth who commanded a more enthusiastic following.

His ability to stir the masses was an asset that others who aspired to places of honor truly envied.

[59] Mrs. James K. Vardaman to Ross A. Collins, November 15, 1928, Byron Dozier to Collins, December 3, 1928, in Spanish American War Records, Pension Number XC2633522, National Archives.

On the stump he attracted and held fascinated multiplied thousands while opponents were speaking to mere hundreds.

Especially was this true in the hey-day of his career.

That he had within him elements that drew many men to him as with hooks of steel is beyond cavil or doubt.

His public career was stormy and tempestuous. He was always in a fight, for he was by nature a fighter and loved to battle with opposing hosts.

That he made mistakes is frankly admitted by those who stood closest to him in his various combats, but they never doubted his earnestness or sincerity.

The *Daily News* for more than a quarter of a century was arrayed against the issues and principles advocated by Vardaman. He was never the political or personal friend of its editor. And yet this writer must confess that at all times he cherished a secret admiration for "The Great White Chief," and marvelled at the man's magnetic personality, his glittering rhetoric, his well rounded sentences, his beautiful oratory, and his ability to stir the masses as they had never been stirred before.[60]

[60] Jackson *Daily News,* June 26, 1930.

EPILOGUE

JAMES K. VARDAMAN lusted for the public spotlight. He wanted people to know him, to respect him. He wanted men to admire him just as he admired the political captains of his boyhood—Senator James Z. George and Congressman Hernando DeSoto Money.

During his childhood Vardaman knew hard times, for his family's poverty had deprived him of a formal education and forced him to work long hours cutting and hauling timber. Fired by a desire to rise above the life he knew as a boy, he yearned to be numbered among those few who stood out from the multitude of farmers and shopkeepers in the simple society of the rural South—the political leaders. To win such a high office as governor or senator—one that would enable him to render service to his people and to win their admiration in return—became the ambition of his life. In pursuing that goal he tried to compensate for his inadequate education by reading avidly. He also became an elegant dresser, who gave minute attention to his personal appearance and maintained a wardrobe that must have strained him financially. After all, if he hoped to be admired, he could not dress like a farmer or the merchant who ran the country store. Like the men of Senator George's generation, he wore his hair shoulder length, clinging to the older style even after men's hair fashions changed. Eventually it became a trademark, distinguishing him from all others: after seeing him, people did not forget him. No other Mississippi politician of his generation acted so flamboyantly.

Vardaman emulated the politicians of his boyhood in other ways. In accord with a code long accepted by southern men, he held white women in exalted esteem and believed men should protect and honor them. Highly conscious of his own honor, he guarded against the taint of personal misbehavior or corruption. He strove to be a gentleman of

382

the old school, one who was friendly and courteous to those about him. For Vardaman that was easy, because he liked people and was a gifted mingler who could amuse others with his stories and humor. During his years in Greenwood, he lived the life he wished: he was the Delta planter, the lawyer, the editor, and the legislator who enjoyed having guests frequent his spacious home, where he entertained them with dinners and parties. Although he attempted to follow the example set by the gentlemen-politicos of the post-Reconstruction South, he eventually cast a far different image. His great energy abetted his drive to reach the top quickly, and he became a much more controversial politician than those who preceded him. In fact, controversy colored his entire political life.

Moreover, Vardaman entered politics during a transition period. The advent of popular primaries made it absolutely necessary for aspiring politicians to appeal to popular issues that could rouse the voters to support them. He proved especially adept under the new system, for he combined personal magnetism with acute perspicacity to come up with a potent formula for appealing to the rural people of his state. Knowing that a barely literate man who toils hard to eke out his living was little moved by colorless speeches on abstract issues, Vardaman stressed subjects close to the hearts of his audiences. He recalled the heroism of the Confederate soldiers, described the virtues of rural life, and appealed to the ego-expanding issue of white supremacy. By demanding larger appropriations for educating white children, less expensive text books, and stricter regulation of railroads, he advocated reforms which his listeners appreciated. A gifted orator, the Mississippian delivered his speeches so stirringly that he went beyond merely entertaining his audiences: he even helped them transcend their narrow little worlds and he moved them as no other speaker they ever heard.

Men reacted strongly to Vardaman. For some he could do no wrong. He thrilled them with his oratory and projected the image of a grand leader. Others considered him a conceited egotist who played the dangerous game of inciting racism to win power. Of course, his political opponents as well as his allies helped to shape his career. In 1903, for instance, he won the governorship with the backing of John Sharp Williams and LeRoy Percy. Three years later, when Vardaman and Williams were pitted against one another in a Senate contest, their former alliance quickly dissolved. Those two able politicians staged a hard fight that Williams barely won by a fraction of one percent of the votes. In 1911 Vardaman faced his other former ally Percy. By that time the "secret caucus" had made Vardaman a martyr in the eyes of many and, confronting weak opposition, he won a smashing victory that carried him to the peak of his political power. Within seven short years America's involvement in World War I so greatly altered the political climate in Mississippi that Vardaman's public career ended as Pat Harrison, another former ally, defeated him in his bid for reelection.

What partly accounted for Vardaman's becoming such a controversial figure was his use of racism. His first stump speeches slightly tapped that issue and found a festering, raw prejudice among Mississippi's whites. The sore had long existed in a state where a white minority worked to suppress a black majority, in a state so deeply resentful of the Reconstruction regime that it readily adopted the 1890 constitution which ultimately eliminated Negroes from voting and holding office. Too many white farmers lived under the vicious crop-lien system that kept them in debt to merchants from birth to death and exacted bone-cracking labor as the price for meager existence. When merchants foreclosed on mortgages and put Negro tenants on those lands, white resentment smoldered all the hotter.

It would not be fair to the man to infer that he became one of the country's most outspoken white supremacists simply because that explosive issue enabled him to gain political power at the hands of a prejudiced constituency. Racism was not confined to Mississippi at the turn of the twentieth century. The whole country, and indeed most of the Western World, then subscribed to racist and nativist phobias. In America the Jew, the Oriental, and the immigrant, as well as the Negro, suffered because of his minority position. Adding fuel to prejudicial fires were the contemporary publications on race that posited the then unquestioned hypothesis that the different races of the world can be scientifically defined and placed on an ascending scale of excellence with the whites at the top and the blacks at the bottom.

Since his youth Vardaman had read insatiably, and his writings and speeches revealed that he delved extensively into contemporary race publications. He expounded rabid views on Negro inferiority not only

because of their political utility, which admittedly entered into the
question, but also because he believed them. Negroes were innately
inferior and to accept them as social and political equals would lead
to intermarriage between blacks and whites—a catastrophe of major
dimensions for the white race. Such mongrelization would cause the
white race to deteriorate and ultimately lose its preeminent position of
master race. His views were not then in the least unusual. During the
time he so vocally incited Negrophobia, not one of his fellow Mississippi politicians ever disagreed with his basic contentions. In Congress
only a few national politicians took issue with his racism. The fact that
for eight years he traveled the country as a popular Chautauqua lecturer, giving over and over only one address, *The Impending Crisis,*
which embodied his racist convictions, indicates that many Americans
sympathized with the views he expounded.

What Vardaman did that so appalled many was to carry an illogical
prejudice to its logical conclusions. If one believes the Negro is irrevocably inferior and that his very presence poses a danger to white
supremacy, why should he be allowed to go to school, vote, and otherwise be on an equal level with his "superiors"? One does not accord
similar privileges to monkeys! To meet the problem honestly, he believed, America needed to repeal the Fifteenth Amendment, eradicate
Negro education, and segregate all blacks. To do otherwise endangered the purity of the white race, the race that throughout history accounted for all man's progress. Besides, under the existing hypocritical
conditions the Negro was allowed only to "taste" the privileges of his
white superiors but never allowed to pursue them, thus unleashing
all the violence, frustration, and animalistic tendencies of his inborn
nature, as well as ruining a good field hand.

Not only did Vardaman present a painfully realistic picture of racism, he did so in raw, unvarnished terms designed to appeal to the
agrarian masses in Mississippi. Sensitive and genteel men could not accept the white supremacy creed in such stark reality. None of his "enlightened" contemporaries recommended granting Negroes social and
political equality with whites, but, like Bishop Charles Galloway, they
tempered their prejudice with benevolent thoughts of economic betterment through education. Thus Vardaman was damned as a racist
demagogue not for what he expounded, which remained essentially

unchallenged, but for the way in which he presented his views and for his audacity in trying to practice what he preached. As governor and as senator, his introduction of Jim Crow laws, his efforts to curb Negro education, his pleas for repealing the Reconstruction amendments, and his refusal to condone Negro public office-seekers all were concrete outgrowths of his basic beliefs on race.

Because Vardaman incited racism, the black man's cause in Mississippi reached low ebb. His use of the issue for political ends was as largely unquestioned as it was inexcusable. He set an example that too many future southern politicians emulated, to the detriment of the Negro. That in the second half of the twentieth century many of Vardaman's racial views are still widely and tenaciously held—in spite of a large body of scientific evidence that disqualifies race as a factor of innate inferiority—shows the far-reaching consequences of the tradition left by the Negrophobes of the early twentieth century, one of the most outspoken of whom was Vardaman. In this respect, at least, he deserves the censure of posterity.

Long after he passed from the political scene, many remembered him as a racist spokesman, but they ignored his legacy as a progressive reformer. In his early writing of the 1890's he espoused an optimistic social philosophy and preached progress. Man could abolish poverty, reduce crime, and improve his life if free to work out his own problems. Society could be improved—provided, of course, it was white society. Like many rural Americans he distrusted the growing power of corporate wealth and believed that banks, railroads, and industries should be regulated for the public good. Because of those attitudes, it is not surprising that he eventually advocated enlightened progressive reforms. As governor, he managed to compile a record of moderate achievements: larger school appropriations, a uniform textbook law, improvements in state charity institutions, stricter regulation of corporate wealth, abolition of convict leasing and reform of the penitentiary system all were improvements that Mississippi needed and for which Vardaman successfully fought. After leaving the governorship his sympathy for the welfare of the "great, silent, slow-thinking, toiling multitude" made him more and more a proponent of reform. By the time he entered the Senate, he supported the programs that the Populists had advocated two decades earlier. As a senator he not only upheld every reform passed by Congress between 1913 and 1916, but he frequently admonished the Wilson administration for being too conservative. Indeed, his voting record closely resembled those of such rural progressives as Robert La Follette of Wisconsin and George Norris of Nebraska.

Despite his consistent work for reform, Vardaman never enjoyed the reputation of a La Follette or a Norris. When men thought of Vardaman they did not remember his campaign to destroy convict leasing, his work for tariff and tax reforms, and his vote for the Child Labor Act. Instead, they remembered that he approved the lynching of black rapists and demanded that Negroes be forever relegated to a caste at the bottom of American society. His flamboyant style and race baiting overshadowed his work for progressive reforms.

Some would declare that a blatant racist could not truly be a reformer. For Vardaman's day such a declaration was scarcely valid. During the Progressive Era most whites, in both North and South, were unconcerned about the plight of the Negro. It was progressivism's major blind spot. The Negro was generally assumed to be of an innately inferior race that could perhaps become more economically comfortable through education but which had little other potential. Vardaman saw the Negro as a threat to white supremacy and he worked to keep him in his lowly state. On the other hand, he realized that serious social and economic problems endangered the welfare of white America, and so he worked to alleviate them. Both as governor and senator, he supported the major reforms of his times.

There was no more conflict between his racism and reform than there was between his racism and high sense of responsibility. As governor, he worked diligently to suppress racial lawlessness and lynch law justice to which he privately subscribed; he had taken an oath to maintain peace and security, and he was determined to do precisely that. Besides, even Vardaman's antipathy towards Negroes had its bounds. As long as blacks docilely kept their "place," he was as interested in seeing that they received justice under the law as he was in seeing that whites benevolently respected that right.

In spite of the solid record of positive reform that Vardaman compiled, Mississippi remained one of America's poorest states. Some charged that Vardaman's hostility to corporate wealth discouraged industries from locating in Mississippi. That was not true, because he worked to regulate only those that ignored the public interest. Thus he vetoed a corporate landowning bill that would have permitted lumber companies to gobble up unlimited forest lands. During the twentieth century Mississippi attracted too many industries that came to escape higher taxes, paid the lowest possible wages, and contributed little to eliminating the state's widespread poverty.

There was a more fundamental reason why Vardaman's progressivism failed to eliminate the problems of Mississippi. During the years he held office Negroes constituted more than half the state's population, but he worked to improve only the lot of the white minority. There was no hope that Mississippi could become a truly progressive state so long as more than half the people were relegated to impoverished subservience. He failed to realize that it was impossible to elevate the whole state while at the same time trying to suppress more than half of its population. What Mississippi needed were programs that would radically improve all educational standards, curb the rising rate of farm tenancy and reduce dependence on one-crop agriculture, and attract those industries which could increase the standard of living. Above all, it needed to root out the cancerous racism that so bitterly divided blacks and whites. Those reforms, most of which were never properly implemented, were not even considered until a later generation; they lay beyond the limits of the progressivism of that day.

The memory of Vardaman's progressive achievements died with him because his rise to power resulted from a highly personal style and because he never forged a lasting political organization through which is reforms could be carried on. He was too jealous of the center stage spotlight to work closely with the one man best equipped to help him form a strong political machine—Theodore G. Bilbo. Even as late as 1915 Vardaman resisted considerable pressure from mutual friends and refused to endorse Bilbo for governor. Vardaman relished every honor as well as every duty that public office brought with it and for that reason rarely delegated authority to subordinates. During his governorship he relied upon his personal rapport with legislators to win support for his programs. In the gubernatorial election of 1907 no one represented the Vardaman faction; no one ran as the leader's hand-picked candidate. When his power reached its zenith in 1911, he again failed as a political organizer; in fact, there is no evidence he even gave it any thought, for his faction was again not represented in the gubernatorial election.

In Mississippi, he supported causes in which he believed and which were popular with his constituency. When he encountered opposition, as in his fight with the McLaurins over convict leasing, he did not dodge. Indeed, he caustically denounced his opponents and worked to defeat them. But when Vardaman went to Washington, his highly personal approach to politics hurt him. His determined opposition to America's entry into World War I brought him into increasing conflict with the Wilson administration. Convinced that he was right, he refused to compromise. Not only did he bolt the ruling of his party caucus on occasion, but he became one of President Wilson's most vehement critics. The same caustic tongue that previously had delighted his Mississippi audiences now began to dismay them. Such denunciation aimed at Republican President Theodore Roosevelt, who had tried to impose a Negro postmaster upon white people, was one thing; directing outspoken criticism at the southern-born Democratic President Woodrow Wilson during a time of international crisis was another.

Because he had long believed the business community possessed too much power and because he strongly advocated American isolation in international affairs, it is not surprising that Vardaman opposed American entry into World War I. What was surprising was that a man who had risen to political power because of his adroit ability to feel out and utilize popular sentiment should, with unwavering courage, follow such an unpopular course even after a surging wave of wartime patriotism seized the American public. He not only bucked popular sentiment, he also ignored political realities by refusing to follow Wilson's leadership. In fact, he had so irrevocably burned all his political bridges by 1918 that President Wilson stripped him of his patronage with little objection from Mississippi.

Here Vardaman's basic honesty worked against him. He believed the business community pushed American into a war that was not to her interest. His every stand was rooted in the belief that his constituents, indeed the whole country, had gone "mad" in the war hysteria that Wall Street stirred up. He had to voice opposition in hopes of setting the nation right—but few were listening and few were those who regretted his political demise that resulted from his stand.

The Mississippian's career resembled in some ways those of other southern politicians. His flamboyant style, his highly personal approach to politics, his race baiting and his advocacy of reforms all have been manifested in the careers of others, although no one combined those characteristics in quite the way Vardaman did. South Carolina's "Pitchfork" Ben Tillman rivaled him as a racist spokesman, and for a time he, too, worked for reforms that might ease the burdens of the white, small farmers. Yet Tillman's zeal for reform slackened and as time passed he became more and more conservative. The Negrophobia and reforms expounded by Georgia's Tom Watson also resembled Vardaman's; but Watson incited anti-Semitism and anti-Catholicism, neither of which Vardaman ever touched. Bilbo returned to the political scene in the 1930's and became a leading proponent of New Deal reforms; he eventually equalled Vardaman as a race baiter. In the 1960's George Wallace of Alabama and Lester Maddox of Georgia followed the Vardaman approach, for both were blatant racists and both supported reforms for their white constituencies.

Unfortunately for Vardaman's political heirs, times changed. Beginning with the work of Franz Boas in the 1920's, anthropologists and sociologists revolutionized the knowledge of race by proposing that no scientific evidence exists to support the belief that whites are innately superior to blacks. In the mid-twentieth century the old racist beliefs that were so common in Vardaman's time fell into disrepute with a considerable segment of white Americans. By the 1950's the South confronted a new movement, based on the change in public attitude, that aimed at insuring full equality for black Americans. In response to the new civil rights movement, Vardaman's brand of Negrophobia revived. Such state leaders as Alabama's Wallace, Georgia's Maddox, and Mississippi's Ross Barnett helped incite a militant racism, expounding the views that Vardaman had made popular over a half century earlier. But by then racism rested on a set of outdated assumptions, and it could no longer coexist peacefully with reform as in Vardaman's day.

Because southern politicians from Vardaman to Wallace shared the folk culture of the rural South, they managed to rouse the masses of whites to support them far better than did the more dignified political leaders. Though there were exceptions, the leaders of the Vardaman tradition never appealed strongly to large planters, industrialists, and financiers; they were never favorites of "polite" society. Like Vardaman, they failed to realize that it was impossible to alleviate the social and economic problems of the whites, while working to keep blacks impoverished and illiterate.

CRITICAL ESSAY
ON AUTHORITIES

The major obstacle encountered in writing this book was the scarcity of Vardaman papers. A thorough collection of his correspondence might have afforded greater insight into Vardaman's thought and personality; it certainly would have facilitated the research. Only one slim volume of his correspondence has been preserved: the Letter Book of Governor James K. Vardaman contains about four hundred copies of letters written by him during his administration. While those letters contain valuable information on patronage, political developments within the state, and the governor's work to suppress racial lawlessness, one gets the impression that they comprise only the letters Vardaman wanted preserved. Other Vardaman letters that have been discovered are scattered through the papers of John M. Stone, Anselm J. McLaurin, A. S. Coody, John C. Burrus, Harris Dickson, and John Sharp Williams, all in the Mississippi Department of Archives and History at Jackson; the papers of Woodrow Wilson and William Jennings Bryan in the Library of Congress; and the papers of Claude Kitchin and Thomas E. Watson in the Southern Historical Collection at the University of North Carolina at Chapel Hill. The total number of Vardaman letters found in these collections does not exceed thirty.

Although letters written by Vardaman are scarce, a number of manuscript collections contain valuable material about him. In the Mississippi Department of Archives and History, a basic source for the years of Vardaman's public career, are the Records of the Governors, consisting of incoming correspondence received by Governors John M. Stone, Anselm J. McLaurin, Andrew H. Longino, James K. Vardaman, and Edmund F. Noel. Of those collections, the one for Governor McLaurin's administration is most valuable, for it is rich in ma-

393

terial on political developments in Mississippi between 1895 and 1899. Even though the incoming correspondence for Vardaman's administration is sparse, it does contain the reports of Detective Albert J. Hoyt describing Whitecapping activities in Lincoln and Franklin counties.

Mrs. Mary Dinkins, who served as Vardaman's secretary during his Senate years, compiled three scrapbooks of newspaper and magazine articles on Vardaman's activities between 1913 and 1919. Besides the Mary Dinkins Collection, other collections of importance on Vardaman in the Mississippi Archives are the papers of John C. Burrus, Eaton J. Bowers, Charlton M. Clark, Harris Dickson, Dunbar Rowland, and Edgar S. Wilson.

The John Sharp Williams Papers are divided into two parts, one in the Mississippi Archives and the other in the Library of Congress. Both collections are invaluable, for they afford great insight into the thinking and activities of the anti-Vardaman forces between 1906 and 1922. Aside from the Williams Papers, the manuscript collections in the Library of Congress contain little information on Vardaman. In the papers of Woodrow Wilson, Thomas W. Gregory, and Albert S. Burleson there are letters revealing how the decision was reached in 1918 to strip Vardaman of his patronage. There are several valuable references to Vardaman's Senate activities in the William Jennings Bryan Papers. Letters in the Theodore Roosevelt Papers make clear the contempt that Roosevelt held for Vardaman.

The Justice Department Records in the National Archives contain several letters from Albert J. Hoyt describing Whitecapping activities and the low state of race relations in Mississippi. The Spanish-American War Records afford some information on Vardaman's activities during that conflict; letters written in Vardaman's behalf by his wife and friends asking that he be granted a military pension describe his declining health in the 1920's.

In the Southern Historical Collection at the University of North Carolina, the Thomas E. Watson Papers reveal how the former Georgia Populist worked in Vardaman's behalf during the senatorial campaign of 1907. Vardaman expressed his determined opposition to President Wilson's preparedness program in several letters written to Claude Kitchin. Both the Jehu A. Orr Papers and the Franklin L. Riley Papers contain enlightening information on Chancellor Robert B. Fulton's troubles at the University of Mississippi.

PUBLIC DOCUMENTS: STATE AND NATIONAL

The Mississippi *House Journals* (1890–1894, 1904–1912) and the Mississippi *Senate Journals* (1890–1894, 1904–1912) supplied information on Vardaman's career as a state legislator and as governor and also afforded material on the political controversies stemming from the Vardaman-Percy campaigns. Mississippi *Laws* (1890–1894, 1904–1908) contain all statutes passed during Vardaman's terms as state legislator and as governor. The Mississippi *Department Reports* (1903–1909), consisting of biennial reports of the Secretary of State, Superintendent of Education, State Treasurer, Superintendent of the Deaf and Dumb Institute, and the Warden and Trustees of the Penitentiary, were especially useful in covering the Vardaman administration. The *Mississippi Official and Statistical Register* (1904–1912) supplied biographical information on state officials, including members of the legislature.

The reports of a number of state legislative investigations were indispensable. *The Reports of the Penitentiary Investigating Committee on Oakley Farm and Hospital* . . . (Nashville, 1906) contains a transcript of all testimony given before the house Penitentiary Committee in 1906; the majority report contributed to the passage of Vardaman's prison reform program. *Record of the Testimony Taken by the Joint Committee in the Investigation of the Charges Made Against Chancellor Robert B. Fulton by D. H. Chamberlain* (n.p., n.d.) afforded a better understanding of the problems at the University of Mississippi during Vardaman's administration. Two reports were essential for studying the senatorial election of 1910: *Investigation by the Senate of the State of Mississippi of the Charges of Bribery in the Election of a United States Senator* (Nashville, 1910) contains the most detailed testimony on the legislative caucus. There is additional information in Mississippi House of Representatives, *Inquiry into the Charges of Bribery in the Recent Senatorial Contest* (Jackson, 1910).

The basic source for Vardaman's Senate career was the *Congressional Record* for the Sixty-third through the Sixty-fifth Congresses. *The Official Congressional Directory* supplied biographical sketches on all members of Congress.

The Deed Record Books for three Mississippi counties—Holmes, Leflore, and Yalobusha—and one Texas county—Jackson—afforded information on the economic standing of both Vardaman and his fath-

er, William Sylvester. The manuscript returns for the United States
Seventh and Eight censuses give the number of slaves owned by William Sylvester Vardaman.

NEWSPAPERS

The most valuable sources of Vardaman's early career are the two
newspapers he edited in Greenwood, the *Enterprise* (1890–95) and
the *Commonwealth* (1897–1903). Most issues of those papers are in
the chancery clerk's office in Greenwood, Mississippi. Unfortunately
many of the issues are deteriorating and already some are in shreds.
The Commonwealth for 1902 and 1903 is in the Mississippi Department of Archives and History, as is the Winona *Advance* which Vardaman edited in 1883. Several other papers contain material on Vardaman's early career. In the Greenwood chancery clerk's office there
are files of the *Southern Farmer* and the *Yazoo Valley Flag*. Scattered
issues of the Greenville *Democrat* and the Greenville *Times* are in the
Greenville Chancery Clerk's office. The Winona *Times* for 1883–84
is in the Winona Courthouse.

During Vardaman's governorship and senatorship the daily newspapers in Mississippi were almost solidly arrayed against him. The one
exception during his governorship was the Vicksburg *Herald*; while he
was a senator the Vicksburg *Post* supported him. Unfortunately, the
back files of the *Post* for the years 1913 through 1919 have not been
preserved. The two Jackson dailies, the *Daily Clarion-Ledger* and the
Daily News, consistently opposed Vardaman throughout his career,
as did the Biloxi *Daily News* and the Natchez *Daily Democrat.*

Files for *The Issue,* which later became *Vardaman's Weekly,* are in
the Mississippi Department of Archives and History. Only the issues
for 1912 are missing. In addition to *The Issue,* the Jackson *Daily
Clarion-Ledger* and the Vicksburg *Herald,* two weekly newspapers
are especially valuable in providing coverage of the legislative caucus
of 1910 and the primary electon of 1911: the Newton *Record* avidly
supported Vardaman, while the Macon *Beacon* vehemently opposed
him.

Among the country weeklies from which material was gleaned for
the years of Vardaman's administration are the Brookhaven *Leader,*
Cleveland *Enterprise,* Columbus *Commercial,* Gloster *Dispatch,* Liberty *Southern Herald,* McComb *Enterprise,* Magnolia *Gazette,* Meadville *Franklin Advocate,* New Albany *Gazette,* Pontotoc *Sentinel,*
Summit *Sentinel,* and Yazoo City *Herald.*

The leading country weeklies that supported Vardaman during his years in the Senate and that continued to stand behind him after the outbreak of war in 1917 were the Aberdeen *Weekly,* Columbus *Commercial,* Hattiesburg *News,* Brookhaven *Leader,* Magnolia *Gazette,* McComb City *Enterprise,* Ripley *Southern Sentinel,* and the Yazoo City *Yazoo Sentinel.*

AUTOBIOGRAPHIES, MEMOIRS AND CONTEMPORARY ACCOUNTS

Charles H. Otken, *The Ills of the South: or, Related Causes Hostile to the General Prosperity of the Southern People* (New York, 1894) reveals how the crop-lien system drove some farmers to participate in Whitecapping raids.

In *The Facts About the Troubles of the University of Mississippi: The Jim Crow Laws Against Whites at the University* (n.p., n.d.), D. H. Chamberlain, Jr., charged that nonfraternity men suffered gross discrimination at the University and that Chancellor Robert B. Fulton sympathized with the fraternities. After Fulton had been exonerated by a legislative investigation, Chamberlain issued *The Mud Beneath the Whitewash* (n.p., n.d), charging that the chancellor's friends had controlled the investigation.

Throughout his career Vardaman was the subject of controversy. Among the articles that appeared in national publications defending him were Gerrald Harris, "Defense of Governor Vardaman," *Harper's Weekly,* LXIX (February 18, 1905), 236–38, and Harris Dickson, "The Vardaman Idea," *The Saturday Evening Post,* CLXXIX (April 27, 1907), 3–5. Highly critical of Vardaman were James Wilford Garner, "A Mississippian on Vardaman," *Outlook,* LXXV (September 12, 1903), 139–40; John M. Mecklin, "Vardamanism," *Independent,* LXXI (August 31, 1911), 461–63; and Frederick Palmer, "Williams-Vardaman Campaign," *Collier's,* XXXIX (July 27, 1907), 11–12. George Creel, "The Carnival of Corruption in Mississippi," *Cosmopolitan,* LI (1911), 725–35, sharply attacked the activities of the anti-Vardaman forces during the 1910 senatorial caucus.

William Alexander Percy's *Lanterns on the Levee: Recollections of a Planter's Son* (New York, 1941) contains a revealing account of the senatorial campaigns of 1910 and 1911. Percy interpreted his father's crushing defeat at the hands of Vardaman as meaning " 'the bottom rail's on top and it's gwiner stay thar.' "

WORKS ON MISSISSIPPI HISTORY

Indispensable for studying this era of Mississippi history is Albert D. Kirwan, *Revolt of the Rednecks: Mississippi Politics, 1876–1925* (Lexington, 1951). Though marred by some factual errors, it nevertheless presents an able interpretation of political developments within the state for a fifty-year period. The more I worked in this era, the more my appreciation of Kirwan's study increased. Vernon Lane Wharton, *The Negro in Mississippi, 1865–1890* (Chapel Hill, 1947) provides valuable background material. A broad study that illuminates many aspects of Mississippi history during the last three decades of the nineteenth century is James Sharbrough Ferguson, "Agrarianism in Mississippi, 1871–1900: A Study in Nonconformity" (Ph.D. dissertation, University of North Carolina, 1953). Especially helpful was Ferguson's interpretation of the 1890 constitutional convention. Charles G. Hamilton, "Mississippi Politics in the Progressive Era, 1904–1920" (Ph.D. dissertation, Vanderbilt University, 1958) treats much of the same material that Kirwan covered.

A number of more specialized studies are essential for understanding developments within the state during the last quarter of the nineteenth century. Four able articles by Willie D. Halsell are devoted to Mississippi politics: "Democratic Dissensions in Mississippi, 1878–1882," *Journal of Mississippi History,* II (1940), 123–35; "Republican Factionalism in Mississippi, 1882–1884," *Journal of Southern History,* VII (1941), 84–101; "James R. Chalmers and 'Mahoneism' in Mississippi," *ibid.,* X (1944), 37–58; "The Bourbon Period in Mississippi Politics, 1875–1890," *ibid.,* XI (1945), 519–37. May Spencer Ringold, "Senator James Zachariah George: Bourbon or Liberal," *Journal of Mississippi History,* XVI (1954), 164–82, probes some of the paradoxes in the career of Mississippi's most powerful post-Reconstruction leader. Helpful in studying the 1890 constitutional convention is J. S. McNeilly, "History of the Measures Submitted to the Committee on Elective Franchise, Apportionment and Elections in the Constitutional Convention of 1890," *Publications of the Mississippi Historical Society,* VI (1902), 129–40. Robert L. Brandfon, *Cotton Kingdom of the New South: A History of the Yazoo Mississippi Delta from Reconstruction to the Twentieth Century* (Cambridge, Mass., 1967) describes economic developments in the Delta during the years Vardaman resided in that section. Robert W. Harrison, *Levee Districts and Levee Building in Mississippi: A Study of*

State and Local Efforts to Control Mississippi River Floods (Stone-ville, Miss., 1951) supplied information necessary for understanding the political controversies that raged in the Delta during Governor McLaurin's administration.

That President Theodore Roosevelt's closing of the Indianola post office contributed substantially to Vardaman's election as governor in 1903 is well demonstrated by Willard B. Gatewood, "Theodore Roosevelt and the Indianola Affair," *Journal of Negro History,* LIII (1968), 48–69. Mary Floyd Summers, "Edgar Stewart Wilson: The Mississippi Eagle, Journalist of the New South" (Ph.D. dissertation, Mississippi State University, 1962) supplies some information on President Roosevelt's patronage referee in Mississippi; unfortunately Summers' work is a disappointing study of an intriguing figure.

Lyda Gordon Shivers, "A History of the Mississippi Penitentiary," (M.A. thesis, University of Mississippi, 1930) explains how the Var-daman forces managed to enact the prison reform bill in 1906. Two studies present conflicting interpretations of the significance of Robert B. Fulton's forced resignation from the chancellorship of the University of Mississippi: Grover Cleveland Hooker, "The Origin and Development of the University of Mississippi with Special Reference to Its Legislative Control" (Ph.D. dissertation, Stanford University, 1932–33) sharply condemns Vardaman for opposing Fulton and for intervening in the affairs of the University. James Allen Cabaniss' *A History of the University of Mississippi* (University, Miss., 1949) presents a more sympathetic interpretation of Vardaman's role in the Fulton controversy. That some of the reforms advocated by Vardaman were enacted by the Mississippi legislature immediately after he left the governorship is demonstrated by Charles G. Hamilton, "The Turning Point: The Legislative Session of 1908," *Journal of Mississippi History,* XVI (1964), 93–111.

William Sidney Coker, "Pat Harrison: The Formative Years, 1911–1919" (M.A. thesis, University of Southern Mississippi, 1962) is a sound study of Harrison's early career. To date the only work of merit on Bilbo is Larry Thomas Balsamo, "Theodore G. Bilbo and Mississippi Politics, 1877–1932" (Ph.D. dissertation, University of Missouri, 1967).

GENERAL WORKS

A study that aided greatly in understanding sectional developments in the American South during the years Vardaman was active in public affairs is C. Vann Woodward's, *Origins of the New South, 1897–1913* (Baton Rouge, 1951). The importance of Vardaman's veto of the corporate landowning bill in 1906 is better understood after reading Paul W. Gates, "Federal Land Policy in the South, 1866–1888," *Journal of Southern History,* VI (1940), 303–30. That Vardaman's interest in prison reform was shared by many other southern progressives is revealed in Jane Zimmerman, "The Penal Reform Movement in the South During the Progressive Era, 1890–1917," *Journal of Southern History,* XVII (1945), 462–92.

By far the most important secondary source for Vardaman's years in the Senate is Arthur S. Link, *Wilson* (5 volumes to date, 1947–1965). Link's shorter synthesis, *Woodrow Wilson and the Progressive Era, 1910–1917* (New York, 1954) is also helpful. A survey of the role played by southern congressmen during Woodrow Wilson's presidency is presented in the first two chapters of George Brown Tindall's *The Emergence of the New South, 1913–1945* (Baton Rouge, 1967). James Holt's *Congressional Insurgents and the Party System, 1909–1916* (Cambridge, 1967) reveals how closely Vardaman's views on domestic and foreign affairs resembled those of such midwestern Republicans as Robert M. La Follette and George W. Norris. Two able dissertations have made important contributions in evaluating the role of southern congressmen during Wilson's administration: John W. Davidson, "The Response of the South to Woodrow Wilson's New Freedom, 1912–1914" (Ph.D. dissertation, Yale University, 1954); Anne Firor Scott, "Southern Progressives in National Politics, 1906–1916" (Ph.D. dissertation, Harvard University, 1957).

In "The South and the 'New Freedom': An Interpretation," *The American Scholar,* XX (1951), 314–24, Arthur S. Link argues that pressure exerted by the "radical" southern progressives pushed President Woodrow Wilson farther to the left in his reform programs between 1913 and 1916. Two scholars have written articles opposing Link's interpretation: Richard M. Abrams, "Woodrow Wilson and the Southern Congressmen, 1913–1916," *Journal of Southern History,* XXII (1956) 417–37; Howard W. Allen, "Geography and Politics: Voting on Reform Issues in the United States Senate, 1911–1916," *Journal of Southern History,* XXVII (1961), 216–28. Other articles by Link that are helpful in understanding Vardaman's career are: "The Progressive Movement in the South, 1870–1914," *North Carolina Historical Review,* XXIII (1946), 172–95; "The Cotton Crisis,

The South and Anglo-American Diplomacy, 1914–1915," in John Carlyle Sitterson (ed.), *Studies in Southern History in Memory of Albert Ray Newsome* (Chapel Hill, 1957), 122–38. Kathleen L. Wolgemuth has written two articles describing how Negroes lost patronage and influence during the Wilson administration: "Woodrow Wilson's Appointment Policy and the Negro," *Journal of Southern History*, XXIV (1958), 457–71; "Woodrow Wilson and Federal Segregation," *Journal of Negro History*, XLIV (1959), 158–73.

For a detailed account of America's struggle to maintain neutrality prior to entry into World War I, see Ernest R. May, *The World War and American Isolation, 1914–1917* (Cambridge, Mass., 1959). Especially helpful in assessing the importance of Vardaman's opposition to American entry into the war is Timothy G. McDonald, "Southern Democratic Congressmen and the First World War, August 1914– April 1917: The Public Record of Their Support for or Opposition to Wilson's Policies" (Ph.D. dissertation, University of Washington, 1961).

Biographies of some of Vardaman's contemporaries have been useful in this work. Two works that have served as models are Francis Butler Simkins, *Pitchfork Ben Tillman: South Carolinian* (Baton Rouge, 1944) and C. Vann Woodward, *Tom Watson: Agrarian Rebel* (New York, 1938). Others that have proved helpful are: Dewey W. Grantham, Jr., *Hoke Smith and the Politics of the New South* (Baton Rouge, 1958), Monroe Lee Billington, *Thomas P. Gore: The Blind Senator from Oklahoma* (Lawrence, Kansas, 1967), and George C. Osborn, *John Sharp Williams: Planter-Statesman of the Deep South* (Baton Rouge, 1943). A. S. Coody, *Biographical Sketches of James Kimble Vardaman* (Jackson, 1922) was a campaign biography and contains little information of value.

INDEX

Abbay, R. F., 64
Ackerman, Miss., 357
Adams, Julius: leased convict, 31–32; influence on Vardaman, 156
Adams, Wirt: investigates penitentiary system, 157
Adamson Act, 282–83
Advance (Winona), 8–12
Agrarianism: demand for constitutional convention, 43–45; praised by Vardaman, 87–88, 106–107, 183–84, 283–85
Air Force: in World War I, 320
Alaskan Railroad Act, 280
Alcorn Agricultural and Mechanical College, 122; J. L. Gillespie removed as trustee, 129–30; Vardaman's policies toward, 182
Aldrich-Vreeland Act, 298
Alexander, Bruce, 353
Alexander, Charlton H.: Vardaman opponent, 203 n22; 1910 senatorial candidate, 205, 230, 233–34, 236–37, 248; clash with Vardaman, 263; death of, 263–64
Alexander, George, 225
Allen, "Private" John: 1899 senatorial candidate, 76; supports Vardaman in 1903, pp. 111–12; as railroad lobbyist, 146 n95; as Percy aide, 204n 27, 223, 248; in 1911 senatorial campaign, 238 n18
Amite County, Miss.: whitecapping in, 136–37
Amory, Miss., 357
Anderson, Albert C.: and Dulaney bribery scandal, 221; Vardaman aide, 331, 377
Anderson, William D.: Vardaman opponent, 203 n22, 214; 1910 senatorial candidate, 205, 213–14; prosecutor in bribery investigation, 219
Anthracite coal industry: investigated, 364
Anti-Catholicism, 82–83, 366
Anti-Semitism: opposed by Vardaman, 39–40, 291–92, 369; as a factor in Whitecapping, 135 n53; 1911 campaign issue, 254
Armed Ship Bill, 314–17
Arms Embargo: advocated by Vardaman in 1915, pp. 301, 304
Army: criticized by Vardaman, 319–20, 367
Ashurst, Henry F., 296
Atterbury, J. T., 128–29, 204
Aviation Act of 1917: weakens Vardaman politically, 340

Baker, Ray Stannard, 114. *See also* Negroes
Banks, George H.: opponent of Vardaman, 203 n22; and Mississippi senate investigation of bribery, 226
Barksdale, Ethelbert: challenges Bourbon Democrats, 9; supports subtreasury plan, 46
Batesville, Miss.: Vardaman prevents lynching, 133
Beauvoir, 123
Beilis, Mendel, 292
Belmont, August, 264–65
Belmont prison farm: purchased by state, 151
Berry, Dr. J. P.: and penitentiary investigation, 162–63; defended by Emmett Cavett, 162
Bew, J. R.: criticizes Vardaman, 68; as McLaurin aide, 70
Bilbo, Theodore Gilmore: praised by

403

Vardaman, 200; charges Dulaney with bribery, 217–18; and Senate investigation of bribery, 220–21, 225–26, 227; and 1910 campaign, 239–44; and 1911 campaign, 253–54; attacked by Henry, 253; relationship with Vardaman, 254, 331–33, 341–42, 372–75, 378–79; attacked by legislature in 1911, pp. 257–58; dispute with Brewer, 329–31; 1915 gubernatorial candidate, 331–33; proposes deal to Ward, 336–37; 1918 congressional candidate, 345; defeated, 359; and state tax commission, 371–72; comparison with Vardaman, 390

Bird, Elder L. H.: supports Vardaman in 1910, p. 212

Birmingham, Ala., 351, 380

Bishop, D. H.: reappointed to University of Mississippi faculty, 170

Blakeslee, H. E., 148 n101

Bloomfield, Horace, 147

Blue Mountain, Miss., 253

Boddie, Van Buren: Vardaman opponent, 203 n22; Percy aide, 214; fight with Bilbo, 242

Boers, 84

Bolivar County, Miss.: and 1896 congressional campaign, 65–66

Bolshevik Revolution: Vardaman's view of, 362–63, 368. See also Communism

Bond sale: Vardaman's role in Mississippi transaction of 1904, pp. 124–25

Bondurant, Alexander L.: reappointed to University of Mississippi faculty, 170

Borah, William E.: opposition to Espionage Act, 325; praised by Vardaman, 370

Bourbons: and Mississippi politics, 43, 92

Bradley, Richard L.: on penitentiary board, 153; supports Vardaman, 154, 155

Brady, Thomas, Jr.: opposes Whitecaps, 141; Vardaman aide, 377

Brame, Lex, 259

Brandeis, Louis D.: influence on Federal Reserve Banking Act, 276; influence on Federal Trade Commission Act, 277; appointment to Supreme Court supported by Vardaman, 292

Brann, William C.: influence on Vardaman, 86

Brantley, Colonel A. H., 11–12

Brewer, Earl: 1907 gubernatorial candidate, 183; elected governor in 1911, p. 254; absence of program, 262; alienation from Vardaman, 328; and penitentiary investigation, 328–29; dispute with Bilbo, 329; attack on Bilbo and Vardaman, 322

Brookhaven, Miss.: anti-Whitecap meeting, 141

Bruce, Blanche K., 378

Bryan, William Jennings: and government ownership of railroads, 179; editor of Commoner, 196; at 1912 Democratic convention, 264–65; influence on Federal Reserve Banking Act, 276; resigns as Secretary of State, 305

Bulletin (Lexington), 22

Bullitt, William C., 365

Burch, Luther: as Vardaman aide, 377

Bureau of War Risk Insurance, 298

Burkitt, Frank: Populist leader, 49; denounced by Vardaman, 51, 52 n37; supports Vardaman, 109, 206, 260–61, 331

Burleson, Postmaster General Albert S.: denounced by Vardaman, 370

Burnett Bill, 283

Byrd, Adam M.: Vardaman opponent, 203 n22; 1910 senatorial candidate, 205; 1910 congressional candidate, 243–44

Calhoun, Solomon S., 159

Cannon, F. S.: Percy aide, 209

Cannon, Joseph G., 196

Carnegie, Andrew: criticized by Vardaman, 87, 197

Carnegie Foundation: grant to University of Mississippi, 171

Carroll, Charles, 199

Carrollton, Miss., 5–6

Cashman, John G.: Vardaman appointee, 273, 351, 352, 353

Castleman, Steve: accuses Bilbo of bribery, 329–30

Catchings, Thomas C.: and 1896 congressional campaign, 64–68; and 1898 congressional campaign, 70–72

Cates, George C., 184–85

Caucus (legislative) of 1910, pp. 207–15

Cavett, Emmett: and penitentiary investigation, 162; as Vardaman opponent, 354

Chalmers, James R., 9–10

Chamberlain, Duncan H., Jr.: attacks fraternities, 171–73

Chamberlain, George E.: supports Vardaman, 358

Charleston, Miss., 357

Child Labor Act (1916): enactment of, 281–82; opposed by Pat Harrison, 338; declared unconstitutional, 367

China: nationalist uprising, 84

Choctaw Indians: interests defended by Vardaman, 291

Clarksdale, Miss.: Vardaman hung in effigy, 317

Clapp, Moses E.: opposes Armed Ship bill, 316n

Clark, Champ, 262

Clark, Charlton M., 271–72

Clarke, James P.: advises John Sharp Williams, 270; and Ship Purchase bill, 303

Clayton Act of 1914, pp. 277, 279

Cleveland, Grover: presidential candidate, 50–51; opponent of free silver, 54; criticized by Vardaman, 87; veto of literacy test, 283

Cleveland, Miss.: condemnation of Vardaman, 317

Cloture: rule adopted by Senate, 316

Cochran, R. F.: denounces Vardaman, 355–56

Coleman, S. R.: attacks Vardaman, 41; Vardaman supporter, 120

Collins, Ross: elected as attorney general, 254–55; withdraws suit against Vardaman, 260; 1920 gubernatorial candidate, 371–72; supports Vardaman, 377

Collins, Thomas, 317

Colored Farmers Alliance, 35

Commercial (Columbus), 107

Commissioner of Agriculture (Mississippi), 148

Committee on Public Information, 340

Commonwealth (Greenwood): founded by Vardaman, 58; supports Vardaman in 1903, p. 107

Communism: Red Scare, 368. See also Bolshevik Revolution

Conner, Mike S., 338, 339

Conscription: opposed by Vardaman, 319–20. See also Selective Service Act

Convict lease system: opposed by Vardaman, 31–32, 48; abolition of, 151, 200. See also Penitentiary system

Covington bill, 277

Coody, A. S.: Vardaman aide, 377

Cook, Samuel C., 217

Cook, W. F., 171 n66

Copiah County, Miss., 3

Cosmopolitan Magazine, 261

Cotton crisis of 1914–15, pp. 298–302

Cowan, Will, 22

Cowart, Joseph Oliver: and Dulaney bribery scandal, 222–23

Cox, Minnie M.: postmaster at Indianola, Miss., 100–101

Critz, Frank A.: 1899 gubernatorial candidate, 75; 1903 gubernatorial candidate, 103, 110–11, 112; Vardaman opponent, 203 n22; 1910 senatorial candidate, 205, 214

Cromwell, Oliver: and Colored Farmers' Alliance, 35

Crosby, T. H., 76

Culberson, Charles A., 279

Culpepper, S. B.: Dulaney bribery scandal, 221

Cummings, W. F.: Vardaman appointee, 273

Cummins, Albert B.: as a progressive, 115; debate with Vardaman, 285–86; opposes Armed Ship bill, 315, 316 n44

Cunningham, James A.: denounces Bilbo, 242

Cutrer, John W., 62

Daily Clarion-Ledger (Jackson): on
Vardaman's appointments, 127; on
acquittal of accused rapist, 134; on
case of E. E. Jackson, 156; on prison
reform, 165; on Vardaman's appeal,
255–56; wishes Vardaman well, 267;
denounces Vardaman, 316–17
Daily News (Jackson). *See Evening
News* (Jackson)
Daily Picayune (New Orleans): Vardaman interview in 1903, p. 113
Dalton, Kit, 238
Davis, Jeff: supports Vardaman, 183
Deaf and Dumb Institute, 123, 130
Democratic convention (national): in
1904, p. 130; in 1912, pp. 264–65;
in 1916, pp. 338–39
Democratic platform (national): on
Panama Canal Act, 294–95; on Ship
Purchase Act, 309
Democratic primary: of 1903, pp. 102–
12; of 1907, pp. 177–90; of 1911,
pp. 230–55; of 1912, pp. 262–63; of
1915, pp. 331–33; of 1918, pp. 342–
58; of 1919, pp. 371–73; of 1922,
pp. 375–79
Democratic primary law of 1902, pp.
96–97
Dicken, J. A., 238
Dickson, William A., 244
Dinkins, Mary, 377
Dispatch (Columbus), 273
Dispatch (Vicksburg), 71, 94
Dixon, Thomas, 199
Doddsville, Miss.: scene of lynching,
133
Dulaney, Lorraine C.: McLaurin supporter, 62; Vardaman opponent,
120; and convict lease system, 154;
charged with bribery, 217–18, 220–
21, 223–25, 228

East St. Louis, Ill.: race riot, 326–27
Eastland, James, 133
Edwards, George R.: Vardaman's sec-
retary, 177; dispute with Noel,
257 n66
Electoral commissioners: appointed
(1904) by Vardaman, 129
Ellis, W. A.: and bill to abolish fra-
ternities, 169. *See also* Fraternities
Elmer, James, 171 n66

Elmer, Will, 171 n66
Emergency Fleet Corporation, 323
Enterprise (Greenwood): purchased
by Vardaman, 22; supports Vardaman in 1917, p. 341
Espionage Act of 1917: Vardaman opposes, 324–25; weakens Vardaman
politically, 340; repeal urged by
Vardaman, 362
Evening News (Jackson): defends
Vardaman, 131; penitentiary investigation, 163; on 1907 senatorial
campaign, 190; Percy's attack on
Vardaman, 212; criticism of Vardaman, 246, 378–79; attack on Burkitt,
261. *See also* Sullens, Frederick

Falkner, John W. T.: Vardaman aide,
273, 339
Farmers' Industrial League, 136
Farmers' Progressive League, 136
Farmers' Protective Association, 136
Farmers' Union: support for Varda-
man, 183; and Earl Brewer, 328
Federal Farm Loan Act, 284
Federal Reserve Banking Act: passage
of, 276–77; as affected by Overman
Act, 323
Federal Tariff Commission: opposed
by Vardaman, 310. *See also* Tariff
Federal Trade Commission, 277–79
Ferguson, S. W.: levee board scandal,
62
Flood Control Act (1917), pp. 284–
85
Foltz, J.H., 31–32
Force Bill: opposed by Vardaman,
36; influence on 1890 constitutional
convention, 44
Ford, Henry: Vardaman's views on,
369
Fox, Mary Ann. *See* Vardaman, Mary
Ann Fox
Foy, Malcomb P., 214
France, Joseph I.: opposition to Es-
pionage Act, 325
Franklin County, Miss.: Whitecapping
activities, 142–44
Franklin, Oscar, 142
Fraternities: at the University of Mis-
sissippi, 168–69, 171–72
Free Silver, 53–54, 62

Fulton, Robert B.: as chancellor of University of Mississippi, 167–68; lobbying activities, 169; and grant from Carnegie Foundation, 171; attacked by Daniel Chamberlain, 172; effects of his dismissal, 175

Gallinger, Jacob H., 278 n28
Galloway, Charles B.: dispute with Vardaman, 131; views on Negroes, 385
Gardiner, A. T., 20–21
Garner, James W., 113–14
Garrison, Lindley M.: on World War I preparedness legislation, 305
George, James Z.: influence on Vardaman, 6–7, 382; as Bourbon leader, 43; leader of 1890 constitutional convention, 44–45; opposes subtreasury plan, 46; supported by Vardaman, 46–47
Germany: and submarine warfare, 304–305, 310–13; 314; Zimmerman telegram, 314
Gibbs, Washington: leader of anti-Vardaman forces, 211–12; attacked by Bilbo, 240
Gillespie, J. L.: as Vardaman's partner, 23; supports Vardaman, 56–57; on 1896 congressional election, 67; as McLaurin aide, 69–70; charged with corruption, 129–30
Glass, Carter, 276
Glover, James Alcorn: restriction of Negro education, 148; attacked by Daniel Chamberlain, 172
Godbold Wells, Miss.: political rally, 238
Goldstein, Nathan, 63
Good Roads Act, 284
Gordon, James: appointed to Senate, 202
Gore, Thomas P.: on Adam Patterson appointment, 287; resolution on armed ships, 311n
Grant, Madison, 370
Great Britain: Panama Canal Act, 294; declares cotton contraband, 300; arms merchant ships, 310–11; power in League of Nations, 366
Greenwood, Miss.: Vardaman's residence there, 16–21; and Vardaman victory rally in 1903, pp. 112–13
Gregory, Thomas W.: and removal of Vardaman appointees, 352
Grey, Edward: cotton crisis, 300
Gronna, Asle J.: against break with Germany, 314; opposes Armed Ship bill, 315, 316 n44; votes against war, 318 n52; opposes Espionage Act, 325
Gulf and Ship Island Railroad: and use of convict labor, 48; attacked by Bilbo, 240; accuses Vardaman of using free pass, 246–47. See also Railroads
Gulfport, Miss.: and Vardaman victory celebration, 113; condemnation of Vardaman, 317

Hall, Mrs. W. J.: and Dulaney bribery scandal, 222, 223
Hardwick, Thomas: and amendment to War Revenue Act, 321–22 n64
Harrison, Benjamin, 100
Harrison, Pat: and 1916 Mississippi Democratic convention, 338–39; senatorial candidacy, 342–47, 353–54, 355–56; endorsed by Wilson, 358; denounced by Vardaman, 371
Hattiesburg, Miss.: and Vardaman victory celebration, 113
Hay-Pauncefote Treaty: and Panama Canal Act, 294
Hearst, William Randolph, 130
Hebron, Bell, 225
Hebron, John L.: Vardaman aide, 120, 127, 210, 238, 364, 377; appointed to levee board, 129; works for prison reform, 165–66, 200; and dismissal of Fulton, 174 n77; purchases The Issue, 267; supports Bilbo, 332; senatorial candidate, 336, 337; supported by Vardaman, 338
Henry, John J.: penitentiary warden, 154; and case of E. E. Jackson, 155; transfers prisoners to Sandy Bayou, 159; removed from office by Vardaman, 166; charges Vardaman guilty of corruption, 217; attacks Bilbo, 253
Henry, Pat: spokesman for Catchings,

66; 1898 congressional candidate, 70; defends Bilbo and Hobbs, 330
Henry, R. H.:editor of *Daily Clarion-Ledger,* 30; convention delegate, 95; on Vardaman's appeal, 255–56
Herald (Biloxi): on Vardaman's inaugural address, 119
Herald (Vicksburg), 166, 180
Herald Star (Kemper): defends Vardaman, 340
Hibbler, Stacy: Vardaman opponent, 203 n22
Hill, David B., 50
Hill, Wilson Shedric: supports Vardaman in 1903, p. 111; support for Percy, 204 n27; and Vardaman-Williams patronage dispute, 272
Hilson, Eli, 139
Hitchcock, Gilbert M.: and Federal Reserve Banking Act, 276; and Ship Purchase bill, 304
Hobbs, B. T.: attack on Percy, 213
Hobbs, George A.: dispute with Brewer, 329
Hog Island Shipyard: criticized by Vardaman, 324
Hollis, Henry F.: and amendment to War Revenue Act, 321–22 n64
Holly Springs, Miss., State Normal School: appropriation vetoed by Vardaman, 121–22
Holmes, C. F.: defends Vardaman, 176
Holmes County, 4
Hoover, Herbert: criticized by Vardaman, 322, 370–71
House, Colonel Edward M., 311
Hoyle, J. M., 119
Hoyt, Albert J.: and Whitecap investigation, 140–44
Hudson, J. S., 209
Hudson, S. S.: defeated for reelection, 254–55; suit against Vardaman, 259
Hughes, William, 275
Humphreys, R. G., 20
Hunt, Walter N., 107
Hunter and Stevens prison farm, 151

Immigration: restriction supported by Vardaman, 283
Immunity Bill, 257–58

Impending Crisis, The, 198–99
Income tax: Vardaman's action in 1913, pp. 274–75
Independent (New York), 90
Indianola, Miss., 100–101
International Harvester Company, 280
Interstate Commerce Commission: as affected by the Overman Act, 323
Issue, The: founded, 196; racist views, 197–98; unprofitable, 199; sold by Vardaman, 267; defense of Vardaman, 349; renamed *Vardaman's Weekly,* 364. See also *Vardaman's Weekly*
Isthmian Canal Locomotive Engineers Union, 180
Italians: lynchings in New Orleans, 39. *See also* Lynching

Jackson County, Texas, 4
Jackson, E. E.: penitentiary investigation, 155–56, 161
Jackson, Miss.: Vardaman's inauguration, 116; lynching prevented by Vardaman, 133–34; 1910 legislative caucus, 206–15; Vardaman rallies, 244–45, 250, 255, 267, 332, 376–77; Vardaman's return in 1917, p. 349; Vardaman's funeral, 380
"Jackson Ring", 106
James, Frank, 238
James, T. R., 258
Jayne, J. M., 62
Jews. *See* Anti-Semitism
Jim Crow law, 121, 287
Johnson, Hiram W.: racist views, 270; supports Vardaman, 358; praised by Vardaman, 370
Johnson, J. W.: reappointed to University of Mississippi faculty, 170
Johnson, Oscar: 1920 gubernatorial candidate, 371–72
Johnson, Paul: defeats Bilbo, 359
Johnson, Stewart, 134
Johnston, Joseph F., 271
Jones County News: on Bilbo's campaign, 242–43
Jones, Henry, 36
Jones, Sam P., 34
Jones, Thomas D., 280
Jones, Wesley L.: debate with Vardaman, 286

Joyner, W. H.: congressional candidate, 335–36
Justice Department: and Hog Island Investigation, 324

Kearney, Belle, 375
Kern, John W., 281
Kincannon, Andrew Armstrong, 175
Kincannon, James Clayton, 153
King, W. H., 209
Kirby, William F.: against break with Germany, 314; opposes Armed Ship bill, 316 n44
Kitchin, Claude: opposition to preparedness, 306; praised by Vardaman, 370
Knut, Sergeant Prentiss, 259
Kyle, John Curtis: Vardaman opponent, 203 n22; 1910 senatorial candidate, 205, 209

Labor agents, 135, 139
Labor unions: favored by Vardaman, 87, 280, 281–83, 367–68
La Follette, Robert M.: as a progressive, 115, 268, 293, 387; his *Weekly Magazine,* 196–97; support for income tax 275; Seaman Act, 281; against break with Germany, 314; opposes Armed Ship bill, 315, 316 n44; vote against war, 318 n52; and amendment to revenue act of 1917, pp. 321–22 n64; opposition to Espionage Act, 325; defended by Vardaman, 326; attack on Wilson, 365; praised by Vardaman, 370
Lane, Harry: as a progressive, 269; opposes Armed Ship bill, 316 n44; vote against war, 318 n52
Lansing, Robert: and cotton crisis, 300; proposal to disarm ships, 310–11; attack on Wilson, 365
Lauderdale Springs, Miss.: political rally, 240–41
Laughter, Michael H., 4
Law and Order Executive Committee: in Lincoln County, 141, 142; in Franklin County, 143
Leader (Brookhaven): editor's attack on Percy, 213
League of Nations: criticized by Vardaman, 361–62, 365–66

Lee, Luke, 269
Lee, Robert C.: prosecutes Whitecaps, 144; and Vardaman-Williams patronage dispute, 272
Lee, Robert E., 350
Leftwich, George J.: anti-Vardaman leader, 214; role in Dulaney bribery investigation, 219
Lemon Hotel, site of Dulaney bribery scandal, 220
Lincoln County, Miss.: scene of Whitecapping, 140–42
List, Henry: murdered by Whitecaps, 139
Lodge, Henry Cabot: opponent of income tax, 275
Longino, Andrew H.: and 1896 congressional campaign, 64–68; criticism of Vardaman, 68, 1899 gubernatorial candidate, 75; as governor, 91–92; joins anti-McLaurin forces, 94; supports primary law, 96; attacked by Vardaman, 97–98; 1903 senatorial candidate, 105–106; and Vardaman's inauguration, 116; state finances, 124; action against Whitecaps, 137; 1920 gubernatorial candidate, 371–72
Loper, Floyd, 353
Lorimer, William, 248
Lowry, Robert: suppresses racial violence, 35; Bourbon leader, 61
Lusitania, 304–305
Lyell, Garland, 207
Lynching: justified by Vardaman, 36–38, 88–89, 109; Vardaman's work to suppress, 132–34. *See also* Italians; Rape-lynch complex

Maddox, Lester, 390
Madison, James S.: speaker of the house, 43; candidate for reelection, 48
Maer, Percy W.: Vardaman appointee, 273; resignation of, 353
Magruder, William Wailes, 165
Mahon, Hugh Kirby: Vardaman opponent, 203 n22
Mayes, Edward, 171 n66
Mayes, Lucius, 171 n66
Mayes, Robert B.: Vardaman ap-

pointee, 128; issues injunction against McLaurin, 158
McAdoo, William G.: and cotton crisis, 298; attacked by Vardaman, 370
McCabe, Henry C., 53
McComb, Miss.: Vardaman rally in 1910, p. 252
McCool, James F., 75
McDermit, J. H.: attack on Vardaman, 354
McDonald, Will Tate: bribery investigation, 219
McDowell, James, 203 n22
McKinley, William: attacked by Vardaman, 236
McLaurin, Anselm J.: supported by Vardaman, 47–48; 1895 gubernatorial candidate, 53; and levee board policies, 62–63; vetoes Capitol bill, 69; and 1898 congressional election, 71–72; refuses to commission Vardaman, 74; 1899 senatorial candidate, 76; senatorial politics, 90; as Democratic convention delegate, 95; influence in 1903 primary, 111–12; son-in-law appointed by Vardaman, 128; appointees removed by Vardaman, 128; and 1904 presidential election, 130; and prison affairs, 151; attacks Vardaman, 160; and penitentiary investigation, 162; influence on 1907 senatorial campaign, 182–83; death of, 201
McLaurin, Henry: Vardaman opponent, 120; and convict lease system, 154–55, 157–58; defends E. E. Jackson, 156; losses charged to his plantation, 157; sued by Vardaman, 158–59; attacked by Vardaman, 160
McLaurin, S. L.: anti-Vardaman leader in 1910, p. 214
McLaurin, Walter: attacked by Vardaman, 160
McLaurin, Judge William K.: accused of drunkenness, 69; not reappointed by Longino, 91; Vardaman opponent, 120
McLemore, Jeff: resolution on armed ships, 311–12
McNair, Stephen D., 153
McNeilly, J. S., 61

McNeilly, M. S.: and Dulaney bribery scandal, 223
McReynolds, James C.: appointment opposed by Vardaman, 288
Merchants: victims of Whitecapping, 134–35
Meridan, Miss.: Vardaman-Williams debates of 1907, pp. 185–89; Vardaman parade in 1911, pp. 252–53; Harrison rally in 1918, pp. 355–56
Meteor (Crystal Springs): on Bilbo campaign, 243
Military Affairs Committee: Vardaman resigns from, 307
Miller, Anthony: Vardaman supporter, 120; and penitentiary investigation, 161; prison reform, 166
Miller, C. C., 93, 94
Miller, R. N., 222–23
Miller School, 175
Minnesota Commission on Public Safety: attack on La Follette, 326
Mississippi Baptist: attacks Vardaman, 107
Mississippi Democratic convention: in 1883, pp. 10–11; in 1899, pp. 78–79; in 1912, p. 263; in 1916, pp. 338–39; in 1920, pp. 374-75
Mississippi Democratic executive committee: refuses to call 1900 convention, 93; opposes early primary (1910), pp. 232–33
Mississippi Hedge Company, 20
Mississippi Press Association: addressed by Vardaman, 26; meets in Greenwood, 29; excursion to St. Louis, 29–30
Mississippi senate: and investigation of Dulaney bribery scandal, 218–26
Mississippi Society, 271–72
Mississippi Supreme Court: Sandy Bayou case, 159. See also Penitentiary system
Mobile and Ohio Railroad, 146. See also Railroads
Money, George P., 23
Money, Hernando DeSoto: Vardaman's cousin, 3; influence on Vardaman, 6–7, 382; supports agricultural bill, 8–9; Bourbon leader, 43; introduces Vardaman to Cleveland, 51; favors annexation of Hawaii,

81; convention delegate, 95; 1903 senatorial candidate, 105–106; supports Vardaman in 1903, p. 111; and 1904 presidential election, 130; resigns from U. S. senate, 177
Money, James: wounded in gun battle, 25
Money, Pierson, 5
Money, William Vardaman: editor of Winona *Advance,* 8–12
Monroe Doctrine: endangered by League of Nations, 366
Montgomery, Isaiah T.: supported by Vardaman, 39
Montgomery, W. A., 75
Montgomery, William Alexander, 166
Moore, Charles J.: investigates Vardaman's contingent fund, 216, 260
Moore, Edward Harris: McLaurin supporter, 62, Vardaman opponent, 120
Moore, Percy L., 12
Morgan, J. P.: criticized by Vardaman, 86–87,197
Morris, Rupert C., 172
Morrison, S. A., 173
Muscle Shoals, Ala., 308, 369

National Association of State Universities, 168
National Colored Democratic League, 287
National Defense Act, 307–308
National Democratic Fair Play Association, 286
Negro Pastor's Association: opposes Vardaman, 111
Negroes: Vardaman's views of, 34–39, 88–90, 102–103, 132–33, 187–88, 193–94, 198–99, 270, 285–91, 326–27, 369–70, 384–86; attempted uprisings, 35, 135–36; threat of rape, 36–38; issue in prohibition campaign, 42; and distribution of school fund, 44, 54–56, 77–78, 148; victims of Vardaman's racism, 59–60; opposition to Vardaman, 111; Ray Stannard Baker on South's view of, 114; Jim Crow law, 121; vagrancy law, 121; and Holly Springs State Normal School veto, 121–22; removed as electoral commissioners,

129; Galloway and Ward dispute over, 131; lawlessness against suppressed by Vardaman, 133–45; and Whitecap terrorism, 134–45; John Sharp Williams' views of, 181, 188–89. *See also* Rape-lynch complex; Vardaman, James Kimble: racist views
Neil, Coral Johnson: and Dulaney bribery scandal, 221–22
Neshoba County Fair: Pat Harrison's speech at, 343–45
Neville, Jim, 240
New Freedom, 267–68
New Nationalism, 268
New Orleans: Italians lynched in 1891, p. 39; Vardaman's statement of opposition to war, 317
Newman, A. M.: as a Whitecapper, 138; opposes Whitecap investigation, 143; conviction, 143–44
News (Indianapolis): on Vardaman's 1911 election, 255
Newton, Miss., 242
Neyland, C. H., 166
Niles, Henry, 144
Noel, Edmund F.: nominated for district attorney, 10–12; as sponsor of primary law, 96; 1903 gubernatorial candidate, 103–104, 110–11; 1907 gubernatorial candidate, 183; supported by Vardaman, 192; programs advocated as governor, 200; dispute with Vardaman, 200–201; and method of selecting McLaurin's successor, 201–202; opposes Vardaman in senatorial election of 1910, p. 210; action on senatorial caucus, 214; and legislative investigation of bribery, 218–19; opposed to early primary, 232–33; attacked by Bilbo, 240; and special session of 1911, pp. 257–58; attempts to bar Vardaman from Senate, 259; attacked by 1912 legislature, 260–61; senatorial candidacy of, 342–43
Norris, George W.: as a progressive, 268, 293, 387; praised by Vardaman, 196; opposes Armed Ship bill, 315, 316 n44; vote against war, 318 n52

Oakley prison farm: purchased by

state, 151; converted to stock farm, 152–53; case of E. E. Jackson, 155–56; investigated, 161–63. *See also* Penitentiary system

O'Gorman, James: on Panama Canal Act, 294; on Ship Purchase bill, 304; opposes Armed Ship bill, 316 n44

Outlook, The: on Vardaman's election in 1903, pp. 113–14

Overman Act: supported by Vardaman, 323

Paine, Thomas, 34

Palmer, U. S. Attorney General A. Mitchell: criticized by Vardaman, 368

Panama Canal Act: Vardaman's stand on, 294–97; opposed by Harrison, 338

Paris Peace Conference: criticized by Vardaman, 361

Parker, Alton B., 130, 264

Passing of a Great Race, The, 370

Patterson, Adam E.: appointment opposed by Vardaman, 287–88

Patronage: Vardaman's handling of, 127–30; dispute with Williams, 272–73

Penitentiary system: reforms advocated by Vardaman, 31–32; Vardaman's work for reform, 150–67; scandal in, 328–29. *See also* Convict lease system

Pennsylvania: anthracite coal investigation, 364

People's Party. *See* Populist Party

Percy, LeRoy: opponent of McLaurin, 61, 63, 66, 67, 71–72, 94, 95; and 1898 congressional election, 71–72; praised by Vardaman, 72; supported Vardaman, 111, 112n, 383; Vardaman opponent, 128–29, 182, 212, 231–33, 247–48, 384; on 1907 senatorial election, 180; 1910 senatorial candidate, 203–204, 213, 214–15; on Bilbo's charge of bribery, 217–18; advocates early primary, 231–32; and 1911 senatorial campaign, 233–39, 248–49; on Witherspoon's victory, 244; resignation called for, 261; on 1912 presidential election, 262

Percy, Walker: support for LeRoy Percy, 204; challenges Bilbo, 241

Percy, Will: support for LeRoy Percy, 204, 223; investigates Vardaman's financial records, 215

Percy, William Alexander: on father's senatorial campaign, 237

Philippines: Vardaman opposes acquisition of, 83–84; independence bill, 288–89

Pinkerton Detective Agency: and suppression of Whitecapping, 140 n75

Pitchfork, The, 329, 330

Planer, Hezekiah: attacked by Vardaman, 163, 164 n47

Poindexter, J. O., 227

Populist Party: in 1892 campaign, 49–51; electoral commissioners, 129; Williams's view of, 179; Vardaman's view of, 179; support for Vardaman, 206; influence on Vardaman, 269–70, 280

Pontotoc, Miss., 332–33

Post (Vicksburg), 273, 351

Powell, Murry, 171 n66

Powell, Robert: 1899 gubernatorial candidate, 75; son suspended from University of Mississippi, 171 n66; University trustee, 173–76

Preparedness (World War I): controversy over, 305–309; weakens Vardaman politically, 334–35

Presidential election: of 1904, p. 130; of 1912, pp. 262–65; of 1916, p. 339

Preston, Miss., 5

Prewitt, J. E., 20

Price, Walter, 227

Primary (Democratic) election law: enactment of, 96–97; amended, 123

Prison reform. *See* Penitentiary system

Prohibition: campaign for in Winona, 12–15; campaign for in Greenwood, 40–41; national law favored by Vardaman, 290–91; provided for in Selective Service Act, 320

Puckett, David, 156–57, 165

Puerto Rico: territorial status opposed by Vardaman, 289

Quinn, Hilary M.: purchases *The Is-*

sue, 267; 1915 gubernatorial candidate, 331
Quinn, Percy, 244

Race riot: Leflore County, 35; East St. Louis, 326–27
Racism: factor in 1903 election, 114–15. *See also* Negroes; Vardaman, James K.: racism; Rape-lynch complex
Railroads: rate discrimination, 9; convict leasing, 48; merger bill vetoed by Vardaman, 146; government ownership of, 179; Alaskan Railroad bill, 280; Adamson Act, 282–83; Railroad Administration, 323. *See also* Gulf and Ship Island Railroad
Raney, J. L., 220–21
Rankin Prison Farm: conditions at, 150; case of David Puckett, 156–57; investigation of, 165
Ransdell, Joseph E., 284
Rape-lynch complex: and Vardaman, 37–38, 88–89. *See also* Lynching; Negroes; Vardaman, James K.: racism
Red Bank, Miss: condemnation of Vardaman, 317
Red Scare, 368. *See also* Bolshevik Revolution
Reed, James A.: on Federal Trade Commission, 278; defends La Follette, 326; praised by Vardaman, 370
Reformer (Raleigh): on LeRoy Percy's election, 231
Reily, W. Marion, 331
Revenue Act: of 1914, pp. 299–300; of 1916, pp. 309–10; of 1917, pp. 321–22
Richardson, Bonner, 20
Ricks, Fanny J., 172 n68
Ricks, John, 172 n68
Rising Tide of Color, The, 370
Robbins, J. Q., 346
Robertson, Stokes, 171 n66
Robertson, Walter W.: Percy aide, 209; and controversy during caucus of 1910, p. 213; legislative investigation, 226–27

Robinson, Ann Burleson. *See* Vardaman, Anna Burleson Robinson
Robinson, Douglas, 15
Robinson, Douglas, Jr., 15, 17 n42
Rockefeller, John D.: criticized by Vardaman, 86, 197
Roosevelt Hotel, 317
Roosevelt, Theodore: attacked by Vardaman, 98–102; relations with Edgar S. Wilson, 98; and Indianola Post Office, 100–102; as issue in 1903 primary, 104–106; refuses to name post office after Vardaman, 131; and New Nationalism, 268; antitrust policies, 277; supported by Vardaman, 325
Rowland, Dunbar: mimicked by Vardaman, 19; defends Chancellor Fulton, 174; and silver service controversy, 200–201
Rublee, George: on Federal Trade Commission, 277, 278
Rush, W. T., 20–21
Russell, Lee: as gubernatorial candidate, 345, 371–73; split with Bilbo, 374–75; support for Vardaman, 377
Russia. *See* Bolshevik Revolution; Red Scare
Ryan, Thomas Fortune, 264–65

St. Louis, Mo.: Democratic convention of 1904, p. 130
Sanders, Wiley N.: repudiation of Vardaman, 346
Sandy Bayou. *See* Convict leasing; Penitentiary system
Santiago, Cuba, 75, 81–83
School appropriation bill, 123
Schurz, Carl, 81
Scott, Charles: McLaurin opponent, 61, 63, 65, 66, 67; Vardaman supporter, 111; gubernatorial candidacy supported by Vardaman, 183, 192
Seay, R. S., 222
Secret ballot: in legislative caucus of 1910, p. 208
"Secret Caucus": of 1910, pp. 201–15; investigation of, 218–27; denounced, 230–31
Sedition Act: opposed by Vardaman, 325–26; repeal urged by Vardaman, 362

Selective Service Act, 320, 340. *See also* Conscription
Sentinel (Grenada): on Vardaman's 1918 defeat, 359
Sentinel (Ripley): defends Vardaman, 216
Shands, Garvin D., 171, 173–76
Sheppard, Morris, 269
Sherman, Lawrence Y., 325
Sherman Silver Purchase Act, 54
Ship Purchase Bill: opposed by Vardaman in 1915, pp. 302–304; supported by Vardaman in 1916, p. 309; reduces Vardaman's political strength, 334, 336–37
Ship Registry Law, 298
Sidon, Miss., 15, 16–17
Sillers, Florence W., 376
Sillers, Walter: McLaurin aide, 62, 64, 68; spokesman for Longino, 66; and congressional campaign of 1898, pp. 71–72; opposes Vardaman, 111
Sisson, Thomas U.: 1907 gubernatorial candidate 183; alienated from Vardaman, 336–37
Small, Sam, 34
Smith, Charles C., 166, 329
Smith, Hoke: cotton crisis, 299, 300, 301
Smith, Murray F., 61, 72
Smith-Hughes Act, 284
Smith-Lever Act, 285–86
Somerville, P. S., 62, 66
Southern Association of Colleges and Secondary Schools, 168
Southern Farmers' Alliance, 46. *See also* Colored Farmers' Alliance
Southern Railroad, 146. *See also* Railroads
Southern States Exposition, 20
Spanish-American War: Vardaman's participation in, 73–75; effect on Vardaman, 297; Vardaman's pension, 379–80
Stamps, Mary, 220
Stephens, Hubert D.: 1922 senatorial candidate, 375–76
Stevens, W. F., 128
Stoddard, Lathrop, 370
Stoddard, Walter: gun battle with Vardaman, 24–25

Stone, Jim, 171 n66
Stone, John M., 61, 62
Stone, William J.: on Ship Purchase bill, 302, 303; opposes Armed Ship bill, 316 n44; vote against war, 318 n52
Stovall, P. S.: opponent of McLaurin, 61; 1915 gubernatorial candidate, 331
Street, Hugh N.: opposes popular primaries, 47; elected speaker of house, 48; forms alliance with Vardaman, 51–52; presides over 1910 caucus, 208; 1910 senatorial candidate, 214; defense of Vardaman, 216
Strong, Joe, 156, 165
Submarine warfare. *See* Germany: submarine warfare
Subtreasury plan, 46
Sullens, Frederick: attacks Vardaman, 246–47; attempts to bar Vardaman from Senate, 259; on Harrison's campaign, 344–45; denunciation of Vardaman, 346; removal of Vardaman's appointees, 352; eulogy on Vardaman, 380–81. See also *Evening News* (Jackson)
Sullivan, William V.: elected to Senate, 90; defeated as convention delegate, 95
Sunflower County, Miss.: state prison farm, 151
Sunflower Tocsin (Indianola): criticism of Vardaman, 68
Supreme Court: rulings criticized by Vardaman, 367
Sussex, 312–13. *See also* Germany: submarine warfare
Sutherland, H. L., 62

Taft, William Howard: vetoes literacy test, 283
Talbert, Polk: Vardaman supporter, 120, 216
Tally, John R., 331
Tariff: Underwood Act, 274–75; rate increases of 1916, p. 310. *See also* Federal Tariff Commission
Tax Commission (Miss.), 371–72
Taylor, LeRoy, 166
Taylor, Swep J.: Vardaman aide, 127,

210, 217, 249, 355, 364; purchases *The Issue,* 267; Bilbo supporter, 332
Terrell, Robert R.: appointment opposed by Vardaman, 288
Thigpen, C. W., 242
Thomas Emmet N.: at Vardaman's inauguration, 117; speaker of house, 120 n7; upholds Vardaman's veto, 122; 1907 gubernatorial candidate, 183
Thompson, R. H., 170
Tillman, Benjamin: influence on Vardaman, 86; support for Vardaman, 183; comparison with Vardaman, 390
Times (New York): on Vardaman's 1910 campaign, 211
Times (Winona), 13–14, 22
Tradings with the Enemy Act, 325
Truly, Jeff: Vardaman opponent, 128; and Sandy Bayou case, 159; as gubernatorial candidate in 1907, p. 183; and 1910 senatorial election, 208
Tuberculosis: establishment of open air sanatorium, 126
Tucker, W. F., 173
Tucker, William F.: Dulaney bribery investigation, 219
Tupelo, Miss.: Judge Robbins denounces Vardaman, 346

Underwood Tariff Act, 274–76. *See also* Tariff
Underwood, Oscar, 262–63, 265
Uniform Textbook Law: enactment, 123; appointment of commissioners, 125
United States Volunteer Infantry: fifth regiment, 74
U.S.S. *Mississippi*: silver service controversy, 200–201
University of Mississippi: Vardaman's policies toward, 167–76; investigation of, 168–69
Upshur, T. H.: gun battle with Vardaman, 24–25

Vardaman, Aletha, 17, 351, 380
Vardaman, Anna Burleson Robinson, 15, 18, 331, 380

Vardaman, Bessie, 17
Vardaman, Gideon Smith, 4 n6
Vardaman Jeremiah, 3
Vardaman, John Fox, 4 n6
Vardaman, John (brother of James K.): influence on James K. Vardaman, 126–27, 375; helps brother in 1922 primary, 379
Vardaman, James Money, 17
Vardaman, James Kimble: family background, 3–5; reading habits, 5–6, 19–20; as editor of Winona *Advance,* 8–12; attacks Edmund Noel's nomination as district attorney, 10–12; advocate of prohibition, 12–15, 40–42; personal habits, 18–20; as attorney, 20–21; purchases Greenwood *Enterprise,* 22; gun battle, 24–25; speech to Mississippi Press Association, 26; editorials on behalf of civic improvements, 26–29; foe of capital punishment, 30–31; advocate of prison reform, 31–32, 150–67; as a progressive, 33, 192–93, 194–95, 196–97, 269–70, 363, 368, 387–88; views on religion, 33–34; racism, 34–39, 54–56, 59–60, 77–78, 82–83, 88–90, 102–103, 109, 114–15, 131, 132–33, 187–88, 193–94, 197–99, 270, 285–91, 326–27, 357–58, 369–70, 384–86; advocate of lynch law, 36–37, 88–89, 109; views on women, 37–38; opponent of anti-Semitism, 39–40, 291–92, 369; elected to state legislature, 43; support for constitutional convention, 45–46; voting record in state legislature, 47–48; candidate for speaker, 48; chairman of appropriations committee, 49; views on Populists, 49–51, 269–70; presidential elector, 50–51; considered for assistant secretary of agriculture, 51; elected speaker, 51–52; and 1895 gubernatorial campaign, 53–58; advocate of free silver, 53–54; founds Greenwood *Commonwealth,* 58; relationship with Anselm McLaurin, 60, 63, 64, 67–73, 90–91; in 1896 congressional campaign, 64–65, 67–68; and district nominating conven-

tion of 1896, p. 67; and 1898 congressional election, 70–72; relations with LeRoy Percy, 72, 212–13, 235–36; defeated for Democratic executive committee, 72–73; and Spanish-American War, 73–75, 297; and 1899 gubernatorial candidacy, 75–79; views on American foreign policy, 81–83; anti-imperialist, 83–85, 288–89; anti-Catholicism of, 82–83, 366; editorial policies of *Commonwealth*, 85–86; views on big business, 87, 146–48, 171, 196–97, 307, 308, 311–13, 324, 367–68, 387–88, 389–90; leads opposition to Democratic executive committee, 93–95; criticism of Longino, 97–98, 138–39; views on Roosevelt, 98–102, 104–105; on Booker T. Washington, 98–99; on Minnie Cox affair, 100–101; and 1903 gubernatorial campaign, 102–103; administration as governor, 116–76; legislative addresses, 117–19, 145–46, 192–94; relationship with legislature, 119–20; as a political leader, 120–21, 126–27, 388–89; appropriations vetoed by, 121–22; state bond sale, 124–25; attitude toward press, 125; and yellow fever epidemic, 125–26; urges better treatment of insane, 126; use of patronage, 127–30, 272–73; works to suppress racial lawlessness, 133–45; campaign against Whitecapping, 139–45; attitude toward corporate wealth, 146–48, 171, 196–97; vetoes railroad merger bill, 146; vetoes corporate landowning bill, 147–48; files suit against McLaurin, 158–59; denounces Emmett Cavett, 163; and removal of Chancellor Fulton, 167–76; senatorial candidacy in 1907, pp. 177, 181–82; political philosophy, 179, 269–70; on 1907 gubernatorial campaign, 183, 192; participation in revival, 184–85; debate with Williams, 185–89; reaction to defeat in 1907, pp. 191–92; Chautauqua lecturer, 198–99; relations with Bilbo, 200, 228, 254, 331–33, 337, 341–42, 372–75; silver service controversy, 200–201; 1910 senatorial candidate, 202–215; contingent fund investigation, 215–17; on Bilbo-Dulaney bribery scandal, 227–28; agrees to early (1910) primary, 232; and Jackson rally of 1910, pp. 244–45; 1911 senatorial campaign, 249–53; and 1912 presidential election, 262–65; relations with William Jennings Bryan, 264–65; relationship with President Wilson, 265–66; relationship with John Sharp Williams in Senate, 270–73; committee assignments, 270–71; Senate record, 273–92; and Underwood Tariff Act, 274–76; and fight for income tax, 274–76; antitrust policies, 277–79; support for labor, 280, 281–83, 367–68; support for agrarian interests, 283–85; works for flood control, 284–85; and Panama Canal Act, 294–97; row with Senator West, 296; attitude toward World War I, 297; opposition to Ship Purchase Bill, 302–304; on *Lusitania* crisis, 304–305; in praise of Wilson's "Peace without Victory" speech, 313; opposition to preparedness, 305–309; opposes break with Germany, 314; opposes Armed Ship bill, 315–17; votes against war, 317–19; opposes conscription, 319–20; record on war legislation, 319–27; criticizes Hoover, 322; opposes Espionage Act, 324–25; opposes Sedition Act, 325–26; defense of Charles C. Smith, 329; on Bilbo-Brewer bribery case, 330–31; supports W. H. Joyner, 335–36; on 1916 presidential campaign, 339; and 1918 senatorial campaign, 347–51, 356–58; ill health of, 350, 357, 377–78, 380; loss of patronage, 351–53; denounced by President Wilson, 358, 378; criticism of Wilson's foreign policy, 361–62; views of demobilization, 362–63, 366–67; attacks Versailles Treaty, 365–66; chairman of Senate Committee on Manufactures, 364; views of Henry Ford, 369; on 1920 gubernatorial campaign, 371–73; and 1922 senatorial campaign, 375–79; death of, 380

Vardaman, James Kimble, Jr., 17, 351

Vardaman, Margaret Newland, 4 n6
Vardaman, Elizabeth, 4 n6
Vardaman, Mary Ann Fox, 4, 5
Vardaman, Minnie, 17, 380
Vardaman, Sarah Talbot, 4 n6
Vardaman, William Sylvester (father of James K.), 3–5
Vardaman, William Sylvester (brother of James K.), 4 n6, 126–27, 273, 353, 375
Vardaman Club, 249
Vardaman's Weekly: Vardaman's editorship, 364–71; and 1922 campaign, 377. See also *Issue, The*
Vagrancy law, 121
Venable, William Webb: as congressional candidate, 335–36
Versailles Treaty: attacked by Vardaman, 365–66
Vicksburg, Miss.: Vardaman victory celebration, 113

Wallace, George C., 390
Walthall, Edward C.: supported by Vardaman, 47; resignation of, 71; death of, 90
War Revenue Act. *See* Revenue Act of 1917
War Risk Insurance Act, 320–21
Ward B. F.: influence on Vardaman, 7–8, 14, 126–27; at Vardaman's inauguration, 116; defense of Vardaman, 131; deal with Bilbo, 336–37; supported by Vardaman, 338; racist views of, 369–70
Ward, Will, 336–37
Warehouse Act, 284
Washington, Booker T., 98–99
Water Valley (Miss.) Rifles, 74
Watkins, H. Vaughn: Vardaman aide, 127, 210, 217, 249, 355, 364; Bilbo supporter, 332
Watson, Tom: support for Vardaman in 1907, pp. 183–84; anti-Semitism, 292; attacks President Wilson, 365; praised by Vardaman, 370; compared with Vardaman, 390
Wear, B. H., 8
Weaver, James B., 50
Weekly Jeffersonian, 184. *See also* Watson, Tenn.
Wells, Ben, 341

Wells, William Calvin, Jr.: Vardaman supporter, 120; and case against David Puckett, 156–57; and penitentiary investigation, 161, 162; defends Vardaman, 164
West, William Stanley, 296
Weyl, Walter, 365
White supremacy. *See* Negroes; Vardaman, James K.: racism
Whitecaps: violence in 1894, p. 55; attack Negroes, 97; terrorist campaigns, 134–45; anti-Semitism, 135 n53; suppression of, 139–45
Whitefield, Albert H., 150, 159
Whitefield, Mrs. Cary, 88
Wiggins, Miss., 317
Wilkinson, M. H., Whitecappers, 142
Willard, Frances E., 13
Williams, Christopher Harris "Kit," 111, 177
Williams, John Sharp: anti-McLaurin leader, 95; Vardaman supporter, 111; and 1904 presidential election, 130; related to Chancellor Fulton, 175; 1907 senatorial candidate, 177, 180–81; political philosophy of, 179; on race problem, 181, 188–89, 287 n52; debate with Vardaman, 185–89; reaction to victory in 1907, p. 191; Vardaman opponent, 203 n22, 296, 383–84; on Dulaney bribery scandal, 218; on Byrd-Witherspoon campaign, 234, 244 n33; on 1911 senatorial campaign, 248, 252, 253; opposes scheme to bar Vardaman from Senate, 259; ignores legislature's instructions, 260; on 1912 presidential election, 262–65; relationship with President Wilson, 265; relationship with Vardaman in Senate, 270–73; fight for income tax, 275–76; reelection to senate, 334–35, 336, 337–38; supports Harrison, 338, 347; removal of Vardaman's appointees, 351–52; denounced by Vardaman, 371; on Hubert Stephens, 376
Williams, William: dispute with Vardaman, 130; as penitentiary director, 153, challenges Vardaman, 154–55

Wilson, Edgar: Roosevelt appointee, 98; on 1903 election, 113

Wilson, G. A., 47

Wilson, Woodrow: presidential candidate, 262–65; relationship with Vardaman, 265–66; New Freedom, 267–68; on Vardaman-Williams patronage dispute, 272–73; antitrust policies, 277; conservative appointments of, 280; vetoes literacy test, 283; and repeal of Panama Canal Act, 294–96; and Ship Purchase Bill, 302–304; and preparedness, 305–309; on *Sussex* crisis, 312; and Armed Ship bill, 314–15; removes Vardaman's appointees, 351–53; endorses Harrison, 358; criticized by Vardaman, 361–62, 365–67; denounces Vardaman in 1922, p. 378

Winona, Miss., 3

Witherspoon, Samuel A.: and 1910 congressional campaign, 243–44; senatorial ambitions of, 334–35; death, 335

Woman suffrage: Vardaman's view on, 290

Wood, Walker, 339

Works, John D.: opposes break with Germany, 314; opposes Armed Ship bill, 361 n44

World War I: Vardaman's attitude toward, 297; cotton crisis, 298–302;

demobilization criticized by Vardaman, 366–67

Wright, Charles E.: attacked by Vardaman, 58–59

Yalobusha County, Miss., 3, 5

Yazoo-Mississippi Delta: Vardaman's early residence there, 15–17; control of state legislature, 44; and school fund issue, 54–55, 89; factional fighting in, 60–68, 70–72; political scandals, 96; and primary election law, 96; influence in primary of 1903, p. 112, influence in legislature of 1904, p. 120; Vardaman's levee board appointments in, 128–29; labor agents in, 139; Percy's political activities in, 204; and Flood Control Act in 1917, pp. 284–85; opposition to 1916 tax commission in, 371–72

Yazoo and Mississippi Valley Railroad: sued by state, 91–92; leased convicts, 152. *See also* Railroads

Yazoo City, Miss., 228

Yellow fever epidemic, 125–26

Yerger, Lawrence, 328–29

Yerger, William G.: opponent of McLaurin, 61, 71

Yewell, T. O., 242

Zimmermann telegram, 314. *See also* Germany